# *Śrī Gāyatrī Sahasranāmam*

(1000 Divine Names of *Śrī Gāyatrī Mātā*)

*

**Dr. Ramamurthy N.**

M.Sc., B.G.L., CAIIB, CCP, DSADP, CISA, PMP, CGBL, Ph.D.

*

*

Title: *Śrī Gāyatrī Sahasranāmam*
(1000 Divine Names of *Śrī Gāyatrī Mātā*)

First Edition: 2020

Author: **Dr. Ramamurthy N,**
http://ramamurthy.jaagruti.co.in/



Number of pages: 394

ISBN (13): 978-93-82237-74-7

Price: ₹ 700.00

*****

# Table of Contents

*****

# Dedication

मातृ देवो भव – *Mātru Devo Bhava*

This book is dedicated with devotion to all those who chant *Gāyatrī Mantra* regularly. There cannot be even an iota of doubt that all will be blessed.

*Dr. Ramamurthy N*

*****

# Blessings

*Śrī Gurubhyo Namaḥ*

*Dattatreya Hare Krişņa Unmattānanda Dāyakaḥ*
*Digambara Mune Bāla Pişaca Jnāna Sāgarā* ||

*Śāntam Dāntam Tapo Nişţam Śāntānanda Yatīśvaram* |
*Bajāmi Yaminām Śreśţam Avadhūtam Aharniśam* ||

*Stuto Mayā Varadā Veda Mātā Prcodayantī Bhavane Dvijātā*
*Āyuḥ Prutivyāntraviņam Brahmavarcasam*
*Mahyantatvā Prajātum Brahmalokam*

*Śastras* say "*Na Gāyatryāḥ Paro Mantraḥ*". To illustrate this a small story –

One poor man, who had been worshiping Gayatri regularly, became depressed because of his poverty and went to worship some low profile Goddess for money. *Mantra Siddhi* occurred and the angel asked him what he wanted, with the mind to bestow what he wanted.

The man only heard the voice of the angel and said that he wanted to see her, to which the angel said, "The fruit of your Gayatri Upasana is burning me without coming before you".

Thus as we know, the best of mantras is Gayatri.

By publishing this 1000 name of such Gayatri with meaning, the author **Dr. Ramamurthy** has done great charity for this spiritual world.

Any worship will result in full benefits, if the meaning is comprehended and performed. Therefore, this is a very useful book for all those who worship Gayatri.

I pray to the Almighty Mother to publish many more spiritual treasures in the form of author books

I pray to the Almighty Mother that all the devotees understand the supremacy of the author and buy and use this book and become recipients of Ambal's grace and that this spiritual work of the author should grow further.

We are very happy to see that Dr. Ramamurthy has compiled and published this book in Tamil also for all devotees. We pray to Goddess Srividya Maha Saubhagya Parashodashi daily, for him and his family and for all the loved ones who read this book to get Ambika's blessings and achieve the quadrupedal purusharthas.

Let everyone enjoy and live happily.

Happiness Truth Auspiciousness

Always in the service of *Sri Devi*.

*Jaya Jaya Jagamba – Sri Gurudevadatta*

With love

Ayyarmalai श्रीप्रणवानन्द स्वामिन:
2020 *Srividya Parambika Trust*

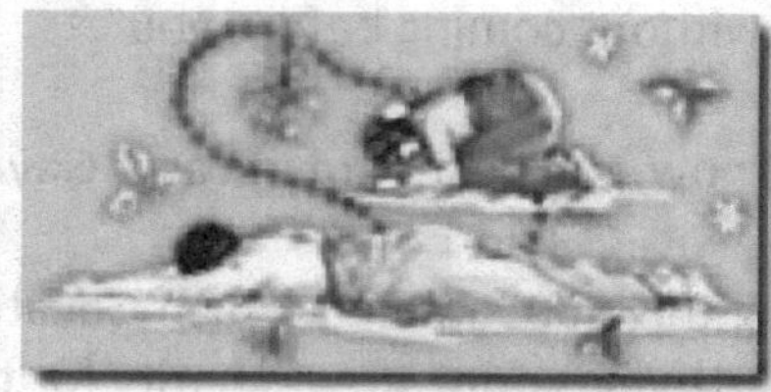

*****

# Introduction

ॐ श्री गुरुभ्यो नमः । *Oṃ Śrī Gurubhyo Namaḥ* ।

We have *Sahasranama Stotrams* on almost all the Gods/ Goddesses. These verses are split into 1000 names and archana is performed to the concerned God.

When anybody hears the word *'Sahasranama'*, immediately *Sri Vishnu Sahasranama Stotra* will only first come to the mind. Sometimes, may also be reminded of *Sri Lalita Sahasranama Stotra*.

When there are *Sahasranama Stotrams/ Namavalis* on every other God, what is the specialty of these two. *Sri Vishnu Sahasranama Stotra* is in the midst of an *Itihasam* called *Mahabharata*. *Sri Lalita Sahasranamam Stotra* is the core within *Brahmanda Puranam*.

Both these – *Itihasam* and *Puranam* – are written by *Sri Veda Vyasa*. *"Vyāsa Rūpāya Viṣṇave"* – *Sri Vishnu* is in the form of *Vyasa*. Hence the *Sahasranama Stotras* written by him, naturally, have glory.

But, *Vyasa* himself has written one more *Sahasranama Stotra* – not so popular. It is a part of *Sri Devi Bhagavatam – Sri Gayatri Sahasranama Stotra*.

All of us are aware that sage Vyasa has written 18 *Maha–Puranas* and 18 *Upa–Puranas*. He himself has listed them also. He has mentioned one *purana 'Bhagavatam'* both in the lists of 18 *Maha–Puranas* and 18 *Upa–Puranas*. One is a *Maha–Purana* and the other one is *Upa–Purana* – one is *Sri Vishnu Bhagavatam* and the other one is *Sri Devi Bhagavatam*. Which is *Maha–purana* and which is *Upa–purana* is a debatable question till date? This is beyond the scope of this book and we do not enter into it.

The *Purana*, called *Sri Devi Bhagavatam* contains 12 *Skandams*. In this text – in the 12th *Skanda*, 7 chapters (from 1 to 7) explain about Goddess *Gayatri Devi* and describe her attributes and glories. *Gayatri Kavaca Stotram* is given in chapter 12–3 and *Gayatri Hrudaya Stotram* is given in chapter 12–4.

Chapter 12–6 gives *Sri Gayatri Sahasranama Stotram* – a very low profile – not so popular sacred text. Since this Sahasranamam is also written by same *Veda Vyasa*, there is no doubt this is also powerful and has equal glory.

The aim of this book is to bring this not so popular *Sahasranamam* to limelight. The verses and 1000 names are provided both in Samskrutam and English with lucid meaning in English. Normally any text relating to Devi is supposed to be secretive. This could be one more reason for this text being not so popular.

Originally it was intented to give meanings for each of the 1000 names. But out of enthusiasm and with the blessings of Gurus and Sri Devi, it ended up as a commentary (Bhashyam) – relating each name to other Sahasranamas like Vishnu, Lalita, Shiva and Sri Lalita Trishatee, Rudram and all – and comparing with various Upanishats, Puranas and other Veda statements. How this could be possible without the grace of Sri Devi?

Generally, it is very difficult to read Samskruta words in English with proper pronunciation. It is apt to read them in Samskruta script itself. But to benefit those who cannot read Samskruta script the *mantras* have been given in English also. The Samskruta words, when transliterated into English are denoted in *italics*. Normally diacritical marks will be used for transliteration of Samskruta words into English. But general readers are not fully conversant with diacritical marks and hence they find it difficult to read. Hence, it has not been used in this book in normal texts. But for proper pronunciation it has been used in *mantras* and in some words.

Humble *pranams* are due to *Pujyasri Pranavananda Swamiji* of Ayyarmalai, who provoked the author to write this book. He has given his blessings and some pleasantries about the author and the book.

The efforts put in by 11 years old grand-daughter of the author Sow. Akshaya is very much appreciated. She went through the entire book for any corrections and confirm easy understanding. She also helped the author in designing the beautiful wrappers.

Hearty thanks to all the good–hearted souls who enabled this book to be presented in this fashion. Attempts have been made to give this book as much error free as possible. Still if there are any errors, apologies are sought. If the errors are given as feedback, it will enable the next edition to be fault free.

There is no doubt that *Sri Gayatri Devi* will shower her full compassion and blessings to all those who read this book.

This book has also been published in Tamil language simultaneously by the same author.

Our humble *pranams* to all our *Gurus*.

Chennai
2020 **Dr. Ramamurthy N.**

*****

# Śrī Gāyatri Devī

The word *Gāyatri* means, whoever sings it, will be protected. *Veda* says; "*Gāyantam Trāyate Yasmāt Gāyatri Yabidhīyate*". When we say sings, it does not mean like singing a song. It is chanting with affection and focus. Whoever chants this *mantra* with devotion and love, they will be protected. Hence this name.

We used to have *Upaniṣats* about various Gods. We have two *Upaniṣats* about *Gāyatri* viz., *Gāyatrī Upaniṣat* and *Gāyatrī Rahasya Upaniṣat*. Do we need any more explanation about the glory of the *Gāyatri*?

*Gayatri* is the personified form of popular Gayatri Mantra, a hymn from Vedic texts. **She** is also known as *Savitri* and *Vedamata* (mother of Vedas). Gayatri is often associated with Savitr, a solar deity in the Vedas.

Normally Gayatri and Saraswathi are understood as one and the same goddess. But, Gayatri is Mother and Saraswathi is daughter. Gayatri has some powers of Saraswathi. In a way, Gayatri is Mother of all Gods. She can take any female form like Saraswathi, Lakshmi, Kali, Durga, Santoshi, Jwala Mukhi, Vaishnavi, Parvati, etc. Brahma is the consort of Saraswathi.

Gayatri Devi and Gayatri Mantra are always treated as synonyms. Gayatri was the name initially applied to a meter of the Rig Veda consisting of 24 syllables. In particular, it refers to the Gayatri Mantra and the Goddess *Gāyatrī* as that mantra personified. The Gayatri mantra composed in this triplet form, is the most famous. Most of the scholars identify Gayatri as the feminine form of Gayatra, another name of the Vedic Solar god, which is also one of the synonyms of Savitri and Savitr. However, the transition period of mantra turned into personification is still unknown. There are different sources available to construct her development through ages.

In *Mahānārayāṇa Upanishat* of *Krishna Yajurveda*, *Gayatri* is described as white–coloured (श्वेतवर्णा – *Śvetavarṇā*), having the gotra of sage Vishwamitra (सान्ख्यायनस गोत्रा – *Sānkhyāyanasa gotrā*), 24 lettered (चतुर्विंशत्यक्षरा – *Caturviṃśatyakṣarā*), three–quartered (त्रिपाद – *Tripāda*), six–bellied (षट्कुक्षिः – *Ṣaṭkukṣiḥ*), five–headed (पञ्चशीर्षः – *Pañcaśīrṣaḥ*) and the one used in *Upanayana* of *Dvijas*[1] (उपनयने विनियोग: – *Upanayane Viniyogaḥ*).

As mentioned in *Taitteeriya Sandhya Bhashyam*, the three quarters of *Gayatri* is supposed to represent the first 3 Vedas (*Ṛg*, *Yajus*, *Sāma*). The six bellies are supposed to represent 4 cardinal directions, along with the two more directions, *Ūrdhva* (Zenith) and *Adhara* (Nadir). The five heads represent 5 Vedangas, namely, *Vyākaraṇa*, *Śikṣā*, *Kalpa*, *Nirukta* and *Jyotiṣa*.

By citing from *Gayatri Tantra*, the text *Mahārṇava Mantra,* gives the significance of *Gayatri Mantra's* 24 letters and its representation that are discussed in the next chapter.

*Dhyana* verse for any God will describe the form of that God. The form of *Sri Gayatri Devi* as per the below *Dhyana* verse would be;

रक्त श्वेत हिरण्य नील धवलैर्युक्तां त्रिनेत्रोज्ज्वलां
रक्तां रक्तनवस्रजं मणिगणैर्युक्तां कुमारीमिमाम् ।
गायत्रीं कमलासनां करतल व्यानद्ध कुण्डाम्बुजां
पद्माक्षीं च वरस्रजं च दधातीं हंसाधि रूढां भजे ॥

*Rakta Śveta Hiraṇya Nīla Dhavalairyuktā Trinītrojjvalāṃ*
*Raktāṃ Raktanavasrajaṃ Maṇigaṇairyuktāṃ Kumārīmimām* ।
*Gāyatrīṃ Kamalāsanāṃ Karatalavyānaddhakuṇḍāmbujāṃ*
*Padmākṣī Ca Varasrajaṃ Ca Dadhatīṃ Haṃsādhirūḍhāṃ Bhaje* ॥

*Sri Narayana* said to *Narada* – Now hear the Dhyanam of Sri Gayatri Devi that grants all desires that will do good to the *Sadhakas* (the practisers).

- The Gayatri Devi has five faces; one of which is of white colour and the other four are of pearl, Vidruma, golden and Nilakantamani colours respectively.
- Each face has got three , lotus like eyes;
- On the head there is a crown of jewels and the digit of the Moon is shining there.

[1] *Dwijas* are – twice born – often referring to Brahmins – one birth from the mother's womb – the second birth during *Upanayana*.

- Her body is composed of the twenty–four tattvas.
- She has ten hands –
    - On the top right and left hands there are two lotuses;
    - Lower down, there are disc and conch shell;
    - Lower down, there are rope and skull;
    - Lower down, there are noose and goad;
    - On the bottom hands right and left she is making signs of "No fear" and "ready to grant boons".
- Riding on the Swan (the Pranas)
- Seated on a lotus (creation);
- Who is bright and decorated with gems and jewels of red, white, green, blue, yellow and other variegated colours;
- On whose neck is suspended the garland of red flowers.

I worship that Kumari (virgin) Gayatri Devi.

Note: The colours are the various emotions and feelings.

*****

# Śrī Gāyatri Mantram

*Gāyatri mantra* is mentioned as "*Gāyatrīm Chandasām Mātaḥ*" – *chandas* here means *Vedas* – *Gāyatri* is the mother of all *Vedas*.

In *Shrimad Bhagavad Gita*, Lord *Krishna* says "Among the *mantras*, I am in the form of *Gāyatri*" (10.34).

Only after *Upanayana*, a boy becomes eligible to learn *Vedas* and other holy *mantras*. Before chanting any *mantra*, or before performing any *Pooja* or worship, *Gāyatri mantra* has to be chant first – else the other *mantras* or *Poojas* will not yield any results.

*Gāyatri mantra* is not about any particular God. In some schools, it is mentioned that *Gāyatri* is about the Sun God. But it is not so. Some other schools say that this is about *Gāyatri*, one of the consorts of Lord *Brahma*. It is about *Brahmam*, the ultimate goal of the life. *Brahmam* and Lord *Brahma* are different. It is specified that only the nature is the greatest among all.

The *Gāyatri mantra* has 24 letters as:

ॐ – *Oṃ* – the *Praṇava mantra* – prefixed like any other *mantra*.

भूः भुवः स्वः – *Bhūḥ Bhuvaḥ Svaḥ* – *Vyāhruti mantras* – prefixed to add power/ strength.

तत्सवितुर्वरेण्यं भर्गो देवस्य धीमहि धियो यो नः प्रचोदयात् ।

*Tatsavituḥ Vareṇyam Bargo Devasya Dhīmahi Dhiyo Yo Naḥ Pracodayāt*

Normal apparent meaning of this is – let us meditate upon the *Brahmam* mentioned as *Savitā* and represented by *Praṇava mantra Oṃ*. It is that *Brahmam* indicated through the three *vyāhruti mantras*. It the brightness of the divine nature. It is that *Brahmam* who create, protect and destroy the three worlds – Earth, space between heaven, called as the upper world and the intervening galaxy. Let that *Brahmam* direct and move our knowledge in the right direction (towards him).

An ordinary ceiling fan with a speed of around 900 rotations per minute creates so much sound. In that case the planets and other members of the Sun family have a speed of around 20,000 rotations per minute. Then what would be the decibel of the sound created – can we imagine?[2] That sound is the *praṇava mantra 'Oṃ'* – says *Gāyatri*. Sage *Viśwāmitra* realised this sound through his penance and taught to his students. They all unanimously named this sound as *'Oṃ'*. *Oṃ* is that *Brahmam,* since it is eternal in all the three tenses. This is the first revolutionary idea of naming the formless *Brahmam*. In *Shrimad Bhagavad Gita* (8–12) also Lord *Krishna* says *"Oṃiti Ekākṣaram Brahma"*.

Let us look at some more aspects of *Gāyatri mantra*.

*Om Bhūḥ Bhuvaḥ Svaḥ* –

- *Om* – *praṇava mantra* prefixed
- *Bhūḥ* – the earth
- *Bhuvaḥ* – the planets
- *Svaḥ* – the galaxy

*Tatsavituḥ Vareṇyam* –

- *Tat* – that (*Brahmam*)
- *Savituḥ* – the Sun God (stars)
- *Vareṇyam* – worshipable or respectable

Once the name and form of a person is known, it is easy to search and find him. *Viśwāmitra* says – it is easy to realise the formless *Brahmam* with the name *Oṃ* and with the lights of stars. For a mathematician, if

---

[2] In mid-2010, astronomers at the University of Sheffield, with the support of NASA managed to record the vibrations (eerie musical harmonies) produced by the magnetic field in the outer atmosphere of Sun. Huge magnetic loops known as coronal loops were observed coiling away from the outer layer of the sun's atmosphere, which behave like sound waves traveling through a wind instrument, *'Om'* i.e. vibrate like strings on a musical instrument.

the value of x is known as 2 then he will immediately find the value of y in the equation 2x + 2y = 0. Same case is *Viśwāmitra*'s. One school's view is that this *Viśwāmitra* was the first person to teach the *Gāyatri mantra* to *Rāma* and *Lakṣmaṇa*.

*Bargo Devasya Dhīmahi* –

- *Bargo* – light
- *Devasya* – God
- *Dhīmahi* – to be meditated upon

Sage insists to us – search the formless *Brahmam* with the available light, through meditation. He further insists to chant the *mantra Oṃ*. He also teaches us how to pray.

*Dhiyo Yo Naḥ Pracodayāt* –

- *Dhiyo* – knowledge
- *Yo* – who
- *Naḥ* – us all
- *Pracodayāt* – lead in the correct path

Oh! *Brahmam*, please lead our knowledge in the correct path to reach you.

The earth called *Bhūḥ*, the planets addressed as *Bhuvaḥ* and the entire galaxy termed as *Svaḥ*, are all rotating at enormous speed. The sound created on account of this rotation is *'Oṃ'* denoting the *Brahmam*. *Tat*, that *Brahmam*, *savituḥ* – reveals in the light (*bargo*) illuminated by the stars. We all need to worship (*vareṇyam*) and meditate upon (*dhīmahi*) him (*devasya*). He (*yo*) will take our (*naḥ*) knowledge (*dhiyo*) in the right path (*pracodayāt*) towards him.

One God is associated with each of the 24 letters in *Gāyatri mantra* as below;

| # | Letters | | God |
|---|---|---|---|
| 1. | तत् | *Tat* | *Gaṇapati* |
| 2. | स | *Sa* | *Narasimhar* |
| 3. | वि | *Vi* | *Viṣṇu* |
| 4. | तुः | *Tuḥ* | *Śiva* |

| # | Letters | | God |
|---|---|---|---|
| 5. | व | *Va* | *Kriśna* |
| 6. | रे | *Re* | *Rādhā* |
| 7. | णि | *Ni* | *Lakshmi* |
| 8. | यं | *Yam* | *Agni* |
| 9. | भ: | *Bhaḥ* | *Indra* |
| 10. | गो | *Go* | *Saraswathi* |
| 11. | दे | *De* | *Durgā* |
| 12. | व: | *Vaḥ* | *Hanumān* |
| 13. | य | *Ya* | *Prithvi* |
| 14. | धी | *Dhī* | *Sūrya* |
| 15. | म | *Ma* | *Rāma* |
| 16. | हि | *Hi* | *Sīta* |
| 17. | धि | *Dhi* | *Candra* |
| 18. | यो | *Yo* | *Yama* |
| 19. | यो | *Yo* | *Brahmā* |
| 20. | नः | *Naḥ* | *Varuṇan* |
| 21. | प्र | *Pra* | *Kāli* |
| 22. | चो | *Co* | *Hayagrīva* |
| 23. | द | *Da* | *Hamsa* |
| 24. | यात् | *Yāt* | *Tulasi* |

Lord *Agni* dwells in the face of *Gāyatri Devi*, *Brahmā* the creator dwells in the forehead, *Viṣṇu* the protector in the heart and the lord *Śiva* the destroyer in the top most part of head.

Thus, *Gāyatri Devi* and *Gāyatri Mantra* are combination of all Gods.

There are two important aspects to note – first *Gāyatri mantra* should not be chant as any other verses (*shlokas*). This is a *Veda mantra*. The lifeline of *Veda* is *svara*. Hence, it has to be chant with appropriate *svaras*. Secondly, in the word *'dhiyoyonaḥ'* the last syllable ('f' like sound) has to be apparent. Else it gives a negative meaning. Thus, having chant in an inappropriate manner and in an urgency, the *mantra* should not be blamed for not being generous in the resultant fruits. Hence, by learning it properly from an appropriate teacher, let us all chant, how much small quantity ever possible and reap the fruits.

**The importance of *Gāyatri Mantraḥ*;**

From the very words of *Kānchi Paramācārya* himself – Chanting of *Gāyatri mantra* is the primary task among those mentioned in *Śāstras*.

*Tripam Evatu Vedebhyaḥ Pādam Pādamadūtuham – Manusmruti*

Each *pāda* of *Gāyatri mantra* has been taken from three *Vedas* – says *Manu*. We have left most of the parts of *Vedas* – at least this should be continued – else what is the way out for us?

The *Gāyatri mantra* is the essence squeezed out by tightening the three *Vedas Rig, Yajur* and *Sāma*. That is the reason it is called as "*Tripāda Gāyatri*". *Atharva Veda* has a separate *Gāyatri mantra* of its own. When *Vedas* talk about *Gāyatri,* it is mentioned as the *Gāyatri mantra* includes the power of all the other *mantras*. This is the one, which gives power to all other *mantras*. Without chanting this no other *mantra* is capable of blessing any fruit or result. For purification of body, we take bath. For purification of mind we have to chant *Gāyatri mantra*.

Those who have left chanting *Gāyatri mantra* for three generations, will never get any welfare. *Taitrīya Àraṇyaka* says "*Sahasra Paramā Devī Śata Madyā Daśāvarā*" – chanting *Gāyatri mantra* 1000 times is the best, at least 100 times have to be chant and least 10 times.

Whatever be the danger period, everyone should chant at least 12 times each of morning, noon and evening without fail. These three are the peace periods of a day. Morning is the time all the living beings wake up. Mind would be in peace at that time. Evening everyone will be at relax after completing the daily cores. That is also a peaceful time. During noon the rays of the Sun will be in straight. Everybody is a kind of tired and mind needs peace at that time. All these three periods have to be meditated and worshiped as *Gāyatri, Sāvitrī* and *Saraswatī*.

*Gāyatri* has to meditated in the morning in the form of *Brāhmī,* consort of *Brahma,* in the noon *Roudhrī,* consort of *Rudra* and in the evening *Vaiṣṇavī,* consort of *Viṣṇu*.

Recently, Dr. Howard Steingeria, an American Scientist, collected various *mantras*, hymns and invocations from different parts of the world and tested for the strength in his laboratory and found out that our *Gāyatri Mantra* produced 110,000 sound waves per second. This was the highest and was found to be the most powerful hymn in the world. Through the combination of sound or sound waves in a particular frequency, this *mantra* was capable of developing specific potentialities, which we call spiritual. The Hamburg University initiated this research both on the mental and physical plane of creation.

The *Gāyatri mantra* is broadcast daily from 7:00 to 7:15 p.m. over Radio Paramaribo, Surinam, South America for the past two years and in Amsterdam Holland for the past six months. They say that in the evening after hectic day's work, hearing this makes the life peaceful and also people get a quality sleep during night, so that they start fresh next day.

We understand people doing various things through hypnotism.

- The hypnotism that would lead us to liberation is *Gāyatri mantra*.
- The hypnotism viz., *Gāyatri mantra* is the one which will enable us to control all the desires and get the full fruit of taking this birth.

*Gāyatri* should be imagined in the form of a mother and worshipped. Thougth God is available in all forms, the form of a mother so affectionate and pretty. *Vedas* affirm that *Gāyatri* is in that form of mother.

There are umpteen *mantras*. Before chanting them, we used to announce the desire for which that *mantra* is chant – *sankalpa* (solemn vow or determination to perform, desire in the heart or mind). But the desire for *Gāyatri mantra* is cleansing of the mind – removing the mental contamination. All other *mantras* lead to cleansing of mind at the end. But the immediate and the only result of *Gāyatri mantra* is removing the pollution in the mind.

*Paramācārya* has ordained three important areas:

1. Perform *Sandhyāvandam* all the three times daily without fail.

2. Chant *gāyatri* mantra for 1,000 times at all possible times – *sahasra gāyatri*
3. Follow fasting on all *Ekādaśi* days.

Thus, advises divine *Kānchi Paramācārya*. Our humble pranams to his lotus feet.

**Significance of chanting *Gāyatri mantra* 12 times:**

Chanting *Gāyatri mantra* 12 times has enormous implication. In every *Yajñopavīta*, the *brahma* knot has to be made by chanting *Gāyatri mantra* 12 times. Then only the *Yajñopavīta* gets vibration and holiness.

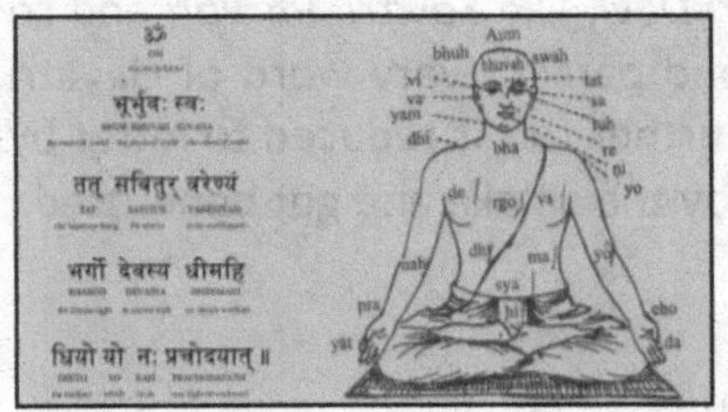


Again, whenever we change the *Yajñopavīta* one has to chant *Gāyatri mantra* for 12 times, before removing the old one. This is in a way handing over of charge – power transfer from the old one to the new one. This small piece of task is not in vogue with all, for the basic reason of ignorance.

In the same manner, when someone bows to the elders, the elder has to chant *Gāyatri mantra* for 12 times before blessing the other person. For instance, if *Lakṣmaṇa* bows to *Rāma*, by the time *Lakṣmaṇa* starts to bow, till he completes announcing *abhivādanam*, *Rāma* has to chant *Gāyatri mantra* for 12 times. Then he has to bless whatever is needed by *Lakṣmaṇa*. With the power of *Gāyatri mantra* whatever be the legal desire, it will be satiated.

Hence, all are requested to chant *Gāyatri mantra* for 12 times at all possible times. Thus, the chanter will be benefitted with mammoth benefits.

These are all very small nuances, easily follow–able with very huge paybacks. People are ready to follow these, if properly taught. Only the unawareness is the cause.

If people want to achieve in their life, the primary requirement is knowledge and understanding. Chanting of *Gāyatri mantra* will purify the mind and improve the understanding capacity. Consequently, the knowledge has to develop and will be ready to face any challenging tasks. Let everyone be benefitted.

*****

# Śrī Gāyatri Kavacam

श्री गायत्री कवचम्

(*Sri Devi Bhagavatam* – 12.3)

The word *Kavacam* literally means shield. In Tamilnadu, *Skanda Shashti Kavacam* is more famous. While chanting *Sri Devi Mahatmyam* we used to chant *Sri Devi Kavaca Stotram*. In a way, these are all prayers seeking to protect us organ by organ, in every direction and in every possible way.

Here this is a prayer to *Sri Gayatri Devi* requesting to protect us. In the beginning different forms of *Sri Gayatri Devi*, like *Savitri*, *Parvati* and so on to protect us in all directions. Second part is every word of Gayatri Mantra to protect us organ by organ. Further this is reduced to letter by letter of the *Gayatri Mantra*. Let us enjoy the shloka and get benefitted.

नारद उवाच । *Nārada Uvācha* ।

स्वामिन् सर्वजगन्नाथ संशयोऽस्ति मम प्रभो ।
चतुःषष्ठिकलाभिज्ञ पातका द्योगविद्वर ॥ १

*Svāmin Sarvajagannātha Samshayo 'Sti Mama Prabho* |

*Chatuḥ Ṣaṣṭikalābhigya Pātakā Dyogavidvara* || 1

Sage Narada asked Sri Narayana – Oh Bhagavan! You are the Lord of this world; You cannot shew favour and disfavour both; You are specially versed in the sixty–four Kalas (areas of learning); You are the chief of the Yogis. I therefore surrender to you to solve a doubt of mine.

मुच्यते केन पुण्येन ब्रह्मरूपः कथं भवेत् ।
देहश्च देवतारूपो मन्त्ररूपो विशेषतः ॥ २

*Muchyeta Kena Puṇyena Brahmarūpaḥ Katham Bhavet* |

*Dehaścha Devatārūpo Mantrarūpo Viśeṣataḥ* || 2

By what *punyam* a man can become free from all his sins and limitations and he can realise and become of the nature of Brahmam.

कर्म तच्छ्रोतुमिच्छामि न्यासं च विधिपूर्वकम् ।
ऋषिस्छन्दोऽधिदैवं च ध्यानं च विधिवद्विभो ॥ ३

*Karma Tatchrotumichchāmi Nyāsam Ca Vidhipūrvakam* |

*Ruṣischando'dhidaivam Ca Dhyānam Ca Vidhivatvibho* || 3

Oh Lord! And what are duly the *Rishis*, *Chandas*, *Devatas*, *Dhyanam*, *Nyasa*, etc., of this meritorious act? I want to hear.

श्रीनारायण उवाच । *Śrī Nārāyaṇa Uvācha* ।

अस्त्येकं परमं गुह्यं गायत्रीकवचं तथा ।

पठनाद्धारणान्मर्त्य: सर्वपापै: प्रमुच्यते ॥ ४

*Astyekam Paramam Guhyam Gāyatrīkavacham Tathā* |

*Paṭhanāddhāraṇānmareyaḥ Sarvapāpaiḥ Pramuchyate* || 4

Sri Narayana said – Oh Narada! There is but one and the only way to this and that is very secret. I will disclose that to you. It is the Gayatri–Kavacha. It can destroy all sins.

सर्वान्कामानवाप्नोति देवीरुपश्च जायते ।

गायत्रीकवचस्यास्य ब्रह्मविष्णु महेश्वरा: ॥ ५

*Sarvānkāmānavāpnoti Devīrūpaścha Jāyate* |

*Gāyatrīkavacasyāsya Brahmaviṣṇumaheśvarāḥ* || 5

Therefore, to recite or to hold it on one's body enables the man to become free from all his sins and to get all his desires fulfilled and he gets the *Sayujya Mukti* with the *Devi* (be merged with Devi).

ऋषयो ऋग्यजु: सामाथर्वश्छन्दांसि नारद ।

ब्रह्मरूपा देवतोक्ता गायत्री परमा कला ॥ ६

*Ruṣayo Rugyajuḥ Sāmātharvaśchandāmsi Nārada* |

*Brahmarūpā Devatoktā Gāyatrī Paramā Kalā* || 6

Now hear the *Rishis*, Chandas, etc., of this *Kavacha* – Brahma, Vishnu and Maheshvara are the Rishis; the Rik, Yajus, Sama and Atharva Vedas are the Chandas; the Parama Kala Gayatri of the nature of Brahmam is the Devata;

तद् बीजं भर्ग इत्येषा शक्तिरुक्ता मनीषिभि: ।

कीलकं च धिय: प्रोक्तम् मोक्षार्थे विनियोजनम् ॥ ७

*Tad Bījam Bharga Ityeṣā Śaktiruktā Manīṣibhiḥ* |

*Kīlakam Ca Dhiyaḥ Proktam Mokshārthe Viniyojanam* || 7

*'Tad'* in Gayatri is the *Beeja*; *'Bharga'* is the Shakti; and *'Dhiyah'* is the *Keelaka*; and Its *Viniyoga* (application) is in getting the Moksha (liberation).

चतुर्भिर्हृदयं प्रोक्तं त्रिभिर्वर्णै: शिर: स्मृतम् ।
चतुर्भि: स्याच्छिखा पश्चात् त्रिभिस्तु कवचं स्मृतम् ॥ ८

*Caturbhirhrudayam Proktam Tribhirvarṇaiḥ Śiraḥ Smrutam |*
*Chaturbhih Syācchikhā Paścāt Tribhistu Kavacham Smrutam* ॥ 8

As part of *Anganyasam* – With the first four syllables touch the heart; with the next three letters touch the head; with the next four letters touch the tuft on the crown of the head; with the next three letters on the *Kavacha*;

चतुर्भिर्नेत्र मुद्दिष्टं चतुर्भि: स्यात्तदस्त्रकम् ।
अथ ध्यानं प्रवक्ष्यामि साधाकाभीष्ट दायकम् ॥ ९

*Caturbhinetra Muddiṣṭam Caturbhiḥ Syāttadastrakam |*
*Atha Dhyānam Pravakśyāmi Sādhakābhīṣṭadāyakam* ॥ 9

With the next four letters on the eyes and with the last four letters make the *Nyasa*, all over the body repeating '*Astraya Phat*'.

Oh Narada! Hear now the *Dhyanam* of *Gayatri*, that grants all desires.

मुक्ता विद्रुम हेमनील धवलच्छायैर्मुखस्त्री क्षणैर्युक्तामिन्दुनि
बद्धरत्न मुकुटां तत्वार्थवर्णात्मिकाम् ।
गायत्रीं वरदाभयाङ्कुशकशा: शुभ्रं कपालं गुणं
शङ्खं चक्रमथारविन्दयुगलं हस्तैर्वहन्तीं भजे ॥ १०

*Muktā Vidruma Hemanīla Dhavalācchāyairmukhaistrī Kśaṇai–*
*ryuktāminduni Baddharatna Mukuṭām Tattvārthavarṇātmikām |*
*Gāyatrīm Varadābhayāmkuśakaśāḥ Śubhram Kapālam Guṇam*
*Śamkham Cakramathāravindayugalam Hastairvahamtīm Bhaje* ॥ 10

The Gayatri Devi has five faces; one of which is of white colour; and the other four is of pearl, Vidruma, golden, and Nilakantamani colour respectively.

Each face has got three eyes; on the head there is a crown of jewels and the digit of the Moon is shining there. Her body is composed of the twenty–four tattvas.

She has ten hands – on the top right and left hands there are two lotuses; lower down, there are disc and conch shell; lower down, there are rope and skull; lower down, there are noose and goad; and on the bottom hands right and left she is making signs of "No fear" and "ready to grant boons".

Thus, meditating on Sri Gayatri, one is to recite the *Kavacha* thus;
Note: The form of Gayatri Devi was explained in a previous chapter also.

गायत्रीं पूर्वत: पातु सावित्री पातु दक्षिणे ।
ब्रह्मसन्ध्या तु मे पश्चादुत्तरायां सरस्वती ॥ ११

*Gāyatrī Paratha Pātu Sāvitrī Pātu Dakśiṇe |*
*Brahmasandhyā Tu Me Paścāduttarasyām Sarasvatī* ‖ 11

Let Gayatri Devi protect me from East; Savitri Devi protect me from South; The Brahma–Sandhya Devi protect me from West and Devi Sarasvati protect me from North.

पार्वती मे दिशं रक्षेत्पावकीं जलशायिनी ।
यातुधानी दिशं रक्षेद् यातुधान भयङ्करी ॥ १२

*Pārvatī Me Diśam Rakśetpāvakī Jalashāyinī |*
*Yātudhānī Diśam Rakśed Yātudhāna Bhayankarī* ‖ 12

Let my Mother Parvati Devi protect me in all directions. Let Jalashayini protect the southeast; Yatudhani protect my South–west; Yatudhana Bhayankari protect my North–east;

पावमानीं दिशं रक्षेत् पवमान विलासिनी ।
दिशं रौद्रीं च मे पातु रुद्राणी रुद्ररूपिणी ॥ १३

*Pāvamānīm Diśam Rakśet Pavamānavilāsinī |*
*Diśam Roudrīm Cha Me Pātu Rudrāṇī Rudrarūpiṇī* ‖ 13

*Pavamanavilasini* my north–west; *Rudrarupini Roudrani* protect me from bottom. *Vaishnavi* protect my nether regions.

ऊर्ध्वं ब्रह्माणि मे रक्षेदधस्ताद्वैष्णवी तथा ।
ऐवं दश दिशो रक्षेत् सर्वाङ्गं भुवनेश्वरी ॥ १४

*Ūrdhvam Brahmāṇi Me Rakśedadhastādvaiṣṇavī Tathā |*
*Evam Daśa Diśo Rakśetsarvāngam Bhuvaneśvarī* ‖ 14

Let Brahmani protect my top. Thus, let me protected from all directions.

Note: Having got protected in all directions by different forms of Sri Devi, now it is moving on to each letter of Gayatri Mantra to get protected.

तत्पदं पातु मे पादौ जङ्घे मे सवितु: पदम् ।
वरेण्यं कटिदेशे तु नाभिं भर्गस्तथैव च ॥ १५

*Tatpadam Pātu Me Pādou Janghe Me Savituḥ Padam* |
*Vareṇyam Kaṭideśe Tu Nābhim Bhargastathaiva Cha* || 15

Let the word *'Tat'* in the *Gayatri mantra* protect my legs; *'Savituh'* protect my Knees; *'Varenyam'*, protect my loins; *'Bhargo'*, my navel.

देवस्य मे तद्धृदयम् धीमहीति च गल्लयो: ।
धिय: पदं च मे नेत्रे य: पदं मे ललाटकम् ॥ १६

*Devasya Me Taddhrudayam Dhīmahīti Cha Gallayoḥ* |
*Dhiyaḥ Padam Ca Me Netre Yaḥ Padam Me Lalāṭakam* || 16

Let *'Devasya'* protect my heart; *'Dhimahi'* protect my neck; *'Dhiyah'*, protect my eyes; *'Yah'*, protect my forehead;

न: पातु मे पदं मूर्ध्नि शिखायां मे प्रचोदयात् ।
तत्पदम् पातु मूर्धानं सकार: पातु भालकम् ॥ १७

*Naḥ Pātu Me Padam Mūrdhni Śikhāyām Me Pracodayāt* |
*Tatpadam Pātu Mūrdhānam Sakāraḥ Pātu Bhālakam* || 17

*'Nah'* protect my head; and *'Prachodayat'* protect the tuft on the crown of my head.

चक्षुषी तु विकारार्णस्तुकारस्तु कपोलयो: ।
नासापुटम् वकारार्णो रेकारस्तु मुखे तता ॥ १८

*Chakśuṣī Tu Vikārārṇastukārastu Kapolayoḥ* |
*Nāsāpuṭam Vakārārṇo Rekārastu Mukhe Tathā* || 18

Again, let the *'Tat'* of the twenty–four syllabled Gayatri protect my head; *'Sa'*, protect my forehead; *'Vi'* protect my eyes; *'Tu'* my cheeks; *'Va'*, protect my nostrils; *'Re'*, my mouth;

णिकार ऊर्ध्वमोष्ठं तु यकारस्त्वधरोष्ठकम् ।
आस्यमध्ये भकारार्णो गोर्कारश्चिबुके तथा ॥ १९

*Ṇikāra Ūrdhvamoṣṭham Tu Yakārastvadharoṣṭakam |*

*Āsyamadhye Bhakārārṇor Gokāraścubuke Tathā* || 19

*'Ni'* protects my upper lip; *'Yah'* protect my lower lip; *'Bha'* within my face; *'Rgo'*, protect my cheeks;

देकार: कण्ठदेशे तु वकार: स्कन्धदेशकम् ।

स्यकारो दक्षिणं हस्तं धीकारो वामहस्तकम् ॥ २०

*Dekāraḥ Kaṇṭhadeśe Tu Vakāraḥ Skandhadeśakam |*

*Syakāro Dakśiṇam Hastam Dhīkāro Vāmahastakam* || 20

*'De'*, my throat; *'Va'* my shoulders; *'Sya'* my right hand; *'Dhi'* my navel;

मकारो ह्रदयं रक्षेद्धिकार उदरे तथा ।

धिकारो नाभिदेशे तु योकारस्तु कटिं तथा ॥ २१

*Makāro Hrudayam Rakśeddhikāra Udare Tathā |*

*Dhikāro Nābhideśe Tuyokārastu Kaṭim Tathā* || 21

*'Ma'*, my heart, *'Hi'*, my belly; *'Dhi'*, my navel; *'Yo'* my hips;

गुह्यं रक्षतु योकार ऊरू द्वौ न: पदाक्षरम् ।

प्रकारो जानुनी रक्षेच्चोकारो जङ्घदेशकम् ॥ २२

*Guhyam Rakśatu Yokāra Ūru Dvou Naḥ Padākśaram |*

*Prakāro Jānunī Rakśeccokāro Janghadeśakam* || 22

*'Yo'*, my secret organs; *'nah'*, my thighs, *'Pra'*, my Knees; *'Cho'* my shanks,

दकारं गुल्फदेशे तु यकार: पदयुग्मकम् ।

तकारव्यञ्जनं चैव सर्वाङ्गं मे सदावतु ॥ २३

*Dakāram Gulphadeśe Tu Yakāraḥ Padayugmakam |*

*Takāro Vyanjanam Chaiva Sarvāngam Me Sadā Avatu* || 23

*'Da'* my heels; *'Ya'* my legs and let *'ta'* protect all my organs.

इदं तु कवचं दिव्यं बाधाशतविनाशनम् ।

चतु:षष्टिकलाविद्यादायकं मोक्षकारकम् ॥ २४

*Idam Tu Kavacam Divyam Bādhāśatavināśanam |*

*Catuḥṣaṣṭikalāvidyādāyakam Mokśakārakam* || 24

This divine *Kavaca* of the *Devi Gayatri* can baffle hundreds and thousands of obstructions and evils; can grant sixty–four *Kalas* (arts) and further bless with liberation also.

मुच्यते सर्वपापेभ्य: परं ब्रह्माधिगच्छति ।
पठनाच्छ्रुवणाद्वापि गोसहस्रफलं लभेत् ॥ २५

*Muchyate Sarvapāpebhyaḥ Param Brahmādhigacchati |*
*Paṭhanācchravaṇādvāpi Gosahasraphalam Labhet* || 25

By the glory of this *Kavaca*, man can become free from all evils and can attain the state of Brahma. Moreover, whoever reads or hears this acquires the fruits of making a gift of a thousand cows.

इति श्रीमद्देवी भागवत महापुराणेऽष्टादशसाहस्रयां संहितायां द्वादशस्कन्धे
गायत्रीमन्त्रकवचवर्णनं नाम त्रुतीयोऽध्याय: ॥

*Iti Śrī Devī Bhāgavata Mahāpurāṇe Dvādaśaskandhe*
*Gāyatrīmantrakavacam Sampūrṇam* ||

Here ends the Third Chapter of the Twelfth Book on the description of the Kavacha of Sri Gayatri Devi in the Mahapuranam Sri Mad Devi Bhagavatam of 18,000 verses by Maharsi Veda Vyasa.

*****

## *Śrī Gāyatrī Hṛudaya Storam*

श्री गायत्री हृदय स्तोत्रम्

(*Sri Devi Bhagavatam* – 12.4 )

नारद उवाच । *Nārada Uvāca* ।

भगवन्देवदेवेश भूतभव्य जगत्प्रभो ।
कवचं च शृतं दिव्यं गायत्री मन्त्रविग्रहम् ॥ १

*Bhagavandevadeveśa Bhūtabhavya Jagatprabho* ।

*Kavacaṃ Ca Śṛtaṃ Divyaṃ Gāyatrīmantravigraham* ॥ 1

अधुना श्रोतुमिच्छामि गायत्रीहृदयं परम् ।
यद्धारणाद्भवेत्पुण्यं गायत्रीजपतोऽखिलम् ॥ २

*Adhunā Śrotumicchāmi Gāyatrīhṛdayaṃ Param* ।

*Yaddhāraṇādbhavetpuṇyaṃ Gāyatrījapato'khilam* ॥ 2

Sage Narada said – Oh Bhagavan! I have heard from you all about the Kavacha and the Mantra of Sri Gayatri. Oh, Deva Deva! Oh you, the Knower of the present, the past and the future! Now tell about the Hrudaya, the highest, the interior or esoteric Essence of the Gayatri, holding which, if one repeats the Gayatri, he acquires all the *punyam* (merits), I am desirous to hear this.

श्री नारायण उवाच । *Śrīnārāyaṇa Uvāca* ।

देव्याश्च हृदयं प्रोक्तं नारदाथर्वणे स्फुटम् ।
तदेवाहं प्रवक्ष्यामि रहस्यातिरहस्यकम् ॥ ३

*Devyāśca Hṛdayaṃ Proktaṃ Nāradātharvaṇe Sphuṭam* ।

*Tadevāhaṃ Pravakṣyāmi Rahasyātirahasyakam* ॥ 3

Sri Narayana said – Oh Narada! This subject on the Hrudaya of Gayatri is explicitly written in the Atharva Veda. Now I will speak on that, the great secret, in detail. Listen.

विराड्रूपां महादेवीं गायत्रीं वेदमातरम् ।
ध्यात्वा तस्यास्त्वथाङ्गेषु ध्यायेदेताश्च देवताः ॥ ४

*Virāḍrūpāṃ Mahādevīṃ Gāyatrīṃ Vedamātaram* |

*Dhyātvā Tasyāstvathāṅgeṣu Dhyāyedetāśca Devatāḥ* || 4

First, consider the Gayatri, the Devi, the Mother of the Vedas as of a Cosmic Form (Virat rupa) and meditate all the Devas as residing on Her Body.

पिण्ड ब्रह्मण्डयोरैक्याद्भावयेत्स्वतनौ तथा ।

देवीरूपे निजे देहे तन्मयत्वाय साधकः ॥ ५

*Piṇḍabrahmaṇḍayoraikyādbhāvayetsvatanau Tathā* |

*Devīrūpe Nije Dehe Tanmayatvāya Sādhakaḥ* || 5

Now in as much as the *Pinda* and *Brahmanda* are similar, consider yourself as of the form of the *Devi* and meditate within yourself on the *Devatas*.

नादेवोऽभ्यर्चयेद्देवमिति वेदविदो विदुः ।

ततोऽभेदाय काये स्वे भावयेद्देवता इमाः ॥ ६

*Nādevo'bhyarcayeddevamiti Vedavido Viduḥ* |

*Tato'bhedāya Kāye Sve Bhāvayeddevatā Imāḥ* || 6

अथ तत्सम्प्रवक्ष्यामि तन्मयत्वमयो भवेत् ।

गायत्रीहृदयस्यास्याप्यहमेव ऋषिः स्मृतः ॥ ७

*Atha Tatsampravakṣyāmi Tanmayatvamayo Bhavet* |

*Gāyatrīhṛdayasyāsyāpyahameva Ṛṣiḥ Smṛtaḥ* || 7

गायत्रीछन्द उद्दिष्टं देवता परमेश्वरी ।

पूर्वोक्तेन प्रकारेण कुर्यादङ्गानि षट् क्रमात् ।

आसने विजने देशे ध्यायेदेकाग्रमानसः ॥ ८

*Gāyatrīchanda Uddiṣṭaṃ Devatā Parameśvarī* |

*Pūrvoktena Prakāreṇa Kuryādaṅgāni Ṣaṭ Kramāt* |

*Āsane Vijane Deśe Dhyāyedekāgramānasaḥ* || 8

Thus, the pundits, the Knowers of the Vedas, say this He is not yet fit to worship the Deva and he is not an Adhikari as yet who has not been able to make himself a Deva; therefore, to establish the knowledge of the oneness of the Deva and himself, he is to meditate the Devas within his body.

Oh Narada! Now I will speak on the Hrudaya of Gayatri, knowing which every man becomes able to become all the Devas. Listen. The Rishi of this Gayatri Hrudaya is Narayana; the Chandas is Gayatri; and Sri Parameshvari Gayatri is the Devata. Perform the Nyasa of this as mentioned before and taking your seat in a lonely place, meditate intently on the Devi with your heart and head well collected.

अथार्थन्यासः ॥ द्यौमूर्ध्नि दैवतम् ॥

*Athārthanyāsaḥ* ॥ *Dyaumūrdhni Daivatam* ॥

Now I am speaking of the Arthanyasa. Hear.

दन्तपङ्क्तावश्विनौ ॥ उभे सन्ध्ये चौष्ठौ ॥ मुखमग्निः ॥ जिह्वा सरस्वती ॥

*Dantapaṅktāvaśvinau* ॥ *Ubhe Sandhye Cauṣṭhau* ॥

*Mukhamagniḥ* ॥ *Jihvā Sarasvatī* ॥

Meditate on the Swarga Devata on your head; the twin Ashvins on the rows of the teeth; the two Sandhyas on your upper and lower lips; the Agni, Fire, within your mouth; Sarasvati, on the tongue;

ग्रीवायां तु बृहस्पतिः ॥ स्तनयोर्वसवोऽष्टौ ॥ बाह्वोर्मरुतः ॥ हृदये पर्जन्यः ॥

*Grīvāyāṃ Tu Bṛhaspatiḥ* ॥ *Stanayorvasavo'ṣṭau* ॥

*Bāhvormarutaḥ* ॥ *Hṛdaye Parjanyaḥ* ॥

Brihaspati on the neck; the eight Vasus on the two breasts; the Vayus, on the two arms; the Parjanya Deva on the heart;

आकाशमुदरम् ॥ नाभावन्तरिक्षम् ॥ कट्योरिन्द्राग्नी ॥

*Ākāśamudaram* ॥ *Nābhāvantarikṣam* ॥ *Kaṭyorindrāgnī* ॥

Akasha, on the belly; Antariksham (the middle space) on the navel; Indra and Agni, on the loins;

जघने विज्ञानघनः प्रजापतिः ॥ कैलासमलये ऊरू ॥

*Jaghane Vijñānaghanaḥ Prajāpatiḥ* ॥ *Kailāsamalaye Ūrū* ॥

Prajapati, the condensed form, as it were, of Vijnana, on the hip joints; the Kailash mountain on the two thighs;

विश्वेदेवा जान्वोः ॥ जङ्घायां कौशिकः ॥ गुह्यमयने ॥

*Viśvedevā Jānvoḥ* ॥ *Jaṅghāyāṃ Kauśikaḥ* ॥ *Guhyamayane* ॥

ऊरू पितरः ॥ पादौ पृथिवी ॥ वनस्पतयोङ्गुलीषु ॥

*Ūrū Pitaraḥ* ॥ *Pādau Pṛthivī* ॥ *Vanaspatayoṅgulīṣu* ॥

ऋषयो रोमाणि ॥ नखानि मुहूर्तानि ॥ अस्थिषु ग्रहाः ॥

*Ṛṣayo Romāṇi* ॥ *Nakhāni Muhūrtāni* ॥ *Asthiṣu Grahāḥ* ॥

असृङ्मांसमृतवः ॥ संवत्सरा वै निमिषम् ॥

*Asṛṅmāṃsamṛtavaḥ* ॥ *Saṃvatsarā Vai Nimiṣam* ॥

अहोरात्रावादित्यश्चन्द्रमाः ॥

*Ahorātrāvādityaścandramāḥ* ॥

प्रवरं दिव्यां गायत्रीं सहस्रनेत्रां शरणमहं प्रपद्ये ॥

*Pravaraṃ Divyāṃ Gāyatrīṃ Sahasranetrāṃ Śaraṇamahaṃ Prapadye* ॥

The Vishvedevas on the two knees; Vishvamitra on the shanks; the Sun's northern and southern paths, the Uttarayana and Dakshinayana on the anus; the Pitrus on the thighs; the Earth on the legs; the Vanaspati on the fingers and toes; the Rishis on the hairs of the body; the Muhurtas on the nails; the planets on the bones; the Ritus (seasons) on the blood and flesh; the Samvatsaras on the Nimisha (twinkling of eye) the Sun and the Moon on the day and night respectively. Thinking thus, repeat "I take refuge of the Divine Holy Gayatri, the Chief and most Excellent One, the Thousand eyed and I take refuge wholly unto Her".

ॐ तत्सवितुर्वरेण्याय नमः ॥ ॐ तत्पूर्वाजयाय नमः ॥

*Oṃ Tatsaviturvareṇyāya Namaḥ* ॥ *Oṃ Tatpūrvājayāya Namaḥ* ॥

तत्प्रातरादित्याय नमः ॥ तत्प्रातरादित्यप्रतिष्ठायै नमः ॥

*Tatprātarādityāya Namaḥ* ॥ *Tatprātarādityapratiṣṭhāyai Namaḥ* ॥

Then repeat;

I bow down to *Tat Savitur Varenyam,*
I bow down to the Rising Sun on the East,
I bow down to the Morning Aditya,
I bow down to the Gayatri, residing in the Morning Sun and
I bow down to all.

प्रातरधीयानो रात्रिकृतं पापं नाशयति ॥

*Prātaradhīyāno Rātrikṛtaṃ Pāpaṃ Nāśayati* ॥

सायमधीयानो दिवसकृतं पापं नाशयति ॥

*Sāyamadhīyāno Divasakṛtaṃ Pāpaṃ Nāśayati* ॥

सायंप्रातरधीयानः अपापो भवति ॥

*Sāyaṃprātaradhīyānaḥ Apāpo Bhavati* ॥

सर्वतीर्थेषु स्नातो भवति ॥ सर्वैर्देवैर्ज्ञातो भवति ॥

*Sarvatīrtheṣu Snāto Bhavati* ॥ *Sarvairdevairjñāto Bhavati* ॥

अवाच्यवचनात्पूतो भवति ॥ अभक्ष्यभक्षणात्पूतो भवति ॥

*Avācyavacanātpūto Bhavati* ॥ *Abhakṣyabhakṣaṇātpūto Bhavati* ॥

अभोज्यभोजनात्पूतो भवति ॥ अचोष्यचोषणात्पूतो भवति ॥

*Abhojyabhojanātpūto Bhavati* ॥ *Acoṣyacoṣaṇātpūto Bhavati* ॥

असाध्यसाधनात्पूतो भवति ॥ दुष्प्रतिग्रहशतसहस्रात्पूतो भवति ॥

*Asādhyasādhanātpūto Bhavati* ॥

*Duṣpratigrahaśatasahasrātpūto Bhavati* ॥

पङ्क्तिदूषणात्पूतो भवति ॥ अमृतवचनात्पूतो भवति ॥

*Paṅktidūṣaṇātpūto Bhavati* ॥ *Amṛtavacanātpūto Bhavati* ॥

अथाब्रह्मचारी ब्रह्मचारी भवती ॥

*Athābrahmacārī Brahmacārī Bhavatī* ॥

Oh Narada! Whoever recites this Gayatri Hrudaya in the morning finds all the sins committed in the night all destroyed! Whoever recites this in the evening gets his sins of the day all destroyed! Whoever recites this in the evening and in the morning can rest assured to have become free of sins; he gets the fruits of all the Tirthas; he is acquainted with all the Devas; he is saved if he has spoken anything that ought not to have been spoken; if he has eaten anything that is not fit to be eaten; if he has chew and sucked anything that ought not to have been chew and sucked; if he has done anything that ought not to have been done and if he has accepted hundreds and thousands of gifts that ought never to have been accepted. The sins incurred by eating with the others in a line cannot touch him. If he speaks lies, he will not be touched by the sins thereof; even if a non–Brahmachari recites this, he will become a Brahmachari.

अनेन हृदयेनाधीतेन क्रतुसहस्रेणेष्टं भवति ॥

*Anena Hṛdayenādhītena Kratusahasreṇeṣṭaṃ Bhavati* ॥

षष्टिशतसहस्रगायत्र्या जप्यानि फलानि भवन्ति ॥

*Ṣaṣṭiśatasahasragāyatryā Japyāni Phalāni Bhavanti* ॥

अष्टौ ब्राह्मणान्सम्यग्ग्राहयेत् ॥ तस्य सिद्धिर्भवति ॥

*Aṣṭau Brāhmaṇānsamyaggrāhayet* ॥ *Tasya Siddhirbhavati* ॥

Oh Narada! What more shall I say to you of the results of Gayatri Hrudaya than this – that whoever will study this will acquire the fruits of performing thousand sacrifices and repeating the Gayatri sixty thousand times. In fact, he will get Siddhi by this.

य इदं नित्यमधीयानो ब्राह्मणः प्रातः शुचिः सर्वपापः
प्रमुच्यत इति ॥ ब्रह्मलोके महीयते ॥

*Ya Idaṃ Nityamadhīyāno Brāhmaṇaḥ Prātaḥ Śuciḥ Sarvapāpaḥ*
*Pramucyata Iti* ॥ *Brahmaloke Mahīyate* ॥

The Brahmana, who daily reads this in the morning will be freed of all the sins and go upwards to the Brahma (Loka) and is glorified there.

इत्याह भगवान् श्रीनारायणः ॥

*Ityāha Bhagavān Śrīnārāyaṇaḥ* ॥

This has been uttered by *Bhagavan Narayana* Himself.

इति श्रीदेवीभागवते महापुराणे द्वादशस्कन्धे गायत्री हृदयं नाम चतुर्थोऽध्यायः ॥

*Iti Śrīdevībhāgavate Mahāpurāṇe*
*Dvādaśaskandhe*
*Gāyatrīhṛdayaṃ Nāma Caturtho'dhyāyaḥ* ॥

Here ends the Fourth Chapter of the Twelfth Book on Gayatri Hrudaya in the Mahapuranam Shrimad Devi Bhagavatam of 18,000 verses by Maharsi Veda Vyasa.

*****

# Śrī Gāyatri Sahasranāmam

The *Devi Bhagavata Purana* (देवी भागवतपुराण), also known as the *Shrimad Devi Bhagavatam* or the *Devi Bhagavatam*, is a Samskruta text that belongs to the Purana–genre of Hindu literature. This text is considered as one of the Maha–puranas or upa–puranas – as already discussed.

This text consists of 12 Skandas (sections) with 318 chapters and 18,476 verses. Along with Sri Devi Mahatmya, it is one of the most important works in Shaktism, a tradition within Hinduism that reveres Devi or Shakti (Goddess) as the primordial creator of the universe and the Brahmam (ultimate truth and reality). It celebrates the divine feminine as the origin of all existence, the creator, the preserver and the destroyer of everything, as well as the one who empowers spiritual liberation.

While all major Puranas mention and revere the Goddess, this text centers around her as the primary divinity. The underlying philosophy of this text is Advaita Vedanta–style monism combined with devotional worship of Shakti (feminine power).

Since all the purana–s is written by Veda Vyasa only, naturally this Devi Bhagavatam also. In this book, 6th chapter in the 12th Skandam describes Sri Gayatri Sahasranamam. This is in a way a dialogue between sage Narada and Sri Narayana. Although Sri Narayana told this to Sage Narada, it was created for all of us to live on.

This Sahasranamam Stotra has three parts – First part including Dhyana verse, main part and the end part. Each part contains respectively 9 + 146 + 10 = total 165 verses. These three parts are discussed with meaning in the following three chapters.

These 146 verses of the main part are split into 1008 names of Sri Gayatri Devi. The beauty here is all the names are in Samskruta alphabetical order covering all the 52 letters (*akashrams*).

Most of the names are common with Sri Lalita Sahasranama, Sri Lalita Trishatee, etc. This implies that all are forms of the same Sri Devi/ Para–Devata/ Brahmam. Wherever possible the names are compared with that of Sri Lalita Sahasranamam and others.

A table with a small comparison of Sri Gayatri Sahasranamam with other major two Sahasranamas viz., Sri Vishnu Sahasranamam and Sri Lalita Sahasranama.

| | **Sri Gayatri Sahasranama** | **Sri Vishnu Sahasranama** | **Sri Lalita Sahasranama** |
|---|---|---|---|
| Presiding Deity | Gayatri Devi | Vishnu | Lalita Devi |
| # of verses in the First Part | 9 | 22 | 50 |
| Dhyana Verse(s) | 1 | 8 | 3 |
| No of verses in the Main Part | 146 | 108 | 182.5 |
| No of verses in the End Part | 10 | 32 | 86 |
| # of names | 1,008 | 1,000 | 1,000 |
| Author | Veda Vyasa | Veda Vyasa | Veda Vyasa |
| Part of | Devi Bhagavatam | Mahabharata | Brahmanda Puranam |
| Dialogue Between | Sage Narada and Sri Narayana | Bheeshma and Pandavas | Hayagriva and Sage Agastya |
| Repetition of names | ~31 | ~35 | Nil |

Let us try to comprehend the 1000 names and enjoy the benefits.

*****

## *Śrī Gāyatri Sahasranāma Pūrva Bhāgaḥ*

*Pūrva Bhāgaḥ* – First part – a kind of preamble to the Gayatri Sahasranama Stotram that is to be followed.

नारद उवाच । *Nārada Uvāca* ।

भगवन् सर्व धर्मज्ञ सर्व शास्त्र विशारद ।
श्रुति स्मृति पुराणानाम् रहस्यम् त्वन्मुखाच्छ्रुतम् ॥ १

*Bhagavan Sarva Dharmajña Sarva Śāstraviśārada* ।
*Śruti Smṛtipurāṇānāṃ Rahasyaṃ Tvanmukhācchrutam* ॥ 1

Narada said – Oh Bhagavan! Oh All–knowing One! Oh, you well versed in all the Shastras! I have heard from your mouth all the secrets of Shrutis and Smritis.

सर्वपापहरम् देव येन विद्या प्रवर्तते ।
केन वा ब्रह्मिविज्ञानं किं नु वा मोक्षसाधनम् ॥ २

*Sarvapāpaharaṃ Deva Yena Vidyā Pravareate* ।
*Kena Vā Brahmavijñānaṃ Kiṃ Nu Vā Mokṣasādhanam* ॥ 2

ब्राह्मणानां गति: केन केन वा मृत्युनाशनम् ।
ऐहिकामुष्मिक फलं केन वा पद्मलोचन ॥ ३

*Brāhmaṇānāṃ Gatiḥ Kena Kena Vā Mṛtyu Nāśanam* ।
*Aihikāmuṣmika Phalaṃ Kena Vā Padmalocana* ॥ 3

वक्तुमर्हस्यशेषेण सर्वं निखिलमादित: ।
*Vaktumarhasyaśeṣeṇa Sarve Nikhilamāditaḥ* ।

Now I ask you, Oh Deva! How can the knowledge of that Veda Vidya (Learning) be obtained by which all sins are rooted out and destroyed, how is Brahmajnanam obtained and how can Moksha be obtained? How can the death be conquered and how can the best results be obtained in this world and in the next?

Oh Lotus–eyed One! You ought to describe fully all these to me.

श्रीनारायण उवाच । *Śrīnārāyaṇa Uvāca* ।

साधु साधु महाप्राज्ञ सम्यक् पृष्टं त्वयानघ ॥ ४

*Sādhu Sādhu Mahāprājña Samyak Pṛṣṭaṃ Tvayā'nagha* ॥ 4

Sri Narayana said – Oh Narada! Oh, Highly Learned One! Sadhu! Sadhu! You have now put a nice question indeed!

शृणु वक्ष्यामि यत्नेन गायत्र्यष्ट सहस्रकम् ।
नाम्नां शुभानां दिव्यानां सर्वपाप विनाशनम् ॥ ५

*Śṛṇu Vakṣyāmi Yatnena Gāyatryaṣṭasahasrakam* ।
*Nāmnāṃ Śubhānāṃ Divyānāṃ Sarvapāpavināśanam* ॥ 5

सृष्ट्यादौ यद्भगवता पूर्वं प्रोक्तं ब्रवीमि ते ।
अष्टोत्तर सहस्रस्य ऋषिर्ब्रह्मा प्रकीर्तित: ॥ ६

*Sṛṣṭyādau Yadbhagavatā Pūrve Proktaṃ Bravīmi Te* ।
*Aṣṭottarasahasrasya Ṛṣirbrahmā Prakīrtitaḥ* ॥ 6

छन्दोऽनुष्टुप् तथा देवी गायत्री देवता स्मृता ।
हलो बीजानि तस्यैव स्वरा: शक्तय ईरिता: ॥ ७

*Chando'nuṣṭup Tathā Devī Gāyatrīṃ Devatā Smṛtā* ।
*Halo Bījāni Tasyaiva Svarāḥ Śaktaya Īritāḥ* ॥ 7

अङ्गन्यास करन्यासावुच्येते मातृकाक्षरै: ।
अथ ध्यानं प्रवक्ष्यामि साधकानां हिताय वै ॥ ८

*Aṅganyāsa Karanyāsāvucyete Mātṛkākṣaraiḥ* ।
*Atha Dhyānaṃ Pravakṣyāmi Sādhakānāṃ Hitāya Vai* ॥ 8

Now I will describe one thousand and eight names of the Gayatri Devi. Listen attentively. These all sin–destroying auspicious names were composed by Brahma and first recited by Himself.

Its Rishi is Brahma; the Chandas is Anushtup; the Devata is Gayatri;

Its Beeja is Halovarna (consonants) and its Shakti is Svaravarna (vowels). Perform the Anga Nyasa and the Kara Nyasa[3] by the Matrika varnas (that is, by the fifty syllables).

---

[3] Anga Nyasa – Touching the limbs of the body with the hand accompanied by appropriate Mantras. Kara Nyasa – assignment of the various pares of fingers and hand to different deities which is usually accompanied with prayers and corresponding gesticulations.

रक्त श्वेत हिरण्य नील धवलैर्युक्तां त्रिनेत्रोज्ज्वलां
रक्तां रक्तनवस्रजं मणिगणैर्युक्तां कुमारीमिमाम् ।
गायत्रीं कमलासनां करतल व्यानद्ध कुण्डाम्बुजां
पद्माक्षीं च वरस्रजं च दधातीं हंसाधि रूढां भजे ॥ ९

*Rakta Śveta Hiraṇya Nīla Dhavalairyuktā Trinītrojjvalāṃ*
*Raktāṃ Raktanavasrajaṃ Maṇigaṇairyuktāṃ Kumārīmimām* |
*Gāyatrīṃ Kamalāsanāṃ Karatalavyānaddhakuṇḍāmbujāṃ*
*Padmākṣī Ca Varasrajaṃ Ca Dadhatīṃ Haṃsādhirūḍhāṃ Bhaje* ॥ 9

Now hear its Dhyanam, that will do good to the Sadhakas (the practisers).

- The Gayatri Devi has five faces; one of which is of white colour and the other four are of pearl, Vidruma, golden and Nilakantamani colours respectively.
- Each face has got lotus like three eyes;
- On the head there is a crown of jewels and the digit of the Moon is shining there.
- Her body is composed of the twenty–four tattvas.
- She has ten hands –
    - On the top right and left hands there are two lotuses;
    - Lower down, there are disc and conch shell;
    - Lower down, there are rope and skull;
    - Lower down, there are noose and goad;
    - On the bottom hands right and left she is making signs of "No fear" and "ready to grant boons".
- Riding on the Swan (the Pranas)
- Seated on a lotus (creation);
- Who is bright and decorated with gems and jewels of red, white, green, blue, yellow and other variegated colours;
- On whose neck is suspended the garland of red flowers.

I worship that Kumari (virgin) Gayatri Devi.

Note; The colours are the various emotions and feelings. The above same dhyana verse has been explained earlier chapters also.

Thus ends the first part (Poorva Bhaga) Sri Gayatri Sahasranamam.

*****

# 1000 Divine Names on *Śrī Gāyatri Devī*

ध्यानम् – *Dhyānam*

रक्त श्वेत हिरण्य नील धवलैर्युक्तां त्रिनेत्रोज्ज्वलां
रक्तां रक्तनवस्रजं मणिगणैर्युक्तां कुमारीमिमाम् ।
गायत्रीं कमलासनां करतल व्यानद्ध कुण्डाम्बुजां
पद्माक्षीं च वरस्रजं च दधातीं हंसाधि रूढां भजे ॥

*Rakta Śveta Hiraṇya Nīla Dhavalairyuktā Trinītrojjvalāṃ*
*Raktāṃ Raktanavasrajaṃ Maṇigaṇairyuktāṃ Kumārīmimām* ।
*Gāyatrīṃ Kamalāsanāṃ Karatalavyānaddhakuṇḍāmbujāṃ*
*Padmākṣī Ca Varasrajaṃ Ca Dadhatīṃ Haṃsādhirūḍhāṃ Bhaje* ॥

The meaning of this *Dhyana* verse has already been provided in the earlier chapters.

1. अचिन्त्यलक्षणा – *Acintyalakṣaṇā*

- *Acintya* – She is beyond thought, imagination and contemplation.
- *Lakṣaṇā* – She is also is usually a super crazy, fun girl who looks like a princess. Her looks and humour can make both men and women crazy about her.

2. अव्यक्ता – *Avyaktā*

- She is in an unmanifested or devoid of form. She is the Prakrit on account of subtleness of its nature and also denoting the Brahmam, which is the subtlest of all and who by virtue of that subtlety is the ultimate support (Ashraya) of Prakrit.
- *Avyakta* as a category along with *Mahat* (Cosmic Intelligence) and *Purusha*.
- The Bhagavad Gita (III.42) retains the psychological categories altogether and drops out the Mahat and the Avyakta (Unmanifest), the two objective categories.

3. अर्थमातृमहेश्वरी – *Arthamātṛmaheśvarī*

- She is the controller of the earth and the entire universe.
- Controller of all devas starting from Brahma.

4. अमृता – *Amṛtā*

- Who is in the form of *Amrutha* (nectar) – *Amruthasvarupini*.
- One who lives in the center of the ocean of nectar.

5. अर्णवमध्यस्था – *Arṇavamadhyasthā*

- One who lives in the middle of an ocean.
- In this context ocean may mean the ocean of milk. Gayatri Devi lives in the ocean of milk alongwith Sri Narayanan.
- 61st name of Sri Lalita Sahasranamam – *Sudhā Sāgara Madhyasthā* – is worth comparing here.

6. अजिता – *Ajitā*

- One who cannot be conquered.
- One who can be conquered only through *yoga*
- The literature *Kāmikā* describes each of *Tantras* to the organs of **Her** body. Here the *Tantra* called *Ajitā* is mapped to her knees.

7. अपराजिता – *Aparājitā*

- This is comparable with the 6th name above – *Ajitā*.
- As per *Devi Purana*, after conquering the king of demons named *Padman*, **she** is known in the three worlds by the epithet *Aparājitā* (unconquerable).
- According to *Chāndogya Upanishat*, the ocean of milk, is located in the city of *Aparājitā*, which can be reached by worshipping her with attributes (*Saguṇopāsanā*).
- *Aparājitā* for *Sri Devi* worshippers is like *Kailash* for *Shiva* worshippers and *Śree Vaikuṇtam* for worshippers of *Vishṇu*.

8. अणिमादिगुणाधारा – *Aṇimādiguṇādhārā*

- **She** is in the form of all these *siddhis* and also gives them to the devotees
- 224th name of Sri Lalita Sahasranamam – *Mahāsiddhiḥ* – is worth comparing here.
- Attainments (*siddhis*) are of eight types as detailed below;

| Aṇimā | Reducing one's body to the size of an atom and roaming around without being seen by others. |
|---|---|
| Mahimā | Expanding one's body to an infinitely large size |
| Garimā | Becoming infinitely heavy |
| Laghimā | Becoming almost weightless |
| Prāpti | Having unrestricted access to all places. |
| Prākāmva | Getting all desires without any restriction. |
| Lesitvā | Control of all movable or immovable things. |
| Vasitvā | The power to subjugate all. |

In addition to the above there are various other *siddhis* like, creating passions like erotic and heroic as per one's wish, not becoming slaves of happiness, sorrow, chillness, heat, desires, aversion, etc.

9. अर्कमण्डलसंस्थिता – *Arkamaṇḍalasaṃsthitā*

- She is seated in the solar system.
- 275th name of Sri Lalita Sahasranamam – *Bhānu Maṇḍala Madhyasthā* – conveys the same meaning.

10. अजरा – *Ajarā*

- Always looking young as pubescent
- 358th name of Sri Lalita Sahasranamam – *Taruṇee* – conveys the same meaning.
- She, as a young girl, lives in *Vişhṇu Granthi* and screams to pierce it (only *Yogis* can hear this sound).

11. अजा – *Ajā*

- One who is unborn. She does not have any origin and hence no end also.
- The same message is conveyed in Sri Lalita Sahasranamam – 866th name – *Ajā* and in 174th name *Nirbhavā*.
- The *Śvētāśvatara Upanishat* (IV–5) – The one, unborn; was not born, will not be born;
- In another *Shruti* we read as – unborn and will not be born again; *Najāto Najanishyate*.
- In *Devi Upanishat* also (26th *rig*) we read as;

  *Yasyā Anto Na Vidyāte Tasmāduchyatenantā* I

*Yasyā Jananam Nopalabyate Tasmātuchyatojā* II

- When there is no birth, naturally there is no end also.

12. अपरा – *Aparā*

- Nobody is there other than herself.
- During the great dissolution **She** only was there.
- Aparā is the three states awaken (Jāgrath), dream (Swapna) and deep sleep (Sushupti). Para is the fourth state.
- *Parā* and *Aparā* are the twofold ether.
- *Parā* – the other person, *Aparā* – dependent on self, i.e., it respectively means an enemy and a friend.
- *Parā* has the qualities of *Sachitānanda* and *Aparā* is pure form.
- *Parā* – superior and *Aparā* – inferior. *Shruti* says, "*Brahmam* is the servant. *Brahmam* is ferry–men;
- *Nityā Shoḍashikārnava* (8th chapter, 2nd verse onwards) explains that *Sri Devi's pooja* is of three types – *Parā, Aparā and Parāpara*. *Para* is worshipping with non–duality in mind (however it is done). *Apara* is worshipping *Śree Chakra*. *Parāpara* is worshipping different types of idols.
- *The speech is of two types – Parā and Apara. Aparā includes Pashyantee, Madyamā and Vaikharee.*
- *Shrimad Bhagavad Geeta* (IX–29) says that the *Brahmam* is of these two types; I have neither foe nor friend.

*Na Me Dveshyosti Na Priyaḥ*

- *Parā* – he who is far off, *Aparā* he who is near. *Shrimad Bhagavad Geeta* (XIII–15) – "I am far and near".

13. अधर्मा – *Adharmā*

- One who is devoid of vices (*adharmas*).
- Actually, she is devoid of both virtued and vices (dharmas and adharmas).
- *Dharma* indicates a sort of limitations or restrictions. That is, the controls for the caste, religion and other *āshramās* respectively are called *dharma*. If these are broken, it is *adharma*. In this context also, **she** is not bound by these distinctions. Hence *Sri Gayatri Devi* is beyond *dharma* and *adharma*.
- 245th name of Sri Lalita Sahasranamam – *Dharmādharmavivarjitā* – is worth comparable in this regard.
- *Dharma* is a quality or character. For instance, to be hot is a

character, hence *dharma*. One who has a character is called *dharmee*. If the fire loses its character of heat then it is *adharma* (In *Rāmāyana*, Sita requests [not orders] fire to be cool with *Hanumān – Sheeto Bhava Hanumataḥ* – hence it was cool). If one loses its character it is *adharma*. *Sri Gayatri Devi* is not bound by any character and hence **She** does not have *dharma* or *adharma*.

14. अक्षसूत्रधरा – *Akṣasūtradharā*

- She wears a rosary, string of beads.

15. अधरा – *Adharā*

- She stands on her own without the support of anyone.
- She only supports others, why does she need a support.
- Adhara (अधर) refers to the "lower lip". It is one of the six minor limbs (*upāṅga*) used in dramatic performance, according to the *Nāṭyaśāstra* chapter 8. With these limbs are made the various gestures (*āṅgika*), which form a part of the histrionic representation (*abhinaya*). She is in charge of this.

16. अकारादिक्षकारान्ता – *Akārādikṣakārāntā*

- She is in the form of Samskruta alphabets starting from '*A*–अ' ending with '*Kśa*–क्ष'
- Such a form is called "*Varṇa Mātrukā Svarūpiṇī*"
- Samskruta alphabets (the fifty–two letters from *A* to *Ksha*), that is the fifty–two *shakti*s from *Amruta* to *Kshamāvati*;
- **She** shines with these letters and the corresponding presiding deities.
- Counting these fifty–two letters backwards and forwards we obtain a hundred and four *shaktis*, – called *Akśara Mālā* each of these reside in ten petals.
- This name is comparable with the 529th name of Sri Lalita Sahasranamam – *Sarvavarṇopa Śobhitā*.

17. अरिषड्वर्गभेदिनी – *Ariṣadvargabhedinī*

- She destroys the six enemies – internal to the body/ mind viz. *kama* (lust), *krodha* (anger), *lobha* (greed), *mada* (pride), *moha* (attachment) and *matsarya* (jealousy).

18. अञ्जनाद्रिप्रतिकाशा – *Añjanādripratikāśā*

- She shines in black colour (*Krishna Varna*) similar to Anjana mountain.

19. अञ्जनाद्रिनिवासिनी – *Añjanādrinivāsinī*

- She lives in the Anjana mountain.

20. अदितिः – *Aditiḥ*

- *Aditi* is one of the wives of sage *Kashyapa* and she is the mother of all the Devas.
- Sri Gayatri Devi is that *Aditi*.

21. अजपा – *Ajapā*

- The exhale and inhale of breath together is called *Hamsa Mantra* or *Ajapā Mantra*. This is a *mantra* about *Sri Devi* in general or Sri Gayatri in particular and hence **She** is *Ajapā*.
- The *Ajapā mantra* has been described in *Dakshiṇāmūrti Samhita*; "Without repetition (*japa*), Oh *Devesi*, that which brings to the practitioners of *mantra* the attainment (the result) of the repetition, is called *Ajapā*, which breaks as under the noose of the *samsāra*"

22. अविद्या – *Avidyā*

- *Avidyā* or ignorance is *Māyā*. She is *Māyā* and hence *Avidyā*.
- *Gayatri Devi* hides herself by the veil of *Avidyā* (lack of knowledge).
- **She** makes her devotees happy by removing the noose of *avidyā* and leads them to *Brahmam*, which is to be attained by liberated souls only.

23. अरविन्दनिभेक्षणा – *Aravindanibhekṣaṇā*

- Her eyes are like lotus flowers.
- Lord Sri Krishna is also called as "*Pankaja Netrāya*", which means lotus eyed.

24. अन्तर्बहिःस्थिता – *Antarbahiḥsthitā*

- She lives both outside and inside of every devotee.
- Normally devotees to outward looking worship. Once they mature, they can perform inward looking worship and identify the Devi inside.
- This name is comparable with the 870th name of Sri Lalita Sahasranamam – *Antarmukhasamārādhyā* and 871st name – *Bahirmukhasudurlabhā*.

25. अविद्याध्वंसिनी – *Avidyādhvaṃsinī*

- Earlier in 22nd name it was mentioned that she is *Avidyā*. Here it is affirmed that she destroys the ignorance of the devotees.
- She removes the veil called Maya of the devotees and gives darshan to those who perform inward looking worship.

26. अन्तरात्मिका – *Antarātmikā*

- She lives in the heart (*Antarātmā*) of the devotes.

27. अजा – *Ajā*

- She is *Prakruti Svarūpinī*, who does not have any birth/ origin.
- This is a repetition of 11th name.

28. अजमुखावासा – *Ajamukhāvāsā*

- One who resides in one of the faces of Lord Brahma.

29. अरविन्दनिभानना – *Aravindanibhānanā*

- One whose face radiates/ shines like a lotus flower.

30. अर्धमात्रा – *Ardhamātrā*

- She is the *Ardhamātra, Bindu* in the Pranava Mantra 'Om'.
- The *Nityāshoḍashikārnava* (*Yoginihrudaya* I-28) says, the *Ardhamātra* (i.e. the dot or *Bindu* of *Oṃ* or *Hreem*) is in the forehead in

the form of a light; above that there is the *ardhachandra* (crescent) in the same form (i.e. of light) and it is a quarter of that - i.e. one *mātrā* consists of 256 *lavas*; 128 in *ardhamātrā* and 64 in *ardhachandra*);

*Deepākāro'rrdha Mātrashcha Lalate Vrutta Ishyate* I
*Ardhachandrastathākāraḥ Pādamātras Tadoordhvataḥ* II

31. अर्थदानज्ञा – *Arthadānajñā*

- She is happy to bestow all four *puruṣārthas* to her devotees.
- There are four *puruṣārthas* viz., *Dharma* (righteousness, moral values), *Artha* (prosperity, economic values), *Kama* (pleasure, love, psychological values) and *Moksha* (liberation, spiritual values).

32. अरिमण्डलमर्दिनी – *Arimaṇḍalamardinī*

- She destroys all the enemies of her devotees.
- When it is said as enemies it is all inward enemies like what is mentioned in the 17th name – *kama* (lust), *krodha* (anger), *lobha* (greed), *mada* (pride), *moha* (attachment) and *matsarya* (jealousy).

33. असुरघ्नी – *Asurāghnī*

- One who extinguishes the demons (*Asuras*) like *Bhanḍāsurā*, *Mahishāsurā*, etc.
- This name is similar to the 318th name of Sri Lalita Sahasranamam – *Rākshasaghnee*.

34. अमावास्या – *Amāvāsyā*

- She is in the form of *Amavasya Tithi Devata* – *Amavasya Tithiroopa*.
- There are Devis pertaining to each of *tithis* called *Tithi Nitya Devis*. She is in the form *Amavasya Tithi Nitya Devi*.

35. अलक्ष्मीघ्न्त्यजार्चिता – *Alākṣmīghnyajārcitā*

- *Mātangi Devi* was responsible to remove *Alakshmi* – opposite of *Lakshmi*, goddess of wealth.
- That *Mātangi Devi* made *archana* to Gayatri Devi.

36. आदिलक्ष्मी: – *Ādilakṣmīḥ*

- She is in the form of *Ādilakṣmī Devi*.

37. आदिशक्ति: – *Ādiśaktiḥ*

- She is in the form of *Ādiśakti* – the Mahamaya.

38. आकृति: – *Ākṛtiḥ*

- She is in a gigantic form.
- The *Navavarnams* of the *Sri Cakra* are also called as *Ākṛti-s.* She is synonymous with *Sri Cakra.*

39. आयतानना – *Āyatānanā*

- One who has a broad face.

40. आदित्यपदविचारा – *Ādityapadavicārā*

- One who removes all the obstrucles in the path of the Sun's movement.
- While performing *Sandhyavandana* – we used to give *Argyam* – 3 times in the morning and evening and 2 times in the afternoon. This water chant with *Gayatri Mantra* (*Gāyatriyā Abhimantritena Āpaḥ*) goes as an arrow and kills the demons, who disturb the movement of the Sun.

41. आदित्यपरिसेविता – *Ādityaparisevitā*

- One who is worshipped by the Sun God.

42. आचार्या – *Ācāryā*

- One who is in the form of an *Ācāryā.*
- The Jagadgurus or heads of mutts are normally called as *Ācāryā*-s. For instance, *Shankaracharya*.
- One who initiates the mantra to the disciples are also called as *Ācāryā*-s. She is the head of all *Ācāryā*-s.

- It is the practice in some localities to call any guru as *Ācāryā*. She is the guru for all and hence aptly called as *Ācāryā*.

43. आवर्तना – *Āvartanā*

- One who is protecting the whole universe.

44. आचारा – *Ācārā*

- *Acharams* are set of rules that has been analyzed and researched by our sages for our well-being. She follows the Acharams religiously.
- Or it can also be construed as She is responsible to set the *Acharams* through the sages.

45. आदिमूर्तिनिवासिनी – *Ādimūrtinivāsinī*

- She lives alongwith *Ādimūrti*, i.e. *Brahmam*.
- In other words, she is the *Brahmam*.

46. आग्नेयी – *Āgneyī*

- She is the dwelling place for *Agni*.

47. आमरी – *Āmarī*

- She is eternal – ever living.
- She is the one who gave the ever-living status to *Devas*.

48. आद्या – *Ādyā*

- She is the oldest – *Ādiswaroopinee*.

49. आराध्या – *Ārādhyā*

- One who is worshipped by all.

50. आसनस्थिता – *Āsanasthitā*

- One is relaxingly settled on a divine seat.

51. आधारनिलया – *Ādhāranilayā*

- One who dwells in the *Mūlādhāra* of the body
- *Mūlādhāra* is the lower abdomen in the body, just beneath the backbone. **She** resides in the Lotus in that place.
- This name is the same to the 514th name of *Sri Lalita Sahasranamam – Mūlādhārāmbujārūḍhā.*

52. आधारा – *Ādhārā*

- One who dons the whole world.
- She is the *Ādhāra Śakti*.

53. आकाशान्तनिवासिनी – *Ākāśāntanivāsinī*

- She lives in the *ahankāram* inside the *Ākāśa Tatvam*.
- Out of the *kalās* of the five primary elements, the *kalā* of ether *tatva* is called *Shāntyateeta*. *Gayatri Devi* is in that form.
- The ether *tatva* is the unison of *Shiva-Shakti*.

54. आद्याक्षरसमयुक्ता – *Ādyākṣara Samayuktā*

- *Ādyākṣara* is the first letter '*A*-अ'[4]. She is merged with this letter.

55. आन्तराकाशरूपिणी – *Āntarākāśarūpiṇī*

- There is a subtle hidden cave in the heart of every soul. She dwells there in the form of ether.
- *Ākāsha* means sky, ether, vacuum, place, etc. There is subtle ether in the heart of every human being. This is worshipped as *Parabrahmam* or *Devi*.
- *Brahma Sūtra* says, the small ether is *Brahmam*;

  *Dahara Uttarebhyaḥ*.
- The *Chāndogya Upanishat* (VIII-1-1) says, there is in this city of *Brahmam* the small lotus house and in it that small ether that should be sought for. Hence the ether of the heart is said to be *Brahmam*;

---

[4] The first Thirukural starting with "Akara mudala..." starts with the first letter of the Tamil alphabet is worth comparing here.

- The same is advised by *Śree Appayya Deekshitar* in his book called *Ratnatraya Parīkṣai*.
- 609th name of *Sri Lalita Sahasranamam – Daharākāśarūpiṇī* – also conveys the same sense.

56. आदित्यमण्डलगता – *Ādityamaṇḍalagatā*

- She exists in the solar system.
- One who is in the midst of the solar orbit.
- It is a method of worshipping *Sri Devi* meditating upon **Her** in the Sun's disc.
- It is also described that *Bhānumaṇḍala* is the *Anāhata cakra*. *Sri Devi* is in the form of *Kuṇḍalini* there.
- 9th name above also conveyed the same message.
- 275th name of *Sri Lalita Sahasranamam – Bhānu Maṇḍala Madhyasthā* – also conveys the same sense.

57. आन्तरध्वान्तनाशिनी – *Āntaradhvāntanāśinī*

- She removes the ignorance of the devotees.
- Ignorance is the *maya*. Only when it is removed, Sri Devi can be realized. She removes it and hence the *upasaka* can understand her.

58. इन्दिरा – *Indirā*

- *Indirā* means Lakshmi. She is Lakshmi, the goddess of wealth.

59. इष्टदा – *Iṣṭadā*

- She bestows anything sought for by the devotees.
- All the legal (not only within the laws of the nation, but also with the laws of Shastras) wishes are satisfied by her.

60. इष्टा –*Iṣṭā*

- Most sought after Devi by the devotees.

61. इन्दीवरनिभेक्षणा – *Indivaranibhekṣaṇā*

- One who has beautiful eyes like a blue lotus flower.

- It may be noted that in the 23rd name it was mentioned as she has lotus like eyes.

62. इरावती – *Irāvatī*

- *Irā* means earth. She originated from earth.
- Gayatri Devi has taken many incarnations. One such incarnation is Sita, who originated from Earth.

63. इन्द्रपदा – *Indrapadā*

- Indra got his post because of the blessings of Gayatri Devi.
- Normally anyone who does heavy penance, would get the post of Indra, but of course with the blessings of her.

64. इन्द्राणी – *Indrāṇī*

- She is in the form of *Sachidevi*, consort of Indra.
- Earlier it was mentioned that She is in the form of the Devis in-charge of all the 52 letters of Samskrutam. *Indrāṇī* is one such form and she is in that form.

65. इन्दुरूपिणी – *Indurūpiṇī*

- She is in the form of Moon.
- She is so beautiful like a Moon.

66. इक्षुकोदण्डसंयुक्ता – *Ikṣukodaṇḍasaṃyuktā*

- She holds a bow made of sugarcane in her bottom left hand.
- *Sri Devi* has a bow made of sugarcane in her left hand. It's symbolic form of the mind.
- Sugarcane is full of moisture; Sugarcane bow is a weapon, though it is sweet; again, it is sweet, though it is a weapon. It shows that *Sri Devi's* mind is full of benignity. Is it not **Her** mind full of sweetness and graciousness?
- The presiding deity of sugarcane bow is *Mantrinī* representing the power of intellect (*Buddhi Shakī*).
- *Shyamala* is a *Shakti* created by *Sri Devi* out of her sugarcane bow as an embodiment of mind energy.

- Usually Cupid (Manmatha) is said to have a sugarcane bow. This bow was given to him by **her**.
- Though not normal Gayatri Devi images, all the Lalita Devi images will have a sugarcane bow in her hand.

67. इषुसन्धानकारिणी – *Iṣusandhānakāriṇī*

- She is very efficient in fixing arrows.
- In the previous name it was mentioned that she holds a bow made of Sugarcane. Sugarcane bow always goes with arrow made of five flowers. Hence this name.

68. इन्द्रनीलसमाकारा – *Indranīlasamākārā*

- She shines like a Blue Sapphire gem.

69. इडापिङ्गलरूपिणी – *Iḍāpiṅgalarūpiṇī*

- *Iḍā, Piṅgala* and *Suśumna Naḍis* are integrated in the body. She is in those forms.

70. इन्द्राक्षी – *Indrākṣī*

- She is the Devi in the name of *Śatākṣī*.
- Both *Indrākṣī* and *Śatākṣī* are one and the same.
- Chapter 7-28 of Sri Devi Bhagavatam describes the glory of *Śatākṣi Devi*, another form of Durga.
- Some people refer this *Śatākṣī Devi* as *Śākambari Devi* also.

71. ईश्वरीदेवी – *Īśvarī Devī*

- One who blesses all wealth (*aishwaryam*) to her devotees.
- **She** is the *Īśvarī*, the *shakti* of the universal absolute.
- The quality of *Īśvara* is Lordship, activity, independence, consciousness, etc. Since *Sri Devi* is with all these qualities, **She** is called *Īśwari*.

72. ईहात्रयविवर्जिता – *Īhātrayavivarjitā*

- She satisfies the three types of wishes of her devotees.

- Three types of wishes – *Lokaishana, Vithaishana* and *Putraishana* – wishes on the world (could be earth), wishes on money and wishes on the sons, daughter, grand-son, etc. She grants all these wishes.
- In other way, wishes of four types Dharma, Artha, Kama and Moksha. Once when the first three are satisfied people will be ready to seek Moksha. Hence only the first three are mentioned here.
- It can also be construed as the basic three wishes like food, clothing and shelter. These are blessed by her.

73. उमा – *Umā*

- The letter *'U'* relates to *Shiva, Mā* means *Lakshmi* (auspicious). Hence *Umā* means the auspiciousness of *Shiva*.
- **She** limits (*Mā*) *Shiva* (*'U'*).
- *Sri Devi* was born as daughter to *Himavan* and his wife *Mena* and had the name *Parvati*. **She** started to do ardent penance even at the age of 5 aiming to marry *Parameshwara*. Hence *Mena* became anxious and wanted to prevent *Parvati* from doing penance. I.e. **She** called *Parvati* as *'U'* and said *Mā* (not to do penance). Hence the name *Umā*.
- The *Soota Samhita* (IV-1-20) says, "I adore the supreme experience which destroys the noose of earthly existence, which purifies even *Sadāshiva*, called *Umā*, which produces the bright state and manifests in many kinds of worlds.
- In *Linga Purāṇa, Shiva* says to *Sri Devi* - In my *Praṇava* there are letters *A-U-M* (UMA) in the form of *Vishnu, Shiva* and *Brahma*. These letters are in the order in the *Praṇava*, with the three notes (*mātrās*) and with the highest pluta.
- The *Mahāvāshista* says - Uma is so called because it contains the essence of the *Praṇava*;

  *"Omkāra Sāra Shaktitvāt Umetiparikeerttitā"*
- According to the *Shiva Sūtra* (I-13) *Uma* means the *Iccha Shakti* of *Yoginis*.
- In Samskrutam the word *Umā* can further mean 'tranquility', 'splendour', 'fame' and 'night'. She is in all these forms.
- As per the statement; *Uma Devi Vinayake – Umā* is the deity worshipped at the *Vināyaka Peeṭa* and again based on *Umā Sindhuvane* – at the *Sindhuvana*.
- *Umāshatvārshikee Matā* – a girl of six years old is called *Uma*.
- *Kenopanishat* says *Uma* invocated *Brahmam* to *Indra*.

74. उषा – *Uṣā*

- *Uṣā* means dawn. She is the light during dawn
- Usha is mythological daughter of heaven and sister of night. It is the auspicious *Brahma Muhurta – Ushat Kalam*.
- This is the Devi to be worshipped during that *Ushat* period.

75. उडुनिभा – *Uḍunibhā*

- One who provides light for the stars to shine.
- *Kaṭopanishat* (II-2-15) says, The Sun, the Moon and the stars do not shine by themselves. **She** only illuminates all these.

76. उर्वारुकफलानना – *Urvārukaphalānanā*

- She is always cheerful like the fruit of a cucumber.
- The *maha-mrutyunjaya mantra –*

*Om Tryambakam Yajāmahe Sugandhim Puṣţivardhanam* |
*Urvārukamiva Bandhanān Mrityor Mukṣīya Māmritat* ||

The specialty of the cucumber fruit is – The cucumber climber spreads on the ground. Hence the fruit after it is ripe, cannot remove itself from the climber, but the climber removes itself from the fruit. In the same way, the worldly affairs would get out of the Atman instead of the soul.

- That is the reason the cucumber fruit is given special treatment with regard to liberation.

77. उडुप्रभा – *Uḍuprabhā*

- She is in water like colour.
- Actually, water is colourless and She also.

78. उडुमती – *Uḍumatī*

- She is in the form of a night.
- The colour of night is black/ dark. Sri Gayatri Devi also is black in colour.

79. उडुपा – *Uḍupā*

- *Uḍu* means Moon. She is in the form of a Moon.

- *Uḍu* also means a boat. She is like a boat helping the devoting to cross the ocean of *samsara*.
- *Uḍu* also means a star. She is in the form of all stars.

80. उडुमध्यगा – *Uḍumadhyagā*

- As mentioned in the previous name, *Uḍu* means star. She lives in the midst of the stars.

81. ऊर्ध्वम् – *Ūrdhvam*

- *Urdhvam* means upwards. Heaven is upward to us. She lives in the heaven.
- Heaven and *moksha* are attainable goals for the devotes of *Sri Devi*. **She** guides to reach the goals easily.

82. ऊर्ध्वकेशी – *Ūrdhvakeśī*

- One who has her hairs raised upwards.
- This means that she has her hairs as lock raising upwards.

83. ऊर्ध्वाधोगतिभेदिनी – *Ūrdhvādhogatibhedinī*

- In the upper world there are two paths (*gati*) – heaven and hell. She distinguishes the both.
- Those who do good things go to heaven. Those who do bad go to hell. She makes people to enjoy or suffer as per their deeds.

84. ऊर्ध्व बाहुप्रिया – *Ūrdhva Bāhupriyā*

- She likes the devotees who raise their shoulders and worship her.

85. ऊर्मिमालावाग्ग्रन्थदायिनी – *Ūrmimālāvāggranthadāyinī*

- *Ūrmimālā* = garland of waves. Vāg = speech. She confers the ability for smooth speech like a garland of waves to her devotees.
- *Bharati,* another name of *Saraswathi* is the Goddess of speech. *Gayatri* and *Bharati* are the same.

86. ऋतम् – *Ṛtam*

- She is full of compassion, creativity, reliability, generosity, loyalty and love on her devotees.

87. ऋषि: – *Ṛṣiḥ*

- A *Rishi* is a person who has wisdom, can call upon the deity, has spiritual knowledge and is able to control his senses. She is in that form.
- *Rishis* are the people who got the *Vedas* and/ or *Mantras* in their mind. She was responsible for them to get these.

88. ऋतुमती – *Ṛtumatī*

- She is a menstruous woman.
- Puranas say that goddesses and even rivers have menstruation.

89. ऋषिदेव नमस्कृता – *Ṛṣideva Nāmasakṛtā*

- One who is bowed by *Rishis* and *Devas*.

90. ऋग्वेदा – *Ṛgvedā*

- Out of the four *Vedas*, *Rig Veda* is supposed to be the greatest. She is in that form.

91. ऋणहर्त्री – *Ṛṇahareri*

- She enables the devotees to clear of the debts.
- *Ṛṇa* = debt. A man is indebted[5] to *Devas*, *Rishis* and *Pitrus*. Every man is trying to repay the debts to them during daily *Brahma-yagnam*.
- Other than these there are other debts to other fellow human beings and animals. She wards off the people from all these debts.
- **She** is not indebted to the devotees. **She** bestows more than what is expected by them.

[5] This does not include vehicle loan, home loan, etc.

- 754th name of Sri Lalita Sahasranamam – *Aparṇā* – also conveys the same meaning.

92. ऋषिमण्डलचारिणी – *Ṛṣimaṇḍalacāriṇī*

- *Ṛṣimaṇḍala* = groups of sages or *Saptarishi Mandalam*. *Cāriṇī* = follower or disciple. She behaves as a disciple of all the sages (*Rishis*).
- That is, she is attracted towards the worship by devotees.

93. ऋद्धिदा – *Ṛddhidā*

- She gives everything to her devotees more than what they wanted.
- When anyone is given more than what he wants, he will never feel the requirement again. Next his mind will focus on her Upasana and will want to reach liberation.

94. ऋजुमार्गस्था – *Ṛjumārgasthā*

- She always follows the moral path.
- She makes her devotees to always to follow the moral path.

95. ऋजुधर्मा – *Ṛjudharmā*

- She always follows the moral and preaches moral to her devotees.

96. ऋतुप्रदा – *Ṛtupradā*

- *Ṛtu* = season. There are six seasons in year viz.
    - *Vasanta Ritu* or Spring,
    - *Grishma Ritu* or Summer,
    - *Varsha Ritu* or Monsoon,
    - *Sharad Ritu* or Autumn,
    - *Hemanta Ritu* or Pre-winter and
    - *Shishir Ritu* or Winter.
- It is she who enables and controls these seasons.

97. ऋग्वेदनिलया – *Ṛgvedanilayā*

- In the 90th name above, it was mentioned that she is in the form *Rig Veda*. Now here it is mentioned that she lives in *Rig Veda*.

- There are lots of hymns praising *Sri Devi* in *Rig Veda* and hence it can be construed that she lives in *Rig Veda*.

98. ऋज्वी – *Ṛjvī*

- She is very easy to move with.
- That is, she is easily attainable, of course, by proper worship.
- 817th name of Sri Vishnu Sahasranamam – Sulabha – also says that he can be attained easily.

99. लुप्तधर्मप्रवर्तिनी – *Luptadharmapravartinī*

- She brings life to the missed out dharmas.
- Since she follows the complete dharma, anything missed out earlier also brought back into practice.

100. लूतारिवरसम्भूता – *Lūtārivarasambhūtā*

- A spondylitis kind of disease is called *Lūtā*. Chanting Gayatri Mantra is a best cure for this disease.

Thus ends 100 divine names on *Sri Gayatri Devi* from 1 to 100

*****

101. लूतादि विष हारिणी – *Lūtādiviṣahāriṇī*

- She removes the poison due to the bite of spider and other insects/ animals.
- She removes in the senses – her *mantra* removes.

102. एकाक्षरा – *Ekākṣarā*

- She is in the form of single lettered Pranava Mantra *'Oṃ'*
- She is also in the form of single lettered Shaakta Pranava Mantra *'Hreem'*.
- The illusion (*Maya*) which is the pure *Satva* form or ignorance is single letter form. She is *maya.*

103. एकमात्रा – *Ekamātrā*

- In the previous name it was mentioned that She is in the form of single letter. Single letter can be of more than one *matra*. Here it is more stressed that She is in the form of single *matra*.

104. एका – *Ekā*

- She is only one – no-two.
- **She** is alone because **She** is without a backup.
- She is an example for Advaita philosophy.
- Almost all the Shakta texts are based on Advaita philosophy.
- The *Brahmam* without any quality is called *Ekā*.
- *Sri Adi Shankara* in his commentary of *Vishnu Sahasranāma* for the 725th name – *Ekaḥ* mentions; since he is the concluded truth without any kind of differences that are internal or that relates to similar external objects or to dissimilar object, he is *Ekaḥ*.
- *Chāndokya Upansihat* (6-2-1) says; *'Ekamevātvteeyam'*.
- In *Devi Upanishat* also we read as;

  *"Ekaiva Sarvatra Vartate, Tasmāduchyate Ekā"* ।

105. एकनिष्ठा – *Ekaniṣṭhā*

- She looks everybody and everything as one.
- She does not bias between people and things and takes care of everybody in the same way.

106. ऐन्द्री – *Aindrī*

- One who bestow energy (*shakti*) to Indra.

107. ऐरावतारूढा – *Airāvatārūḍhā*

- One who rides on *Airāvata* elephant.
- It is a known fact that Indra only rides on *Airāvata*, the white elephant originated from the Milky ocean. But She is Indra and hence this name.

108. ऐहिकामुष्मिक प्रदा – *Aihikāmuṣmika Pradā*

- **She** bestows whatever asked for by the devotees both in this and the other worlds including the salvation.
- She bestows her devotees bliss in this world and liberation in the other world.

109. ओङ्कारा – *Oṅkārā*

- She is *Praṇava Swaroopinee.*
- She is the essence of the *Praṇava Oṃ.*

110. ओषधी – *Oṣadhī*

- She is in the form of medicine for all diseases in this world.
- The medicine for the disease called *samsārā* is **She** only.
- For the 287th name *Oushadhaḥ* and 578th name *Bheshajam* in *Viṣhṇu Sahasranāma*, Sri Adi Shankara has commented as medicine for the disease of worldly affairs.
- For the disease of hunger food is the only medicine. In the same fashion to get the worshipping initiation, chanting of these 1000 names is the only way out.

111. ओता – *Otā*

- The word *Otā* in Samskrutam has lots of meanings like – invoked, summoned, interwoven, addressed, there, etc.
- She is in the form of sutra (a rope), the embodiment of all beings binding all the living beings.

- The *antaḥkaraṇa* (अन्तःकरण) "the inner cause" refers to the totality of two levels of mind, namely the *buddhi*, the intellect or higher mind, and the manas, the middle levels of mind which (according to theosophy) exist as or include the mental body. She sits in the *antaḥkaraṇa* of all living beings and binds all of them.

112. ओतप्रोत निवासिनी – *Otaprota Nivāsinī*

- She spreads in the entire *Brahmandam* that originated from the *Brahmam*.

113. और्वा – *Aurvā*

- She is *Vāḍavāgniswarūpiṇī*.
- *Vāḍavāgni* (marefire) — One of the five natural forms of *Agni* (holy fire). This form, represents Agni's most fearful form hidden under the sea, ever ready to destroy the world. She is in that form.

114. औषधसम्पन्ना – *Auṣadhasampannā*

- She is related to - interconnecting all *Auṣadhams* – medicines.
- In the $110^{th}$ name above, it was mentioned that she is in the form of Auṣadhi – medicines.

115. औपासनफलप्रदा – *Aupāsanaphalapradā*

- She bestows the results/ fruits related to *Aupāsana*.
- Aupāsana (औपासन) refers to "fire sacrifice of the grahastas". All the householders are supposed to grihastha's do this duty twice a day (*nitya karma*). She blesses the results of this rite.

116. अण्डमध्यस्थिता देवी – *Aṇḍamadhyasthitā Devī*

- She is the Devi, who lives in the midst of the *Andam*.
- *Andam* is the *Brahmandam*, i.e. the universe. She lives in the middle of this universe.
- Our Earth, space and the stellar zone constitute one galaxy (*Brahmāṇḍam*). Universe (*Brahmāṇḍa maṇḍalam*) consists of millions of such galaxies. *Sri Devi* sinks this entire universe.

- *Taitrīya Upanishat* (III-6-1) says that the *Brahmam* is established in the superior radiance-space – fixed there; *Parame Vyoman Pratishṭitaḥ*. This ether is of two types – Macrocosm and Microcosm (*Brahmāṇḍam* and *Pindāndam*). Both are tools to identify the *Brahmam*. **She** is in that bright form.

117. अःकारमनुरूपिणी – *Aḥkāramanurūpiṇī* (*Visargarūpiṇī*)

- The last vowel of Samskrutam, *Aḥ* is called *Visargam*. She is the deity in that form.
- *Visargam* is a specialty of Samskruta language. It is very important in mantras. She is in that form.

118. कात्यायनी – *Kātyāyanī*

- She is the *Katyayani Devi*.
- She is a daughter of sage *Katyayana* or *Katar*. Hence *Katyayani*.
- 556th name of Sri Lalita Sahasranamam is also the same name – *Kātyāyanī*.
- The *Vāmana Purāṇa* says - this is the name of the deity in the collective form of the brightness (*tejas*) of all the *Devas*.
- According to the *Kālikā Purāṇa*, this is the deity at *Oḍyāṇa Pīṭa*.
- According to *Devi Purāṇa, Kam – Brahmam, Shiras* – stone. Since *Sri Devi* supports the whole world and is omnipresent there, **she** gets this name as *Kātyāyanee*.
- Elders say that the name *Kātyāyani* only evolved as *Kāttāyee* in villages.
- *Gopika* ladies worshipped *Kātyāyanee* during *Mārgaseersha* month and got *Krishna* as their husband.
- In the *Devi Kavacha* (prelude of *Devi Maahaatmya)*, it has been mentioned that the sixth, out of the nine names of *Durga*, is *Kātyāyanee*.

119. कालरारी – *Kālarātrī*

- *Gayatri Devi* took the incarnation of *Kālarātrī* to destruct the demons and protect the *Devas*.
- It has been mentioned in *Varāha Purāṇa* that *Kālarātrī* is the destruction energy originated from *Tamo* character of *Rudra*.
- As a pre-announcement of one's death, a person will get a dream in

the night previous to death. That night is called *Kālarātri*.

- In *Brahmastuti* of *Saptashatee* (first chapter) it has been mentioned that *Kālarātri* is the dissolution at the end of *kalpa* and *Moharāthree* is the great destruction. **She** is in those both the forms.
- In some schools it has been mentioned that in *Rāmayanā*, *Kālarātri* only took the incarnation as *Sitā* to kill *Rāvana*.
- In *Laghu Shoḍanyāsa*, *Kālarātri* is one of the names of 12 *Devis*.
- It can be also be taken as – **She** is in the form of *Kālaratri* mentioned in the *Devata Nyāsā* of *Mahāshoḍanyāsa*.

120. कामाक्षी – *Kāmākṣī*

- One with beautiful eyes.
- One who has (beloved) *Kāmeshwara* as her eyes.
- One who bestows all desires of **Her** devotees by **Her** eyes.
- One who has *Saraswathi* (*Kā*) and *Lakshmi* (*Mā*) as **Her** eyes.
- Kanchipuram is one of the 108 *Shakti Peetams*, where *Sri Devi*'s waist (the place where the waist band, *Kānchi*, is worn) fell.
- *Brahma* performed a sacrifice in this place seeking the powers of creation. *Sri Devi* as *Kamakshi* fulfilled *Brahma*'s desires.
- *Kāma* (Cupid) was destroyed by *Paramashiva*'s third eye and restored to life by *Sri Devi*'s vision. Hence *Kamakshi*.
- 62nd name of Sri Lalita Sahasranamam is also the same name – *Kāmākṣī*.

121. कामसुन्दरी – *Kāmasundarī*

- She bestows a beautiful form to her devotees, as they want.
- *Shivakāmasundari* who beauty attracted lord Shiva to her.

122. कमला – *Kamalā*

- She is so beautiful like a lotus flower.
- Every chakra of the body is lotus like with various number of petals. Sri Devi lives midst the lotus in each of the chakras.

123. कामिनी – *Kāminī*

- One who is most liked (by the devotees).
- Those who desire liberation desire, to obtain **Her** by knowledge. Hence *Kamini*.

124. कान्ता – *Kāntā*

- One who is most beautiful.
- Since **She** is effulgent, **she** looks like the Ultimate beauty. The luster is the beauty and brightness of the body.
- *Kam – Brahmam. Anta* - final. Unconditioned *Brahmam* is her final form. This is the last philosophy of *Sri Devi*'s form without any quality (*nirguṇā*). To start as a teacher, followed by *saguṇā* form and *nirguṇā* form is made perceived by **Her**.
- The presiding deity of the eleventh night of the dark fortnight of the lunar month is called *Kānta*. **She** is in that form. **She** is in the form of all the presiding deities of all the days and nights and hence this is very apt.
- 329th name of Sri Lalita Sahasranamam is also the same name – *Kāntā.*

125. कामदा – *Kāmadā*

- One who fulfills all the desires of her devotees.
- *Kāmada* means *Shiva* – that is one who destroyed Cupid. *Kāmada* means, one who is auspiciously united with the destroyer of *Kāma*.
- Hereditary property is called *Dāyam*. *Sri Dev* has *Kāma* as *Dāyam*. Her association with *Kāma* is timeless.
- 63rd name of Sri Lalita Sahasranamam *Kāmadāyinī* – is worth comparable here.

126. कालकण्ठिनी – *Kālakanṭhinī*

- One who is the consort of *Kāla Kanḍar*.
- She controls the *kala* (time period) through her neck and hence *Kālakanṭhi.*
- Lord *Parameshwara*, when he swallowed the venom, it stayed in his neck and hence his throat has become black in colour. Hence, he is called *Nīlakanṭar* or *Kālakanṭar*. The consort of that *Kālakanṭar*.
- *Vāyu purāṇa* says, "In the presence of a multitude of *Devas*, *Pishāchas*, serpents and demons, the virulent poison became transfixed in the throat; hence I am called *Kālakanṭar*".
- According to the *Devi Purāṇa*, among the sixty-eight sacred places, *Kālanjara* is a place where *Kalakanṭā* is worshipped. The presiding *Devi* in that place is mentioned here in this name.

- *Kala* – a soft low sound, *kanta* – throat, i.e. a soft low sound proceeds from her throat and hence *Kāḷakaṇṭinee*.
- There is a story in the *Linga Purāṇa* that in order to destroy the demon *Dārukā*, Lord *Shiva* created *Kālakaṇṭhee*.
- 464th name of Sri Lalita Sahasranamam is also – *Kālakaṇṭhī*.

127. करिकुम्भस्तनभरा – *Karikumbhastanabharā*

- *Karikumbha* = frontal globe of an elephant. She has breasts like the frontal globe of an elephant.

128. करवीरसुवासिनी – *Karavīrasuvāsinī*

- *Karavīra* = the dwelling place of Goddess Lakshmi. Sri Gayatri Devi lives well in that place (*Suvāsinī*).
- In other words, there is no difference between Goddess Lakshmi and Sri Gayatri Devi.

129. कल्याणी – *Kalyāṇī*

- One who is in an auspicious form.
- Sri Devi is the complete auspicious.
- *Kalyā* – good words, *ana* – to utter. *Kalyām* + *Anatee* = one who always utters good words.
- According to the Padma Purana – in the Malaya Mountain, she is worshipped as Kalyani.
- 324th name of Sri Lalita Sahasranamam is also – *Kalyāṇī*.
- Again the 2nd name in Sri Lalita Trishati is also *Kalyāṇī*. Sri Adi Shankara's, commentary of this name is; auspiciousness is happiness. This happiness in worldly activities, as per *Veda* (*Taitireeya*, etc.), is health and youth – that is, happiness enjoyed by this body right from general human till four-faced Brahma. These are all atom sized drops from the complete bliss. Sri Devi is the complete bliss. As per *Veda* – *Vignānamānandam Brahma* – She is the complete bliss in the form of *Brahmam*, without any blemish.

130. कुण्डलवती – *Kuṇḍalavatī*

- One who is in the form of *Kundalini* energy.
- *Kundalini* shakti is in the form of a snake coiled in 3.5 rounds

beneath the backbone of the body. She is in that form

- The three rounds respectively represent the letters *'A'*, *'O'* and *'M'*. The half round is the half scale. That implies *Kundalini* corresponds to *Oṃ* – the *Praṇava mantra*.
- **She** is breathing like the snake sleeping in *Moolādhāra*. The breath of this *Kundalini*, the energy of the soul, is the vital life (*prāṇan*). One can hear the sound of this breath by completely closing the ears. If it is not heard, it is told that death is nearing.

131. कुरुक्षेत्रनिवासिनी – *Kurukṣetranivāsinī*

- One who lives in Kurukshetra.
- *Kurukshetra* is the place where the *Mahabharata* battle did happen. This is also indicated as place of *Dharma* (righteousness). Hence the results of the action of giving away things is much more than the same action in other places.
- The virtue that is got by the giver is equal to the sin got by the receiver. Hence, he has to do adequate expiation to remove the sin. But it has been mentioned that if he receives anything in *Kurukshetra*, there is no expiation for this and hence the giver gets limitless virtue.

132. कुरुविन्ददलाकारा – *Kuruvindadalākārā*

- She shines like a ruby (*Kuruvinda*)
- She is like a shape of the ruby called *Kuruvinda*.

133. कुण्डली – *Kuṇḍalī*

- In the 130th name above, it was mentioned that she is in the form of *Kundalini* energy.
- The form of *Kundalini* is explained in detail in the 10th *verse* of *Soundaryalaharee*.
- The method of awakening the sleeping *Kundalini* energy and taking it to *Brahmarandhram* has been described in the *Yoga Shastra*. The *Kundalini* energy wakes up, reaches the *Brahmarandhram* and rains the nectar in the *nādis* by – ardent devotion, the results of adoration and the blessings of the teacher in addition to the *Haṭayoga* methods. In the present days for laymen like us, only the first method is best suitable – *Sri Kanchi Kamakoti Paramacharya* has explained. (The book *Deivathin Kural*, 6th Volume, Page 783...).

- The main theme of the songs sung by *Siddhas* is to awaken the *Kundalini* energy and to bring it to the *Brahmarandhram*. The same is the main object of the famous song *"Ādu Pambe"* and the gestures made during the dance for this song.
- *Chooḍalai Upākhyānam* in *Yoga Vāshitam* advises as – As the smell in a flower is recognised, the mind called *Puryashṭakam* can also realise the *Kundalini*, which is available inside the self.
- The *Vāgbhava Beeja* is also called as *Kundalini*. Hence it can also be interpreted as **She** is in the form of *Vāgbhava Beeja*.
- *Sri Adi Shankara* in his commentary of *Viṣhṇu Sahasranāma* for the 907th name – *Kunḍalī* mentions – *Viṣhṇu* is in the form of *Adi Sesha* – a snake.
- It is told that the entire *Vinayagar Agaval* written by *Aouvaiyar* in Tamil talks about *Kundalini*.

134. कुमुदालया – *Kumudālayā*

- *Kumudam* means flowers like Lily, *Kairavam*, *Rakta Pankajam* and Red Lotus. She blossoms like a group of these flowers.
- Earlier, in the 67th name, it was mentioned that she has an arrow made of 5 flowers. Lily is one of the five flowers.

135. कालजिह्वा – *Kālajihvā*

- She has her tongue protruding outside to slay the demons. That type of tongue is called *Kālajihvā*.

136. करालास्या – *Karālāsyā*

- She has a horrible and coming out face to destroy the enemies.
- She humourously kills the asuras in a flippant way and hence such a face description.

137. कालिका – *Kālikā*

- She is free from enemies.
- There cannot be any enemies to Sri Devi and even if there is any, she will convert them to a friend or kill them.
- *Kālikā Purana* describes, Sri Devi and Parameshwara and has lots of nuances and stories.

138. कालरूपिणी – *Kālarūpiṇī*

- She is in the form of time (*kalam*).
- She only decides/ controls the time.
- *Devi Upanishat* mentions that **She** is in the form of a minute time period.

139. कमनीयगुणा – *Kamanīyaguṇā*

- She is with all the good qualities.
- One who possess the six good qualities – viz., peace, co-operation with others, war, marching with the armies, encamped, arranging the forces and allies. *Kāmandakaneeti shastra* (ethical code) describes these the six characters one should have.
- The *Puranas* give out the following six as great characters; Prosperity, righteousness, fame, wealth, wisdom and dispassion. **She** is filled with these characters.

140. कान्तिः – *Kāntiḥ*

- One who is in the form of effulgence.
- The body which attracts others is called luminous or refulgent.
- *Veda* says Sun, Moon, etc., are luminous only because of the effulgence of the Supreme Being.

*Na Tatra Sooryo Bhāti Na Chandra Tārakam Nema Vidyuto Bhānti Kuto'yamagniḥ*
*Tameva Bhāntamanubhāti Sarvam Tasya Bhāsā Sarvamidam Vibhāti* ll

- *Kānti* indicates the *Icchā shakti*.
- The same sense in conveyed in Sri Lalita Sahasranamam – 329th name *Kāntā*, 465th name *Kāntiḥ* and 465th name *Kāntimatī*.

141. कलाधारा – *Kalādhārā*

- One who is an embodiment all the sixty-four forms of arts.
- **She** has all the 64 arts in **Her** form.
- In the Bhashyam for the 236th name in Sri Lalita Sahasranamam – *Chatuḥṣaṣṭikalāmayī* – Sri Bhaskara Raya gives the list of 64 arts. But there are differences from the list given by others. However, it has been agreed by all that there are in total 64 arts.
- *Kalā* also means *Tantra*. It has been mentioned in *Soundaryalaharee* that there are 64 *Tantras*. *Sri Devi* has all these as **Her** form.

142. कुमुद्वती – *Kumudvatī*

- One who is an assemblage of lotuses.
- She is like a pond filled for lily flowers.

143. कौशिकी – *Kauśikī*

- One of the meanings of the word *Kauśikī* is Moonlight. She shines like a cool Moonlight.
- Another meaning is cytology, which is a science concerned with the structure and function of plant and animal cells. She is the cells in every living being and hence this name.

144. कमलाकारा – *Kamalākārā*

- One who shines like a lotus flower.
- One who is in the shape of a lotus flower. She holds a lotus flower in one of her hands and also sits on a lotus flower. Hence, she looks like a lotus.

145. कामचारप्रभञ्जिनी – *Kāmacāraprabhañjinī*

- She demolishes those who have own pleasures.
- *Kāmacāra* can mean one's own pleasure, moving freely, sensuality, selfishness, etc. She controls all these.

146. कौमारी – *Kaumārī*

- One who is always young.
- An 8-year-old little girl is called as *Kaumārī*. Sri Devi is in that form.
- *Kaumārī* is one of the 8 *Matrukā Devis*, in the middle layer of *Chatusrā* (*Noopurā*) of *Sri Chakra*. Sri Gayatri Devi in that form.
- *Kaumārī* is one of the eight mothers. Sri Devi took various forms for killing the demons and *Kaumārī* is one such form.
- Various gods/ Devas gave their female forms to help Chandi Devi to annihilate the demons. Among them *Kaumārī* is Kumara's female form.

147. करुणापाङ्गी – *Karuṇāpāṅgī*

- One who embodiment of pity, compassion, empathy, merci and what not.

- *Shrimad Bhagavatam* says – the good dispositions are of four types;
  - o Friendship with those who are happy without being envious (*maitree* or friendship),
  - o Compassion for those who are suffering (*karuna*),
  - o Gladness to see the righteous (*muditā*) and
  - o Overlooking or not mindful of the sinful (*upekshā*).

These four tendencies contribute to clarity of mind and purify it.

- In *Lalita Trishati* also the compassion of *Sri Devi* is described in various names like, 9th name *Karuṇāmruta Sāgarā*, 151st name *Kaṭākshasyandi Karuṇā* and 153rd name *Kārunya Vigraha*.
- In the meditation verse of Sri Lalita Sahasranamam also it has been mentioned as; *Aruṇām Karuṇā Tarangidākshim* – stressing *Karuṇā*, the compassion.

148. ककुबन्ता – *Kakubantā*

- She is the form of all the directions.
- She is in all directions.

149. करिप्रिया – *Karipriyā*

- On whom elephants are attracted to.
- All animals do love her and elephant also.

150. केसरी – *Keśarī*

- One who a lion as her vehicle.

151. केशवनुता – *Keśavanutā*

- Most respected by Bhagawan *Keshava*.

152. कदम्बकुसुमप्रिया – *Kadamba Kusumapriyā*

- One who is fond of *kadamba* flowers.
- Since **She** is fond of *kadamba* trees, a *kadamba* jungle has been set up outside her *Chintāmaṇi* (*graha*) house.
- In Sri Lalita Sahasranamam – 60th name *Kadambavanavāsinee*, 323rd name *Kadambakusumapriyā* (this very same name).
- This refers the goddess *Meenakshi*, who is blessing the devotees at Madurai.

- The 11th name in *Sri Lalita Trishatee* is *Kadamba Kusumapriya*. *Sri Adi Shankara*'s, commentary for this name is; *Kadamba* tree is one of the *Kalpaka* trees (*deva* tree). Inner-self is a group of Satva quality of five elements. Similarly, *Kalpaka* tree is a common name for five types of trees viz., *Santānam, Harisantānam, Mantāram, Pārijātam* and *Kadambam*. The five parts of inner self is mind, intellect, volition, ego and heart. Mind is the *satva* part of wind. Intellect is the *satva* part of fire. Similarly, volition – water, ego – earth and heart or combined inner-self *satva* part of ether. Hence *kadamba* is mind; one who resides in the forest of mind is called *Kadambavanavāsinee*. *Kadambakusumā* is the expansion of the mind. Knowledge and expansion are inseparable forms. There is no knowledge without expansion and vice versa. Hence for *Sri Devi*, who is in the integrated form of knowledge on subjects and *tattvas*, is very much of fond of *kadamba* flower in the form of expansion of mind.

153. कालिन्धी – *Kālindī*

- *Kālindī* means Yamuna river. She is in that form.
- *Kālindī* also means the snake in the Yamuna river, on whose head Krishna danced.

154. कालिका – *Kālikā*

- This is a repetition of 137th name above.

155. काञ्ची – *Kāñcī*

- She is the holy city of *Kāñcī* viz., Kancheepuram.
- Kamakshi is the presiding deity of Kancheepuram. Earlier in 120th name we read that She is that Kamakshi. Hence, she is *Kāñcī*.
- *Kshetram* is a place is made ready through the rules of *mantra, tantra* and *yantras*, or naturally ready for nearing godliness is called *Kshetram* – for instance Kancheepuram, Banaras, Kāmaroopa, etc. **She** is in the form of all these *Kshetras*.

156. कलशोद्भवसंस्तुता – *Kalaśodbhavasaṃstutā*

- Sage Agastya is called *Kalaśodbhava*, since he was born in a pot (*kalasam*). She was worshipped by him.

- Fundamentally, there are 12 originators of Srividya tradition (path) – *Manu*, Moon, *Kubera*, Lopāmudrā, Cupid, *Agastya*, Agni, Sun, *Nandi*, *Skanda*, *Shiva* and *Krodhabhattāraka* (*Durvāsa*). Sage Agastya is one among them.

157. कामामाता – *Kāmamātā*

- She is mother of *Kāma* – cupid.
- *Sri Parameshwara* acquired reduced Manmata to ashes. Upon request of *Sri Devi*, **He** gave back the life to Cupid. Hence, she is mother of *Kāma*.
- There are four *puruṣārthas* viz., *Dharma* (righteousness, moral values), *Artha* (prosperity, economic values), *Kama* (pleasure, love, psychological values) and *Moksha* (liberation, spiritual values).
- In the 31st name it was mentioned that She satiates the *Artha* wish. Now here she satisfied *Kāma* wish of all the devotees.

158. क्रतुमती – *Kratumatī*

- She is in the form of all sacrifices – *yagnas*.
- Anything and everything are offered in the holy fire with the mantra *Svāhā* or *Svadhā*. *Svāhā* or *Svadhā* are consorts of Lord Agni. *Svāhā Devi* act as carrier of offerings to Devas and *Svadhā* takes the role of a carrier of offerings to Pitrus. She is in both the forms of *Svāhā* or *Svadhā*. Hence, she is all *yagnas*.

159. कामरूपा – *Kāmarūpā*

- Her form is so beautiful and attractive.
- **She** is in the form of *Kāmagyā* in *Kāmaroopa Kshetram*.
- There is a separate chapter called *Kāmaroopa Kshetra Māhātmya* in *Kālikā Purāṇa*.

160. कृपावती – *Kṛpāvatī*

- One who shows intense compassion (*Kṛpā*) on her devotees.
- All the forms of *Sri Devi* are with compassion.
- **She** bestows compassion without expecting anything in return.

161. कुमारी – *Kumārī*

- One who;
  - Removes sorrows and poverty,
  - Destroys enemies,
  - Enhance of wealth and strength
  - Provide long life
- A girl of 2 years age is called *Kumārī*
- 148th name *Kaumārī* is almost similar to this.

162. कुण्डनिलया – *Kuṇḍanilayā*

- One who lives in the holy fire vessel (*agni Kuṇḍa*).
- She lives in the *Kundalini* of human body. 130th and 133rd names above can also be referred.

163. किराती – *Kirātī*

- She is in the form of Durga. *Kirātī* is another for *Durga*.
- She takes the form of Durga to annihilate the demons to protect the Devas.

164. कीरवाहना – *Kīravāhanā*

- One who has a parrot as her vehicle.

165. कैकेयी – *Kaikeyī*

- In Ramayana she took the role *Kaikeyī*. Though it was a negative role and everybody hated her, she took that role to begin the demolition of Ravan and other demons.

166. कोकिलालापा – *Kokilālāpā*

- One who has a voice like a quill.

167. केतकी – *Ketakī*

- *Ketakī* (*Taazhampoo*) is a flower which had been worn on Lord

Shiva's head. She is in that form. However, it is not much used during worship of any God.

- In *Natyashastra*, *Ketakī* is a gesture (screw-pine). She shows that hand sign.
- *Ketakī* also refers to peepal tree, which is called as kings of trees. In any category, she is the greatest. Among the trees she is *Ketakī*.

168. कुसुमप्रिया – *Kusumapriyā*

- *Kusuma* is a kind of flower, which is liked by her. On the whole she likes all the flowers.
- *Kusuma* is one of the eight deities (yoginis) of the *Yogin cakra*. She likes her.

169. कमण्डलुधरा – *Kamaṇḍaludharā*

- In the form of a young *Brahmacarinee*, she has a *Kamaṇḍalu* in her hand.

170. काली – *Kālī*

- One who is in the form of *Kali*.
- One who decides the time is called *Kali*. She is in that form.
- The *Mahakali* is the deity worshipped at Ujjain as the consort of *Shiva* in the form of *Mahakala*.
- **She** as *Mahakali*, is worshipped as the deity of the first story in *Saptashatee*.
- *Kali* also means one who is black in colour. *Sri Gayatri Devi* has been mentioned as black in colour in many a place. When **She** takes the rude form, **she** is black in colour.

171. कर्म निर्मूल कारिणी – *Karma Nirmūla Kāriṇī*

- She nullifies the *karma*-s of her devotees.
- The initial part of *Vedas* is called *Karma Kanda*, which defines the *karmas* to be performed by all. The later part is called Vedanta or *Gnana Kanda*. Once people perform all the karmas and mature themselves, they can practice *Gnana Kanda* and obtain *Gnana*. Initially She is in the form of *Karma Kanda* and make her devotees mature to obtain *Gnana*.

172. कलहंसगतिः – *Kalahaṃsagatiḥ*

- Her walking is similar to that of Hamsa bird.

173. कक्षा – *Kakṣā*

- The word *Kakṣā* in Samskrutam has many a meaning. One such is the orbit of planets and natural satellites. It is she who controls the planets and natural satellites to move along with orbit without deviation.

174. कृतकौतुक मङ्गला – *Kṛtakautuka Maṅgalā*

- She has a beautiful conjugal bride form.
- She makes everyone in the conjugal form. That is, she bestows auspicious marriage life to all her devotees.

175. कस्तुरी तिलका – *Kasturī Tilakā*

- One who is adorned with a vermillion mark on the forehead.
- *Kasturi* means deer musk.
- The word *Tilakā* means the hair falling on the forehead. Her form is so beautiful with *Kasturi* and *Tilaka*.
- It is the practice that *Sumangali* ladies (ladies living with their husbands) to wear *Kasturi* on the starting place of the hair in the forehead.
- *Kasturi Tilakā* means female elephant. **She** is worshipped by ladies; whose walk is comparable to that of female elephants.

176. कम्रा – *Kamrā*

- She is a versatile lady.
- She is a very gorgeous lady.

177. करिन्द्रगमना – *Karindragamanā*

- One who has an elephant as her vehicle.

178. कुहू: – *Kuhūḥ*

- Earlier it was mentioned that there are presiding devatas for each of the *Thithis* called *Thithi Nitayas*. Here She is the deity in-charge of *Amavasya* (New Moon Day).

179. कर्पूरलेपना – *Karpūralepanā*

- One whose aroma is like camphor (*Karpoora*).
- Her aroma spreads in all directions and attracts the devotees.

180. कृष्णा – *Kṛṣṇā*

- One who is black in colour. In this Sahasranamam this has been mentioned multiple times.

181. कपिला – *Kapilā*

- *Kapila* is a great sage, one of the incarnations of Vishnu. She is his consort and hence *Kapilā*.
- The great sage *Kapila* reduced to ashes 6 sons of Sagara, who while searching for the sacrificial horse of their father taken away by Indra, fell in with him and accused him of having stolen it.
- He is also said to have been the founder of the Sāṅkhya system of philosophy.
- The word *Kapilā* has lots of meanings - A dog, Incense, A form or fire, The tawny colour, The Sun, Name of a country, a brown cow, a kind of perfume, a kind of timber, the common leech, a female elephant of the south east and so on. She is in all these forms.

182. कुहराश्रया – *Kuharāśrayā*

- She lives in a cave like place within the body. This again indicate the Sushumna nadi through which the Kundalini energy passes. Hence, she is the kundalini energy.
- Again, the word Kuharam has lots of meanings like yoni, lips (adharam), prakriti, samsara path (margaka), secret (guhyam), stree cihnam. It all relates to her.

183. कूटस्था – *Kūṭasthā*

- One who is the location of ignorance (Maya).
- *Kooṭa* means – cheating, hidden, lie, etc. The true bliss form of the soul, is hidden by ignorance and made to whirl in the cycle of births and deaths. **She** only is the head of this ignorance and deludes the souls.
- *Shrimad Bhagavad Geeta* (XII-3) also says;
  *"Kooṭasthamachalam Dhruvam"*.
- It means that **She** is the abode of the above said ignorance.
- In addition, *Kooṭa* also means – peak of a hill, a smith's large hammer, etc.
  - She is idle like a peak of a hill, without any work and immobile.
  - The lathe of an iron smith is called as *kooṭa*. To change the shape of anything, it will be beaten with a huge hammer after heating it with high temperature. But the shape of the lathe does not change. In the same fashion **She** is without any change.
- **She** is in the halls (*kooṭas*) like *Vāgbhava*, etc.
- *Kooṭa* also indicates the entrance of a city. Taking it to indicate the triangle of a *Sri Chakra*, it can be considered that **She** resides there.
- *Kooṭa* means society, meeting, etc. The entire society of this universe is with *Sri Devi* and hence this name.
- 896th name in Sri Lalita Sahasranamam is also the same name – *Kūṭasthā*.

184. कुधरा – *Kudharā*

- One who holds the entire earth.
- One who protects the entire earth.

185. कम्रा – *Kamrā*

- This name is a repetition of 176th name.

186. कुक्षिस्थाखिलविष्टपा – *Kukṣisthākhilaviṣṭapā*

- She protects the entire universe.
- She controls and manages the entire universe.

187. खड्गखेटकरा – *Khaḍgakheṭadharā*

- *Khaḍgam* is one type of weapon. She has it in one of her hands.
- She has many weapons including *Khaḍgam* to annihilate the demons and protect us all.

188. खर्वा – *Kharvā*

- One who a girl who chooses her own husband.
- Who else can choose a husband for her?

189. खेचरी – *Khecarī*

- One who shows the path (*gati*) to liberation.
- She bestows all types of knowledge to her devotees.

190. खगवाहना – *Khagavāhanā*

- *Khaga* means moving in air. She has the capacity to move in air or she uses air itself as her vehicle.
- Eagle or swan can fly in air. She has these birds as her vehicle.

191. खट्वाङ्गधारिणी – *Khaṭvāṅgadhāriṇī*

- One who is armed with a club, etc.
- *Khaṭvānga* is a club with a human skull at its end.
- *Khaṭvā* also means a cot. Hence it can be taken as **She** has the leg of a cot as a weapon.

192. ख्याता – *Khyātā*

- One who is a well-known celebrated *Devi*.
- 395th name of Sri Lalita Sahasranamam – *Prasiddhā* – also conveys the same sense.

193. खगराजोपरिस्थिता – *Khagarājoparisthitā*

- *Khaga* = bird, *Rāja* = king, *Upari* = on. *Sthitā* = She sits.
- King of birds is Eagle – Garuda. She sits on Garuda bird.

194. खलघ्नी – *Khalaghnī*

- There are various types of *Agni*. She is in all such forms which includes *Khala* type also.
- The word *Khala* means a lot – granary, earth, soil, place, contest and so on. She is in each of these forms.

195. खण्डितजरा – *Khaṇḍitajarā*

- She is an ageless lady.
- Earlier it was mentioned that she is always young. Here it is mentioned that she does not has age. That is, she never becomes old and hence always young.

196. खण्डाख्यानप्रदायिनी – *Khaṇḍākhyānapradāyinī*

- She gives sweet stories lady. *Khyāna* means story. For instance – *Lalitopākhyāna* – story of *Lalita*.
- We have lot many sweet stories about her. She is the heroin of all such sweet stories.

197. खण्डेन्दुतिलका – *Khaṇḍendutilakā*

- She has a third eye like a crescent Moon on her forehead.
- In lot many places it has been mentioned that She is three eyed. The third eye is what is mentioned here.

198. गङ्गा – *Gaṅgā*

- She is like the holy river Ganga.
- Earlier in the 153rd name, it was mentioned that she is like river Yamuna. This means that she has the forms of all the rivers.
- The *Brhannāradeeya Purāṇa* says, "The Supreme name of *Ganga* is the fire that consumes the forest of sin because Ganga is the remover of the disease of *samsara*. Therefore, it should be sought with much effort. Hence, **she** is said to be in the form of *Ganga* also.
- *Devi Purana* explains in another way - "As **She** has three steps, the three paths of Ganga, the three qualities, etc."; for it says, "Bali was bound by three steps, the Ganga came from three places, heaven, etc., by the three qualities *satva*, *rajas* and *tamas*. **She** performs the

functions of creation, preservation and destruction; hence **She** is called *Triguṇā*".

- Lord Shiva has Ganga river on his head. Hence, he is called as Gangadhara. She is his consort.

199. गणेशगुहपूजिता – *Gaṇeśaguhapūjitā*

- *Gaṇeśa* = Lord *Ganesha*. *Guha* = Lord *Karthikeya*. She is worshipped by both.

200. गायत्री – *Gāyatrī*

- One who is in the form of Gayatri.
- One who protects those who praise her – i.e. those who chant her mantra.
- Veda says "*Gayatreem Chandasam Mataḥ*" – Gayatri mantra is the mother of all mantras.
- In Shrimad Bhagavat Geeta (X-35) Lord Krishna says; *Gāyatree Chandasāmaham*. In *Koorma Purana* also the same is conveyed as; *Gayatri Chandasamasi*.
- According to *Padma Purāṇa, Gāyatree* is a daughter of a shepherd (*Gopakanya*), a junior wife of *Brahma*. Once when *Brahma* was performing a sacrificial fire (*Yaga*), he called his wife *Savitri*. She told that *Lakshmee* and others are yet to come and that she would come with them. With this *Brahma* got wild and brought a daughter of a shepherd from *Shakti* (*gopakanyā*) and told *Viṣhṇu* that they would go quickly to the *yaga* and there is a *Devi* called *Gayatri* there. *Viṣhṇu* also said "She is given by me to you: you marry her as per the *Gandarva* method". *Brahma* did so. (For the word *Gopakanya* – *Go* has several meanings. One of them is *Veda*. Those who guard *Veda* are *Gopar*).
- *Gayatri* protects those who recite her mantra. *Gayatri kalpa* says;
  "*Gāyantam Trāyate Yasmāt Gāyatree Tena Gadyate*".
- *Devi Purana* says; *Gāyanāt Gamanatvāpi Gāyatree Tridashārchitā* – *Devas* worship *Gayatri* by singing and nearing her.
- *Chāndogya Upanishat* (3-12-1) says; *Gāyatree Cha Trāyate Cha* – singing and protection.
- *Mahā Vāshista Rāmāyana* says; *Gāyatree Gāyanātmatvāt* – Since **She** is in the form of songs, **she** is called *Gāyatree*.
- *Padma Purāṇa* says that *Sri Devi* is in the form of *Gayatri* – "Especially after taking bath in the holy *pushkara*, my *mantra* has to

be recited. I dwell in the eight letters (eight letters in every group). I am always omnipresent;

- Ordinarily recited *Gayatri mantra* has 3 groups and the complete *Gāyatree mantra* has four. It is told that *Brahma* absolved the first three groups as a capsule form of *Rig*, *Yajur* and *Sāma Vedas*. The fourth one is a gist of *Atharva Veda*. It is said that since this is a very special one, to know it, we need to have *Upanayana* again.
- It is well known that *Shrimad Ramayana* includes *Gayatri mantra* and the 24 verses are read as *Gayatri Ramayana*.
- *Tripura Tāpinee Upanishat* advises that *Panchadashee mantra* has the meaning of *Gayatri mantra* in every group.
- This has also been explained in *Nitya Shodashikarnavam*.
- In *Mahāshoḍanyāsa* (*Prapancha Nyāsa*), it has been mentioned that **She** is in the form of three *Guṇas*.
- The meaning and glory of *Gāyatrī* and her mantra, have been discussed in a different chapter elaborately. She is nothing different from *mantra*.
- 420th name in Sri Lalita Sahasranamam is also *Gāyatrī*.

Thus ends 100 divine names on *Sri Gayatri Devi* from 101 to 200

*****

201. गोमती – *Gomatī*

- *Gomati* is a river falling into Ganges and name of another river falling into the Indus. She is in the form of all rivers including these.
- *Gomati* is a place abounding in herds of cattle. She is the Gomata and hence this name.
- *Gomati* is the name of a Vedic hymn or formula to be repeated during expiation for killing a cow. She is in the form of all mantras including this.

202. गीता – *Gītā*

- *Gītā* is a sacred song or poem, religious doctrines declared in metrical form by an inspired sage. She is in that form.
- Everyone is aware of *Shrimad Bhagwat Gita*, part of *Mahabharata*, advised by Lord Krishna to Arjuna. There is some low-profile text called *Sri Devi Gita*[6], part of *Sri Devi Bhagavatam*, advised by *Sri Devi* herself to Himavan (Himalaya mountain). She is nothing different from her *Gita*.

203. गान्धारी – *Gāndhārī*

- All of us are aware that *Gāndhārī* is wife of *Dhrudarashtra* in *Mahabharata*. She is a pativrata, who intentionally closed her eyes with a cloth, since her husband is blind. Sri Gayatri Devi is in that form.

204. गानलोलुपा – *Gānalolupā*

- *Gāna* = song, singing. She is very eager or longing for hearing her devoting singing songs.
- She has desire/ appetite for songs. Hence devotees can easily satisfy her with songs and get their wishes satiated.

205. गौतमी – *Gautamī*

- Gautama Maharishi was a Rigvedic sage. His wife Ahalya is called

[6] The author of this book has written separate books on Sri Devi Gita both in Tamil and English.

*Gautamī*, whose story all of us are aware her story in Ramayana. She is in her form.

- The Godavari is India's second longest river after the Ganga. The Godavari splits into two branches which are called Vriddha-Gautami (Gautami-Godavari) and Vasishta-Godavari. As mentioned earlier She is in the form of all rivers including this.

206. गामिनी – *Gāminī*

- One whose gait is like that of an elephant.
- It is usual to compare the gaits of males to elephant. But here for a change it has been compared with that of a female.

207. गाधा – *Gādhā*

- She is so beautiful like wife (Rathi Devi) of Cupid.
- *Gādhā* is name of a *Sāman*. She is in the form of all *Vedas* including *Sāma Veda* which again includes *Gādhā*.

208. गन्धर्वाप्सरसेविता – *Gandharvāpsarasevitā*

- She is worshipped by *Gandharvas* and *Apsaras*.
- *Gandharvas*, are celestial musicians and *Apsaras* are celestial dancers. She is worshipped by them.
- This implies that the songs of *Gandharvas* are an important part of every *pooja*.
- The word *Gandharva* also means horse. *Sri Devi* was worshipped by them.
- The songs of *devas* are called *Gandharvam*. **She** was served with such songs.
- In *Mahāshoḍanyāsa* (*Devata Nyāsa*), we read that **She** was worshipped by thousand crores *Gandharva* races.
- 636th name in Sri Lalita Sahasranamam is also *Gandharvasevitā* – गन्धर्व सेविता.

209. गोविन्दचरणाक्रान्ता – *Govindacaraṇākrāntā*

- She is the one who can easily approach Sri Govinda. Other than our Sri Devi, nobody else can easily approach Sri Govinda.
- She is the one who frequently visits Sri Govinda.

210. गुणत्रयविभाविता – *Guṇatrayavibhāvitā*

- She manifested with all the three gunas.
- In her Saguna form she has all the three qualities.

211. गन्धर्वी – *Gandharvī*

- Earlier in 208th name it was mentioned that she is worshipped by Gandharvas. Here she herself is in the form of a Gandharvi.

212. गह्वरी – *Gahvarī*

- She is so glorified that she is tough to reach.
- *Gahvarī* means that she is in a cave. Hence tough to reach.
- Multiple times it has been mentioned that she is in the form of Kundalini energy in a cave.

213. गोत्रा – *Gotrā*

- She is in the form of the earth.
- *Gotrā* means the earth or herd of cows. She is in both the forms.

214. गिरीशा – *Girīśā*

- *Himavan* is the king of mountains. Being his daughter, **she** is called as *Haimavatee* and *Girīśā*.
- She is the head of all the mountains.

215. गहना – *Gahanā*

- She is inaccessible by bad people.
- She is hard to understand unless through devotion.

216. गमी – *Gamī*

- She is moving everywhere so that she is omnipresent.

217. गुहावासा – *Guhāvāsā*

- She lives in a cave. This has been mentioned multiple places in this Sahasranama.

- One who is the mother of *Guhā* (Lord *Murugā*).
- The root word *Guhoo* means to cover. The *jeevas* veiled by ignorance are called *Guhās*. Just as sparks come from the hot iron so do the souls have come out from the Self.

218. गुणवती – *Guṇavatī*

- She is a personification of good qualities.
- One who is the treasure house of qualities.
- The *Sānkhya* doctrine says that though the qualities are specifically three viz. *satva*, *rajas* and *tamas*, they have endless modifications. **She** is the treasure house of all such qualities.
- This is comparable with 604th name in Sri Lalita Sahasranamam – *Guṇanidhiḥ* – गुण निधि:.

219. गुरुपापप्रणासिनी – *Gurupāpapraṇāsinī*

- She destroys great sins like sins on gurus (teacher).
- In Devi Gita (7-36-26) it is said that when Lord Parameshwara becomes angry, Guru can save; but when the Guru becomes angry, even by Lord Parameshwara cannot do anything. It is she who has to come to the rescue.

220. गुर्वी – *Gurvī*

- She is a great mother.

221. गुणवती – *Guṇavatī*

- This name is repetition of 218th name above.

222. गुह्या – *Guhyā*

- One who is most secretive both in form and meanings.
- *Guhyā* means one who dwells in a cave, i.e. heart.
- **She** is secretive and dwelling in our heart. Hence, **she** can be identified only by inward search.
- The word *Guhyā* can be considered to mean *Jeevātma* (soul), *Paramātmā* (supreme) and the union of both. The presiding deity

who can bestow these results is called *Guhya*.

- *Sri Adi Shankara* in his commentary for *Vişhņu Sahasranāma* for the 542nd name – *Guhyaḥ* – one who can be understood by the secret *Upanishats* or one who dwells in the secret cavity viz., heart. 545th name – *Guptaḥ* – **He** is beyond speech and mind.
- *Kaṭopanishat* (I-2-12) says;

  *"Esha Sarveshu Bhooteshu Kooṭātmā na prakāshate"*.
- The very same name is 624th name in Sri Lalita Sahasranamam – *Guhyā* – **गुह्या.** This can also be compared with 707th name in Sri Lalita Sahasranamam – *Guhayaroopiṇee*.

223. गोप्तव्या – *Goptavyā*

- She is most secretive in hearts atmas.
- One who does the task of protector.
- *Sri Devi* takes up the protection function to sustain the created universe – when **Her** *satva* quality predominates.

224. गुणदायिनी – *Guṇadāyinī*

- Earlier in 218th and 221st name it was mentioned that She is qualities personified.
- Here it is mentioned that she bestows good qualities to her devotees.

225. गिरिजा – *Girijā*

- This is similar to 214th name गिरीशा – *Girīśā*.
- **She** is daughter of Himavan, king of mountains.

226. गुह्यमातङ्गी – *Guhyamātaṅgī*

- **She** is in the form *Brahma-vidyā* (*Brahma-vidyā svaroopinee*). This *Brahma-vidya* is secretive. Hence, she is *Guhya*.
- *Sri Devi* was once born as the daughter of sage *Matanga* and was thus known as *Mātangee*. Typical of women living in jungles, she wears earrings made of palm leaf and headgear made of wild flowers. The very sound of the Veena in her hands killed her enemies. The parrot in her hand was *Brahma-Vidya* personified.
- *Mātangee* is one of the 10 *Dasha Maha Vidya Devis*. That *Mātangee* is in-charge of *Brahma-Vidya*. *Sri Gayatri Devi* is in her form.

227. गरुडध्वजवल्लभा – *Garuḍadhvajavallabhā*

- *Sri Vishnu* is *Garuḍadhvaja* – has *Garuḍa* in his flag. *Sri Vishnu* is fond of her.
- *Kanakatārā Satavam* of *Sri Adi Shankara* says;

*Geerdevateti Garuḍadhvajasundareeti* I

228. गर्वापहारिणी – *Garvāpahāriṇī*

- She destroys the arrogance of her devotees.
- One who is with pride. **She** has the great ability of creating this world, protecting it and finally merging it with herself. Hence, **she** has pride.

229. गोदा – *Godā*

- One who is very happy through *go dhan* – giving out a cow.
- *Go* also means the earth. Hence, she is very happy through *go dhan* – giving out *earth*.

230. गोकुलस्था – *Gokulasthā*

- One who lives in Gokula – alongwith Sri Krishna.

231. गदाधरा – *Gadādharā*

- She holds mace, a weapon, in one of her hands.

232. गोकर्णनिलयासक्ता – *Gokarṇanilayāsaktā*

- She lives at Gokarna – the starting place of Cauvery river.

233. गुह्यमण्डलवर्तिनी – *Guhyamaṇḍalavartinī*

- She is very secretive.
- She lives in a cave – heart of her devotees.
- She lives in a cave – *sushumna nadi* and moves as Kundalini energy.

234. घर्मदा – *Gharmadā*

- She creates heat and makes the water of ocean as vapour and hence causes the rain.

235. घनदा – *Ghanadā*

- One who creates the cloud and hence causes the rain.
- This name goes together with the previous name creating the same sense.

236. घण्टा – *Ghaṇṭā*

- One who wears a girdle with tinkling bells. The small gems inside the bells make a soft pleasant sound.
- The anklets worn on *Sri Devi*'s feet have bells fixed with gems. They make a sweet and soft jingle while oscillating.
- One who is the primal mystic sound. While pronouncing the words *Om*, *Hreem*, etc., the last syllable *'m'* sounds in an elongated way. After plucking the strings of Veena, or after ringing the bells in temples, if we allow the sound to subside on its own, it subdues mildly in a reverse telescopic way. She is in the form of such a mind-blowing sound.

237. घोरदानवमर्दिनी – *Ghoradānavamardinī*

- One who extinguishes great demons.
- By destroying the evil habits of the demons, **she** shows good path to him also.
- Demons are monsters bound by ignorance. Actions arising out of ignorance with selfish goals, take the form of Devils.
- She kills the demonistic characters of her devotees.
- A person attains external bliss when the immortal soul power wins over the demonic forces, which raise their head from time to time within the mind.

238. घृणिमन्त्रमयी – *Ghṛṇimantramayī*

- She is in the form of shining/ glowing mantras.
- The Gayatri mantra is shining/ glowing like anything. She is in that form.

239. घोषा – *Ghoṣā*

- She makes huge noise during battle.
- The enemies are threatened by her *Ghoṣā* (noise) itself.

240. घनसम्पातदायिनी – *Ghanasampātadāyinī*

- She orders the clouds to pour rain.
- She offers adequate rain to this earth that is needed for the living beings to live on.

241. घण्टारवप्रिया – *Ghaṇṭāravapriyā*

- She becomes happy on hearing the sound of bells.
- During puja the bell is rung differently at appropriate times. She is happy to hear this.

242. घ्राणा – *Ghrāṇā*

- She is in-charge of all aromas.
- *Ghrāṇā* also means the nose of a bull. A rope or string is put through a bullock's nose for a bridle to control it. She in that form, also controls people who are looking like a bull.

243. घृणिसन्तुष्टकारिणी – *Ghṛṇisantuṣṭikāriṇī*

- She makes the Sun pleased.

244. घनारिमण्डला – *Ghanārimaṇḍalā*

- She protects her devotees from many enemies.
- Enemies mentioned here need not mean external enemies. There are various internal enemies. She destroys those enemies and protects the atman.

245. घूर्णा – *Ghūrṇā*

- *Ghūrṇam* means diverting from outside matters or circulating. On account of bliss, her naturally reddish eyes are further red-tinged and rotates without interest in outside matters.

246. घृताची – *Ghṛtācī*

- She is in the form of Saraswathi.
- She is in the form night (*rātri*).

247. घणवेगिनी – *Ghaṇaveginī*

- Her hurricane speed is incomparable – supersonic speed.

248. ज्ञानधातुमयी – *Jñānadhātumayī*

- She is made of complete knowledge.
- She offers complete knowledge to her devotees.

249. चर्चा – *Carcā*

- She has concern over her devotees and make then knowledgeable all subjects.

250. चर्चिता – *Carcitā*

- She always adorned with Sandal and other perfumes.
- She smells so stunning.
- **She** is full of aroma of divine sandal, flowers like *Kadamba*, *Parijatham*, etc.
- Devotees apply all the fragrances like Sandal, eaglewood, European saffron, *javvadu*, *Kasturi*, cow-bezoar, etc., on her.

251. चारुहासिनी – *Cāruhāsinī*

- One who has a charming smile.
- It has been mentioned by some – The Moon is thy sweet smile – This saying means there is a certain stage of consciousness (*Prabodha*) which gives the highest bliss and which should be known from a teacher alone.
- *Cāruhāsinī* is also a 4 x 14 syllabic chandas (meter). She is in that form also.
- 242nd name in Sri Lalita Sahasranamam *Cāruhāsā* – is worth comparable here.

252. चटुला – *Caṭulā*

- She is shining like a lighting.

253. चण्डिका – *Caṇḍikā*

- One who is with anger.
- **She** is angry with those who do not have devotion on **Her**.
- Anger is one of the characters of *Brahmam*. Hence, *Chaṇḍikā* is *Brahmam* itself.
- Because she killed the demons *Chandan* she is *Caṇḍikā*.
- As mentioned in *Devi Bhagavatam*, it can be construed that **She** is in the form of seven-years-old girl; *Chaṇḍikā Saptavarshā Syāt*.
- From *Saptashatee*, it is understood that the combined form of *Mahākālee*, *Mahālakshmee* and *Mahāsaraswatee* is called as *Chaṇḍika*.
- 755th name in Sri Lalita Sahasranamam also – *Caṇḍikā*.

254. चित्रा – *Citrā*

- *Citrā* is the 15th titi nitya Devi. Earlier it was mentioned that she is in the form of all the *titi nitya Devi*s. *Chitra Nitya* lives in the outside ether. She is in that form *Citrā* also.

255. चित्रमाल्यविभूषिता – *Citramālyavibhūṣitā*

- She shines with a garland made of various colours.

256. चतुर्भुजा – *Caturbhujā*

- One with four hands.
- *Sri Devi* has four hands – two from each shoulder in front and back. The Four hands only have been indicated in the forms usually contemplated during meditation. Hands come first and foremost whenever we try to concentrate on the form mentioned in the *Dhyana Shloka* (meditation verse).
- The four *Devi*s who are the commandants of *Sri Devi*'s army viz., *Ashwaruda*, *Sampatkaree*, *Mantrinee* and *Varahee*, may be deemed to be the four hands of *Sri Devi*.
- The *Manta*s pertaining to the above four *Devee*s are indicated by

this name. She is in the form of those mantras.

- 7th name in Sri Lalita Sahasranamam is also *Chaturbāhusamanvitā*.
- 766th name in Sri Vishnu Sahasranamam is *Chaturbāhu*.

257. चारुदन्ता – *Cārudantā*

- She has a very good-looking tooth.
- 25th name in Sri Lalita Sahasranamam says *Shuddha Vidyāngkurākāra Dvijapankti Dwayoojjwalā*. This means that she rows of teeth shining like sprouts of *Shuddha Vidya*.
- *Shuddha Vidyā* refers to the superior *Shoḍashāksharī Mantra*. It consists of 16 letters or *beejās*. *Beejās* also mean seeds. The teeth look like the two sprouts from the seeds – the upper and lower rows.
- *Sri Devi*'s two rows of teeth are compared to the sprout of *Vidya*.

258. चातुरी – *Cāturī*

- She is the most skillful/ clever lady.

259. चरितप्रदा – *Caritapradā*

- She is a philanthropist imparting moral education to all.
- She has a holy story (Caritam). Her story is most powerful that even when it is heard or recollected in the mind, the devotee gets full benefits. This has been announced by *Sri Devi* herself in the 12th chapter of *Sri Devi Maahaatmyam*.

260. चूलिका – *Cūlikā*

- She is the top most among all Gods/ Goddess.

261. चित्रवस्त्रान्ता – *Citravastrāntā*

- She shines with a colourful dress.

262. चन्द्रमःकर्णकुण्डला – *Candramaḥkarṇakuṇḍalā*

- She wears the Moon as ear studs.

- From the statement (flowing smoothly like water) *Kātilolakātilola*, it is very clear that the ear studs enhance the beauty of a lady – Two ladies talk to each other;

  First lady: *Kā Atilola* – who is very beautiful?

  Second lady: *Kātil lola* – one who wears rings in ears.
- *Sri Adi Shankara* has installed ear studs to *Sri Devi* in most of the important temples.
- In *Soundaryalahree Sri Adi Shankara* says that because of the ear studs of *Sri Devi*, lord *Parameshwara* lives long.

263. चन्द्रहासा – *Candrahāsā*

- She has a scimitar (a sword like weapon) in one of the hands.
- Sri Devi has lots of weapons in her hands and this is one among them.
- She has a charming smile. It has been mentioned that the Moon is thy sweet smile – This saying means there is a certain stage of consciousness (*Prabodha*) which gives the highest bliss and which should be known from a teacher alone.
- The 242nd name in Sri Lalita Sahasranamam – *Chāruhāsā* – is worth comparable here.

264. चारुदात्री – *Cārudātrī*

- She only makes the Moon illuminate.
- *Dātrī* also means foster-mother. She is like a foster mother for Moon.

265. चकोरी – *Cakorī*

- She is like a female cakora (Greek partridge) bird.
- Cakora is like king of birds and hence she is of that form.

266. चन्द्रहासिनी – *Candrahāsinī*

- She is in dazzling white colour like a cool Moon.
- When she smiles her teeth shines like a Moon.
- Her face shines so bright that the Moon becomes shy.

267. चन्द्रिका – *Candrikā*

- One who gives, like a Moon, soothing for those who suffer from distress.

268. चन्द्रधात्री – *Candradhātrī*

- She makes the Moon beam illuminating the ocean of good fortune.

269. चौरी – *Caurī*

- A female thief. Earlier it was mentioned that she is in all the 64 arts. Stealing is one of the 64 arts. She is expert in that art also.
- She keeps her energy (shakti) as a secret and hence not visible to others.

270. चौरा – *Caurā*

- She crushes the sins of her devotees.

271. चण्डिका – *Caṇḍikā*

- This is a repetition of 253rd name.

272. चञ्चद्वागवादिनी – *Cañcadvāgavādinī*

- One who speaks sprightly and clearly without ambiguity.

273. चन्द्रचूडा – *Candracūḍā*

- One who wears a Moon (crescent Moon).
- One who is wearing a comely crescent moon in **Her** crown.
- Her third eye on the forehead is a crescent Moon.

274. चोरविनाशिनी – *Coravināśinī*

- One removes all the thieves. She removes the theft itself.
- The word thief here does not only mean the external, but internal thieves also.
- In 269th name above, it was mentioned that she is a female thief. Only a thief can recognize other thieves. Hence first she becomes a thief, before searching and removing all the other thieves.

275. चारुचन्दनलिप्ताङ्गी – *Cārucandanaliptāṅgī*

- One whose body (all the organs) smeared with scent of sandal paste.
- 434th name of Sri Lalita Sahasranamam *Chanḍanadravadigdhāngee* – also communicates the same meaning.

276. चञ्चच्चामरवीजिता – *Cañcaccāmaravījitā*

- She is waved with fans made of cane.

277. चारुमध्या – *Cārumadhyā*

- She has an elegant hip area, called middle place.

278. चारुगती – *Cārugatī*

- Her walking is so gaiety.
- Since she has a small waist her walk is so graceful.
- She controls the orbit of Moon.

279. चन्दिला – *Candilā*

- She shines like silver.

280. चन्द्ररूपिणी – *Candrarūpiṇī*

- She is in the form of a Moon. Actually, she is the Moon.
- *Sri Devi* is always there in the form of a Moon and hence no need of *Āvāhana* (deifying) and related *mudrās* (signs of hand), when puja is performed treating Moon as Devi.
- In the story of Abhirami Battar at Thirukadaiyoor, we all know that Sri Devi threw her ear stud and showed a Full Moon on a New Moon day.

281. चारुहोमप्रिया – *Cāruhomapriyā*

- She is always present in all great *yagnas* (homas).
- She is always happy by all *yagnas*.

- She is in the form of homa-kunda (the vessel for holy fire).

282. चार्वाचरिता – *Cārvācaritā*

- One with best/ great/ perfect practices.

283. चक्रबाहुका – *Cakrabāhukā*

- One having a cakra (discuss) in one of her hands.
- Being consort of Vishnu, she has Sudarshana Chakra in her hands.
- During the battle with demons, each of the God gave his weapon to her. In this regard Sri Vishnu gave Sudarshana Chakra to her.

284. चन्द्रमण्डलमध्यस्था – *Candramaṇḍalamadhyasthā*

- One who is residing in the center of the Moon's disc.
- It has been mentioned that the full moon is present in the *Sahasrāra Kamala* in the head. **She** is residing in the center of that moon.
- It can also be interpreted as – *Sri Devi* woken up from the *Mooladhara* breaks through the six *chakras* and reaches the Lord *Parameshwara* in the *Sahasrara Kamala*, called *Chandra maṇḍala*.
- If one contemplates *Sri Devi* in the Moon's disc in the sky on a full Moon day and worships **Her** by chanting this *Sahasranama*, he gets long life devoid of all diseases. This method is also named as *Ayushkara Prayoga*.
- In the *Shiva Purana* it has been mentioned as – *Shiva* resides in the head of fire and *Sri Devi* resides in the center of the Moon's disc.
- The inherent meaning is that the Moon's disc is the *Sri Chakra* itself.
- It has been mentioned in the *Tantra Sāstrās* that *Sri Devi Upasakas* have to do *Sri Vidya Sandhyavandhana* in every session and at mid-night, after the routine and normal *Sandhyavandhana*. At that time *Sri Devi* has to be meditated as **She** is the in the Moon's disc.
- In 280th name above it was mentioned that She is in the form Moon itself.
- 240th name in Sri Lalita Sahasranamam *Chandramaṇḍalamadhyagā* -– also coveys the same sense.

285. चन्द्रमण्डलदर्पणा – *Candramaṇḍaladarpaṇā*

- She reflects the Moon.

- Earlier it was mentioned that She is the Moon. Now it is said that she reflects the Moon. Because she is everywhere, she reflects anything and everything.

286. चक्रवाकस्तनी – *Cakravākastanī*

- Her breasts are like *Cakravāha* bird.
- *Cakravāha* is a raga in Carnatic classical music. *Cakravāha* is also a kind of bird called ruddy goose or Brahmany duck. Her breasts are compared to this bird.

287. चेष्टा – *Ceṣṭā*

- She shows a naughty gesture.

288. चित्रा – *Citrā*

- This is a repetition of 254th name.

289. चारुविलासिनी – *Cāruvilāsinī*

- One who is esteemly playful – showing the same thing in different forms.
- Illusion (*Māyā*) is of two types – hiding the existing one (*Āvaranam*) and showing the same things in different forms (*Vikshepam*), i.e. showing the unrealistic form as a real one.
- *Vilāsam* means pastime, play, erotic actions, etc. *Cāru* is elegant or pleasing. She possesses all these.

290. चित्स्वरूपा – *Citsvarūpā*

- She is *Chit Swaroopinee*. She is in the form *Chinmaya*.
- She is in the form of *Chit* and hence always knowledgeable.
- The word *Chit* means flawless *Brahmam*. *Sri Devi* emerged from the fire of *Chit*, that is knowledge. In other words, *Sri Devi*'s real form emerges from the sacrificial fire of knowledge for the purpose of annihilating ignorance.
- *Shakta Shastras* say that only the *chit* (pure consciousness) plays by reflecting in different forms.
- *Atma* is the dynamic form of *Sri Devi* – omnipresent, omnipotent,

love in all forms (*Sat*, *Cit* and *Ananda* – that is existence, knowledge and bliss).

- *Kameshwara* is the form of *Atma* – self. That means – He likes everything and liked by everything and hence the *Cit Atma* is *Kameshwara*. The mental differentiation of *Dvaita* will be burnt in the *cit* blaze of *Kameshwara*. Hence *Jeeva* has merged with *cit-atma* – self. The balance is only a '**null**' – The form of *Chinmaya*.
- The 124th name of *Sri Lalita Trishatee – Sarvamangalā – Sri Devi* is the *Cit* energy nothing different from *Brahmam*.

291. चन्द्रवती – *Candravatī*

- *Candravatī* means several forms of ladies. She is in all such forms.
- Particularly *Candravatī* means a princess. She always is a princess.

292. चन्द्रमा – *Candramā*

- She is the presiding deity of Moon.
- In many a place in this Sahasranamam it has been mentioned there She and the Moon are one and the same. The same is being stressed in this name.

293. चन्दनप्रिया – *Candanapriyā*

- She is fond of Sandal.
- Traditionally *Sri Devi* is worshipped with sandal paste offerings Sandal paste. It is one of the important offerings during the worship.
- Sandal paste is also offered to Brahmins, Sumangali ladies and small girls. When they are offered with Sandal, she becomes happy.

294. चोदयित्री – *Codayitrī*

- She inspires her devotees.
- One who inspires into right action.
- *Kaṭopanishat* (II-3-2,3) says – since **She** inspires fear;

*Mahadbhayam Vajramudyatam*

"It is a great terror, a raised thunderbolt"; *Brahma Sūtra* (I-3-39) explains that thunderbolt (*Vajra*) in this context is *Brahmam*.

295. चिरप्रज्ञा – *Ciraprajñā*

- She is eternal bliss.
- She is eternal knowledge – *Sanātana Vidyā Swarūpiṇī.*

296. चातका – *Cātakā*

- She is a firm decisive person like a *Cātakā* bird.
- *Cātakā* bird is ordinarily called as Jacobin cuckoo, Clamator jacobines, pied cuckoo or the pied crested cuckoo. This bird is famous for its stubbornness to complete the task undertaken. Sri Devi is also in a similar way, will definitely complete task under taken by her and also will enable her devotees in the same fashion.

297. चारुहेतुकी – *Cāruhetukī*

- She is an elegantly conditioned lady.

298. छत्रयाता – *Chatrayātā*

- She always moves with an umbrella.

299. छत्रधरा – *Chatradharā*

- She acts as a parasol for her devotees.
- She offers shade to her devotees and do not allow to them to suffer.

300. छाया – *Chāyā*

- She is her own shadow.
- She is like shadow for her devotees.
- In the previous name it was mentioned that she offers shade. Here it is mentioned that she herself is shadow.

Thus ends 100 divine names on *Sri Gayatri Devi* from 201 to 300

*****

301. छन्दःपरिच्छदा – *Chandaḥparicchadā*

- One who is well versed in Vedas. One who is the essence of all *Vedas*.
- One who created the *Vedas*. She is in-charge/ leader of Vedas.
- The word *Chandaḥ* would mean – word, *Veda*, *Gāyatree*, meter and so on.
- Any prose with *Chandaḥ* (meter) and svaram is called *Veda*. If there is no svaram and only *Chandaḥ* is available it is called *kavya* (epic). She is an expert in both.
- *Veda* says "*Gāyatreem Chandasām Mātaḥ*" – *Gāyatree mantra* is the mother of all *mantras*.
- In *Srimad Bhagavat Geeta* (X-35) Lord *Sri Krishna* says;
  *Gāyatree Chandasāmaham*.
- In *Koorma Purana* also the same is conveyed as;
  *Gāyatree Chandasāmasi*.
- *Chandaḥ* is one of the 6 *Vedāngas* – organs of *Vedas*.

302. छायादेवी – *Chāyādevī*

- She is in the form of a shadow.
- There are two people viz., shadow and light in the cavity – the heart. She is in the form of both. Those who know *Brahmam* call them shade and light. The meaning is that as both, shadow and light, enter the cavity of the heart and both contradict each other;

303. छिद्रनखा – *Chidranakhā*

- *Chidra* means hole. It is She who makes the hole.
- In this *Sahasranama*, multiple times it has been mentioned that She lives in a cave of the heart or *sushumna*. Here that cave is mentioned as hole.

304. छन्नेन्द्रियविसर्पिणी – *Channendriyavisarpiṇī*

- She comes near to those who has sub-judicated their senses.
- *Sri Devi* promotes righteousness in her devotees, like control of senses, cleanliness, wealth and devotion to god.

305. छन्दोऽनुष्टुप्प्रतिष्ठान्ता – *Chando'nuṣṭuppratiṣṭhāntā*

- Earlier it was mentioned that she is in the form of all types of *Chanda*-s. *Anuṣṭup* is a chandas with 4 padas of 8 characters each, totaling 32 letters. She resides in that form also.

306. छिद्रोपद्रवभेदिनी – *Chidropadravabhedinī*

- She helps her devotees to identify and overcome the deceitful *yogis*.
- A *yogi* is normally identified by the external attire. From the outward look a genuine and deceitful yogi cannot be distinguished. She helps her devotees to identify and avoid the guile yogis.

307. छेदा – *Chedā*

- She circumvents those who do sins.
- She enables her devotees to avoid sins.
- *Cheda* again means hole and She lives in the hole called heart of the *upasakas*.

308. छत्रेश्वरी – *Chatreśvarī*

- She treats herself as student. There is no end for learning. She has thirst for learning and updating. If not updated the person will become outdated.
- *Chatra* means a student or umbrella.
- Regarding she in the form of umbrella and providing shade and all it has already been discussed.

309. छिन्ना – *Chinnā*

- Literal meaning of *Chinnā* is harlot/ sternutation/ sneezing. Actually, sneezing is removal of irritation. It is she who removes the irritations of the life of the devotees.

310. छुरिका – *Churikā*

- In one sense *Churikā* means darba – which is a holy grass used in all

Vedic religious activities – be it *para* or *apara*. She is in that form. That means it is she who conducts all the Vedic rites.

- Typical of any Samskruta word, *Churikā* also has lots of meanings like – knife, axe, etc. Earlier itself it was mentioned that she is in the form of all weapons. It includes this also.

311. छेदनप्रिया – *Chedanapriyā*

- She is an expert in piercing. She pierces through the narrow Sushumna nadi, pass through all the chakras including piercing through the *grantis* (knots).
- Almost all the Shakta texts, virtually in all the places, talk about the Kundalinee energy piercing through Sushumna nadis. This means that Sri Devi and Kundalini are synonymous.

312. जननी – *Jananī*

- *Janani* means mother. She is the mother of all.
- She is Jaganmata – mother of the universe. She is also called as Jagatjanani.
- The supreme mother – When we are in deep trouble, the first word uttered by us involuntarily is *Ma*. Human beings are afflicted by three kinds of *Tapas* (difficulties), which cannot be solved by the mother in her human form. The possession of the power to resolve these difficulties makes **Her** the "Superior Mother". Worshipping **Her**, who has given birth to the whole world, will prevent birth again in this world from the mother's womb.
- All the *mantras* originated from **Her** and hence the name *Janani*.
- In Lalita Shasranama it has been mentioned in more than one place that She is the mother. For instance, 457th name – *Mātā* – माता. Even the starting name is *Srimātā*.

313. जन्मरहिता – *Janmarahitā*

- It is she who saves her devotees from next birth.
- In almost all the phala shrutis of Devi verses like Sri Lalita Sahasranamam, Lalita Trishati, Devi Mahatmyam, Devi Bhagavatam and so on, it has been stressed that those who chant the mantras will definitely reach Moksha. They will be liberated from next birth.

314. जातवेदा – *Jātavedā*

- She is *Agniswaroopinee* – she is in the form of fire (*Agni*) god.
- *Durgā Sooktam*, within *Rig* Veda goes like this "जातवेदसे सुनवाम... – *Jātavedase Sunavāma...*". Its meaning is – We offer our oblations to the Fire of Devi to cross over this very difficult ocean of worldly existence.

315. जगन्मयी – *Jaganmayī*

- She contains the whole world within her.
- She is contained in this world.
- She is omnipresent – she is all pervasive in the whole universe.

316. जाह्नवी – *Jāhnavī*

- She is in the form of river Ganges.
- River Ganges is daughter of sage Jahnu and hence Ganga is called *Jāhnavī*. As earlier mentioned, our Devi is in that form.
- As earlier mentioned, the black water of Yamuna river and the white water of Ganges river mix in the Triveni junction, but still maintain their own individuality (colour) for some distance.

317. जटिला – *Jaṭilā*

- She is mixed with her own devotees.
- There is no difference between Atman and Sri Devi. Both are one and the same. This is real advaitam – mixing of *jeevatma* and *paramatma*.

318. जेत्री – *Jetrī*

- She is always a triumphant.
- One who is the conqueror of ignorance (*Avidyā*).
- **She** helps the devotees to win over it. **She**, who is the form of knowledge herself, bestows knowledge and wins over ignorance.

319. जरामरणवर्जिता – *Jarāmaraṇavarjitā*

- One who relieves her devotees from the fear of cycle of birth and death.

320. जम्बुद्वीपवती – *Jambudvīpavatī*

- One who lives in *Jamboodveepam*.
- There are seven islands around *Manidveepam* in the Meru Mountain, the residence of Sri Devi. They are;
    a. *Jambootdveepam* (Land of berries – Asia),
    b. *Kushadveepam* (land of darba grass – Oceania including Indonesia and the Philippines excluding Australia)
    c. *Plaksha Dveepam* (land of the fig trees – South America)
    d. *Pushkara Dveepam* (land of lakes – North America)
    e. *Shaalmali Dveepam* (land of the silk cotton trees – Australia)
    f. *Krauncha Dveepam* (land of the *krauncha* birds or the demoiselle crane – Africa)
    g. *Shaaka Dveepam* (land of the trees – Europe).
- The 15 Titi nitya Devis live in these *dveepam* on rotation in each of eras (*yugas*). *Nityā Devees* are in the form of the worlds and time and their interchange. Accordingly, *Sri Dev* dwells in the *Mahāmeru* during the first year of *Kruta Yuga* (*Kruta* era). *Nitya Devee*s starting from *Kameshwaree* till *Jvalamalinee* live in other *Dveepams* and seven oceans. *Chitra Nitya* lives in the outside ether. In the next years they rotate their places of living - each *Nitya Devi* (including *Sri Devi*) moves to next place. In the same way in the following years they move to adjacent places. In the sixteenth year they return to the original places. Each of the *Nitya Devi*s becomes the Moon of *Meru* in one year. *Tantrarāja Tantra* (28th chapter) explains this in detail.

321. ज्वाला – *Jvālā*

- One who is in the form of flames.
- One who dwells in the center of the fort of fire built by *Jvalamalini*.
- The chapter 7-31[7] in Sri Devi Bhagavatam is titled "Sri Devi Appeared as Flame". To annihilate the demon *Tarakan*, devas, including Brahma and all, did penance and prayed to Sri Devi. She appeared as torch or flame. Devas were scared and cried. Then she changed her form into a beautiful girl.
- According to *Lalithopakyana*, in the course of the battle with *Bhandasura*, in order to protect the army, *Sri Devi* instructed *Jvalamalini* to build a fort of fire with 100 *yojanas* area and 30

[7] The 10 chapters from this 7-31 to 7-40 are combined called as Sri Devi Gita.

*yojanas* height, in the center of which **She** staged with **Her** army.

- She is surrounded by sparks of fire and yet remains unaffected.

322. जयन्ती – *Jayantī*

- She is always victorious.
- She makes her devotees also to be victorious in all fair acts.

323. जलशालिनी – *Jalaśālinī*

- She is in the form of bashfully beautiful water fall or flowing river.

324. जितेन्द्रिया – *Jitendriyā*

- She has her senses sub-judicated.
- *Vamana Purana* says – *Sri Devi* promotes righteousness in her devotees, like control of senses, cleanliness, wealth and devotion to god; *Jitendriyatvam Shoucham Cha Māngalyam Bhaktireva Cha* I

325. जितक्रोधा – *Jitakrodhā*

- One who has conquered her anger.
- In 253rd name it was mentioned that she is very angry. Here it is contradicted. Even who has conquered the anger, has to be angry on the enemies while fighting with them. That is what mentioned in 253rd name.
- She destroys the tendency to get angry of her devotees.
- 462nd name in Sri Vishnu Sahasranamam is also the same name – *Jitakrodhā*.

326. जितामित्रा – *Jitāmitrā*

- One who has conquered all enemies.
- Multiple times it has been mentioned that enemies are not only external. But also, internal. Every human has six internal enemies – lust, anger, stinginess, libidinous, recklessness and amusement. In an earlier name it was mentioned that She suppresses the anger of the devotees. Here it is mentioned that she destroys all the enemies.
- 524th name in Sri Vishnu Sahasranamam is also the same name – *Jitāmitrā*.

327. जगत्प्रिया – *Jagatpriyā*

- One who is a favourite of this entire universe.
- She is liked by all not only human beings, but also by all living things.
- She is fond of everybody and everything.

328. जातरूपमयी – *Jātarūpamayī*

- One who is splendidly beautiful.
- She offers stunning beauty to her devotees.

329. जिह्वा – *Jihvā*

- One who has a long tongue. In the form as *Kali* she has a long tongue.
- As *Sarasvati*, who causes speech, she ever resides in the tongues of all beings.
- **She** is in the form of the tongue, which recognises the taste. The organ tongue has two roles to play – recognizing the taste and speech. She is for both.

330. जानकी – *Jānakī*

- In Ramayana, she took the incarnation as Janaki daughter of King Janaka.
- To annihilate Ravana and other demons, she took the role Janaki.

331. जगती – *Jagatī*

- Earlier it was mentioned that she is in the form of all types of Chanda-s. Again in 305th name it was mentioned that she is in the form of *Anuṣṭup* chandas. A verse in Jagati chandas will have 4 padas of each 12 characters. Now she is in the form of Jagati chandas.

332. जरा – *Jarā*

- In the 10th name she was addressed as *Ajarā*. Here it is contradicted. She has a form of an old. Like the simile that the darkness goes away automatically when the ray of The Sun is struck – for the darkness called old age, **she** is like Sun. That is, **she** bestows knowledge that the body and soul are different and that the youth and old age are only for the body.

- She takes the form of old-age during Sandhya time.
- She is not affected by the time.

333. जनित्री – *Janitrī*

- She is a mother.
- In the 312th name above also, she was indicated as a mother.
- In a normal family itself, the children will move affectionately with the mother and with a mild respect with the father. As a mother of the universe, we take liberty while moving her. That is the reason she is often called as mother.

334. जह्नुतनया – *Jahnutanayā*

- Daughter of sage *Jahnu*. She is in the form of river Ganga. This has to be cross referred with 313th name *Jāhnavī*. 198th name also can be referred.

335. जगत्त्रयहितैषिणी – *Jagattrayahitaiṣiṇī*

- One who bestows wealth to all the three worlds.
- **She** is in all the three worlds.
- 614th name in Sri Vishnu Sahasranamam – *Lokatrayashraya* can be compared.
- In *Shrimad Bhagavad Gita* (III-22) *Sri Krishna* says – there is nothing in three worlds that has not been done be me;
  "*Na Me Pārthāsti Kartavyam Trishu Lokeshu Kinchana*".

336. ज्वालामुखी – *Jwālāmukhī*

- One who has the flame as her face.
- The term *Jwala* means flame – the physical manifestation of Jwala is always a set of eternal flames.
- A story known to most of us. When *Daksha*, father of *Sati Devi* (in one of **Her** incarnations) despised **Her** consort, Lord *Shiva*, **she** could not tolerate it and left **Her** body. Lord *Parameshwara* was roaming

carrying her body. Sri Vishnu cut her body into pieces with his chakra. Each piece of her body fell at 108 different places all over India. These 108 places became the Shakti Peetams.

- The tongue of Sri Devi fell at a town and a Nagar parishad in Kangra district in the state of Himachal Pradesh. The presiding deity of this temple is called *Jwālāmukhī*.

337. जपवती – *Japavatī*

- She always chants the name Brahma as japam. A japam is defined as pious repetition of a holy name or sacred *mantra*, practiced as a spiritual discipline.
- She bestows her blessings on those who chant Gayatri Japam.
- *Shrimad Bhagavad Gita* (X-25) says that He is in the form of *Japa Yagnam* also; *Yagnānām Japayagnoosme*.

338. ज्वरघ्नी – *Jvaraghnī*

- She is best medicine for any type of fever – feverish fire.

339. जितविष्टपा – *Jitaviṣṭapā*

- She is winner of this entire universe.
- She has won the minds of her devotees.
- She has won every battle she fought with demons.
- She has won all her organs and help her devotees also to win over the organs.

340. जिताक्रान्तमयी – *Jitākrāntamayī*

- She is so victorious that everybody is astonished over her victory.
- This name is in continuation of previous name.

341. ज्वाला – *Jvālā*

- This is a repetition of 321st name.

342. जाग्रती – *Jāgratī*

- *Jāgram* means to awake. *Jagrati* – the soul being in conscious state.

Her name at this state is *Vishvaroopa*. This Vishvaroopa is the state of the soul in the conscious state. Hence, she is *Jagrati*.

- She is in the awakened state of mind.
- There are five states of the Jeeva – awaken (*Jagrat*), dream (*Swapna*), deep sleep (*Sushupti*), swoon (*Tureeyam*) and transcendental (*Tureeyatheetham*). She is in all these states.

343. ज्वरदेवता – *Jvaradevatā*

- She is the goddess of all fevers.
- In the 338th name above it was mentioned that She is the medicine for any fever. Here it is mentioned that she is the lord of fever.
- This implies that fever is a special type or an important disease. Further since there are many types of fevers, it has to be mentioned as all fevers. Chanting of this *Sahasranāma*, is to get rid of the fever(s).

344. ज्वलन्ती – *Jvalantī*

- She becomes happy when black mustard is offered into holy fire in the *yagnas*.
- As per tantric methods, gayatri homa is done by offering black mustard, to satisfy Sri Gayatri Devi.

345. जलदा – *Jaladā*

- *Jaladā* means cloud. She is in the form of cloud bestowing adequate water to living beings.
- She is a water giver.

346. ज्येष्ठा – *Jyeṣṭhā*

- She is the biggest. Nothing greater or bigger than her.
- She is the supreme bliss. One who has an immensely great form.
- When contemplating the *Brahmam*, *Veda* mentions contradicting characters. Smaller than the smallest, bigger than the biggest – *Anoranīyān Mahato Mahīyān*.
- In *Sri Rudram* when bowing to Lord Shiva – 6th paragraph starts with "*Namo Jyeṣṭhāya Ca*". He is the biggest.
- Again, the *Camakam* – 2nd paragraph starts with "*Jyeṣṭyam Ca Me*". Requesting to make me great.

347. ज्याघोषस्फोटदिङ्मुख्यै – *Jyāghoṣasphoṭadiṅmukhī*

- She clearly permeates the directions and intermediate quarters with her bows.
- She is an all pervade. She protects this whole universe from all directions. This was also discussed in the *kavaca* chapter earlier.
- The 10 Devis of Dasha Maha Vidya (The 10 Cosmic Powers of the Divine Mother) originated from 10 different directions (4 primary, 4 corners, top and bottom) only.

348. जम्भिनी – *Jambhinī*

- She destroys the demons with her teeth.
- In the form of Kali, she had big teeth and tongue. She used to bite and kill the demons and drink their blood.

349. जृम्भणा – *Jṛmbhanā*

- It is she who makes the buds to blossom.

350. जृम्भा – *Jṛmbhā*

- She is always a blossomed flower like.
- This name has to be read in conjunction with the previous name.
- Flower buds will blossom and shrivel on the same day, whereas *Sri Devi*'s feet remain permanently lustrous and thus they win over flowers.
- Shrimad Bhagavatam (5-20-10) lists various kinds of flowers.

351. ज्वलन्माणिक्यकुण्डला – *Jvalanmaṇikyakuṇḍalā*

- She shines with the ear jewels (kundela) studded with gem stones.
- An ornament in the ears is very important, especially to Sumangali ladies. In Tamil, even *Shiva* is described as "*Todudaiya Seviyan*" – one who has studs in his ear.
- 28th verse of *Soundaryalaharee* says that – even after consuming the great venom *Shiva* continued to live on account the shakti of ear Kundalam of Sri Devi. On the other hand, even after consuming nectar, *Devas* get destroyed (during dissolution); *Sudhāmaptāsvādhya*...

352. झिञ्झिका – *Jhiñjhikā*

- She creates and protects even the lowest ranked living beings like Shrimp.
- *Sri Devi* has such a broad mind so that **She** does not distinguish any soul from *Brahma* onwards till a worm
- It is indicated as, though there is a huge difference between a worm and *Brahma*, as a mother **She** has equal affection with all.
- 285th name in Sri Lalita Sahasranamam – *Ābrahmakīṭajananī* – आब्रह्म कीट जननी – She is the mother from Brahma till a worm. **She** gave birth to all these beings.

353. झणनिर्घोषा – *Jhaṇanirghoṣā*

- She attracts with the chimes of her Bracelet.
- She does not need anything to attract her devotees. Still this name specifies the greatness of her shining bracelet.

354. झंझामारुतवेगिनी – *Jhañjhāmārutaveginī*

- She is so strong like frightening thunder storm or thunderbolt.
- The thunderbolt in the hands of Indra, made of the backbone of a sage is supposed to be the strongest weapon. That is the reason that weapon is compared here.

355. झल्लरीवाद्यकुशला – *Jhallarīvādyakuśalā*

- She can be made happy by playing the Cymbals instrument.
- She is always fond of music. Cymbals is a fast instrument and hence she very much likes the instrument and hence the player also.

356. ञरूपा – *Ñarūpā*

- She is so beautiful/ majestic like a bull.
- One of her vehicles is Nandi. Nandi is supposed to be most beautiful/ majestic of all bulls. Hence the comparison here.

357. ञभुजा – *Ñabhujā*

- She has courage, valour and strength like a bull.

- As mentioned in the previous name, again Nandi is taken as a simile in this context.

358. टङ्कबाणसमायुक्ता – *Ṭaṅkabāṇasamāyuktā*

- *Tanka* = sword. *Bana* = arrow. She is an expert in using sword, arrow, etc., in a battle.
- She has every other type of weapon in her hand and she is an expert in using all of them.
- A weapon will act as intended by the person who takes aim. Here these weapons will act as per the wish of *Sri Devi*.

359. टङ्किनी – *Ṭaṅkinī*

- She has all types of weapons in her hand and chisel is also one among them. She is expert in using this also.

360. टङ्कभेदिनी – *Ṭaṅkabhedinī*

- The word Tanka has lots of meanings. The best suitable in this context is caste. She distinguishes various castes.
- She prescribes the dharma for each of the caste and make everyone follow his dharma and act accordingly.

361. टङ्कीगणकृताघोषा – *Ṭaṅkīgaṇakṛtāghoṣā*

- She makes loud noise like Rudra Ganas.
- Her noise can be considered as loud and scary laughter.
- During war times with demons, the loud and scary laughter of *Sri Devi* has been mentioned in many places.

362. टङ्कनीयमहोरसा – *Ṭaṅkanīyamahorasā*

- One who lives in the heart (*vakshastal*) of the great *Mahavishnu*.
- She in the form Lakshmi lives in the heart of Vishnu.

363. टङ्कारकारिणी देवी – *Ṭaṅkārakāriṇī Devī*

- One who howls loudly during battle and all.

- It is very usual for those who fight in the battle to shout loudly. It is called *Kosham* in Samskrutam.
- It has been mentioned in Sri Devi Mahatmyam that even the lion vehicle of Sri Devi shouted loudly and the demons were scared of it.

364. ठ ठ शब्द निनादिनी – *Ṭha Ṭha Śabda Ninādinī*

- She terrifies her enemies with *Tha Tha* sound itself.
- In continuation of the previous name, this name also talks about Sri Devi making horrible noise in the battles.

365. डामरी – *Ḍāmarī*

- She is the in the form of *Damari Devi*.
- There are 10 Devis surrounding Sri Devi in her Chintamani house. They are; *Dāmaree, Dhankāriṇee, Nārnā, Tāmasee, Sthānvee, Dhākshāyanee, Dhātree, Nāree, Pārvatee* and *Phatkāriṇee*.
- Sri Devi is in all those forms including *Ḍāmarī*

366. डाकिनी – *Ḍākinī*

- She is the in the form of *Ḍākinī*.
- The female Imp attending Sri Devi *Ḍākinī*. She is in her form also.
- This and the previous name imply – it is she who is in the forms of her own attendant and surrounding herself. When she is everybody in this world, naturally her attendants also.

367. डिम्भा – *Ḍimbhā*

- The word *Ḍimbhā* in Samskrutam has lots of meanings like – new born baby, recently formed embryo, young animal, child, body, uterus and so on.
- She is in all such forms.

368. डुण्डमारैकनिर्जिता – *Ḍuṇḍamāraikanirjitā*

- One who killed the demon called *Ḍuṇḍamāra*.

369. डामरीतन्त्रमार्गस्था – *Ḍāmarītantramārgasthā*

- There is a lot of variances in Sri Vidya tantras. One such is *Ḍāmarī Tantra*. It is she who explains that path of that tantra.

370. डमड्डमरुनादिनी – *Ḍamaḍḍamarunādinī*

- *Ḍamaru* is a percussion instrument in the hands of Lord Shiva. It creates *Ḍamaḍ Ḍamaḍ* sound. It is she who enables *Ḍamaru* to make the sound.
- Lord Nataraja holds this *Ḍamaru* instrument in his hand. During his dance, the 16 sound waves of Maheshwara Sutra originated from this *Ḍamaru*. She is the cause for the origin of such sounds.

371. डिण्डीरवसहा – *Ḍiṇḍīravasahā*

- *Ḍiṇḍī* is a wind instrument. It is she who enables *Ḍiṇḍī* to make the rhythmic sound.

372. डिम्भलसत्क्रीडापरायणा – *Ḍimbhalasākrīḍāparāyaṇā*

- She is fond of playing alongwith small children.
- Philosophically thinking – *Ashṭāvakra Samhita* (*Gita*) (II-25) says – Sri Devi says – the souls originate from me, in the form of boundary-less ocean, as natural waves. They hit each other, play for some time and abscond after some time. She only makes the souls to play in such a way.
- The word *Lalita* is derived from *'Lālanam'*, that is one who is always engaged in playing games – one who plays with all creatures with motherly affection. *Sri Gayatri Devi* is *Lalita Devi* and hence playful.

373. ढुण्ढिविघ्नेशजननी – *Ḍhuṇḍhivighneśajananī*

- She is the mother of *Ḍhuṇḍhi Vignesh* – Ḍhuṇḍhi *Ganapati*.
- It is told that there are 32 types of Ganapatis at a high level. *Ḍhuṇḍhi Ganapati* is one among them. He has four arms. His hands hold the single tusk, the rosary (*Rudrakaha*), the hatchet (Kuthara - an axe) and a pot of jewels (Ratnapatra). He is Red in Colour. She is his mother.

374. ढक्काहस्ता – *Ḍhakkāhastā*

- *Ḍhakkā* is a large drum. She holds this in one of her hands. She also plays it.

375. ढिलिव्रजा – *Ḍhilivrajā*

- She is integrated with the group called *Ḍhili*.

376. नित्यज्ञाना – *Nityajñānā*

- She has eternal/ permanent/ continuous knowledge.
- She is a personification of knowledge.
- In the 308th name above it was mentioned that she is a student – a continuous learner. Resultantly she has eternal knowledge.
- Sri Vishnu Sahasranamam 454th name – ज्ञानमुत्तमम् – *Jnānamuttamam* – can be compared here.

377. निरुपमा – *Nirupamā*

- She is without form.
- Sri Devi has been described with various forms, including that of *Virat* form (*Vishwaroopa*). In reality she is formless. The sense of this name is; since **She** is omnipresent there is no form relating to characters.
- *Brahmam* is nameless and hence formless. To reach that Brahmam one has do *Nirguna/ Niroopa upasana*. To start with, till the person matures, he can do *Saguna/ Saroopa upasana*. But this cannot continue. One has to leave the boat after reaching the other shore. In that way one has to mature and realise formless Brahmam. *Sri Devi* will grace us to become capable of transcending the abyss of plurality and comprehend Her as the Formless Absolute.
- **She** acquires a body or form as **she** pleases – The quality of a shape or body is like the "Solid Ghee", which can also lose its shape when warmed. This implies that **she** is with form as well as is formless.
- Sri Lalita Sahasranamam 814th name – *Amūrtā* – also says that she is without form or shape.
- Sri Vishnu Sahasranamam 720th name – *Amūrtimān* – also conveys the same sense. *Sri Adi Shankara* comments on this name – **he** is formless because he does not have the bondage and actions (*karmas*).

378. निर्गुणा – *Nirguṇā*

- She is without any quality or character.
- This name goes hand-in-hand in tune with the previous name. When Sri Devi is formless, naturally she is without any quality. When she has a form, she has to be described with some qualities.
- It can also be interpreted as meditation with qualities is *Suguna Upasana* (meditation imagining some form). In due course when it becomes meditation with meaning, it becomes *Nirguṇa Upasana* (meditation on the formless and attribute-less).
- In *Śvētāśvatara Upanishat* (VI-11) we read *Sākṣī Chetā Kevalo Nirguṇaśca* – Witness, the philosopher, one who is uncontaminated and who is free from characters.
- This has been explained in *Matsya* and *Padma puranas*. The traits of *Devas* are their identities; characters are related to bodies. Since *Sri Devi* is in the form of *Chit*, **she** has no characters neither identity.
- Sri Lalita Sahasranamam 139th name – *Nirguṇā* – also says that she is without qualities.
- Sri Vishnu Sahasranamam 840th name – *Nirguṇa* – also conveys the same sense. *Sri Adi Shankara* in his commentary quotes the above said *Upanishat* and *Puranas*.

379. नर्मदा – *Narmadā*

- She is in the form of river *Narmada*.
- Earlier it has been mentioned that she is in the form all rivers. That includes river Narmada also.
- Pilgrims used to do circumambulation (Parikrama) of the holy Narmada river, starting from Omkareshwar, one of the 12 Jyothirlinga temples of Lord Shiva and ending in the same place. It is a formidable spiritual exercise and challenge—an incredible journey of about 2,600 km. This is a pride that no other river has.

380. नदी – *Nadī*

- She is in the form all rivers.
- In Samskrutam all the rivers from East-west are called *Nadī* and they are feminine. All the rivers from North-south are called *Nadaḥ* and they are masculine. In this context we have to take all rivers flowing East-west are Sri Devi's form only.

- Earlier it has been mentioned separately about rivers Yamuna, Narmada and Ganges. Here it is commonly mentioned about all the rivers.
- Shrimad Bhagavatam (5-19-18) gives the names of around 45 rivers flowing in Bharath.

381. त्रिगुणा – *Triguṇā*

- One who is endowed with the three qualities.
- The *Vayu Purana* says, "This *Devi* creates as well as destroys forms, **she** has many forms, many functions and many names, by function and by **Her** sport **She** is threefold in the world, hence **She** is called *Triguṇā*".
- The *Vishnu Purana* also says, "I admire that eternal energy, which is thy energy which is in all beings and in all souls, the basis of the qualities";
- In 378th name above, **she** was mentioned as without qualities. Depending on the qualities of the worshippers, **she** can be worshipped with or without qualities.
- *Devi Purana* explains in another way - "As **She** has three steps, the three paths of Ganga, the three qualities, etc."; for it says, "Bali was bound by three steps, the Ganga came from three places, heaven, etc., by the three qualities *sattva*, *rajas* and *tamas*. **She** performs the functions of creation, preservation and destruction; hence **She** is called *Triguṇā*";
- Sri Lalita Sahasranamam 984th name is also the same – *Triguṇā*.
- Sri Vishnu Sahasranamam 839th name – *Guṇabhruta* – also conveys the same sense.

382. त्रिपदा – *Tripadā*

- She has three legs/ feet.
- That means she has the same form of three footed *Trivikrama* incarnation of Sri Vishnu.
- 534th name of Sri Vishnu Sahasranamam – *Tripada* – also conveys the same sense.

383. तन्त्री – *Tantrī*

- She is in the form of a *Tantri*.

- *Srividya* (*Devi Upasana*) is mainly in two paths – *Vedic* and *tantric*. One who follow *Vedic* paths are called *vaidheekas* and who follow *tantric* paths are called *tantris*. Whichever path is followed the ultimate goal to reach is the Devi – the *Brahmam*.
- Again, there are two kinds of worshipping *Sri Devi* – external (*Bāhyam*) and internal (*Āntaram*). And again, the external has two divisions, *Vedic* and *Tantric*. The internal method is also of two kinds with support (*Sādhāra*) and without support (*Nirādhāra*).
- The various *upacaras* done/ shown during *Devi* worship are called *tantras* and performer is called *tantri*.
- Almost all the *Shakta* related texts are called *tantrams*. The authors of those texts are *tantris*. She is in that form.
- The Veena and the parrot in the hands of *Sri Devi* became the *Shaktis* known as *Yantrini* and *Tantrinee*.

384. तुलसीतरुणासीतरुः – *Tulasītaruṇātaruḥ*

- She is in the form of Tulasi among the plants.
- Tulasi (Holy basil) is a sacred plant used while worshipping lord Vishnu, Krishna and all. It is regarded as an earthly manifestation of the goddess Tulasi/ Brinda. She is regarded as an incarnation of Lakshmi and thus the consort of the Sri Vishnu. The offering of its leaves is mandatory in ritualistic worship of Vishnu and his avatars like Krishna.
- Bilva leaf is to Lord Shiva and similarly Tulasi leaf is to Lord Vishnu.

385. त्रिविक्रम पदाक्रान्ता – *Trivikrama Padākrāntā*

- She is the Trivikrama who measured the three worlds with three feet taking a gigantic form.
- In one sense mother of universe (*Jaganmātā*) and in another sense the *Trivikrama* form measuring all the three worlds.
- Sri Vishnu Sahasranamam 530th name is also the same – त्रिविक्रम – *Trivikrama*.
- She is the consort of Lord Vishnu and there is no difference between him and she.

386. तुरीयपदगामिनी – *Turīyapadagāminī*

- She is the guide to reach the fourth (*Turīya*) state.

- Sri Vidya philosophy is to clearly understand the three states awaken, dream and deep sleep and distinguish the differences between the souls in each of these states Vishva, Taijasā and Prāna. Such an understanding state is called the fourth state or *Tureeya*. Hence, she acquires this name.
- The state mentioned in *Vedas* – *"Shiva Matvaitam Chaturttam Manyante"* is called *Tureeya*.
- The *Tripura Siddhanta* says, as **she** presented herself to *Turiyānandanātha* (a certain teacher) She is known by the name *Tureeya*.
- She is in the swoon (*Tureeya*) state, still further in transcendental (*Tureeyatheetham*) state beyond awaken, dream and deep sleep states (*Vishva, Taijasā* and *Prāgnā*).

*Gāyatree Sashirās Tureeya Sahitā Sandhyā Mayeetyagamairāgyātā Tripure Tvameva Mahatām Sharmapradā Karmanām* (*Lagustuti*)

- Sri Adi Shankara describes this state of mind in detail in the 97th verse of *Soundaryalaharee*.
- The *Shiva Sūtra* (I-11) says, "He is *veeresa*, who enjoys in the threefold way". That is, *Veerendras* are those who realise the fourth state (*tureeya*) in the other three states also (awaken, deep sleep and swoon); *Tritayābhoktā Veereshaḥ*.

387. तरुणादित्यशङ्काशा – *Taruṇādityasaṅkaśā*

- She is the lustre and brightness in like the stormy Sun. Sun is always related to heat. That is the reason an adjective stormy has been prefixed. This makes the Sun to cool. She is the cool Sun.
- She used to be mapped to *Aruṇa* colour, one of the names of the Sun himself.
- Sun is also called as *Rudra*. During great dissolution Sun rises and burns the entire world. On account of this torridly rains and world submerges in the waters. It is she who makes this Sun's activity.
- *Bṛhadāraṇyaka Upanishat* (III-8-11) says, the *Brahmam* is the support of the Sun and other luminaries – *"Etasmin Khalvakshare Gārgi Sooryāchandramasou Vidhrtou Tishtaraḥ"*. She is that Brahmam.
- It has been mentioned that the letter *'Hreem'* is the *Shakta Pranava Mantra*. The *'Ha'* in the *'Hreem'* belongs to the Sun God. Hence there is no difference between she and the Sun.
- We are aware that she has *hamsa* as her vehicle. The word *hamsa*, when derived from the root verb meaning motion (*hanti*) stands for

both the Sun and the vital air known as *prāna*. The consciousness that is our essential core has both the Sun and the *prāna* as indicators (*vāhana*) of its manifested omnipresence. Hence, **she** is the Sun.

388. तामसी – *Tāmasī*

- She is with *Tāmasa* quality.
- Earlier it has been mentioned that she is without quality (*Nirguna*) and again with three qualities (*Triguna*). Out of the three qualities, now *Tāmasa* attribute is mentioned here.
- From *mahat* arose the three-fold egoism, namely *vaikārika* (pure), *taijasa* (passionate) and *tāmasa* (dark). Here, *tāmasa* is the origin of the elements. The rest of the creation belong to *sattva* and *rajas*.
- In 365th name above, it was mentioned that Sri Devi is surrounded by to 10 different Devis. *Tāmasī* is one among them. She is in her form also.

389. तुहिना – *Tuhinā*

- She is the cool brightness of the Moon.
- She is the Moon beam illuminating the ocean of good fortune.
- Earlier in 387th name above, it was mentioned that She is the inform of the Sun. Now it is the turn of the Moon.
- According to 32nd verse of Soundaryalaharee, *sa*–स is the *beejākshara* (seed letter) pertaining to the Moon (*Chandra* or *Sheeta Kiraṇa*). That seed letter is Sri Devi's. This letter occurs twice in the *Pancadashaksharee* (15 lettered) Mantra.
- *Sri Devi* is the one who grants the Moon the quality of emitting, oozing out of nectar – *Amruta* – which in turn grants immortality (*amaratva* – अमरत्व) to the *Devas*.
- Sri Devi is always much pleased when she is worshipped on a Full Moon Day. That too it has been mentioned that she has to be worshipped by looking at the Moon. In that case no need of any invocation (*avahana*) of Devi.
- In 280th name above it has been mentioned that she is the Moon.

390. तुरा – *Turā*

- She reaches her devotees very fast.
- In the 98th name above, it was mentioned that she can be attained

easily. Here it is confirmed that she herself will reach the devotees very fast.

- She becomes very happy even with a small tiny worship and immediately reaches the upasaka to satisfy his/ her wishes.

391. त्रिकालज्ञानसम्पन्ना – *Trikālajñānasampannā*

- One who bestows the knowledge of all the three periods – past, present and future.
- The *Vayu Purana* says – As **She** recollects all actions, past, present and future, **she** is called *Smruti*.
- Sri Vishnu Sahasranamam 4th name – भूत भव्य भवत्प्रभुः – ***Bhūta Bhavya Bhavat Prabhuḥ*** and 290th name is also the same – भूत भव्य भवन्नाथ – *Bhūta Bhavya Bhavannātha*.

392. त्रिवेणी – *Triveṇī*

- At Allahabad the three rivers Yamuna, Ganges and Saraswathi merge together. It is called *Triveni Sangamam*. She is in the form of all rivers and including this *Triveni Sangamam*.
- Though the rivers Yamuna and Ganges are physically merging, the river Saraswathi is said to be *Antarvahini* – flowing from above and merging with the other two rivers.
- The black water of Yamuna river and the white water of Ganges river mix in the *Triveni* junction, but still maintain their own individuality (colour) for some distance.

393. त्रिलोचना – *Trilocanā*

- One who is endowed with three eyes.
- It is mentioned in the dhyana verse of Sri Gayatri Devi that the Moon, Sun and the fire god (Agni) are the three eyes of *Sri Devi*.
- In Sri Lalita Sahasranama, 477th name is the same *Trilochanā*.
- Again, in Sri Lalita Sahasranamam 453rd name – *Trinayanā*, 762nd name *Tryambikā* also conveys that *Sri Devi* is three-eyed.
- She is equal with Lord Shiva – both are in Red colour (this has originated from white), three eyes, crescent Moon, etc., – *Roopa Sāmyam* (quality of form).
- Every upasaka, during *anganyasa* while doing *japa*, has to assume that he/ she has three eyes as "*Netratrayaaya Voushat*". The upasaka becomes the Devi herself.

394. त्रिशक्तिः – *Triśaktiḥ*

- She is of 3 energies (Shaktis) – *Iccha Shakti*, *Jnana Shakti* and *Kriya Shakti*.
- The aggregate of three *shaktis* – *Icchā* (desire), *Jnāna* (knowledge) and *kriyā* (action). *Sri Devi* is in all these three forms and the integrated form also.
- *Iccha Shakti* – the energy of will or desire, *Jnana Shakti* – the energy of knowledge and *Kriya Shakti* – the energy of action – for any and all success, all 3 of these forms of Shakti need to be involved. The process and interplay of these energies is continually cycling within us and without these ingredients, we would become inert.
- If we can consider this in the computer systems – the computer has to work on Hardware, Software and power from SMPS (Switch Mode Power Supply). Hardware is *Kriya Shakti*, Software is *Iccha Shakti* and Power for SMPS is *Jnana Shakti*. Without the Software (Mind), the Hardware (Senses) is dead and without the Hardware Software is also useless. And both are useless without power in SMPS. Hence *Jnana Shakti* is the pivot and the power to SMPS is got by connecting it to Main Power point and this is *Sri Shakti Devi*. Let us all connect ourselves to the Absolute which is like the Main Power point that provides power to SMPS so that the *Iccha Shakti* and *Kriya Shakti* in us are able to perform well.

395. त्रिपुरा – *Tripurā*

- She is *Tripurā*, the highest power.
- She is more ancient than the *Trimoorties* (*Brahma*, *Vishnu* and *Rudra*) and hence *Tripurā*.
- There are various Shakta related texts on *Tripura* – *Tripura Rahasyam, Tripura Siddhānta, Tripura Upanishat, Tripura Tāpinee Upanishat* and so on.
- Sri Devi is normally addressed as *Tripura Sundaree* and sometimes as – *Tripura Bhairavee*. Young Devi Bala is addressed as *Bala Tripura Sundaree*.

396. तुङ्गा – *Tuṅgā*

- She is in the form of *Tuṅgā*.
- *Tuṅga* means heavy, a mountain like. She is the heaviest in the world and hence she is *Tuṅgā*.

- According to *Samarāṅgaṇa Sūtradhāra* (chapter 49) *Tuṅgā* refers to a type of temple classified under the group named *Maṇika*. The *Maṇika* group contains ten out of sixty-four total temples classified under five prime *Vimānas* (aerial car/ palace), which were created by *Brahmā* for as many gods (including himself).

397. तुरङ्गवदना – *Turaṅgavadanā*

- One of meanings of *Turaṅga* is horse. Hence this name will mean that she is horse faced.
- Lord Vishnu has an incarnation as *Hayagriva* – horse faced. He is the lord of knowledge. He was guru of sage Agastya and taught him Sri Lalita Sahasranama, Sri Lalita Trishatee and all.
- Being consort of Vishnu and being part of him, she also has a form with horse face.

398. तिमिङ्गिलगिला – *Timiṅgilagilā*

- She feeds the non-vegetarian whale also.
- Being mother of all living beings she takes care every creature including whale.
- There is saying in Tamil that God feeds even a toad within a rock.

399. तीव्रा – *Tīvrā*

- She is like the rose flower.
- She is compared to rose flower in colour, fragrance, softness and all.

400. त्रिश्रोता – *Triśrotā*

- *Triśrotas* means river Ganga. It has been mentioned that She is in the form of all rivers including Ganga.
- *Triśrota* means three streamed – that is *Triveni*. As mentioned in 392nd name she is in the form of *Triveni Sangamam*.

Thus ends 100 divine names on *Sri Gayatri Devi* from 301 to 400

*****

401. तामसादिनी – *Tāmasādinī*

- She swallows the darkness called ignorance.
- This manifestation of *māyā*, characterised by objective distinctions, is the first creation, the creation of darkness (*tāmasa sarga*), void of consciousness.
- 388th name above can also be referred in this context.
- The deity in *Maṇipoora Chakra,* which indicates that **she** destroys darkness (*tamas* – तमस्) and illuminates the conscience.
- There is darkness of ignorance covering up the spiritual center in the heart where the spark of Absolute Consciousness is situated. **She** destroys the ignorance and gives self–illuminating bliss.
- The *Rig Veda* (X-129) beginning with "there was no being, in that time, nor, was no being – in the beginning darkness was hidden by intelligence," also confirms the above; "*Nāsadāseenno Sadāseet, Tama Āseetatamasā Goolahamadre*".
- From this creation called *tāmasa*, in which the three qualities (*Gunas*) were differentiated, arose the creation of partially manifested, *mahat*. This is the second creation. It is said, "from *avyakta* comes the category of *mahat* in which are distinctly manifested the three *Guṇas*; so also, from *mahat ahamkara* (egoism)". From that (creation of *mahat*) arises the third, the creation of *ahamkara* in which the three *Guṇas* are manifested objectively. It is said, "From *mahat* arose the three-fold egoism, namely *vaikārika* (pure), *taijasa* (passionate) and *tāmasa* (dark), which last is the origin of the elements". Here, as "*tāmasa* is the origin of the elements," it follows that the rest of the creation belong to *sattva* and *rajas*.
- From that *tāmasa* egoism which is called the origin of the elements, arose, with the aid of the *rajas*, creation of the five subtle elements (*tanmātras*). This is the fourth creation.

402. तन्त्रमन्त्रविशेषज्ञा – *Tantramantraviśeṣajñā*

- One who is in the form of all *mantras* and *tantras*.
- It is she who bestows all mantras and tantras to all her devotees.
- It is said that there are seven crores (70 million) of *mantras*. She is in the form of all these *mantras*. Or Her form itself is these *mantras*. The mantras are got by intuition of the sages. Hence, they are called as *Mantradrashtas*. It is she who made those sages to get these mantras.

- Since all the *Tantras* indicate *Sri Devi* Herself and prove Her, she is in the form of all *Tantras*.
- 206th name in Sri Lalita Sahasranamam say *Sarva Tantra Roopa* – सर्व तन्त्र रूपा – One who is the spirit of all *Tantras* in her form.
- 204th name in Sri Lalita Sahasranamam say *Sarva Mantra Svaroopiṇee* – One who is in the form (very essence) of all *mantras*.
- 280th name in Sri Vishnu Sahasranamam say *Mantra* – He himself is *mantra*.

403. तनुमध्या – *Tanumadhyā*

- One who has a slender waist.
- *Tanumadhyā* is the deity worshipped in the country of Kanchi; for it is said, may *Sri Devi, Tanumadhyā*, the consort of *Bilvesvara* residing on the bank of the *Nivā* (river), protect me.
- *Tanumadhyā* is the name of certain meter. With 6 letters for each word it has 24 letters.
- The *Pingala sutra*, says, if there is one *tagaṇa* and *yagaṇa* in each foot it is called *Tanumadhya*.
- 360th name in Sri Lalita Sahasranamam is the same name *Tanumadhyā*.

404. त्रिविष्टपा – *Triviṣṭapā*

- She is the head of all the three worlds. **She** is known by all in the three worlds.
- She is in all the three worlds and she is worshipped by all in the three worlds.
- 627th name of *Sri Lalita Sahasranama, Trijagadvandyā* – also says that **she** is in all the three worlds.
- 646th and 647th names of *Vishnu Sahasranama* – *Trilokatma* and *Trilokesha* can be related here.

405. त्रिसन्ध्या – *Trisandhyā*

- She is worshipped thrice in a day.
- Dvijas have to do Sandhyavandanam three times a day. Gayatri Japam is an important part of Sandhyavandanam.
- It can be reminded that during *Sandhyavandana* we meditate the supreme being is in Sun's disc. Also, *Gayatri* is meditated in Sun's

disc. The verse; *Nama Savithre*.. may be reminded.

- In the *Sri Vidya sandhyavandana*, *Sri Dev*i is meditated at all the three times in Sun's disc.

406. त्रिस्तनी – *Tristanī*

- One who has three breasts.
- The story goes like this – King Malayadhwaja Pandya and his wife Kanchanamalai who performed a yajna seeking a son for succession. Instead a daughter is born who is already 3-year-old and has three breasts. Shiva intervenes and says that the parents should treat her like a son and when she meets her would be, she will lose the third breast. The king crowns her as his successor and when she meets Shiva, she takes her true form of Meenakshi with two breasts.

407. तोषासंस्था – *Toṣāsaṃsthā*

- She is always seen happy.
- She makes her devotees to be always happy.
- 525th name of *Vishnu Sahasranama* – *Pramodana* also convey the same meaning.

408. तालप्रतापिनी – *Tālapratāpinī*

- She is in the form of melody or rhythm in any song.
- Rhythmic and melodious songs will make the audience happy. She is in the form to make her devotees happy.
- She terrifies her enemies with sound of her bow string (*Tāla*) itself.

409. ताटङ्किनी – *Tāṭaṅkinī*

- One who wears the two large earrings.
- One type of ornament worn by ladies in their ears is called *Tāṭanka* (palm-leaf).
- The Sun and the Moon have the fortune to become *Sri Devi*'s eyes, earrings and **Her** breasts.
- *Tāṭanka* is considered to be an auspicious ornament for *Sumangalis* (ladies living with their husbands). *Sri Adi Shankara*, in his *Soundaryalaharee*, (28th verse) describes with awe that *Sri Parameswara* could survive, even after consuming the *Halakala* (poison), only by the power of *Sri Devi*'s *Tāṭankas*.

410. तुषाराभा – *Tuṣārābhā*

- She shines as a dazzling beauty.
- She is so chilly like an iceberg.

411. तुहिनाचलवासिनी – *Tuhinācalavāsinī*

- She dwells in himachal mountain.
- She as Hemavathi, is daughter of Himalaya mountain.
- In the previous name it was mentioned that she is so chill. Since she lives in Himalayas, she is so cool.

412. तन्तुजालसमायुक्ता – *Tantujālasamāyuktā*

- She is like a fiberglass.
- She is so flimsy and transparent to her devotees and hence this name. At the same time to her enemies she is so hard.

413. तारहारावलिप्रिया – *Tārahārāvalipriyā*

- She wears a garland of twinkling stars.
- The gems in her jewels twinkle like stars.

414. तिलहोमप्रिया – *Tilahomapriyā*

- She is happy with sesame offered in the holy fire (yagnas).
- Black sesame homa is performed to satisfy ancestors (pitrus). Earlier it was mentioned that in the form of Swadha Devi, she carries the offerings made in the holy fire to pitrus. She makes the ancestors happy and arrange to bless the offeror.

415. तीर्था – *Tīrthā*

- She is in the form holy sanctified water (*Tīrthā*).
- In any function/ ceremony, it is usual to keep water in a pot (*kalasa*). Devi is invoked in the water. The coconut, mango leaves and darba grass (*koorca*) act as antennae, receive the vibrations of the mantras chant and sanctify the water. Then the water becomes *Tirtha* (holy water). She is in that form.

416. तमालकुसुमाकृती – *Tamālakusumākṛt*

- She is in the colour of *Tamāla* flower.
- *Tamāla* is blue/ blackish in colour. She is in that shade.

417. तारका – *Tārakā*

- She rescues her devotees from all troubles.
- She liberates her devotees to Moksha.
- *Tārā* can also be interpreted to mean the two *Devis* - *Mangala* and *Shukla* or the *Devata* - *Tāraka*.
- *Tārakāsurā* is a demon. He had a boon that he can be killed only by a son of Lord Shiva. Sri Devi incarnated as Hemavati, a daughter of Himavan (Himalaya Mountain). She married Lord Shiva and caused him to create Lord Kumara. Lord *Subramanya* killed *Tārakāsurā*. Behind the scene she was instrumental in killing this demon.

418. त्रियुता – *Triyutā*

- She is inseparable from Trimoortis.
- Brahma, Vishnu and Rudra are Trimoortis. She takes the form of the consorts of all the three and hence intimate to all the three.
- Sri Devi above the Trimoortis, only enable them to do their tasks.

419. तन्वी – *Tanvī*

- She is a slender or delicate woman.
- She is slender to her near and dears. On the other hand, she is very hard to her enemies and others who do not worship her.

420. त्रिशङ्कुपरिवारिता – *Triśaṅkuparivāritā*

- She is the form in which King *Triśaṅku* worshipped.
- The story of *Triśaṅku* is known to all. He was a king of Ayoddhi, earlier to Dasharatha. He wanted to go to heaven with his body as such. Sage Vishwamitra helped to him to satiate his desire. At that he worshipped Sri Gayatri Devi.

421. तलोदरी – *Talodarī*

- One who has a slim waist. In **Her** anthropomorphic form, **she** is beautiful, having a slender waist.
- In the 403rd name above also conveyed the same meaning.
- If the syllable *'A'* to be added the name becomes *A-talodaree*; the *atala* world is her abdomen when **She** assumes the *virāt* form. As per *Devi Gita* (7-33-34);

  *Atalāti Mahālokāḥ Katyadho Bhāgatām Katāḥ*
- 847th name of *Sri Lalita Sahasranama*, also the – *Talodaree*.

422. तिलाभूषा – *Tilābhūṣā*

- She shines in blue colour like the flower sesame plant.
- In multiple places it has been mentioned that she is in black colour – Black in the sense it is bluish black.

423. ताटङ्कप्रियवादिनी – *Tāṭaṅkapriyavādinī*

- One who wears the two large ear studs.
- The Sun and the Moon are the ear studs of Sri Devi.
- 409th name above can also be referred.

424. त्रिजटा – *Trijaṭā*

- *Trijaṭā* means spicy wood-apple. She is in that form or she is fond of that fruit.
- *Trijaṭā* is the daughter Vibhishana in Ramayana. Among the demoness around Sita in Ashokavana, she was the only person who was consoling Sita. Our Sri Devi did that role also.

425. तित्तिरी – *Tittirī*

- She is like a partridge bird.
- Sage *Vaisampayana*, due to some anger, asked disciple *Yagnavalkiyar* to vomit all the Yajur Veda taught by him. He religiously obeyed and the vomited Vedas became Tittiri-s and hence they are called as *Taitrīya Shaka* and became the *Krishna* (black) *Yajur Veda.* She is in the form all Vedas including this.

426. तृष्णा – *Tṛṣṇā*

- She satiates the thirst of her devotees.
- Here thirst does not mean thirst for water, as normally understood – thirst to know the *Brahmam*.
- Animals do understand only hunger and thirst; they do not speak of the known *Brahmam*; they do not see the known, they do not know the future, nor this nor the other world. But that is not the case of human.

427. त्रिविधा – *Trividhā*

- She is of any triplets we can think off. Some are indicated below. She is in the form of all these and more.

i. Three *nādās* as *Tretagnis*, *Tripuras* and *Trayees*.
ii. Trimoortis – Brahma, Vishnu and Rudra
iii. Trigunas – Sattva, Rajo and Tamo
iv. Three *agnis* – *Gārhapatyam*, *Āhavaneeyam* and *Dākshināgni*.
v. Three *Vedas* – *Rig*, *Yajus* and *Sāma*.
vi. Three *poopurams* in *Sri Chakra*
vii. Three lettered *Bālā* mantra.
viii. Three groups in *Panchadashaksharee* – *Vāgbhava*, *Kāmarāja* and *Shakti*.
ix. Three forms of *Kundalini* – *Parā*, *Chit* and *Prāṇa*
x. *Triputee* – *Gnāna*, *Gnanātru* and *Gneyam* (the knowledge, the object of knowledge and the knower)
xi. *Tatvamayee* – *Tat*, *Tvam* and *Ayee*
xii. Three types of worship – *Antaryāga*, *Bahiryāga* and *Mahāyāga*.
xiii. Three areas of the *mantra* – *beejam*, *shakti* and *keelakam*
xiv. Three eyes – Sun, Moon and Agni.
xv. Tripada – *gayatri mantra* has three *padams*.
xvi. Three main functions of the Supreme Being – creation, protection and destruction.
xvii. Three forms – *Stūla*, *Sūkshma* and *Param* or physical, subtle and causal.
xviii. *Sāmudrika Sāstrā* specifies that higher class men and women will have three lines (folds) on their forehead, neck and abdomen.
xix. Three forms – *Mantra*, *Tantra* and *Yantra*
xx. Three groups in Pranava Mantra – *A*, *U* and *Ma*.
xxi. Three worlds – *Bhoo*:, *Bhuva*: and *Suva*:.

xxii. Three states of soul – awaken (*Jāgrath*), dream (*Swapna*) and deep sleep (*Sushupti*).
xxiii. Three tenses – past, present and future.
xxiv. Three *Shaktis* – *Icchā*, *Gnāna* and *Kriya*.

428. तरुणाकृती – *Taruṇākṛtī*

- She is always young.
- 10th and 146th names above also communicate the same message.

429. तप्तकाञ्चनसङ्काशा – *Taptakāñcanasankāśā*

- She shines like a glossing gold.
- The dhyana verse of Sri Lalita Sahasranamam itself says that she is in golden colour.
- 800th name in Sri Vishnu Sahasranamam – *Suvarnabindu* – can be equated here.

430. तप्तकाञ्चनभूषणा – *Taptakāñcanabhūṣaṇā*

- She wears shining gold ornaments.
- Only a pure gold will shine. Hence, she wears pure gold ornaments.
- This name goes hand-in-hand with the previous name. She herself is in gold colour and in addition she wears lots of gold jewels.
- In Sri Lalita Sahasranamam there is many a name stating that she wears gold necklace, gold ear rings, gold bangles, etc., individually. Here in this name, it is given in an integrated fashion.
- 541st name in Sri Vishnu Sahasranamam – *Kanakangadi* – also states that he wears golden ornaments.

431. त्रयम्बका – *Trayambakā*

- One who is three-eyed.
- It was also mentioned in the Dhyana verse of Sri Gayatri that she has three eyes in each of her faces.
- 393rd name above also conveyed the same meaning.
- *Devee Purāṇa* says – **She** has three eyes – they are the Sun, the Moon and Agni.
- The same meaning is conveyed in Sri Lalita Sahasranamam – 453rd – *Trinayanā*, 477th – *Trilochana* and 762nd – *Tryambakā*, names.

- It can also be considered as – **She** is in the form of mother of the three gods – *Brahma*, *Viṣhṇu* and *Rudra*.

432. त्रिवर्गा – *Trivargā*

- One who bestows the triad of human values (aspiration to do meritorious acts, the capacity for it and the means for it).
- According to *Amara* dictionary – *Trivarga* indicates the above three.
- One who is abode of the three objects of desire.
- It has been indicated in many a place that **She** also bestows salvation.

433. त्रिकालज्ञानदायिनी – *Trikālajñānadāyinī*

- She bestows the knowledge of all the three times – past, present and future.
- Great upasakas/ sages used to tell precisely about the future also. It is possible with her blessings only.

434. तर्पणा – *Tarpaṇā*

- The root for the word *Tarpaṇā* is *Trupti* – satisfaction. Tarpana is a kind water offering to satisfy. She gets satisfied with the offerings made by the devotees.
- She makes the devotees get satisfied with her blessings.
- *Devatas* gets satisfied only if the complete meaning of the *mantras* is understood. This is called *tarpaṇam*. Worshipping alone without the knowledge of others is called *rahasya tarpaṇam*. **She** gets satisfied by such worshipping.

435. तृप्तिदा – *Tṛptidā*

- In the previous two names, it was mentioned that She gets satisfied by offerings and Tarpana. When she is satisfied, she makes her devotees get satisfied with all the desires.

436. तृप्ता – *Tṛptā*

- This name is in continuation of the above three names. She is fully sated and makes her devotees also fully satiated.

437. तामसी – *Tāmasī*

- This name is a repetition of 388th name above.

438. तुम्बरुस्तुता – *Tumbarustutā*

- Who has been praised by celestial musicians and singers like *Tumburoo* and others.
- Earlier in the 208th name it was mentioned that she is being praised by Gandharvas and Apsaras. Again in 211th name it was mentioned that she is being praised by Gandharvas. Tumburoo is one of the Gandharvas famous for his singing. Hence it is specifically mentioned that she is happy with his singing.

439. तार्क्ष्यस्था – *Tārkṣyasthā*

- She travels on Garuda using him as a vehicle.
- Being a consort of Lord Vishnu, Garuda becomes vehicle for her also.

440. त्रिगुणाकारा – *Triguṇākārā*

- She possesses all the three qualities.
- In 210th name above, it was mentioned that in the Saguna form she possess all the three qualities viz., Sattva, Rajas and Tamo.
- 839th name in Sri Vishnu Sahasranamam – *Gunabhruta* – also says that he is with qualities i.e. Saguna form.

441. त्रिभङ्गी – *Tribhaṅgī*

- She is in the form of a meter (chandas) of 4 x 32 syllabic instants.
- Earlier it was mentioned that she is in the form of all types of chandas. Again in 251st, 305th and 331st names it was mentioned that she is in the form specific meters. In the same way here also, she is in the form *Tribhaṅgī* chandas which 4 x 32 letters.

442. तनुवल्लरी – *Tanuvallarī*

- Her body – all her organs are so soft and flimsy like a creeper.
- 412th and 419th names above also mentioned that she is soft. At the same she becomes hard when she fights with her enemies.

443. थात्कारी – *Thātkārī*

- She makes '*Thāt*' noise during battle.
- Earlier in 239th, 361st and 364th names also it was mentioned that she makes loud noise during battle.
- In the previous name it was mentioned that she becomes hard while fighting. The warrior has to become and hard and also with anger only one can fight the enemies. In Ramayana also, it is a known fact that Rama is so calm and soft. But during all his battles be it with Tataka, Mareecha, Karan or Ravana, he became angry and fought the battles.

444. थारवा – *Thāravā*

- She makes fear free loud noise during battle.
- Again, this is in continuation of the previous name – describing the nature of the noise. People do get anger on account fear. But in the case of Sri Devi she gets angry just to fight with the enemies and not with fear.

445. थान्ता – *Thāntā*

- She is an auspicious Devi.
- *Sri Devi* is the complete auspicious.
- In Sri Lalita Sahasranamam in lot many places it has been mentioned that she is in an auspicious form – for instance 324th name *Kalyāṇee*.
- Sri Lalita Trishatee describes her form as auspicious – for instance 124th name *Sarvamaṅgalā*.
- The 2nd name in *Sri Lalita Trishatee* is also *Kalyānee*. *Sri Adi Shankara*'s, commentary of this name is; auspiciousness is happiness.

446. दोहिनी – *Dohinī*

- She offers whatever is sought for (legally).
- She is like Kamadhenu or Karpaga Vruksha – giving whatever wishes the devotees put forth and some more than what was not asked for. As a mother she knows what is needed for her children – why should we ask her?

447. दीनवत्सला – *Dīnavatsalā*

- She loves her devotees.
- Literally *Dīna* means poor – poor does not necessarily mean not having wealth or money. It includes that they are poor in not getting the love of a mother. Or they are poor in knowledge of the Brahmam. She loves her devotees and bestows what is lacking with them.
- 349th name in Sri Lalita Sahasranamam – *Vandārujanavatsalā* – communicates the same message.
- 471st name in Sri Vishnu Sahasranamam also – *Vatsala* – means the same sense.

448. दानवान्तकरी – *Dānavāntakarī*

- Destroyer of demons.
- *Dānava* means demon. She slayed the demons like Mahishasura, Dhoomralocana, Chanda, Munda, Raktabeeja, Shumba, Nishumba and so on. Hence this name.
- 5th name in Sri Lalita Sahasranamama – *Devakāryasamudyatā* – The aim of her incarnation is to help Devas. They are frequently disturbed by the demons. She incarnates in one or other form

449. दुर्गा – *Durgā*

- One who is with the name *Durga*.
- **She** is *Durgā* since she killed the demon called *Durgaman*. In *Devi Saptashatee* (11th chapter) and in the *Lakshmi Tantra* of the *Pāncharātra* Sri Devi says – I am going to kill the demon named *Durgaman*, hence my name shall be *Bheema*.
- The same is mentioned in *Kāsi Kanḍa* also
- Or this is the goddess who resides in the place called *Sannati* on the bank of the river, *Bheemarathi*.
- *Durga* protected *Indra* and other *devas* from the mental fear and war, from *Subalan* and others.
- As per *Devi Bhagavatam, Durgā* is, as solicited by king *Subāhu*, established herself under this name at *Banaras*.
- A nine-year-old girl is called *Durga*.
- The verse read for a 9-year girl during *Kanya Pooja* in *Chanḍi Homam* is;

*Durgame Dustare Kārye Bhavatu: Khavināshineem* I
*Poojayāmi Sā Bhaktyā Durgām Dirgārti Nashineem* II

- According to *Devi Bhagavatam* (III-26) the meditation verse for this girl is:

*Durgāt Trāyati Bhaktam Yā Sadā Durgārti Nāshinee* I
*Durgjeya Sarva Devānām Tām Durgām Poojayāmyaham* II

- It is read in *Durgā* Sooktam as; *Durgām Deveem Sharanamaham Prapadye.*
- In *Prapancha Nyāsa* of *Mahāshoḍa Nyāsa*, **she** is said to be in the form of *Kāshṭha*.
- One who has lion as vehicle – that is *Durga*.
- In the *Padma Purana*, in its *Pushkara Kāṇḍa*, it has been mentioned that – He, who is devoted to Goddess *Durgā*, is not stained even by committing heinous crimes, in the manner as the lotus leaf is not affected by water.
- We have lot many stotras/ texts on *Durga – Durga Saptashati, Durgāchandra Kalā Stotra, Durga Sooktam*, etc.
- 189th name in Sri Lalita Sahasranamam is *Durgamā* and 190th name is *Durgā* itself.
- 778th and 779th names in Sri Vishnu Sahasranamam are also *Durgama* and *Durga*.

450. दुर्गासुरनिबर्हिणी – *Durgāsuranibarhiṇī*

- One who killed the demon (asura) called *Durgaman*.
- She killed many monsters, from time to time she will get a corresponding name. For instance, she got the name Chandee because she killed Chandan.

451. देवरीती – *Devarītī*

- She follows a splendourous path.
- She shows a heavenly path to her devotees to follow. She leads along the path of salvation.
- Unless she herself follows a divine path, she cannot show a wonderful to others.
- There are mainly two paths in Sri Vidya worship – *Samaya* and *Koula*. The *Samaya* path has two sub-divisions – *Dakshina* and *Vama*. Within each sub-division there are three methods viz., *Bāhyā* (with tools – outward) and *Āntara* (worshipping without any tools) *Parāpara Pooja* (both the methods mixed). Whatever be the path followed, the goal to reach is *Sri Devi*, the *Brahmam*.

452. दिवारात्रि: – *Divārātriḥ*

- It is she who creates the day and night.
- According to *Kali Purana* – one day (day and night) of *Brahma* is called as *Para*. His day and night are of equal duration and they are called *Parārdham*. But, for Sri Devi, who is subtler than the subtle and minute than the minutest there is no bindings like day, night, year, etc., because she only creates the time and she is not controlled by time.
- *Sri Devi* moves like the Sun and the Moon personifying day and night and thus 'Time'.

453. द्रौपदी – *Draupadī*

- In Mahabharata she was in the form of *Draupadi*.
- Draupadi is one of the great pativratas and Sri Devi was playing that role to help Lord Krishna to reduce the load on the Earth.

454. दुन्दुभिस्वना – *Dundubhisvanā*

- She plays drums (percussion instrument) like *Dundubhi*.
- *Dundubhi* is an onomato poetic word, means ' drum', as used in both war and peace. It is often mentioned from the *Rig Veda* onwards.

455. देवयानी – *Devayānī*

- She leads the way to Brahmam.
- *Devayānī* is a daughter of Indra. Lord Kumara destroyed the demons like Taraka, Soora and all, and saved the Devas. In return Indra offered his daughter to Lord Kumara in marriage. She is in that form of *Devayānī*.

456. दुरावासा – *Durāvāsā*

- With great difficulty upasakas and yogis bring her to their heart to dwell.
- 780th name in Sri Vishnu Sahasranamam – *Durāvāsā* – conveying the same meaning.

457. दारिद्र्योभेदिनी – *Dāridryobhedinī*

- She removes the poverty of her devotees.
- 161st name above also indicated the same sense.

458. दिवा – *Divā*

- One who controls the day.
- In the 452nd name above, it was mentioned she creates the day and night. Here day alone is specified.
- 39th name of Sri Vishnu Sahasranamam – *Āditya* – he is in the form of Sun.
- 232nd name in Sri Vishnu Sahasranamam – *Ahaḥ Samvartaka* – says that he in the form of Sun makes the day.

459. दामोदरप्रिया – *Dāmodarapriyā*

- One who loves *Damodaran*.
- One who is loved by *Damodaran*.
- 367th name in Sri Vishnu Sahasranamam is *Damodara*. Being his consort, this name is very apt.

460. दीप्ता – *Dīptā*

- Her radiance is so splendour.
- Lot many places in this Sahasranamam her shining brightness has been described.
- The luster is the beauty and brightness of the body.

461. दिग्वासा – *Digvāsā*

- She is spread in all directions.
- One who has faces in all round directions.
- **She** has the form of ten directions. *Linga* and *Vayu Purana*-s also confirm the same.
- The *vyāhruti mantra*-s, *Bhoo*: *Bhuva*: *Suva*: are used to bind all the directions.
- **She** is omnipresent.

462. दिग्विमोहिनी – *Digvimohinī*

- **She** attracts all the directions.
- She spreads that aroma in all directions.
- With her pleasant aroma **She** attracts all the directions.
- The 26th name of *Lalita Sahasranāma* – *Karpūraveeṭikāmoda Samākarshidigantarā* says that **she** attracts the four directions towards **Her** by the enjoyable aroma of the betel (*tāmbūla*) emanating from **Her** lotus like mouth,
- **She** has the form of ten directions, says, *Linga Purana*.

463. दण्डकारण्यनिलया – *Daṇḍakāraṇyanilayā*

- One who lives in a forest.
- There are various forests across the globe. She lives in all the forests (*āraṇya*) including *Daṇḍaka* forest.

464. दण्डिनी – *Daṇḍinī*

- One who administers justice by punishing the culprits.
- *Daṇḍaneeti* is the *shastra* which describes the crimes and the corresponding punishments for the criminals.
- The *Devi Purana* says, because **She** leads to certainty men who wander into good and bad ways by restraining and by soothing them, **she** is called *Daṇḍinī*.
- **She** punishes and controls dishonest people and those who do cruel.
- *Sri Adi Shankar* in his commentary of *Vishnu Sahasranāma* for the 924th name – *Dushkrutihā* – says that he destroys the bad act of sin or one who does sinful acts.
- She punishes so that the devotees are cleared off from the sins and seek the lotus feet of *Sri Devi*.

465. देवपूजिता – *Devapūjitā*

- **She** is always worshipped by all *Devas*.
- The *Renuka Purāṇa* says – this *Sandhya* Devi is to be worshipped by *Devas*, the twice-born and by great souls, in sitting down, in lying down, in moving about, in eating and she is *Rebuke* herself.

- Such a message is communicated repeatedly in all the texts just to stress, when such is the case of *Indra* and other *Devas*, how about ordinary people like us – we should also always worship *Sri Devi*.

466. देववन्द्या – *Devavandyā*

- **She** is praised by all *Devas*.
- **She** is praised by all *Devas* including the trinities viz. *Brahma*, *Vishnu* and *Rudra*.

467. दिविषदा – *Diviṣadā*

- One who is always seated in heavens.
- One who always lives in heavens.

468. द्वेषिणी – *Dveṣiṇī*

- One who hates the demons.
- She hates the sinners and punishes them. Otherwise she loves all and no question of hatred by Sri Devi. It is only in the good interest of the person.

469. दानावाकृती – *Dānāvākṛtī*

- One who is attracted towards the demons also.
- In the previous name it was mentioned she hates the demons. Also, it is she, who kills the demons. But still she is attracting the demons also. For instance, in Devi Mahatmyam, an Asura called Shumban was attracted by the beauty of Sri Devi. He sent a messenger by name Sugriva, to Sri Devi asking her to marry him.
- Lot many demons did penance on Sri Devi and obtained various boons. She was attracted by the stringent penance of them.

470. दीननाथस्तुता – *Dīnanāthastutā*

- She is the only refuge for the poor.
- Nobody else can come to the rescue of the orphan like.
- 447th name above can be read with this name.

471. दीक्षा – *Dīkṣā*

- *Deeksha* means destroying the sin of **Her** disciples by invocating the *mantras*. That is the duty of the teachers. **She** is *Deekshita*.
- The *Atharva Samhita* says – *Deekshā,* is the root word from which *Deekshita* is derived. The guru who initiates is called *deekshita*.
- During *yāgās* (sacrificial fire) the master is called as *Deekshitar*. It can be considered that **She** is in that form.

472. दैवतादिस्वरूपिणी – *Daivatādisvarūpiṇī*

- She is in the form of all *Devata*-s.
- It has been mentioned in Sri Devi Mahatmyam all the devas gave their forms to Sri Devi so that she gets all the shaktis for killing of the asuras.

473. धात्री – *Dhātrī*

- She is a giver.
- She gives everything to her devotees to all living things. She is the mother and she gives anything asked for and even something more.

474. धनुर्धरा – *Dhanurdharā*

- She is a good archer.
- She single handedly fought and won the battles with demons. Who else can be better archer?
- 857th name in Sri Vishnu Sahasranamam is also the same *Dhanurdhara*. There it is masculine and here it is feminine word.

475. धेनु: – *Dhenuḥ*

- One who fulfills all the desires.
- Fulfilling all the desires is the nature of the celestial cow *Kāma-dhenu*. She is in that form. *Devi Upanishat* also preys; *"Sā No Mandreṣamūrjaṃ Duhānā Dhenurvāgasmānupa Suṣṭutaitu"*.

476. धारिणी – *Dhāriṇī*

- One who holds the earth.

- The word *Dhāriṇī* means the earth, supports, in the form of, etc. She is the Earth. She supports the Earth. She is in the form of earth. All the meanings are apt for her.

477. धर्मचारिणी – *Dharmacāriṇī*

- One who is devoted to dharma.
- One who promotes righteousness.
- One who makes her devotees to strictly follow the dharma.

478. धरन्धरा – *Dharandharā*

- She only provides the beam of light to Sun and other stars and enable them illuminate.
- Anything which emits light is on account of her.

479. धराधारा – *Dharādhārā*

- One who supports the mountains.
- She herself incarnated as a daughter of a mountain.

480. धनदा – *Dhanadā*

- She gives booty or treasures to the needy.
- She in the form of Lakshmi is in-charge of wealth and she bestows the wealth to all.
- For instance, she as a consort of Lord Krishna, in the form of Rukmini, gave plenty of wealth to Kuchela.

481. धान्यदोहिनी – *Dhānyadohinī*

- One who gives grains to her devotees.
- This name alongwith the previous name combinedly indicated in the 886th name in Sri Lalita Sahasranamam – *Dhanadhānya Vivardhinee* –increasing the wealth and grain.

482. धर्मशीला – *Dharmaśīlā*

- One who is a strict follower of Dharma.

- 477th name above can be read in conjunction with this name.

483. धनाध्यक्षा – *Dhanādhyakṣā*

- She is the head of all wealth. She is goddess Lakshmi and hence in-charge of prosperity.
- This name should be read in conjunction with 480th name above.

484. धनुर्वेदविशारदा – *Dhanurvedaviśāradā*

- One who is an expert in *Dhanur Veda*.
- Dhanur Veda deals with archery. She is an expert in that.
- 474th name above also indicated the same sense.

485. धृती – *Dhṛtī*

- She is a courageous lady. She is without fear.
- She offers fearless courage to her devotees.

486. धन्या – *Dhanyā*

- One who is grateful.
- As means of expressing gratitude to the devotees who worship **Her**, **she** bestows the results.
- **She** bestows wealth. It can also be taken that **She** has wealth.
- *Dhanya* is a certain *Yogini* as mentioned in the *Jyotisha shastra*, namely *Mangala*, *Pingala* and *Dhanya*. She is in that form.
- The *Bhavishyottara Purana* says, during the last period when the soul goes out of the body, four types of thought process may happen. Accordingly, the results may vary. The gist of it is as below;
  a. **Thought *Ārta*;** *Ārta* is the meditation, which arises through illusion, the desire to possess dominion, pleasure, beds, seats, women, scents, garlands, jewels, cloths and ornaments.
  b. **Thought *Raudra*;** *Raudra* is said by the wise to be that meditation, in which arises the desire and not indifference, though he had wounds, fire, beating, cruelty, bodily injury, breaking limbs, etc.
  c. **Thought *Dhanya*;** – *Dhanya* is said by the wise to be that meditation in which arises a thought by the following of the meaning of the *Upanishats* and by the performance of great

vows, etc. about the causes of bondage and liberation and going and coming (reincarnation) and of the tranquility of the five senses and compassion in all beings.

d. **Thought Shuklā**; *Shuklā* is said by the wise to be that meditation in which by practice of Yoga which destroys the constructive imagination the senses are not tainted by material objects; the inner self is fixed on its unity with one reality i.e. *Brahmam*.

- *Shrimad Bhagavad Gita* (VIII-6) says – whatever being a man thinks of at the last moment when he leaves his body, that alone does he attain, Oh Kaunteya, being ever absorbed in the thought thereof.
- 957th name in Sri Lalita Sahasranamam is also the same – *Dhanyā*.
- 754th name in Sri Vishnu Sahasranamam also the same name in masculine form – *Dhanya*.

487. धृतपदा – *Dhṛtapadā*

- **She** is quick paced in walking.
- While singing a song or chanting Vedas people to increase the speed of singing/ chanting in three different ways – She only enables the quick pace.

488. धर्मराजप्रिया – *Dharmarājapriyā*

- **She** is respected by Dharmaraja.
- Dharmaraja is one of the names of *Yama*. She is worshipped, respected and loved by him. Naturally she also loves him as her devotee.
- Fundamentally there are twelve persons who started the Sri Vidya practice. One among them is Dharmaraja/ Yama.

489. ध्रुवा – *Dhruvā*

- She is eternal/ imperishable.
- 388th name in Sri Vishnu Sahasranamam also the same name in masculine form – *Dhruva*.

490. धूमावती – *Dhūmāvatī*

- *Dhūmāvatī Devi* is the seventh among the ten – Dasha Maha Vidyas. She is in that form.

- In *tantra shastras* the word energy will always indicate one with that *Dhūmāvatī Devi*.

491. धूमकेशी – *Dhūmakeśī*

- She is in the form of *Dhūmakeśī*.
- In Devi Mahatmyam, Sri Devi took the form of *Dhūmakeśī* to annihilate the demon *Dhoomralocanan*. She is in that form.
- In Samskrutam the word *Dhūma* means smoke. One of the offering during worship is to show smoke with aroma. She becomes happy with that.

492. धर्म शास्त्र प्रकाशिनी – *Dharma Śāstra Prakāśinī*

- She upholds the Dharma Shastra.
- She brings the Dharma Shastra to limelight.
- Righteousness is her support. Because the *Mahānārāyaṇa Upanishat* (XXII-1) says – Everything is established in *dharma* or by whom *dharma* is supported, i.e., *dharma* becomes the support of all things by **Her;** *"Dharme Sarvam Pratishtitam"*.

493. नन्दा – *Nandā*

- The word *Nandā* indicates river Ganges called as *Alagānanda*. **She** is in that form.
- *Nandā* also means prosperity, delight, happiness, etc. She is in all these forms.

494. नन्दप्रिया – *Nandapriyā*

- She is loved by Sri Krishna son of Nandagopa.
- *Nanda* – Ananda – bliss – She bestows bliss to all.
- She takes her devotees towards bliss.

495. निद्रा – *Nidrā*

- She is in the form of sleep.
- Sleep, here, should not be taken in the sense of lazy sleep what lethargic people do. She is in the form of *Yoga Nidra*.

- In the very first chapter of Devi Mahatmyam, Lord Vishnu was in Yoga Nidra. Brahma and other devas worshipped Sri Devi to free him from Nidra. Sri Devi obliged. Vishnu annihilated the demons Madhu and Kaitapa.
- In *Kālikā Purana* we read as;
  *Tatastu Viṣhṇumāyām Mām Yoganidrām Jaganmayeem* I
- Rest and sleep are must for anyone. As a mother she hugs with affection and gives compulsory rest and peace. It is worth compared to *Devi Mahātmyā* verse –
  *Yā Devee Sarva Bhooteshu Nidrā Roopena Samsthita.*

496. नृनुता – *Nṛnutā*

- She is bowed by all human beings.
- During worship bowing is one of the offerings. Every human who worship does bow to her.

497. नन्दनात्मिका – *Nandanātmikā*

- She is always rejoicing.
- She bestows rejoice to her devotees.
- The garden in *Indraloka* is called *Nandana Arāma,* since it gives pleasure and rest.

498. नर्मदा – *Narmadā*

- This name is a repetition of 379th name above.

499. नलिनी – *Nalinī*

- She is like water lily flower.
- She has a lily flower in one of her hands.
- 142nd name above also conveyed the same meaning.

500. नीला – *Nīlā*

- She is Blue in colour.
- Normally Blue and Black are synonymously used. It is usual to say that Lord Sri Krishna and Lord Sri Rama are also in blue colour. Actually, one variance of blue itself is called Rama Blue.

- In this Sahasranamam itself, in lot many places it has been mentioned that she is in Black (Blue) colour.
- She wears blue diamond studded jewels. That blue colour reflects on her.

Thus ends 100 divine names on *Sri Gayatri Devi* from 401 to 500

*****

501. नीलकण्ठसमाश्रया – *Nīlakaṇṭhasamāśrayā*

- Since Lord *Paramashiva* has venom in his neck, he got the name as *Neelakandan*. She lives alongwith him.
- She is also worshiped by Lord *Paramashiva*. It has been mentioned that there 12 fundamental Sri Vidya methods. One such was created by Lord *Paramashiva* himself.
- It is mentioned in the *Vayu Purana* as; Lord *Paramashiva's* body is white in colour whereas his neck is black (on account venom). Similarly, *Sri Devi*'s body is partly in the form of *Gayatri*, which is white in colour and partly in the form of *Kali*, which is black in colour. (Blue and black are considered as similar colours).

502. नारायण प्रिया – *Nārāyaṇa Priyā*

- Being his consort, she loves Narayana and she is loved by Narayana.
- There is no difference between *Narayana* and *Sri Devi*. In the form *Arddhanaree*, *Sri Devi* is left half of Shankara. In the form of *Shankara Narayana*, *Narayana* is the left half. Hence, they both are one and the same.
- *Naran* means the soul. The last abode of the souls is *Ayana*. Hence *Narayana* also indicates *Shiva*. **She** is the consort of *Shiva*.

503. नित्या – *Nityā*

- One who is permanent and eternal.
- This soul is eternal. Hence the argument of *Kshanigavigyana* that the world vanishes every second is not valid.
- Fifteen *tithi Nityā Devis* are being mentioned in the method of worshipping *Sri Vidya*. *Sri Devi* herself is the 16th *Maha Nitya*.
- *Sri Devi* is delighted seeing the 15 *Nitya Devis* staging the war with the 15 knights of *Bhandasura*. This has the name of a *Nitya Devi* as foremost.
- The meditation *mantras* and *poojas* of these 15 *Nitya Devis* have been described in *Tantra Raja Tantra*. Depending on the expected results (*Kamya phalan*) the meditation will vary. By meditating *Nityā* one can be free from ruins.
- In Sri Lalita Sahasranama, 136th name is the same *Nityā* and again 951st name *Shaswatee* also communicate the same message.
- We read *Avinānāshi Vā Areyamātmā* (IV-5-14) in *Bṛhadāraṇyaka Upanishat*.

504. निर्मला – *Nirmalā*

- One who is free from all impurities.
- **She** does not have the impurity of arrogance.
- **She** is free from the impurity of *Tamo* character.
- **She** does not have the impurity of ignorance. Liberation is the aim of the soul.
- By meditating this name one can be free from the impurity of arrogance.
- 135th name in Sri Lalita Sahasranamam also the same *Nirmalā*.

505. निर्गुणा – *Nirguṇā*

- This is a repetition of 378th name above.

506. निधि: – *Nidhiḥ*

- One who is the treasure house of wealth.
- Since **She** is in the forms of nine nidhis, **she** is called as *Nidhi*. According to Amarakosha, the nine *nidhis* are;

1. *Mahapadma*: Great lotus flower
2. *Padma*: Lotus/ a Himalayan lake with treasures
3. *Shankha*: Conch shell
4. *Makara*: Crocodile/ Antimony
5. *Kachchhapa*: Tortoise or turtle shell
6. *Kumud* or *Mukunda*: a particular precious stone or Cinnabar/ Quick Silver
7. *Kunda*: Jasmine/ Arsenic
8. *Neela*: Sapphire/ Antimony
9. *Kharva*: Dwarf, Cups, vessels baked in fire

507. निराधारा – *Nirādhārā*

- One who rises from *Moolādhāra*. *Ādhāra* can be taken as *Moolādhārā* from where **She** rises upwards.
- One who has no support other than **Herself**, (since **She** herself is the support for all).
- This indicates the *Nirādhāra* (without any support like image, etc.) pooja.

- *Tatrāpi Sā Nirādhārā Yuyudhe Tenachantikā* (*Durga Saptashatee* – 10-23). When *Sri Devi* was fighting with *Sumbhasuran*, **she** was standing in the sky without any support.
- *Sabhagavaḥ Kasmin Pratishtita Iti Sve Mahimna Iti Hovāca* (*Chāndogya Upanishat* VII-24-1). It is replied for the question "Where is that *Brahmam* stationed?" as; it is conspicuous without any support other than self.
- There are two kinds of worshipping *Sri Devi* as external (*Bahyam*) and internal (*Āntaram*). And again, the external has two divisions, *Vedic* and *Tantric*. The internal method is also of two kinds with support (*Sādhāra*) and without support (*Nirādhāra*).
- The *Nirādhāra* worship is by pure intellect – focusing the mind on *Sri Devi*'s image obtained by knowledge. In reality, pure intellect means nothing else, but the supreme *Sri Devi*. Hence for the destruction of *samsara*, one should worship the *Sri Devi*, the very self, the witness, free from the glamour of the manifold universe. By one's own direct experience of *Maheshwari* as the self, **she** should be worshipped with much reverence, this is the worship which leads to salvation.
- As an evidence for this, the verses in the 5th chapter – *Māhātmya Kāṇḍa* of *Sootha Samhitai* can be considered.
- 942nd name in Sri Vishnu Sahasranamam also – *Bhuvobhuva* – conveys the same message – who exists himself without any other support.

508. निरुपमा – *Nirupamā*

- This is a repetition of 377th name above.

509. नित्यशुद्धा – *Nityaśuddhā*

- One who is eternally pure.
- **She** is beyond any impurity in all the three times (tenses); hence this name.
- *Veda* says; *Asparshascha Mahān Shuciḥ* – **She** does not touch anything, elder to all and always pure.
- Another verse of *Veda* says – the body is untidy, but the person inside is clean;

  *Atyanta Malino Deho Dehee Chātyanta Nirmalaḥ*
- 148th name in Sri Lalita Sahasranamam also the same *Nityashuddhā*.
- 600th name in Sri Vishnu Sahasranamam also – *Shiva* – conveys the same message – who is eternally pure.

510. निरञ्जना – *Nirañjanā*

- One who is free from any stain. *Anjana* means black collegium used for eyes. Though it is used for beautification, still it is a stain. She does not need any external tool to beautify her, she is naturally beauty.
- In this context *Anjana* implies ignorance or illusion. The knowledge disappears due to ignorance (owing to its quality of darkness in mind). It has to be construed that *Sri Devi* has no relevance to ignorance or illusion.
- There are three kinds of ignorant souls (*Pashus*);
  a. The *Vijnanākevala*, he who sees the self in the non-self and has arrogance as the only impurity.
  b. The *Pralayakevala*, he who has the impurity of *karma*, which is unperceivable and which gives him new births; he also has the impurity mentioned in 'a' above.
  c. The *sakala*, he who has the impurity of the illusion (*māyā*). He has the idea of duality in all matters. He also has the impurities mentioned in 'b' above.

*Sri Bhāskara Rāya* explains all these, in his book called *Sethu Bandam* (explanation to VI-27 in *Nityāshotasikārnava*).

- *Sri Devi* has no impurities of *sakala* and hence *Niranjana*.
- *Śvētāśvatara Upanishat* (VI-19) indicates *Brahmam* as One who is – *Ni* (more) – *Ranjanam* (happiness/ delight)

  "*Niravatyam Niranjanam*".

511. नाद बिन्दु कलातीता – *Nāda Bindu Kalātītā*

- It is the "*Moola Prakriti*" or Nature that is the origin of mind, intellect and Ego! This Nature is otherwise called as *Parasakthi*. This *Devi* is called '*Bindu*'. From this *Moola Prakriti* have emerged four types of speeches called "*Para, Pashyanthi,* Madhyama and *Vaikharee*". *Sri Lalitha Sahasranama Stotram* says "*Para Prathyak Chithi Rupa Pashyanthi Para Devata Madhyama Vaikhari Rupa Bhakta Manasa Hamsika*". i.e. *Sri Devi* is the embodiment of these four types of speech and the swan of the hearts of her devotees. The combination of these sounds is called Nada.
- *Shabda Brahmam* gives rise to three forms of *shaktis* (*Iccha, Jnana* and *Kriya*). These three energies are also referred as *Bindu, Kala* and *Nada*.

- Sri Arunagirinathar also has written a Thiruppughaz starting with these terms eulogizing his chosen deity Lord Subramanya – "*Nada Bindu Kaladi Namo Namo*".

512. नाद बिन्दु कलात्मिका – *Nāda Bindu Kalātmikā*

- This name stresses what was indicated in the previous name. She is in those forms.

513. नृसिंहिनि – *Nṛsiṃhinī*

- She is in the form of *Nṛsiṃhinī*.
- *Pratyangirā Devi* is also called as *Nṛsiṃhī*, the *Shakti*, the concept of eternal energy.
- Sri Devi was preparing for the battle with asuras like Chanda, Munda, Shumbha, Nishumbha and all. She took the forms of nine Devis called Nava Durga-s. Different Gods gave their features and created Nine Devis. In this regard the feature of Lord *Narasimha* was *Nṛsiṃhinī*. *Sri Devi Kavacam* describes all these Devis.

514. नगधरा – *Nagadharā*

- Daughter of a mountain.
- She took the incarnation as *Hemavati*, daughter of Himavan (Himalayas Mountain).

515. नृपनाग विभूषिता – *Nṛpanāga Vibhūṣitā*

- She is adorned with snake as her jewel.
- Lord Shiva always wears a snake around his neck. His son Ganesha wears a snake as *Yagnopaveetam*. Being in that family, she wears a snake as a jewel.

516. नरकक्लेश शमनी – *Narakakleśa Śamanī*

- She removes the fear of hell from her devotees.
- Those who regularly chant Gayatri Mantra becomes free from all his sins. Where there is no sin in his account, no question of hell also.
- Shrimad Bhagavatam (5-26-7) lists the various punishments for all sins given in the hell. It is very terrific even to read.

517. नारायण पदोद्भवा – *Nārāyaṇa Padodbhavā*

- One who originated from the feet of *Nārāyaṇa*.
- In Vaikunta, Lord Narayana will be lying on the snake Adi Sesha. Goddess Lakshmi sits by the feet of Narayana and pressing his legs. She is goddess Lakshmi.

518. निरवद्या – *Niravadyā*

- One who is flawless/ blemish-less.
- *Avadyā* means not to be revealed; that means flaw or deficiency. These types of flaws are induced only due to ignorance. *Sri Devi*, who is in the form of knowledge, is beyond all these defaces.
- *Śvētāśvatara Upanishat* (VI.19) says defectless and pure – *"Niravadyam Niranjanam"*
- *Avadyā* is the name of one of the hells. *Koorma Purana* says that one who is always (day and night) in the thought of *Sri Devi* does not go to the hell called *Avadya*.
- *Linga Purana* says – One who does not worship the consort of *Sri Devi*, who has blue neck, will be burnt in the hells called *Gorā* onwards till *Māya*. The devotees of *Sri Devi* are protected and liberated from these hells. Hence *Niravadya*.
- *Kurai Onrum Illada Govinda – Thiruppavai* (28) by *Andal* can be compared. Based on this Rajaji also has written a song in Tamil starting with *"Kurai Onrum Illai…"*
- 150th name in Sri Lalita Sahasranamam also the same *Niravadyā*.

519. निराकारा – *Nirākārā*

- One who is not limited to and by any form. There is some specialty in everything we see. The various forms of *Sri Devi* seen by us are illusions. **Her** real form is formless. The sense of this name is; since **She** is omnipresent there is no form relating to characters.
- 137th name in Sri Lalita Sahasranamam also the same *Nirākārā*.

520. नारद प्रियकारिणी – *Nārada Priyakāriṇī*

- One who loves Narada.
- One who is loved by Narada.
- Narada is a son of Brahma born through his mind (*manasa putra*). Being one of consorts of Lord Brahma she and Narada have mutual affection.

521. नानाज्योतिः समाख्याता – *Nānājyotiḥ Samākhyātā*

- She is noted by various types brightness.
- It has been mentioned in many that because of her all the Stars, Sun, Moon, Agni and all get illuminated. She only makes them bright.

522. निधिदा – *Nidhidā*

- One who gives wealth/ treasure to her devotees.
- 480th name above also conveyed the same meaning.

523. निर्मलात्मिका – *Nirmalātmikā*

- One who is free from all froths.
- 504th name above also conveyed the same meaning and can be referred for more commentaries.

524. नवसूत्रधरा – *Navasūtradharā*

- One who wears a new auspicious string (Mangal Sutra) tied by her consort at the time of wedding.
- *Sri Devi* is *Nitya Sumangali*, who is always a *Sumangali*, wearing the *Mangala Sutra*. Although **She** emerged out of *Chidagni Kunda*, already wearing the *Mangala Sutra*, the *Deva*s wanted to see the wedding ceremony of the Holy couple and made **Her** husband tie the string again on *Sri Devi*.
- This *Mangala Sutra* tied by him showered blessings to the entire world. That too for the upliftment of the whole world.

525. नीतिः – *Nītiḥ*

- One who has very good behaviour.
- *Nīti* shastra is a law book on behaviour. It is she who made these shastras and make her devotees to have good behaviour.
- *Dandaneeti* is the *Shastra* which describes the crimes and the corresponding punishments for the criminals. The *Devi Purana* says, because **She** leads to certainty men who wander into good and bad ways by restraining and by soothing them.

526. निरुपद्रव कारिणी – *Nirupadrava Kāriṇī*

- One who clears all obstrucles.
- There are 'n' number of blocks on the way to liberation. She clears all these for her devotees.

527. नन्दजा – *Nandajā*

- She is a daughter of Nandagopa.
- In *Saptashatee* (XI Chapter) *Sri Devi* herself gives advance information that she will born in the house of *Nandagopa* in the womb of *Yashoda*.

  *Nandakhopagruhe Jātā Yashodāgarbhasambhavā* I
- This baby-girl born to Nandagopa-Yashoda couple, was swapped with Baby-Krishna born to the Vasudeva-Devaki couple.
- It has been mentioned in *Shrimad Bhagavatam* (X *Skanda*) that *Sri Devi* was (*Mahāmāyā*) born as daughter of *Nandagopa*.
- The first, sixth and eleventh days of bright lunar fortnight are called *Nanda*. She is in that form.
- According to Murthy Rahasyam, *Saptashatee* – since **She** was born as daughter of *Nandagopa*, **she** is called as *Nanda*.

  *Nandā Bhagavatee Nāma Yā Bhavishyati Nandajā*
- *Padma Purana* says – The river *Sarasvati*, when flows near *Himāchala*, is called as *Nandā*; "*Nandā Himavat Prushte*". She is in that form.

528. नवरत्नाढ्या – *Navaratnāḍhyā*

- She is adorned with jewels fitted with nine gems.
- *Sri Skanda Maha Purana – Sambava Kanda* – 27th chapter says – unable to withstand the luster originating from the eyes of *Sri Parameswara*, the *Devas* got frightened and ran here and there. *Sri Devi* also got scared and got up from the lap of *Sri Parameswara* and walked towards her palace. While doing so, **she** slipped and the nine gems from the anklets scattered on the way. The nine gems scattered from the ankle rings reflected in the illusionary half as nine *Devis*.
- *Sri Bhaskara Raya*, in his commentary for Sri Lalita Sahasranamam for the 235th name *Chatuḥśaśṭi Yupacārāḍhyā* lists down the 64 upacaras to be offered to Sri Devi – offering *Navamaṇi Makutam* (a

crown made of nine gems) is one such *upacara*.

- *Sri Adi Shankara*, in his commentary for Sri Lalita Trishatee for the 67th name *Lalantikā Lasatphālā* mentions that she wears on **Her** forehead the ornament called *Lalantika*, made of Pearls surrounding the nine gems.

529. नैमिषारण्य वासिनी – *Naimiṣāraṇya Vāsinī*

- One who lives in the *Naimiṣa Araṇya – Naimiṣa* forest.
- All our *Puranas* were narrated by sage *Soota* to sage *Sounaka* and others at *Naimiṣāraṇya* at the time of *Satrayāga*. *Sri Devi Bhagavata Purana*[8] also was narrated by him. *Sri Devi* herself seated there was hearing her own stories.
- In Sri Lalita Sahasranamam it has been mentioned that Sri Lalita dwells in *Naimiṣa* forest. Lalita Devi and Gayatri Devi are one and the same. Hence this name.
- In our *Puranas* lot many holy forests (*Puṇyāraṇya*) have been mentioned in and around India – *Daṇḍakāraṇya, Champakāraṇya, Vindhyāraṇya, Vedāraṇya, Vīkṣāraṇya*, etc. *Naimiṣāraṇya* is one such holy forest.
- 463rd name above can also be compared.

530. नवनीतप्रिया – *Navanītapriyā*

- One who is fond of butter.
- Lord Krishna, during his childhood used to be too naughty. He is very much fond of butter. One of his names is *Navaneeta chora* (butter thief). Being his consort, she is also fond of butter.
- Death is for the body and not for the soul. **She** makes her devotees realise this philosophy. Like the curd is churned to get butter, **she** churns the fear of death and creates the knowledge of philosophy and removes the fear.

531. नारी – *Nārī*

- She is a lady.
- Typical of any Samskruta word, the term *Nārī* also has several meanings – a woman, wife, sacrifice, any feminine object and so on. She is in all such forms.

---

[8] This Gayatri Sahasranama is part of *Sri Devi Bhagavata Purana*.

532. नीलजीमूतनिस्वना – *Nīlajīmūtanisvanā*

- The noise created by her is like a thunder sound created by blue clouds.
- In 239th and 361st names above it was mentioned that she makes a loud noise during battle threatening her enemies. That noise is compared here to the thunder noise made by blue clouds.

533. निमेषिणी – *Nimeṣiṇī*

- Her form is such that everybody else feel shy of their beauty.
- Her beauty makes other feel blush – not only ladies, but also gents.

534. नदीरूपा – *Nadīrūpā*

- She is in the form of all rivers.
- 380th name above also conveyed the same message.
- Earlier in different names, it was mentioned that she is in the form of individual rivers like Ganga, Yamuna, Triveni, Narmada, Godavari, Gomati, Gokarna, Cauvery, Jahnavi and all. Now it is stressed again that she is in the combined form of all holy rivers.
- *Mahānārāyaṇa Upanishat* (XIV–1) says –

"*Apāmekā Mahimānam Bibharti*" and again as "*Āpo Vā Idam Sarvam*".

535. नीलग्रीवा – *Nīlagrīvā*

- She is blue necked.
- Lord *Parameswara*, when he swallowed the venom, it stayed in his neck and hence his throat is coloured in blue (black). Hence, he is called *Nīlagrīva*. His consort is also *Nīlagrīvā*. In Sri Rudram Lord Shiva is bowed as "*Namo Nīlagrīvāya Ca*".
- *Vayu purana* says, "In the presence of a multitude of *Devas*, *Pishāchas*, serpents and demons, the virulent poison became transfixed in the throat; hence I am called *Nīlagrīva*".

536. निशिश्वरी – *Niśiśvarī*

- *Niśi* = mid-night. One who is the presiding deity of night.
- In *Mahāshoḍā Nyāsa* (*Prapancha Nyāsa*), it has been said that **She** is in the form of night time.

- **She** is the in the form of day time during dark half of lunar month and night time during bright half of lunar month.
- The letter *'Ha–ह'* represents Sun and the letter *'Sa–स'* represents Moon. In Panchadashaakksharee mantra these two key letters. Thus, *Sri Devi* moves like the Sun and the Moon personifying day and night and thus 'Time'.

537. नामावलिः – *Nāmāvaliḥ*

- One who has different names.
- *Nāma* = name. *Āvaliḥ* = garland or sequence. She has a garland of names. Sri Devi is in different forms like Gayatri, Lalita, Lakshmi, Saraswathi and all. For each of these forms we have Sahasranamas (1000 names). All put together we get infinite names. All those names our Devi's.
- 247th name in Sri Vishnu Sahasranamam – *Asankhyeya* – also conveys that he has uncountable names.

538. निशुम्भघ्नी – *Niśumbhagnī*

- One who smashed the demon *Niśumbhan* (brother of demon *Śumbhan*).
- In Devi Mahatmya, 9th chapter deal with the story of Sri Chandi Devi in the form of Maha Saraswathi, assassinating the demon *Niśumbhan*. Our Gayatri Devi is that Chandi Devi.

539. नाग लोक निवासिनी – *Nāga Loka Nivāsinī*

- One who lives in the world of snakes.
- The *patala* is the world of snakes. All the three worlds are under her control and hence this world also.
- The *Kundalini* energy, is in the form of a snake coiled in 3.5 rounds. She is in that female snake form dwelling in Mooladharam.

540. नवजाम्बूनदप्रख्या – *Navajāmbūnadaprakhyā*

- Her charm is like a new gold.
- Normal gold itself will be shining. A new gold will shine still more brightly. Her elegance is like this.

541. नागलोकाधि देवता – *Nāgalokādhi Devatā*

- She is the presiding deity of the world of snakes.
- In 539th name above, it was mentioned that she lives in the world of snakes. When she lives in a location, naturally she will be the deity of that place – who else can be?

542. नूपूराक्रान्त चरणा – *Nūpūrākrānta Caraṇā*

- Her feet are adorned with anklets and other foot ornaments.
- Earlier it was mentioned that she wears all jewels. Typical of any sumangali lady, she wears foot ornaments also. Hence her feet are shining.

543. नरचित्त प्रमोदिनी – *Naracitta Pramodinī*

- She makes the mind of human beings as most joyful.
- She herself is pleasure personified. Hence, she makes her devotees also delightful.

544. निमग्नारक्तनयना – *Nimagnārakta Nayanā*

- Her eyes are sunk in red.
- Her red luster reflects in her eyes also.
- Her body is red. She has red lily/ lotus on her hand. She wears red Sindhooram on her forehead. She wears jewels studded with red gem stones. She wears dress red in colour. When everything on and around her is red, her eyes also.
- She gets angry only when she fights with her enemies. At that time on account of anger, her eyes become red.

545. निर्घातसमनिःस्वना – *Nirghātasamaniḥsvanā*

- She makes dreadful noise like a thunderbolt.
- In 239th, 361st and 532nd names above described her loud noise. Here again it is re-stressed and compared to the horrible noise thunder.

546. नन्दनोद्याननिलया – *Nandanodyanilayā*

- She lives in a garden of smelling flowers.
- Rejoicing gardens with flowers are surrounding the dwelling place of Sri Devi, namely, *Sri Puram*.

547. निर्व्यूहोपरिचारिणी – *Nirvyūhoparicāriṇī*

- She hangs in the free space in an unmanifested form without any array.
- In her *niroopa* form she shines without any image. Initially she arose as a torch in front of Devas. Since they were scarred, she came out with a beautiful lady form.

548. पार्वती – *Pārvatī*

- The daughter of Mount Himavan, the king of all mountains (Parvata Raja).
- *Himavan* is the king of mountains. Being his daughter, **she** is called as *Pārvatī*, *Haimavatee* and *Girija*.
- *Brahma Purana*, in the *Purusottama Kshetra Mahātmya* says – *Parvati*, who was born from the womb of *Menaka*, wife of *Himavan* in a previous birth, in the next birth is born as *Subhadra*, sister of *Sri Krishna* in the womb of *Devaki*.
- 246th name in Sri Lalita Sahasranamam is also the same – *Pārvatī*.

549. परमोदारा – *Paramodārā*

- One who is extremely generous.
- **She** is supremely generous, readily responding to the prayers of **Her** devotees.
- *Udara* also means very big. **She** is very big both in space and time. Since **She** is very big, **she** is called as *Paramodāra*.
- This name can be split as – *Para* = supreme, *moda* = bliss, *Ārā* = complete. That is, **she** bestows complete and supreme happiness to **Her** devotees.
- If the name is split as – *Parama* + *Uda* + *Āra* = very great water i.e. ocean; ocean here meaning the ocean of worldly existence; *Ārā* = weapons. **She** is the destroyer of the worldly existence of her devotees.

- By prefixing *A* to the name, we get *Aparamodārā*; if this is split as *Aparama + Udāra*. *Apa* = gone, *Rama* = wealth or joy. i.e. for the poor and miserable people, **she** is, *Udāra*.
- 939th name in Sri Lalita Sahasranamam is also the same – *Paramodārā*.

550. परब्रह्मात्मिका – *Parabrahmātmikā*

- **She** only is the *Para-brahmam*.
- According to *Sri Vidya* philosophy, the form of unison of *Shiva* and *Shakti* is the *Parabrahmam*. Here there is no distinction between *Shiva* and *Shakti*.
- **She** is the energy through which the Parabrahmam can be identified.
- *Bṛhadāraṇyaka Upanishat* (verses I-3, 1-4) explains the universal absolute (*Parabrahmam*) becoming two as husband and wife.
- According to the *Svetāsvatara Upanishat* (V-1) – in imperishable and infinite highest universal absolute (*Parabrahmam*), wherein the two, *vidyā* and *avidyā* are hidden, one is imperishable and the other is perishable, **she** who rules these two is different from either;
- 97th verse of *Soundaryalaharee* reads;
  *Mahāmāyā Vishvam Bhramayati Parabrahma Mahishee* II

551. परा – *Parā*

- One who is in the form of sound called *Para*, the transcendent word.
- The power of expression depends upon the correspondence of the words and their meanings. Hence, as the unconditioned *Brahmam* also is included in the sound (*Shabdabrahmam*), *Brahmam* indirectly (*Lakshana*) indicates (as the *Vedāntins* say) by the existence of the words, etc. Because the words which are the physical forms of speech (*Vaikharee*) only express or identify the physical form of *Brahmam* (the *Virāt*) and do not correspond to the pure unconditioned *Brahmam*. The speech is divided into four forms; *Parā*, *Pashyantee*, *Madyamā* and *Vaikharee*.
- To clearly understand these, it is necessary to mention some background information. During great dissolution (*Maha-Pralaya*) when the actions (*karmas*) of beings about to be manifested are not yet ripe, the *Brahmam*, bound by illusion (*māyā*) and by those actions (*karma bhinna māyā* – literal meaning being illusion itself in

the form of actions) is called *ghanibhoota* (the congealed one). When, in course of time, the actions begin to ripen and the former state of un-ripeness disappears, that state is called *vichikrisā* (longing for action). At the moment of ripeness, when the modification of illusion appears, *Brahmam*, endowed with illusion in the form of ripened actions, is called *avyakta* (unmanifested). Hence creation is attributed in the *Smritis* to the *avyakta* – that is the *avyakta* sprung with the three qualities. That *avyakta*, as it is the sprouting root of the universe, is termed as the *kāraṇabindu* (the causal dot). The *Prapanchasāra* says, that Intelligence, the congealed one, desirous of action, attains the state of *kāraṇabindu*. From this *kāraṇabindu* proceeds in order the *kāryabindu* (effective dot). From the latter *nada* (sound); thence the *beeja* (the seed); thus, the three came into being. These three are also called by the words the supreme, subtle (*sookshma*) and physical (*sthoola*). In their nature they partake respectively intelligence (*chit*), combined-intelligence (*achit*) and non-intelligence (*Chidachit*). Hence the *Rahasyāgama* says, that *Bindu* (the causal dot) in the course of time sprouts and become three. Its three divisions are gross, subtle and supreme. These are called, *Bindu*, *nada* and *beeja*. These four, including the *kāraṇa-bindu* in their divine aspect (*ādhi-daivata*) are *avyakta*, *Eshwara*, *Hirānyagarbha* and *Virāt*. They are called by various names and forms in the *Sastras*. They are;

| **Form (*Swaroopa*)** | **Effective Dot (*Kāryabindu*)** | **Sound (*Nada*)** | **Seed (*Beeja*)** | **Causal Dot (*Kāraṇabindu*)** |
|---|---|---|---|---|
| *Ādhidaivata* | *Eshwara*<br><br>*Vāmā*<br>*Icchā Shakti* | *Hiraṇyagarbha*<br><br>*Jyeshtā*<br>*Gnana Shakti* | *Virāt*<br><br>*Roudhree*<br>*Kriyā Shakti* | *Avyakta Brahmam*<br>*Shāntā*<br>*Amibikā* |
| *Ādhibhoutikam* | *Kāmaroopa Peeṭa* | *Poorṇagiri Peeṭa* | *Jālantara Peeṭa* | *Oḍyāna Peeṭa* |

- In the bodily aspect the *Kāraṇabindu* (*adhyātma*) resides in the *Moolādhāra* and is known by the words *shakti* or *pinda* (mono-syllable *mantra*), *Kunḍalinee*, etc. This has been mentioned in *Kalidāsā's Laghustava* (V-1) – there is a *shakti* called *Kunḍalinee*, having known her who is ever engaged in the work of the creation of the universe, a man never again enters a mother's womb as a child (i.e. he has no more birth).
- This is the *kāraṇa bindu* in its non-differentiated condition. When it

sprouts in order to create the three, namely *kāryabindu*, etc., then the unmanifested sound called *Shabdabrahmam* arises from it.

- It is also said as, from this differentiation, that *bindu* comes with an unmanifested sound, that sound is termed as *Shabdabrahmam* by voice experts. This sound, since it is one with the *Kāraṇabindu* and is therefore all-pervading, yet first appears in the *Moolādhāra* of the persons by the power of wind acted upon by the effort of manifestation. In the *Moolādhara* in the body the wind first appears, that acted upon by the effort of a person desiring to speak, produces the all-pervading *Shabdabrahmam*". That *Shabda-brahmam*, which is in the *kāraṇabindu*, when it is manifested remaining motionless (*nishpanḍa*).
- Though the *kāraṇabindu* originated as *shabdabrahmam*, it remains motionless in its own place *Moolādhāra* and hence is called *parā* speech.
- The same *Shabdabrahmam*, produced by the same air proceeding as far as the navel, joined with the reasoning intellect mind (*Manas*), possessing the nature of the manifested *Kāryabindu* with simple motion (*sāmānya spanda*) is named *pashyanti* speech.
- Next the same *Shabdabrahmam*, produced by the same air proceeding as far as the heart, joined with the determining (understanding *Buddhi*), in the manifested sound, endowed with special motion (*vishesha spanda*) is called *madhyamā* speech.
- Next the *Shabdabrahmam*, produced by the same air, proceeding as far as the mouth, developed in the throat, etc., in the form of articulation, capable of being heard by the ears of other's possessing the nature of the manifested *beeja*, with the universal motion (*spashṭatara*) is called *vaikharee* speech.

*Moolādhāre Para Proktā Pashyantee Nabhisam Stitā* I
*Madyamā Bhuddhi Samyuktā Ashṭasthāneshu Vaikharee* II

- Sri Devi is in the forms of all these four types of sound - *Parā, Pashyanti, Madhyamā* and *Vaikharee*.
- It is also explained by *Sri Adi Shankara* in his *Prapancha Sāram* (II-43) that sound which first arises in the *Moolādhāra* is called *Parā*, next the *Pashyanti*; next when it goes as far as the heart and is joined to the understanding Buddhi it is called *Madhyamā*; and the full manifestation is *Vaikharee*. Thus, articulated sound is produced by air;

*Moolādhārāt Prathama Mudito Yashcha Bhāvaḥ Parākhyaḥ*
*Pashchāt Pashyantyatha Hrudayago Bhuddhiyun Madyamāgyaḥ*
*Vyakte Vakharyata Rurudishorasya Jantoḥ Shushumnā*
*Pandhas Tasmādbhavati Pavane PreritāVarṇa Samgnā*

- The same idea is mentioned in *Nityā Tantra* also – the *Parā* form arises in the *Moolādhāra* produced by air; the same air rising upwards, manifested in the *Svādhistāna*, attains the *Pashyanti* state. The same slowly rising upwards and manifested in the *Anāhata*, united with the understanding is termed *Madhyama*. Again, rising upwards appearing in the *Vishuddhi* and comes out from the throat is *Vaikharee*. Thus, though there are four kinds of speech gross minded men who do not understand the first three, think *Vaikharee* alone to be the speech.
- The *Veda* says; hence the men think *Vaikharee* alone to be the speech which is imperfect. That is to say imperfect by not possessing the first three forms;

  *Tasmāt Yatvācho' Nāptam Tam Manushyā Upajeevanti.*
- Another *Veda* statement also (*Rig Veda* I-164-45) says; four are the definite grades of the speech; those Brahmins who are wise know them; three are deposited in secret and motionless; men speak the fourth-grade speech;

*Chatvāri Vāg Parimitā Padani Tāni Vidur Brāmhanā Ye Maneeshinaḥ* I
*Guhā Treeni Nihitā Nengayanti Tureeyam Vācho Manushyā Vadanti* II

- The *Tripurasiddhānta* explains the word *parā* in different ways. As **She** is pleased with *Parānandanātha* (a teacher) **She** is called *Parā*. As **She** is celebrated in the work called *Parānanda*, **she** is *Parā* and as **She** is the supreme source of grace, **she** is *Parā*.
- The *Shiva Tattva* without any dispositions and the *Shakti Tattva*, the cause of the dispositions on account of creation, are one and the same in the *Parā Samvit*.
- As per 32nd verse of *Soundaryalaharee* – '*Sa*-स' represents *Parā* – the ultimate – as in *Parāshakti* – the ultimate power.
- 366th name in Sri Lalita Sahasranamam is also the same – *Parā*.
- 809th name in Sri Lalita Sahasranamam – *Parātparā*, says – **she** is the most supreme of the supreme.

552. पञ्चकोशविनिर्मुक्ता – *Pañcakośavinirmuktā*

- One who dwells amidst the five *koshas* (psychological sheaths of the personality).
- It has been told that there are five sheaths in our body; *Annamaya* (food), *Prāṇamaya* (*prānic* or energy), *Manomaya* (mental), *Vignanamaya* (intellectual) and *Ānandamaya* (bliss). Each of these is covered in the previous one. Hence this name is given to *Sri Devi*, since **She** is in the integral form with *Brahmam* as *Ānandamaya*

sheath. *Taitrīya Upanishat* verse (2-5);

*"Anyontara Ātmānandamayaḥ"*

- However, *Sri Adi Shankara* has quoted that it is not correct to say that *Ānandamaya* sheath is the universal absolute (*Brahmam*) and these two are different. Based on this philosophy, it has been told that *Ānandamaya* sheath is in the form of *Chit Shakti*, which is the luminous form of *Brahmam*. (*Ānandamaya karaṇam* and *Samānādhikaraṇam* of *Sri Adi Shankara*'s commentary for *Brahma Sūtra*). The same method is explained in *Shreekanda Bhashyam* and the books explaining it. Based on this opinion, this name has to be taken as, **she** is in the midst of the five sheaths. That is, *Brahmam* is beyond *Ānandamaya* sheath, but completing it, being witness to all actions and in the form of truth and knowledge.
- In the *Navāvarṇa Pooja*, after the ninth *Āvarṇa* above the *bindu*, *Pancha Panchikā Pooja* is done imagining that there are five thrones. These five *Panchikās* respectively are; five *Lakshmees*, five sheaths, five *kalpalatas*, five *kāmadenus* and five gems. The names of five sheaths are; *Sri Vidya*, *Paramjyothi*, *Parānishkalā Shāmbavee*, *Ajapā* and *Mātruka*. These details are available in the book called *Gnānārnava Tantra*.
- *Sri Vidya* sheath is worshipped in the *Bindu*. The other four are worshipped outside differentiating the individual and the combined ones. Since *Sri Vidya* sheath is worshipped in the *Bindu*, amidst these four, this name to *Sri Devi*.
- The five sheaths can be named as below;
  i. First – *Āntra Drushyānuvitta Samādhi* (inner sightless)
  ii. Second – *Āntra Shabtānuvitta Samādhi* (inner soundless)
  iii. Third – *Bāhya Drushyānuvitta Samādhi* (outer sightless)
  iv. Fourth – *Bāhya Shaptānuvitta Samādhi* (outer soundless)
  v. Fifth – *Bāhya Nirvikalpa Samādhi* (outer not-wavering)
- Sage Durvāsā (Kroda Pattārakar) also mentions that Sri Devi is in the form of the supreme being;

*Anna-prāṇa-manaḥ Prabodha Paramānandaiḥ Shiraḥ Pakshayuk*
*Puchchātmaprakaṭair Mahopanishadhām Vakyaiḥ Prasiddheekrutaḥ* I
*Koshaiḥ Panchabhirebhireva Bhavateemetat Praveenāmiti*
*Jyotiḥ Prajvaladu Jvalātma Chapalām Yo Veda Sa Bramhavit* II

- 428th name in Sri Lalita Sahasranamam – *Panchakoshāntarasthitā* – also conveys the same message.
- 432nd name in Sri Vishnu Sahasranamam – *Mahakosha* – also conveys the same message.

553. पञ्चपातक नाशिनी – *Pañcapātaka Nāśinī*

- One who destroys five great sins.
- There are five great sins (*mahāpāthakās*) – *Brahmahathi* (killing a Brahmin), looting, drinking alcohol, liking of elder's wife and being supportive to those who do the other four sins.
- In Sri Devi Bhagavata – King Janamejaya was a son of King Parikshit and grand-son of Abhimanyu. He asked Sage Shuka that his great grand parents have killed lot many people. What is the expiation for them? Sage Shuka advised King Janamejayan to perform *Chandi Homa*, so that all the Brahmahatti sins of all his fore-fathers would be wiped off.
- Expiation for all these sins has been described in various *Shanthi* books. One such expiation for these sins and completely destroying the very thought of those sins also, is remembering upon the lotus feet of *Sri Devi*. The thought would tempt to do the sins again and again. Hence worshipping *Sri Devi* would completely destroy this thought and generate the thought of good deeds.
- If one has chant with focus (without deviating mind) at least one name out of these 1000 names so much sins are destroyed that nobody could have committed as many sins as in all the 14 worlds.
- 992nd name in Sri Vishnu Sahasranamam – *Paapanashana* – destroyer of all sins.

554. परचित्तविधानज्ञा – *Paracittavidhānajñā*

- One who can understand the mind of others.
- During worship and all, we need not ask anything specifically to Sri Devi. She knows our thought process and bless accordingly.
- While a sin is defined – it is not necessary that one has to do an even task. Even some evil task thought to do in the mind itself is a sin – *manasaa*, *vaacaa* and *karmanaa*.

555. पञ्चिका – *Pañcikā*

- She is the controller of five primary elements.
- Five primary elements are Ether, Air, Fire, Water and the Earth. It is she who creates and regulates all these.
- One other philosophy is that *Sri Devi* is in the form of anything, which has all these five elements.

- The *Virāt* form of Sri Devi – the subtle form of the five elements which is the *Brahmāṇḍam*. **She** is in that *Virāt* form.
- The secret form of these is the five self-characteristics (*Tanmātrās*). These characteristics are the unique features of the five elements, which constitute the physical earth.

| Elements (*Bhūtās*) | Self-Characteristics (*Tanmātrās*) |
|---|---|
| Space (*Ākāśā*) | Sound (*Shabdā*) |
| Wind/ Air (*Vāyu*) | Sense of touch (*Sparsha*) |
| Fire (*Agnī*) | Form/ Colour (*Rūpa*) |
| Water (*Jala*) | Taste (*Rasa*) |
| Earth (*Prithvi*) | Odour (*Gandha*) |

- These characteristics standalone only in the very intricate and atomic state of the elements. The Universe, we perceive is the composite form of these elements and hence each element cannot be perceived separately.

556. पञ्च रूपिणी – *Pañca Rūpiṇī*

- She is in the form of the five primary elements.
- It can also be considered that since **She** is in the form of five or **She** originated in five ways.

557. पूर्णिमा – *Pūrṇimā*

- She is in the form of full Moon.
- One who has her body like a full moon.
- It can be noted that the full moon is present in the *Sahasrāra Kamala* in the head. **She** is residing in the center of that moon.
- In every month during the full moon day, if **She** is worshipped, with these thousand names, in the night by imagining *Sri Devi*'s form on the *Sri Chakra*, the worshipper would himself have the form of the goddess *Gayatri* and he cannot be seen as another one, for it is a sin to see him as anything else.

558. परमा – *Paramā*

- One who is the great in all things and in all ways.
- **She** who limits and shows us the immeasurable *Brahmam*.
- The word *Parama* means "at a distance". i.e. **She** is at a distance for

those who do not have devotion.

- According to *Vishnu Purana*, the supreme being has four forms viz., Male, Twice Born, Time and *Param*. **She** is in the fourth form *Param*.
- This name can also be construed as *Paramātma*.
- 618th name in Sri Lalita Sahasranamam also the same – *Paramā*.

559. प्रीतिः – *Prītiḥ*

- One who easily gets satisfied by her devotees.
- She immediately satisfies the needs of her devotees.

560. परतेजः – *Paratejaḥ*

- One who is the Supreme light.
- The state without light is darkness. The ignorance is the darkness in the mind. Once the light is on, the darkness goes away. When there is knowledge ignorance is removed. When it is dark neither inside nor outside the world is seen. The outside darkness is removed by Sun, Moon, stars, fire and other light galaxies. Sound is also light, because we recognise something with the help of sound in darkness also.
- The above said Sun, etc., are illuminated only by **Her**. Hence, **she** is called as supreme (*param*).
- The *Bṛhadāraṇyaka Upanishat* (IV-4-16) says, "That is light of light";

  *Taddevā Jyotishām Jyotirāya Hopāsadamrutam*.
- *Kaṭopanishat* (II-2-15) says, The Sun, the Moon and the stars do not shine by themselves; for **She** illuminates the mind that illuminates all of these;

  *Na Tatra Sooryo Bhāti Na Chandra Tārakam Nema*
  *Vidyuto Bhānti Kutoyamagniḥ Tameva Bhāntamanubhāti*
  *Sarvam Tasya Bhāsa Sarvamidam Vibhāti*
- *Chāndogya Upanishat* (VIII-3-4) – The sun shines only when he is illuminated by Her; "*Param Jyotirupasampadya*".
- The *Bṛhadāraṇyaka Upanishat* (III-9-10) "The supreme light one attains" – *Jyotis* here means the illuminator, for we see the same meaning given in such places, "the illuminator of the mind" –

  *Mano Jyotiḥ*

561. प्रकाशिनी – *Prakāsinī*

- She shines like anything.

- **She** gives brightness to the Sun himself. *Sri Devi*, who is in the form of Brahmam, resides within the Sun also.
- *Sri Devi* shines as the only brilliant ruler of the universe.
- One who shines with all divine qualities.
- The gist is that **She** shines with various meanings.

562. पुराणी – *Purāṇī*

- She is the heroin of many puranas. There are lot many puranas above her.
- One who is the most ancient being; **She** is primordial.
- **She** was there even before creation of all other beings. **She** only created all.
- Since **She** has ancient qualities, **she** is *Purāṇī*.
- *Purā* = old, *Nava* = new. She is very old and very new as well.
- 498th name in Sri Vishnu Sahasranamam – *Purātana* – who is very ancient.

563. पौरुषी – *Pauruṣī*

- She is a woman – as mentioned in 531st name above.
- She is a lady worshipped by males.
- She is the earliest and greatest lady.

564. पुण्या – *Puṇyā*

- One who is famed for virtue/ righteousness/ holiness.
- Just thinking and communicating the fame of *Sri Devi* will give virtue.
- **She** has the reputation of giving virtue to **Her** devotees.
- One who can be attained only through virtues/ righteousness.
- *Punya*, good actions performed in previous births – only through this **Her** blessings can be attained.
- The *Devi Bhagavatam* says, "Only those ever-righteous ascetics, who are devoted to wisdom, see; but the men of desire see not the holy and beneficent *Devi*";

  *Pashyanti <u>Puṇya</u> Punjā Ye Ye Vedāntas Tapasvinaḥ* I
- It is a virtue to hear about **Her** and to praise **Her.**
- She enables the sinners also to worship her and make then virtuous.
- 687th name in Sri Vishnu Sahasranamam is the same name in masculine form – *Punya*.

565. पुण्डरीक निभेक्षणा – *Puṇḍarīka Nibhekṣaṇā*

- One who has blossomed lotus eyes.
- The eyes of Sri Devi are described in many places in multiple ways. Comparing her eyes to lotus flower has been seen many texts.
- 345th and 556th names in Sri Vishnu Sahasranamam – *Padma Nibhekṣaṇa* and *Puśkarakṣā* – the Lotus eyed.

566. पाताल तल निर्मग्ना – *Pātāla Tala Nirmagnā*

- One who can travel upto the beneath world (*Pātāla Tala*).
- Not everyone can travel to the *Pātāla* world. But she can, being goddess of all the 14 worlds.

567. प्रीता – *Prītā*

- One who easily get gratified by her devotees.
- This has already been mentioned in the 559th name above and being stressed here.

568. प्रीति विवर्धिनी – *Prītivivardhinī*

- She augments the satisfaction of her devotees.
- Only when the desires are satisfied the devotee can focus on meditation, worship and all.

569. पावनी – *Pāvanī*

- *Pāvanī* – of pure form. One whose body is holy and sanctifying both in form and character.
- The very thought of *Sri Devi* washes away all sins and makes one the purest.
- *Pāvanī* also means yellow Myrobalan – she is in that colour.

570. पादसहिता – *Pādasahitā*

- One who is with three feet.
- The meditation verse of Sri Gayatri Devi, itself mentioned that she has three feet.

- 382nd name above also gave the same sense.
- 534th name in Sri Vishnu Sahasranamam is also the same – *Tripada*.
- Literally *Pādasahitā* will mean one with a foot – this has nothing special – no need to mention. Hence its meaning is construed as one addition foot – *Tripada*.

571. पेशला – *Peśalā*

- She has a most beautiful form/ image.
- Her pleasant form has been described in almost every possible place. Originally, she originated as a torch. Devas were scared and she came out in a pleasing form.

572. पवनाशिनी – *Pavanāśinī*

- One who is feeding on air.
- During penance, people used to live without any food through mouth and they only eat air. Sri Devi has done lots of penances and at that time she lives without food or she eats only the air.

573. प्रजापतिः – *Prajāpatiḥ*

- Consort of Lord Brahma.
- Lord Brahma is called *Prajāpati* – being his consort she is called *Prajāpatiḥ*.
- **She** is mentioned as the consort of *Prajāpati*, in *Mahāshoḍa Nyāsam* (*Moorthy nyāsam*).
- 69th name of Vishnu Sahasranamam is also the *Prajapati*.

574. परिश्रान्ता – *Pariśrāntā*

- One who takes rest.
- She has delegated all her tasks to others and they are also perfectly doing the same. Her only chore is to oversee others and to bless the devotees. She does this with ease.
- The literal meaning of *Pariśrāntā* is fatigue or exhaustion. She never gets exhausted. Hence it has to be construed as she removes the fatigue of her devotees.
- In Ramayana also – during the battle with Ravana – sage Agastya advises Aditya Hrudaya Stotram to Rama. It starts with *"Tato*

*Yuddha Pariśrāntam...*" – Rama was seemingly tired of the battle. Then he prayed Lord Surya with this Stotram and went ahead with the war.

575. पर्वत स्तन मण्डला – *Parvata Stana Maṇḍalā*

- One who has a hard rock breast region.
- Breast is one organ that adds beauty to ladies. This has been clearly explained in Samudrika Shastra for Ladies. Devi's breasts have been described in various texts like Soundaryalaharee, Sri Lalita Sahasranamam, Sri Lalita Trishatee, etc.
- 147th name of Sri Lalita Trishatee – *Kaţhina Stana Maṇḍalā* – She has a hard rock breast region.
- Even in this Sahasranama, right from meditation verse, the beauty and nature of her breasts are pronounced in many a place.

576. पद्म प्रिया – *Padma Priyā*

- Lord Vishnu is used to be called as Padmanabhan (48th, 196th and 346th names in *Vishnu Sahasranama*). She is loved by him.
- Being his consort, they mutually have affection over each other.
- *Priya* does not only indicate love, but also the feeling of happiness experienced by just seeing the things one possesses. This meaning is also very apt here.

577. पद्म संस्था – *Padma Saṃsthā*

- She is in the form of assembly of lotus flowers.
- Sri Devi has lots of connection with Lotus flower – She sits on a lotus flower. She has a lotus flower in one of her hands. Her eyes, face, etc., are compared to Lotus flowers. Her feet are always compared to Lotus.
- Every chakra of the body is having lotus flowers of varying petals. She is sitting in all the chakras – especially, thousand petalled Sahasrara Chakra on the head.

578. पद्माक्षी – *Padmākṣī*

- One who has long eyes like the petals of a Lotus flower.
- 24th and 565th names above also mentioned that she has Lotus eyes.
- 7th name in Sri Lalita Trishatee – *Kamalākṣee* – conveys the same

message.

- Again, 16th name in Sri Lalita Trishatee – *Kañjalocanā* – also conveys the same message.
- The seat of Devi is the lotus. Hence a look from her lotus like eyes is able to grant happiness (bliss) and creative activity of the entire world.

579. पद्म सम्भवा – *Padma Sambhavā*

- One who originated from/ with a Lotus flower.
- As Goddess Lakshmi, when she originated from the Milky Ocean itself, she is connected to Lotus flower. She had a lotus flower in her hand.
- The comparison to Lotus is because lotus has not only pleasant smell but also beauty and attractiveness. Being on the lotus implies that *Sri Devi* grants all the *Purushārthās – Dharma, Artha, Kāma* and *Moksha*.

580. पद्म पत्रा – *Padma Patrā*

- The lotus leaves are not affected by water.
- He, who is devoted to Sri Devi, is not stained even by committing heinous crimes, in the manner as water does not stick to lotus leaf.
- The *Padma Purana*, in its *Pushara Kanda* says – The mass of sins though as great as mount Meru is instantly destroyed by worshipping *Devi*.

581. पद्म पदा – *Padma Padā*

- One whose feet are tender/ gentle/ delicate like lotus flower.
- Almost every organ of Sri Devi is compared with Lotus flower on account of its tenderness and fragrance.
- *Sri Adi Shankara,* in his *Soundaryalaharee* 4th *verse* mentions as – **Her** Lotus feet itself bestows more than what is sought for, by the devotees.

582. पद्मिनी – *Padminī*

- She is an excellent woman as tender and as fragrant as Lotus flower.
- Samudrika Lakshna Shastra divides woman based on their beauty. She belongs to the first of the 4 classes defined by that Shastra.

- From 576th name above, the lotus flower and Sri Devi are being mapped in one or other manner.

583. प्रियभाषिणी – *Priyabhāṣiṇī*

- She speaks kindly or agreeably.
- Typical of a mother she speaks softly to her devotees.
- *Priyabhāṣiṇī* is a kind of common hill myna. She is in the form of every living thing and hence this form also.

584. पशुपाश विनिर्मुक्ता – *Paśupāśa Vinirmuktā*

- She liberates her devotees from the bondage of the souls.
- The soul is tied with various affections and all in this world. Unless these are removed, he is not able to think of Moksham. She helps in this regard.

585. पुरन्ध्री – *Purandhrī*

- She looks like a simple home making lady, taking care of house cores.

586. पुरवासिनी – *Puravāsinī*

- She looks like an ordinary town lady.
- She merges with normal people even in looks. Hence this and previous names.

587. पुष्कला – *Puṣkalā*

- One who gives nourishment (bliss or completeness) to all.
- It can be taken as *Pushkalā* – omnipresent.
- In one of the books it is stated that **She** is one of the consorts of *Iyanar – Poorṇā* and *Pushkala*. Both the names mean fullness.
- According to *Sri Devi Bhagavatam* (VII-38-19) the place of *Gayatri* is called as *Shrimad Pushkaram*.
- In Samskrutam the letter *ra* and *la* are not much differentiated. Hence the 804th name in Sri Lalita Sahasranamam – *Pushkarā* also gives the same meaning.

588. पुरुषा – *Puruṣā*

- She bestows all the *Purushartas* to her devotees.
- It has been discussed in various places in this Sahasranamam about the four *puruṣārthas* viz., *Dharma* (righteousness, moral values), *Artha* (prosperity, economic values), *Kama* (pleasure, love, psychological values) and *Moksha* (liberation, spiritual values). She is the one who gives all these.

589. पर्वा – *Parvā*

- She is in the form of festivals.
- People feel much happy while celebrating a festival. She is the cause of it.
- Various festivals and festivities are dedicated to Sri Devi – Navratri (there are four Navratris in a year), throughout the month of Adi, and so on.
- *Sri Devi Gita*, as part of *Sri Devi Bhagavatam* – chapter 7-38 completely deals with various festivals and utsavams of *Sri Devi*. These are pointed out by Sri Devi herself.

590. पारिजात सुमप्रिया – *Pārijāta Sumapriyā*

- She is fond of *Pārijāta* flower.
- Earlier in the 152nd name it was mentioned that she is fond of Kadamba flowers. *Kadamba* is one of the *Kalpaka* trees (*deva* tree). *Kalpaka* tree is a common name for five types of trees viz., *Santānam*, *Harisantānam*, *Mantāram*, *Pārijātam* and *Kadambam*. These five types of trees represent the five parts of inner self – mind, intellect, volition, ego and heart.
- The 323rd name of *Sri Lalita Sahasranamam – Kadambakusumapriyā* –says that **She** is fond of *kadamba* flowers.
- The 11th name in *Sri Lalita Trishatee* is also *Kadamba Kusumapriyā*.

591. पतिव्रता – *Pativratā*

- One who is a great *pativrata*. One who is a devoted spouse.
- **She** is always with the thought as precept consort.
- *Sri Adi Shankara*, in his *Soundaryalaharee*, 96th verse starting with

*Kalatram Vadhātram*, describes *Sri Devi* as the; *Sateenām Acharame* – first among the *Pativratas*.

- For whom *Kameshvara* is the 'worshipped deity' – she is *Parama Pativrata*.
- Our scriptures mention about the greatness of *Pativratas* – *Nalāyinee, Damayantee, Aruntatee, Anasooyā, Sitā, Vāsukee* (consort of *Thiruvalluvar*) and others. Our Devi only takes all these forms.

592. पवित्राङ्गी – *Pavitrāṅgī*

- One who is very pure.
- 509th name above also conveyed the same message.
- In *Shrimad Ramayana* (*Ayodhya Kanda* – 39th chapter) – *Anasooya Devi* says; *Streenām Pavitram Paramam Patireko Vishishyate* ll
  As mentioned in the previous name Anasooya is one of the major *pativratas* – she is the mother of *Dattareya*. Unless is pure, she cannot be a pativrata. Only those who are pure, can be *pativratas*. Hence this name goes alongwith the previous name.

593. पुष्पहास परायणा – *Puṣpahāsa Parāyaṇā*

- She smiles like a blooming flower. One who has a charming smile.
- Her smile not only adds beauty, but also welcomes and makes it interesting to those who want to reach **Her**.
- The *Mantasmita Catakam* of *Mooka Pancashatee* completely describes the smile of *Sri Devi* only.
- The Moon is thy sweet smile – This saying means there is a certain stage of consciousness which gives the highest bliss and which should be known from a teacher alone.
- *Sri Lalita Sahasranamam* talks about the smile of *Sri Devi* in lot many places. To quote a few;
  - 602 – *Darahāsojjavalanmukhee* – One whose face shines with smile.
  - 924 – *Darasmeramukhāmbujā* – One whose lotus face is radiant with a sweet smile.
  - The meditation verse also says *Smitamukheem*.
- 60th name in Sri Lalita Trishatee says *Eeṣatsmitānanā* – one who has a gentle smiling face (Ever smiling).

594. प्रज्ञावतीसुता – *Prajñāvatīsutā*

- She is an intelligent and knowledgeable lady.
- She is in the form of Saraswathi, the goddess of learning. Then do we need to expressly mention about her intelligence and knowledge.

595. पौत्री – *Pautrī*

- One who is in the form of granddaughter – son's daughter.

596. पुत्रपूज्या – *Putrapūjyā*

- One who is worshipped by her son.
- Narada is one of her sons. He always worships her.

597. पयस्विनी – *Payasvinī*

- One who gives Amruta like milk.
- She in the form of cow gives sweet milk to her devotees.
- *Payasvinī* is also the name of a river. She is in the form of all rivers including this.

598. पट्टिपाशधरा – *Paṭṭipāśadharā*

- She showers her affection on devotees as a continuous rainfall.

599. पङ्क्ती – *Paṅktī*

- The word *Paṅktī* in Samskrutam will mean – line, queue, row, series, a set of five, etc.
- In this context we can take the last meaning – a set of five – five primary elements – controller of five primary elements.
- *Paṅktī* also means a chandas or meter of 4 x 10 syllables. She is in that form of *Chandas*.

600. पितृलोक प्रदायिनी – *Pitṛloka Pradāyinī*

- Those who worship Sri Devi with iniquity go to the world of *pitrus* after leaving this body. She paves way for the same.
- Every human desire for happiness in the next world, that is, *Pitruloka*. Worshipping her is the only way out. She bestows the same to her devotees.
- When any soul leaves the body, the karmas done by the son(s) during first 12 days aims at getting a place in the world of Pitrus for the departed soul. It is she who offers that place.

Thus ends 100 divine names on *Sri Gayatri Devi* from 501 to 600

*****

601. पुराणी – *Purāṇī*

- This is a repetition of 562nd name above.

602. पुण्यशीला – *Puṇyaśīlā*

- One who is famed for virtue/ righteousness/ holiness.
- Just thinking and communicating the fame of *Sri Devi* will give virtue.
- One who can be attained only through virtues/ righteousness.
- *Punya*, good actions performed in previous births – only through this **Her** blessings can be attained.
- **She** has the reputation of giving virtue to **Her** devotees.
- *Sri Adi Shankara* also conveys the same message, in his commentary of *Sri Vishnu Sahasranamam* for the 688th name – *Puṇyakeerttiḥ*.
- Sri *Devi Bhagavatam* says, "Only those ever-righteous ascetics, who are devoted to wisdom, see; but the men of desire see not the holy and beneficent *Devi*".
- *Sri Adi Shankara* also conveys the same message, in his commentary to 1st verse of *Soundaryalaharee*.

603. प्रणतार्तिविनाशिनी – *Praṇatārtivināśinī*

- One who removes the troubles/ griefs of her devotees.
- She gives and then removes the difficulties. Later she enable him to attain her.

604. प्रद्युम्न जननी – *Pradyumna Jananī*

- Mother of Pradyumnan.
- Pradyumnan is a son of Rukmini and Lord Krishna. Our Devi was in the form of Rukmini and hence mother of Pradyumnan.

605. पुष्टा – *Puṣṭā*

- One who is well nourished.
- **She** has the 36 *tattvas* as her body. Hence complete in all respects without any flaw. Hence *Puṣṭā*.
- In *Saptashatee* (5th chapter) we read as;

  *Yā Devee Sarvabhooteshu Pushtiroopena Samsthitā* I
  *Namastasyai Namastasyai Namastasyai Namo Nama*: II

- **She** has many qualities and hence *Puṣṭā*.
- **She** is nourished with the juice of *Brahmam*; bliss only gives completion. Since *Sri Devi* is of the form of *Brahmam*, **she** is *Puṣṭā*.
- One who is nourished by Brahmins and hence *Puṣṭā*.
- For instance, one *Shruti* statement – *Brahmaṇaiḥ Poshitam Brahma* and one *Smriti* statement –

  *Brahmayushmat Tadbrāhmanairāyushmat*.
- 801st name in Sri Lalita Sahasranamam is also *Pushṭā*.
- 392nd name in Sri Vishnu Sahasranamam is also *Pushṭa*.
- Srimad-Bhagavatam (4-1-49) says - The thirteen wives of Dharmadevan are Shraddha, Maitree, Daya, Shanti, Tushti, Pushti, Kriya, Unnati, Buddhi, Medai, Didiksha, Hree and Murthy.

606. पितामहपरिग्रहा – *Pitāmahaparigrahā*

- One who is devoted to *Pitamaha*.
- *Pitamaha* literally means paternal grandfather. In this context *Pitamaha* will mean Lord Brahma. She is dedicated to him.

607. पुण्डरीकपुरावासा – *Puṇḍarīkapurāvāsā*

- *Pundarikapuram* is Chidambaram. She lives there as Sivakami, consort of Lord Nataraja.
- *Pundarika* also means Lotus flower. Sri Devi has been connected to Lotus flower in lot many ways.
- The *Chāndogya Upanishat* (VIII-1-1) says, there is *Brahmam* in a small lotus house and in it that small ether that should be sought for. Hence the ether is the heart that is said to be *Brahmam*;

  *Atha Yadasmin Brahma Puredhaharam Pundareekam Vechma*
- 111th name in Sri Vishnu Sahasranamam is *Puṇḍarīkakṣa* – Pervading the Lotus of the Heart

608. पुण्डरीकसमानना – *Puṇḍarīkasamānanā*

- *Pundarika* is Lotus flower. She has her face similar to Lotus.
- *Pundarikan* is lord Vishnu. She is equal to him.

609. पृथुजङ्घा – *Pṛthujaṅghā*

- One who has broad thighs.
- 148th name in Sri Lalita Trishatee – *Karabhoruḥ* – Whose thigh is like

the trunk of an elephant.

- The 39th name in *Sri Lalita Sahasranamam – Kāmeshagyāta Soubhāgya* – she has two beautiful and soft thighs known only to *Sri Kameshwara.*

610. पृथुभुजा – *Pṛthubhujā*

- One who has long arms (shoulders).
- According to Samudrika lakshna Shastra, a Shatria male should have arms extending upto the knees. It has been mentioned in Ramayana that Sri Rama had such arms. Such arms are needed to help in fighting with the enemies with bow and arrow. Here our Devi also fights with various enemies and hence this metaphor.

611. पृथुपादा – *Pṛthupādā*

- One who has long feet. Her feet are so holy and great.
- The hands were mentioned a long in the previous name and now it is the turn of legs.
- Sages say that "What is to be done while in crisis? Just think about the feet of *Sri Devi*. What will do that type of thinking? It makes even *Brahma* and others as servants".
- We all continue to do one or another mistake. While enquiring about the expiation, it is understood that thinking of the feet of *Sri Devi* is the only way out.
- In the 10th verse of *Soundaryalaharee* Sri Adi Shankara says – The shower of nectar, which flows from between two feet, wets all the *nāḍis* in the human body (made of five primary elements).

612. पृथूदरी – *Pṛthūdarī*

- One who has a broad belly region.
- Samudrika Lakshana Shastra says that the hip of the ladies should be thin, but the belly area should be broad. Accordingly, Sri Devi has a broad belly region.
- This also means the Manipooraka Chakra of the human body. She lives there.

613. प्रवालशोभा – *Pravālaśobhā*

- One who shines like coral.

- One who has the luster of coral. She is red in colour like coral.
- For the 293rd name Sri Lalita Trishatee – *Hreemkāramayasouvarṇa Stambhavidruma Putrikā* – Sri Adi Shankara comments – **She** is the main deity occurring as a coral idol in the hall called *'hreem'* supported by golden pillars.

614. पिङ्गाक्षी – *Piṅgākṣī*

- One who has yellowish brown eyes.
- Her beautiful and graceful eyes brownish in colour.

615. पीतवासाः – *Pītavāsāḥ*

- She is dressed in yellow colour.
- The dhyana shloka of Sri Lalita Sahasranamam says – *Peetavastrām* – dressed in yellow.

616. प्रचापला – *Pracāpalā*

- She is highly agile.
- She has lots of activities to do and she does all the task without feeling tired.

617. प्रसवा – *Prasavā*

- One who delivered all the living beings.
- She is Jaganmata – mother of the entire universe. Also, she only creates all the lives. Hence it is apt to say that she delivers all the living beings.

618. पुष्टिदा – *Puṣṭidā*

- One who offers offers nourishment to all her devotees.
- Earlier in the 605th name above, she was mentioned as *Puṣṭā* – who is well nourished. Here it is said that she bestows nourishment to her devotees. Unless she is nourished, he cannot bestow nourishment to others. Hence these two names.

619. पुण्या – *Puṇyā*

- This is a repetition of 564th name above.

620. प्रतिष्ठा – *Pratiṣṭhā*

- She is as peaceful as anything.
- She does not get provoked, unless she is in a war. She is always peaceful.

621. प्रणवागती – *Praṇavāgatī*

- She is the root form of *Pranava Mantra*.
- The *Pranava Mantra* – *'Oṃ'* – originated from her only.
- The letter *'Hreem'* is the *Shakta Pranava Mantra*. She is in that form also.
- 301st name of Sri *Lalita Sahasranamam* – *Hreemkāree*.
- 81st name in *Sri Lalita Trishatee* is *Hreemkāra Rūpā*. 60 names out of 300 in *Sri Lalita Trishatee* start with the letter *Hreem*.

622. पञ्चवर्णा – *Pañcavarṇā*

- She is of five colours.
- In the meditation verse of Sri Gayatri Devi itself, it was mentioned that she has five faces and each face is of white, pearl, coral, golden and blue-gem colours.
- Among the parrots the five colored parrot is the most beautiful. She is also just as beautiful.

623. पञ्चवाणी – *Pañcavāṇī*

- She is of the form of five *vāṇī*-s – voices *Para*, *Apara*, *Pashyanthi*, *Madhyama* and *Vaikharee*. These have already been described in 12th and 511th name above.
- She is of the form of five *pranas* – prana, Apana, vyana, udana and samana – which control the vāṇī-s.

624. पञ्चिका – *Pañcikā*

- This is a repetition of 555th name above.

625. पञ्जरस्थिता – *Pañjarasthitā*

- She lives in all living things.

- She is the Atman. Hence, she lives in all *jeevatmas*.
- She lives in the hearts of all living beings.

626. परमाया – *Paramāyā*

- She is in the form of absolute illusion.
- Sri Devi is the illusion. Illusion is Sri Devi.

627. परज्योतिः – *Parajyotiḥ*

- One who is the Supreme light.
- The state without light is darkness. The ignorance is the darkness in the mind. Once the light is on, the darkness goes away. When there is knowledge ignorance is removed. When it is dark neither inside nor outside world is seen. The outside darkness is removed by Sun, Moon, stars, fire and other illuminated galaxies. Sound is also light, because we recognise something with the help of sound in darkness also.
- The above said Sun, etc., are illuminated only by **Her**. Hence, **she** is called as *Parajyotiḥ*.
- The *Bruhadaranyaka Upanishat* (IV-4-16) says – "That is light of light" – *Taddevā Jyotishām Jyotirāya Hopāsadamrutam*.
- Again, the same *Bṛhadāraṇyaka Upanishat* (III-9-10) says – "The supreme light one attains" – *Jyotiḥ* here means the illuminator, for we see the same meaning given in such places, "the illuminator of the mind" – *Mano Jyotiḥ*
- *Katopanishat* (II-2-15) says, The Sun, the Moon and the stars do not shine by themselves; for **She** illuminates the mind that illuminates all of these.
- *Chāndogya Upanishat* (VIII-3-4) – The sun shines only when he is illuminated by Him – *Param Jyotirupasampadya*.
- *Parajyotiḥ* is the eight-syllable *mantra* described in the fifth chapter of the *Dakshinamoorti Samhita*. She is in that form.
- 806$^{th}$ name in Sri Lalita Sahasranamam is *Parasmaijyotiḥ* – giving the same meaning.

628. परप्रीती – *Paraprītī*

- One who is very kind to others.
- Typically, as a mother she is very kind to all.

629. परागती – *Parāgatī*

- She is the only way out to devotees who want to get liberated.
- *Kaṭopanishat* (III-11) says – **She** is in the form conclusively mentioned in *Vedānta* statements; *"Sākāshta Sā Paragatiḥ"*.
- 12th name of Sri Vishnu Sahasranamam – *Muktānām Paramā Gatiḥ* – giving the same sense.

630. पराकाष्ठा – *Parākāṣṭhā*

- She is the limit or border for this universe.
- This universe is endless and hence limiting it or finding the border is very difficult. Similarly reaching Sri Devi is also not an easy task.

631. परेशानी – *Pareśanī*

- She is the Parameshwari. She is the Sovereign Supreme.
- **She** is the *Eshwari*, the *shakti* of the universal absolute.
- 396th name of Sri Lalita Sahasranamam is *Parameshvaree* – conveying the same message.
- *Sri Adi Shankara* in his commentary of Sri *Vishnu Sahasranamam* for the 377th name – *Parameshwaraḥ* – he is *Parameshwara,* since he has great wealth and supreme ruling power.

632. पावनी – *Pāvanī*

- This is a repetition of 569th name above.

633. पावकद्युती – *Pāvakadyutī*

- One who has a shining luster/ magnificence.
- The gratification of the mind and body gives brightness to the body. That is called luster. **She** has it.
- 768th name of Sri Lalita Sahasranamam – *Dyutidharā* – conveys the same meaning.
- 176th name of Sri Vishnu Sahasranamam – *Mahādyuti* – has the same sense.

634. पुण्यभद्रा – *Puṇyabhadrā*

- A gentle lady full of virtues. *Punya* = virtue, *Bhadra* = a gentle lady.
- One who is famed for virtue/ righteousness/ holiness.
- Just thinking and communicating the fame of *Sri Devi* will give virtue.
- **She** has the reputation of giving virtue to **Her** devotees.

635. परिच्छेद्या – *Paricchedyā*

- One who appears differently for different persons.
- Devotees try to worship her with form (*saroopam*). Whatever form they want, whatever form they imagine, she appears in that form to them. In reality, she is the Brahmam – the Brahmam is *niroopam* (without any form).

636. पुष्पहासा – *Puṣpahāsā*

- She smiles like a flower.
- Smile – laughter without the teeth being visible. Her smile is very soft like a flower blossoms from the bud.

637. पृथूदरी – *Pṛthūdarā*

- This is a repetition of 512th name above.

638. पीताङ्गी – *Pītāṅgī*

- One who wears a yellow dress.
- 615th name above also conveyed the same message.

639. पीतवसना – *Pītavasanā*

- This name also conveys the same meaning as the previous name.

640. पीतशय्या – *Pītaśayā*

- One whose bed/ couch is in yellow colour.
- Her bed is also in yellow colour according to her yellow dress.

641. पिशाचिनी – *Piśācinī*

- One who lives alongwith the group of ghosts.
- In general, all Devi related texts are called tantras. *Tantric* method of Devi worship is more into evil spirit related. Hence this name.

642. पीतक्रिया – *Pītakriyā*

- One who drinks alcohol.
- It has been described that **She** consumes alcohol to bring the *Rajo* quality to the forefront and not to have mercy on the demons.
- In Sri Lalita Sahasranama, in many places like, it has been mentioned that *Sri Devi* drinks alcohol – 333rd name – *Varuṇeemadavihvalā*, 432 – *Madaghoorṇita Raktākshee*, 510 – *Madhupreetā*, 575 – *Mādhveepānālasā* and 717 – *Madhumatee*.

643. पिशाचघ्नी – *Piśācaghnī*

- One who removes evil spirits.
- Earlier in the 641st name above, it was mentioned that she lives with the ghosts or evil spirits. Here she protects her devotees from evil spirits.

644. पाटलाक्षी – *Pāṭalākṣī*

- Her eyes are like blossomed roses.
- Earlier in couple of places, her eyes were compared to Lotus flower. Here it is compared to Rose flower. There could be no one who is not attracted towards rose flower – in the same way with her eyes.

645. पटुक्रिया – *Paṭukriyā*

- One who cleverly does every work.
- Having taken a task, she completes it cleverly to the core – with 100% perfection.

646. पञ्चभक्षप्रियाचारा – *Pañcabhakṣapriyācārā*

- She likes all the five types of taking food.

- She is fond of all these types of foods and methods of eating.
- Taking food is described as five types viz.
    - *Bhashyam* (Food which has to be eaten by mastication),
    - *Choshyam* or *Charvyam* (which has to be devoured or swallowed),
    - *Bhojyam* (which has to be sucked in),
    - *Lehyam* (That which has to be licked) and
    - *Peyam* (drinking, such as juices, water, milk etc.)
- Lord Krishna says in Shrimad Bhagavad Gita (15.14) – it is I who digest all these types of food.

647. पूतनाप्राणघातिनी – *Pūtanāprāṇaghātinī*

- One who killed the demoness called *Pootana*.
- Actually, lord Krishna, as a baby, killed *Pootana*, who was sent by Kamsa to kill him. But there is no difference between Krishna and Sri Devi. Hence, she gets this name.

648. पुन्नागवनमध्यस्था – *Punnāgavanamadhyasthā*

- One who lives (takes rest) in the midst of the Rhizophora mucronate (*Punnaga*) forest.
- She is fond of every flower, which includes *Punnaga*, which gives a beautiful fragrance.

649. पुण्यतीर्थनिषेविता – *Puṇyatīrthaniṣevitā*

- One who lives in all the sacred places.
- Wherever she lives that place becomes sacred.

650. पञ्चाङ्गी – *Pañcāṅgī*

- One who binds her devotees, like a rope or chain binds the elephants.
- Elephants are bound by rope or chain by the mahout just to control it. In that manner she binds her devotees to control them.

651. पराशक्तिः – *Parāśaktiḥ*

- One who is the Supreme energy/ power.

- Among the elementary substances in the body, skin, blood, flesh, fat and bone were derived from energy (*Shakti*). Marrow, semen, breath and vitality (soul) derived from *Shiva*. The tenth one is called *Parashakti*. This has been explained in the *Kāmikāgama*.
- *Parashakti* can also be interpreted as very great energy. (*Parā – Utkrushta* – very great). The principle of *Shaktas* is that just by unison with *Shakti*, *Shiva attains* enormous greatness. In the first verse of *Soundaryalaharee* and other books stress the same principle.
- *Śvētāśvatara Upanishat* (IV-8) says, His supreme *Shakti* is known in different form; *"Parāsya Shaktir Vivdhaiva Shrooyate"*.
- The *Linga Purana*, says, whatever energy is attributed to any substance is *Sri Devi* and the ruler of all energized substance is the great *Shiva*. Those substances, which possess energy are the manifestation of *Shiva*. The wise recognize the energies in substance to be *Sri Devi*.
- The *Shakti* form of the *mantra* called *Para*.
- 572nd name of Sri Lalita Sahasranamam is also same *Parāshaktiḥ*.

652. परमाह्लादकारिणी – *Paramāhlādakāriṇī*

- One who bestows the great bliss.
- She blesses Paramanandam to her devotees.

653. पुष्पकाण्डस्थिता – *Puṣpakāṇḍasthitā*

- One who lives in the stem of the flowers.
- This stem can also be construed as the *Sushumna nadi* through which the *Kundalini* energy travels from *Mooladara* to *Sahasrara*.

654. पूषा – *Pūṣā*

- *Pūṣā* means the Sun. She is in that form.
- It has been mentioned multiple times that Sri Devi is in the form Sun, Moon, stars, Agni and all. That is being reiterated in this name.
- *Pūṣā* is also the name of one of the twelve Adityas – the offspring of Sage Kashyapa and Aditi.

655. पोषिताखिलविष्टपा – *Poṣitākhilaviṣṭapā*

- One who nourishes the entire universe.

- As Jaganmata, it is she who protects this whole world.

656. पानप्रिया – *Pānapriyā*

- One who fond of partaking.
- She is also fond of drinking the divine nectar.
- She is fond of making Devas to drink the divine nectar.

657. पञ्चशिखा – *Pañcaśikhā*

- She has tufts of hair on the head.
- As a symbol of tuft, it is usual to tie five hairs together. This is called *Pancashikha*.

658. पन्नगोपरिशायिनी – *Pannagopariśāyinī*

- She lies on snakes.
- Lord Vishnu always lies on a snake. As his consort she also.
- Snakes are part and parcel of every god(dess) – Lord Shiva wears it on his neck, Lord Vishnu always lies on it, Lord Ganesh wears it as *yagnopaveetam* and so on.

659. पञ्चमात्रात्मिका – *Pañcamātrātmikā*

- One who has five characteristics as arrows.
- In her physical form, *Sri Devi* has five flowers as arrows in her hands viz. Lotus, Red Lotus, Red Lily, Red Jasmine and Mango flower. The characteristics of these arrows are the effect they make on the objects attacked by them viz., to induce happiness, to give taste, to enthrall, to dry out and to kill.
- The secret form of these arrows is the five self-characteristics (*mātrās*). These characteristics are the unique features of the five elements, which constitute the physical earth.

| Elements | *Bhūtās* | Self-Characteristics | *Mātrās* |
|---|---|---|---|
| Space | *Ākāśā* | Sound | *Shabdā* |
| Wind/ Air | *Vāyu* | Sense of touch | *Sparsha* |
| Fire | *Agnī* | Form/ Colour | *Rūpa* |
| Water | *Jala* | Taste | *Rasa* |
| Earth | *Prithvi* | Odour | *Gandha* |

These characteristics standalone only in the very intricate and atomic state of the elements. The Universe, we perceive is the composite form of these elements and hence each element cannot be perceived separately.

Before the evolution of the universe, from the Absolute (*Moola prakriti*), I.*e*. when matter and energy are in a state of indistinguishable union, the elements could be identified by their individual characteristics- space by sound, air by sense of touch and so on. In this state these are called *Tan Matra*s.

- The arrows hit their targets and give their desired effect, as intended by the person who aims them. A sincere devotee targeted by Sri Devi's arrow will experience the good and pleasurable effects of these characteristics. If the devotee is insincere (bad in intention), the arrows also will give only undesirable effects such as agitation or disturbance, maddening or intoxication, etc.
- These arrows have three forms in three different states – in the physical (*Stoola*) state, they take the form of flowers; in the secret (*Sookshma*) state, they are *Mantras*; and in the Vāsanā state they take the form of *Para*, a form of sound.
- *Sri Devi* also has weapons – Sugarcane as bow and flowers as arrow, like Cupid (Manmatha). Hence, she is called as Kameshwaree. As the emotion of love (Srungara rasa) is important to Her, she is endowed with beautiful things as weapons.
- The presiding deity of sugarcane bow is *Mantrinī* representing the power of intellect (*Buddhi Shakti*) and the presiding deity of arrows is *Dandanatha* – commander-in-chief representing the physical power. The *Vag Devis* symbolically emphasise that intellect and power should act in unison.

660. पृथ्वी – *Pṛthvī*

- She is in the form of the Goddess Earth (*Bhoomi Devi*).
- *Moolādhāram* is the place of abode for *Prithvi Tattvam*. The earth is enchanted in that *Tattva*.
- The world is created by the unison of the soul and the earth. She is in both the forms.
- The thirty-six *tattvas* beginning with the earth, created by **Her** is her seat.
- **She** from whom the universe starting from the earth, manifested – since *Māṇḍūkya Upanishat* (7th verse) says –

*"Prapanchopashamam Shiva madhvaitam Chaturtam Manyante"*.

- Sathyabama, most loved wife of Lord Krishna, was an incarnation of *Bhoomi Devi*. Our Devi was in that form also.
- *Sri Adi Shankara* in his commentary of 187th name of *Sri Vishnu Sahasranamam – Govinda* – mentions, since he bore and took out the earth that is being destructed by the demon *Hiranyaksha*, he is *Govinda*.

661. पथिका – *Pathikā*

- She always wanders/ travels.
- She is so dynamic that she cannot be idle in one place and always travels.

662. पृथुदोहिनी – *Pṛthudohinī*

- She bestows everything adequately to her devotees.
- She confers what they asked and something more also. After satisfying their desires, she exploits them to become desireless and aim for liberation.

663. पुराणन्यायमीमांसा – *Purāṇanyāyamīmāṃsā*

- She is in the form of *Purana*-s, *Nyaya* and *Meemamsa*.
- *Meemamsa* lays down the rules defined in the *Vedas* to do *karmas*. It is of two types viz., *Poorva* (ancient) *Meemamsa* and *Uttara* Meemamsa. Those who follow *Poorva Meemamsa* have full confidence in the *Karma Kanda* of *Vedas*. On the other hand, those who follow *Uttara Meemamsa* believe only the *Gnana Kanda* (*Vedanta*-s) of *Vedas*.
- *Nyaya*, literally means 'rules', 'method' or 'judgment'. *Nyaya Shastra* is also called as *Tarka* (Logic) *Shastra* and its author is *Gautama Maharishi*.
- *Puranas* describe about the important events of glorious past. Unlike history, which we learn in schools, *Puranas* aim to impart moral, religious and spiritual instructions. Sage Vyasa has written 18 Maha Puranas and 18 Upa-Puranas. What is mentioned in Vedas are given as a juice in story format in Puranas. *Pura* = old, *nava* = new. It is very old and very new as well.
- She is in the form of all these.

664. पाटली – *Pāṭalī*

- The word *Patali* has several meanings like possessing trumpet flowers, knowing the secret of others, knowing the time and place and so on. She is in all these forms.

665. पुष्पगन्धिनी – *Puṣpagandhinī*

- She smells like a flower.
- She does not need any artificial perfumes. Her natural aroma itself is like flowers. Also, she always wears one or more flowers. Hence her fragrance is enchanting.

666. पुण्यप्रजा – *Puṇyaprajā*

- She is a virtuous lady.
- She makes her devotees also to do virtuous (*punyas*) acts and not to do sins (*papas*).

667. पारदात्री – *Pāradātrī*

- One who gives the other world to her devotees.
- She only can give the *moksha* to her devotees.

668. परमार्गैकगोचरा – *Paramārgaikagocarā*

- She shows the route to the other world to her devotees.
- In the previous name it was mentioned that she only can give moksha to the devotees. Here it is mentioned that she shows the empirical path to *moksha*. It is for us to travel through the path.

669. प्रवालशोभा – *Pravālaśobhā*

- This is a repetition of 613th name above.

670. पूर्णाशा – *Pūrṇāśā*

- She is complete in all respects.
- **She** is complete in **Herself** and omnipresent, **she** is beyond all the controls of universe.

- **She** is complete in all respects. She does not need anything. Hence, **she** is always contented.
- 685th name of Sri Vishnu Sahasranamam is *Pūrṇa* – giving the same meaning.

671. प्रणवा – *Praṇavā*

- She is in the form of *Pranava mantra*.
- Before creating this world, *Brahma* chant the *Praṇava mantra 'Om'*, by joining the first letters of three *Vedas* (*'A'*, *'U'* and *'M'*). Then he chanted *'Bhooḥ'*, *'Bhuvaḥ* and *'Suvaḥ'* and then created the world. It expanded to chant the words *'Mahaḥ'*, *'Janaḥ'*, *'Tapaḥ'* and *'Satyam'* and expanded as seven worlds. Hence the *Pranava*, the names of these seven worlds are called *Vyāhrutis*. **She** is in this form.
- 102nd and 621st names above also can be referred in this regard.
- 957th name of Sri Vishnu Sahasranamam is *Praṇava* – giving the same meaning.

672. पल्लवोदरी – *Pallavodarī*

- She has her belly region as soft as a new-born leaf.
- 612th name above can also be referred.

673. फलिनी – *Phalinī*

- She is in the form of fruits.
- Fruits here does not only mean the vegetable fruits, but results/ fruits of mantras and stotras.

674. फलदा – *Phaladā*

- She bequeaths the results of the mantras and all. In the previous name it was mentioned that she is in those forms.
- Lots of benefits/ fruits are mentioned in the *phalasruti* part of every *stotra, mantra* and all. She bestows all those benefits for all who chant them with focused mind and devotion.

675. फल्गुः – *Phalguḥ*

- She is in the form of river Phalguni.

- Phalguni is the name of a month. She being controller of *kaalaa* (time) she is in the form this month also.
- Phalguni is a river running in Gaya. People used to do ancestors related karmas here. It has a curse from Sita that it should run only beneath the ground.
- Earlier it was mentioned that she is in the form of all rivers. That includes this Phalgini also.

676. फुत्कारी – *Phutkārī*

- She kicks with her legs, when she is angry.
- Nobody can tolerate her anger – she kicks the enemies with her legs.

677. फलकाकृती – *Phalakākṛtī*

- She hits the goal as an arrow hits the aim.
- The arrow hits the aim without any deviation. In the same way she also acts, in a focused manner.

678. फणिन्द्रभोगशयना – *Phaṇindrabhogaśayanā*

- She is lying on top of the head of the snakes.
- Lord Vishnu lies on Adi Sesha snake, which is the head of snakes. As his consort she also lies on this snake.
- 658th name above can also be referred.

679. फणिमण्डलमण्डिता – *Phaṇimaṇḍalamaṇḍitā*

- She is adorned with lots of snakes.
- She wears snakes as jewels.

680. बालबाला – *Bālabālā*

- *Bālā* denotes young girl. She is younger than that young girl.
- Imagining *Sri Devi* as a young girl and worshipping of *Bālā Tripurasundaree*, is the first stage of *Srividya Upasana*.
- She is the girl *Sri Balatripura Sundaree*.
- 965th name of Sri Lalita Sahasranamam is *Bālā*.

681. बहुमता – *Bahumatā*

- She is a highly regarded/ esteemed lady.
- All are not full-fledged Srividya Upasakas. Still people do Gayatri Japam – normally thrice a day all the 365 days. Hence, she is much thought of Goddess.

682. बालातपनीभांशुका – *Bālātapanībhāṃśukā*

- She shines as a rising Sun.
- Her luster is equated to that of rising Sun.
- In the morning, the rising Sun graciously reduces his intensity of the heat emanating from his light, just for us to see his cherry coloured rays. Similarly, *Sri Devi* is also of Crimson colour. (This colour itself is called *Aruna* colour, one of the names of the Sun himself and also the name of his charioteer).
- 6th name of Sri Lalita Sahasranamam – *Udyadbhānusahasrābhā* – Her luster is equal to infinite (thousands) rays of rising Sun.

683. बलभद्रप्रिया – *Balabhadrapriyā*

- She has affection on Balarama.
- *Balabhadra* and Balarama are synonyms. Revathi is his consort. Our Devi is in the form Revathi and hence she and Balarama have mutual affection.

684. बन्द्या – *Bandyā* or वन्द्या – *Vandyā*

- *Bandyā* or *Vandyā* are synonyms – *ba* and *va* or interchangeable in many languages. They have lots of meanings in Samskrutam – A name of the *varṣa nāḍi*, ray of the Sun, Proper to be worshiped or adored, Adorable, Venerable, Laudable, Commendable, Praiseworthy and so on.
- All these are apt to our *Devi*.

685. बडवा – *Baḍavā* or वडवा – *Vaḍavā*

- Similar to the previous name *ba* and *va* or interchangeable.
- She is friendly with her devotees. With a friend we share everything – be it good or bad, positive or negative, *sukha* or *dukkha* and all.

She lends her shoulder for us to cry on and then pacify us in a friendly way.

686. बुद्धिसंस्तुता – *Buddhisaṃstutā*

- *Saṃstutā* can be interpreted as Praised together, eulogized, agreeing together, harmonious, Intimate, familiar, equal to, intended, aimed at and so on.
- Considering any of the above verbs with *Buddhi* (brainpower) will fit in for our *Devi*.
- The summary is she has to be worshipped with attention or focus to reap the full benefit.

687. बन्दीदेवी – *Bandīdevī*

- She confines herself with her devotees.
- She makes her devotees to confine with her. Once they have started worshipping her, they will not move out.

688. बिलवती – *Bilavatī*

- One who dwells in a cave i.e. heart of the devotees.
- **She** is secretive and dwelling in our heart. Hence, **she** can be identified only by inward search.
- She is most secretive and is in caves, beyond the phenomenal universe – the knowledge that cannot be perceived by senses.
- Cave will also mean the place where Kundalini energy normally sleeps – the bottom tip of the back-bone. As Kundalini energy She resides there.

689. बडिशघ्नि – *Baḍiśaghnī*

- She destroys deceitfulness.
- Dishonesty in the mind will never go alongwith worship. Hence first it has to be removed and then concentrate on *Upasana*. She helps the first step of eradicating the deceit.

690. बलिप्रिया – *Balipriyā*

- One who is delighted with the mighty. Strength is not the physical strength – Meditation / mental strength.

- *Dheera* or *Bali*, those who are able to succeed by destroying ignorance. **She** is fond of them.
- One who conquers the enemies like amorousness, desire, etc., can be called as *Bali*. She blesses them with affection.
- During the incarnation as *Vamana*, *Vishnu* had compassion over the emperor *Bali*. This name indicates that form.
- During worship, for the satisfaction of deities, some articles are offered as *bali*. **She** accepts them with hilarity.
- 677th name of Sri Lalita Sahasranamam is also the same – *Balipriyā*.

691. बान्धवी – *Bāndhavī*

- She is a relative with her devotees.
- Earlier she was mentioned as a friend. Now she is indicated as a relative.
- It can also be construed as she binds the relatives, as already mentioned.

692. बोधिता – *Bodhitā*

- She acts as an instructor/ teacher.
- Normally only a guru instructs or initiates. She takes the role of guru also.
- She is a friend, relative and now a *guru* also. She takes all the roles.

693. बुद्धिः – *Buddhiḥ*

- She is the brainpower of all.
- She is the Shakti without which no one/ nothing can act.

694. बन्धूककुसुमप्रिया – *Bandhūkakusumapriyā*

- One who has the luster similar to the *Bandhooka* flower.
- *Bandhooka* (*Bandhujeeva*) is a famous big tree in Bengal. This belongs to Vengai race of trees (Pterocarpus bilobus). This blossoms pretty yellow mixed with red coloured flowers. **Her** luster is similar to that of this flower.
- 964th name of Sri Lalita Sahasranama – *Bandhooka Kusuma Prakhyā* – also conveys the same sense.

695. बालभानुप्रभाकरा – *Bālabhānuprabhākarā*

- 682nd name above can be referred. This name conveys the same meaning.

696. ब्राह्मी – *Brāhmī*

- One who is in the form of *Saraswathi*, the consort of *Brahma*.
- **She** is in the form of speech and hence can be taken as *Vāgeeshwaree*.
- The senior most among the eight mothers. **She** shines alongwith the vehicle swan, the chanting garland (*japamālā*) and *kamaṇḍalu* (a vessel with water used by sages) in hand. **She** killed the enemies just by sprinkling the water from *kamaṇḍalu* through *darbha* (a sacrificial grass).
- 675th name of Sri Lalita Sahasranamam is also the same – *Brāhmī*.
- 668th name of Sri Vishnu Sahasranamam is also – *Brahmī*.

697. ब्राह्मणदेवता – *Brāhmaṇadevatā*

- **She** is the goddess of Brahmins.
- Actually, Brahmin here does not only mean Brahmin by caste. It really means all those who gets Brahmopadesam through upanayana – Brahmin, Kshatriya and Vysyas. All these people do Gayatri Japam thrice a day on all the days. Hence, she is called as *Brāhmaṇadevatā*.
- Normally all the human incarnations of Lord Vishnu will be *kshatriya*, with some exceptions. On the other hand the human incarnations of Lord Shiva and Sri Devi are brahmins.
- 667th name of Sri Vishnu Sahasranama is also *Brāhmana* – in the form of Brahmins.

698. बृहस्पतिस्तुता – *Bṛhaspatistutā*

- One who is worshipped by *Brihaspati*.
- *Brihaspati* is the *Deva-guru*. Earlier itself, it was mentioned that She is revered by all Devas. Hence, she is adored by *Brihaspati* also.

699. बृन्दा – *Bṛndā* or वृन्दा – *Vṛndā*

- *Bṛndā* means sacred plant basil (*Tulasi*). She is in that form.

- According to Sri Devi Bhagavatam, *Tulasi Devi* is one of the consorts of Lord Vishnu. Our Devi is in her form.
- Lord Vishnu is very much fond of *Tulasi* and hence this sacred plant is very much used in his worship.

700. बृन्दावनविहारिणी – *Bṛndāvanavihāriṇī* or

वृन्दावनविहारिणी – *Vṛndāvanavihāriṇī*

- One who lives in basil plant forest.
- In the previous name, it was mentioned that she is in the form of Tulasi plant. Now it is mentioned as she lives in the Tulasi forest.
- Vrindavan also known as Brindaban, is a historical city in the Mathura district of Uttar Pradesh, India. It is located in the Braj Bhoomi region and is where Lord Krishna spent most of his childhood days. Our Devi lives in this city.

Thus ends 100 divine names on *Sri Gayatri Devi* from 601 to 700

*****

701. बालाकिनी – *Bālākinī*

- Her form is so astounding like a line/ series of cranes.
- Cranes usually move in a series line in a pond like military parade. It will be a wonderful sight. In that manner her form is also so amazing.

702. बिलाहारा – *Bilāhārā*

- She removes or tolerates the defects in karmas (action).
- She does everything with 100% perfection. But her devotees, being normal human beings can only try a near perfection and will definitely have defects/ errors. She helps in removing those defects and even if some error remains, she tolerates it.

703. बिलवसा – *Bilavasā*

- She dwells in a cavity or cave – heart of her devotees.
- This has been mentioned in multiple times in this Sahasranama and other Shakta texts.

704. बहूदका – *Bahūdakā*

- The literal meaning is – She is watery.
- The practical meaning would be – she lives in water. Lord Vishnu lives in ocean of milk. Being his consort, she lives in the ocean.

705. बहुनेत्रा – *Bahunetrā*

- She has lots of eyes. In her virat form she has lots of eyes.
- The first line of *Purusha sooktam*, which describes the virat form of *Brahmam*, mention – *Sahasrākṣa* = having 1000s of eyes.
- 283rd name of Sri Lalita Sahasranama is *Sahasrākshee* – having 1000s of eyes.
- 226th name of Sri Vishnu Sahasranama is also *Sahasrākṣa* – having 1000s of eyes.
- 1000 here means thousands of and not exactly.

706. बहुपदा – *Bahupadā*

- She has lots of legs. In her virat form she has lots of legs.
- Again, the first line of *Purusha sooktam*, which describes the virat form of *Brahmam*, mention – *Sahasrapād* = having 1000s of legs.
- 227th name of Sri Vishnu Sahasranama is also – *Sahasrapād*.

707. बहुकर्णावतंसिका – *Bahukarṇāvataṃsikā*

- She wears lots of jewels in ears.
- Sri Devi does not need any jewels. Otherwise also she is naturally beautiful. But the devotees, for their satisfaction, decorate her with lots of jewels.
- One type of ornament worn by ladies in their ears is called *Tāṭanka* (palm-leaf). The Sun and the Moon take the form of this *Tāṭankas* to beautify *Sri Devi*'s face.
- 262nd name above can also be referred.

708. बहुबाहुयुता – *Bahubāhuyutā*

- She has lots of shoulders (hands). In her virat form she has lots of shoulders.
- *Sahasrabāhu* is the name of Kartaveerya Arjuna, who had 1000s of shoulders. He is a disciple of Lord Dattareya. She is in that form.
- 840th name in Shiva Sahasranama is also *Sahasrabāhuḥ*.

709. बीजरूपिणी – *Bījarūpiṇī*

- She is in the form of *Beejaksharas* (root letters).
- *Hreem* is the *shakta pranavam*. It has been mentioned earlier also that she is in that form.
- The great *pancadashakshari* mantra and the *shodashakshari* mantras comprising of 15 and 16 beeja letters respectively. She is in the form of every letter and then combinedly the mantra itself.

710. बहुरूपिणी – *Bahurūpiṇī*

- She has lots of forms.
- In whatever form the Devotees, whatever form they imagine, like to have worship she appears in that form. In reality, she is the Brahmam – the Brahmam is *Nirupam* (without any form).

711. बिन्दुनादकलातीता – *Bindunādakalātītā*

- *Bindu* is the innermost point (ninth *āvarana*) in *Sri Chakra*, representing *Sarvānandamaya Chakram*. The *Shiva Chakra* circle is the *Bindu*. In a Meru it is the top most point.
- Nada is the sound created by the human body. In the 551st name above it was discussed in details about the types of sound and she is in each type.
- According some schools, in the body, *Bindu* is the *Sahasrara Chakra*. **She** dwells there.
- Kala is art. There are 64 arts and she is in all these forms.
- In a combined manner she lives and has excelled in all the types of *Bindu*, *Nada* and *Kala*.

712. बिन्दुनादस्वरूपिणी – *Bindunādasvarūpiṇī*

- In continuation of the previous name, she is in all the forms of *Bindu* and *Nada*.

713. बद्धगोधाङ्गुलित्राणा – *Baddhagodhāṅgulitrāṇā*

- She has a cattle skin as an armour in her fingers (hands).
- It is armour for her devotees and not for her.

714. बदर्याश्रमवासिनी – *Badaryāśramavāsinī*

- One who lives in Badrikashrama.
- Nara-Narayana, the twin sages do penance in Badrikashrama. She also lives there doing service for them.
- As per Bhagavatam Nara-Narayana are incarnations of Lord Vishnu. They only born as Arjuna and Krishna later. She will be too happy to do service to them.

715. बृन्दारका – *Bṛndārakā* or वृन्दारका – *Vṛndārakā*

- She is in the form of Tulasi plant.
- 384th, 699th and 700th names above can be cross connected with this name.

716. बृहत्स्कन्धा – *Bṛhatskandhā*

- She has a broad trunk part in her body.
- The trunk is an anatomical term for the central part of the bodies which extends from the neck and limbs. This part of her body is broad. This is as per Samudrika Lakshana Shastra.

717. बृहती – *Bṛhatī*

- Her part of the body between the breast and backbone is so lovely.
- *Bṛhatī* is that part of the body between the breast and backbone. That is so lovely for our Devi as per Samudrika Lakshana Shastra.

718. बाणपातिनी – *Bāṇapātinī*

- She is an expert in sending the arrows as rain.
- In the 67th name above, it was mentioned that she is an expert in using bow and arrows. Here it is mentioned that she sends the arrows as rain on enemies.

719. बृन्दाध्यक्षा – *Bṛndādhyakṣā* or वृन्दाध्यक्षा – *Vṛndādhyakṣā*

- She is most prominent among the girl friends (*gopika* ladies), starting from Brinda (Vrinda), of Lord Krishna.

720. बहुनुता – *Bahunutā*

- This is a repetition of 681st name above.
- One who is worshipped by many people.
- As already mentioned all those for whom Upanayana has been performed have to do Gayatri Japam thrice a day on all days. Hence, she is worshipped by many people. In fact, she is adored by all.

721. वनिता – *Vanitā*

- One who is loved by all.
- As a mother she has affection with all.
- *Vanitā* is a kind meter. She is in that form.

722. बहुविक्रमा – *Bahuvikramā*

- *Bahu* = many or much or more. *Vikrama* has lots of meanings like – name of a Tamil year, manner, stability, valour, motion, heroism and so on.
- She is in too much of all these forms.

723. बद्धपद्मासनासीना – *Baddhapadmāsanāsīnā*

- She sits in Padmasana posture bound by it continuously.
- She always sits in Padmasana on a lotus flower.

724. बिल्वपत्रतलस्थिता – *Bilvapatratalasthitā*

- Tulasi leaves are most suitable during pujas for Lord Vishnu. Similarly, Bilva leaf is most suitable during pujas for Lord Shiva. Both these are to be used not as single leaf, but as *Tala* – three (triplets) leaves.
- Earlier it was mentioned that she is happy with tulasi leaves. Here it is mentioned that she becomes happy, if any one does puja with Bilva leaves.
- This implies she is in one form or other loved by Lord Vishnu and Lord Shiva as well.

725. बोधिद्रुमनिजावासा – *Bodhidrumanijāvāsā*

- One who lives beneath the Fig tree.
- Bodhi is a tree of wisdom under which perfect wisdom is attained. It is she who is in the form of that tree.
- This is the tree under which buddha got his wisdom.

726. बडिस्था – *Baḍiṣṭhā*

- One who is of old age.
- Since she originated before all, she is the oldest among all.

727. बिन्दु दर्पणा – *Bindu Darpaṇā*

- One who is pleased when **Her** devotees do *Bindu Tarpanā* (offerings).

- During Navavarna puja, the worshippers do *tarpana* in the *Sarvanandamaya Chakra* (*Bindu*). **She** is pleased with the same.
- **She** is happy with the special *arghya pindas*.
- The details of *Bindu* offerings can be found in *Parasurama Kalpa Sūtra, Paramananda Tantra* and *Laghu Stuti*.
- According to the saying; *Binduricchuḥ* – *Bindu* also means the wise men and **She** is pleased by their offerings.
- 974th name of Sri Lalita Sahasranama is *Bindutarpaṇasantushṭā*.

728. बाला – *Bālā*

- One who is in the form of girl or *Sri Balatripura Sundaree*.
- *Bālāmbikā* is a girl of nine years, similar to the form of *Sri Devi* and *Sri Devi* is fond of her. More details can be found in *Lalithopākyānā*.
- *Sri Devi* is pleased by killing of the sons of *Bhanḍa* by *Bāla*.
- Like a small girl **She** is interested in sports and hence she is called as *Bālā*, says *Tripura Sittāntam* –

  *Bālaleelā Vishishṭadbāleti Kathitāpriye* ll
- The *Śvētāśvatara Upanishat* (IV-3) says – Thou art boy or girl;

  *Tvam Kumara Uta Vā Kumāree*.
- 680th name above may also be referred.
- 965th name of Sri Lalita Sahasranama is *Bālā*.

729. बाणासनवती – *Bāṇāsanavatī*

- One who holds bow and arrow in her hands.
- She holds bow made of sugarcane and arrows made of five flowers in her hands.

730. बडवानलवेगिनी – *Baḍavānalaveginī*

- One who moves so fast like *Baḍavāgni*.
- *Agni*, sacrificial fire, is of various kinds, *Gārhapatya*, *Āhavanīya*, *Dakṣiṇa*, *Badavagni*, *Māṃsāgni*, *Medāgni*, *Asthyāgni*, *Majjāgni*, *Śukrāgni*, *Bhūtāgni*, *Ākāśāgni*, *Vāyvagni*, *Tejogni*, *Jalāgni*, *Pārthivāgni*, *Viṣamāgni*, *Tīkṣnāgni*, *Mandāgni* and so on.
- Out of the above types the story of Badavagni thus goes – Lord Shiva woke up from his meditations and looked around to discover a world on the brink of corruption and being unsalvageable. Shiva decided it was time to wipe the slate clean. Shiva, the destroyer,

opened his world destroying third eye attempting to destroy the three worlds. Out came a terrible fire that threatened all existence. There was panic everywhere. Only Saraswathi remained calm. "Shiva's fire burns only that which is impure and corrupt". She took the form of a river and with her pure waters picked up the dreaded fire from Shiva's third eye. Within the folds of her water she carried the fire far away from the earth to the bottom of the sea where it transformed into a fire breathing mare called 'Badavagni', the beast of doom. Our Devi was that Saraswathi at that time.

731. ब्रह्माण्डबहिरन्तस्था – *Brahmāṇḍabahirantasthā*

- She lives both inside and outside of the *Brahmandam*.
- Our Earth, space and the stellar zone constitute one galaxy (*Brahmāṇḍam*). Universe (*Brahmāṇḍamaṇḍalam*) consists of millions of such galaxies. *Sri Devi* sinks this entire universe in **Her** luster.
- If the upasaka can imagine Macrocosm (*Brahmāṇḍam*) and Microcosm (*Pindāndam*) as an integrated one, then only he can realise the *chakras* in the body.
- *Brahmāṇḍa*, is the results from combination of the five gross elements, consisting of sixteen modifications. *Virat* is the individuality of this. *Svarat* is the individuality of the unmanifested, which is the cause of these two. *Samrat* is the root cause of all these.
- The subtle form of the five elements, the *Brahmāṇḍam*, is the Virat form of Devi.
- *Taitrīya Upanishat* (III-6-1) says that the *Brahmam* is established in the superior radiance-space – fixed there. This ether is of two types – Macrocosm and Microcosm (*Brahmāṇḍam* and *Pindāndam*). Both are tools to identify the *Brahmam*. **She** is in that bright form.
  *Parame Vyoman Pratishṭitaḥ.*

732. ब्रह्मकङ्कणसूत्रिणी – *Brahmakaṅkaṇasūtriṇī*

- One who wears the Kankana tied by Lord Brahma.
- Being his consort, she wears the bracelet given by Brahma.

733. भवानी – *Bhavānī*

- The word *Bhava* has three meanings – Lord *Mahadeva*, the human life cycle and Cupid. **She** gives life (*Ānayathee*) to all these three and hence *Bhavānee*.
- Since Lord *Paramashiva* creates all the living things his name is *Bhava*. His consort is *Bhavānee*.
- Out of the eight forms of Lord *Paramashiva*, the form of water is called *Bhava*. His consort is *Bhavānee*. One who gives life to the living form of water is *Bhavānee*. *Sri Rudram* says –
  *Tayonmruḍa Jeevase.*
- The name of *Sri Devi* in *Sthaneshwara Shetra* is *Bhavanee*.
- In the 22nd *verse* of *Soundaryalaharee*, assuming two usages for the word *Bhavānee* the grace of *Sri Devi* is explained. The word *Bhavānee* is used as an exclamation and as a predicate.

A devotee thinks to address *Sri Devi* as Bhavanee! and asks **Her** – why can't you pass your graceful sight on the slave like me? In this regard the devotee just starts with the two words "*Bhavanee* You" – Instantly *Sri Devi* takes the request as "I have to become you". **She** provides the salvation, which is rare even for the *Devas* including *Brahma* also.

*Bhavani Tvam Dāse Mayi Vitara Drushtim Sakaruṇām*
*Iti Sthothum Vanchan Kathayati Bhavāni Tvamiti Yaḥ* I
*Tadaiva Tvam Tasmai Dishasi Nijasāsyujya Padaveem*
*Mukunḍa Brahmendrasputa Makuta Neerājitapadām* II

- *Mahashoḍanyāsam* (*Prapanchanyāsam*) says that **She** is in the form destruction of the Universe.
- 112th name of Sri Lalita Sahasranama is also the same – *Bhavānī*.

734. भीषणवती – *Bhīṣṇavatī*

- One who is in a dreadful form.
- She takes terrible forms to annihilate the demons.
- Her forms like Kali, Pratyangira and all are so fearful even to Devas.
- In lots of places it has been mentioned that her form is so beautiful. She is beautiful to her devotees, even to her enemies. But her form is fearful during the battle.
- 948th and 949th names in Sri Vishnu Sahasranama are – *Bheema* and *Bheema-parakrama* – conveying the same meaning.
- 4th name in Sri Shiva Sahasranama is also *Bheema*.

735. भाविनी – *Bhāvinī*

- One who creates, protects and destructs the whole world.
- She does all the three tasks means she gets it done through Trimoorties. It is she who enables, provides shakti to the Brahma, Vishnu and Rudra to perform their tasks.

736. भयहारिणी – *Bhayahāriṇī*

- One who nullifies the fears of her devotees.
- One who dispels all fears. The fear here, can be construed as fear of birth and death cycle.
- Though in the 734th name above, it was mentioned that her form is so dreadful, her devotees need not scare about her. She removes the fears of her devotees.
- In *Saptashatee* also we read as;
  *Dāridriya Dukkhaḥ Bhaya Hāriṇee Kā Tvadanyā*
- In Sri Chakra, there are Devis to be contemplated on the four sides and in the center of the *Bindu*. Among them the seven Devis pertaining to West are – *Sanjeevani, Mrithyunjayā, Amruta Sanjeevani Bhairavee, Vajreshwaree, Tripura Bhairavee, Bhayahārini* and *Sampath Pradā Bhairavee*.
- *Brahdāraṇyaka Upanishat* (1.4.2) says *"Tveeteeyādhvai Bhayam"* – there is nothing else other than *Sri Devi* and hence no fear.
- 121st name in Sri Lalita Sahasranamam is *Bhayāpahā*.
- 834th and 935th names of Sri Vishnu Sahasranama are *Bhayāpahaḥ* and *Bhayanāshanaḥ*.

737. भद्रकाली – *Bhadrakālī*

- She is in the form of Bhadrakali.
- In tune with the 734th name above, in her fearful form she is Bhadrakali.
- At Srinagaram, Sri Lalita Devi is surrounded six deities viz., *Bandhinee, Bhadrakālee, Mahāmāyā, Yashasvinee, Raktā* and *Lamboshtee*.
- Bhadram means Mangalam or auspicious. Hence this form is most auspicious.
- There is one *Veda Shanti Patam* beginning with *"Bhadram Karnebhiḥ ..."*

738. भुजङ्गाक्षी – *Bhujaṅgākṣī*

- Her eyes are like snakes.
- The beauty of *Sri Devi*'s face undergoes momentary changes and the motion of her two eyes is compared to the fast movement of snakes, which increases her beauty.
- The beauty of the eyes of Sri Devi has been described in many a place in this Sahasranama and other texts also.

739. भारती – *Bhāratī*

- She is in the form of *Bharati*.
- Bharati is Saraswathi, goddess in-charge of education. It has earlier also mentioned that our Devi is in the form Saraswaṭhi, i.e. Bharati.

740. भारताशया – *Bhāratāśayā*

- One who meditates upon *Bharati* (Saraswathi) is called *Bharata*. She sits in his heart.
- She lives in the hearts of her devotees who all meditate upon her with focus and attention.

741. भैरवी – *Bhairavī*

- The consort of *Bhairava*.
- Since *Bhairavā* does the three functions, he is in terrific form. **She** is his eergy.
- It is a natural quality of ladies to get scared. *Bheeru* – woman. All women taken collectively are called *Bhairavam*. Since **She** is in that form, she is *Bhairavee*.
- In the eighth *Āvarana Devatā Tripurāmbā Chakresvaree mantra*, in the middle division, when '*R*' is eliminated, it is known as *Bhairavee mantra*. *Sri Devi* is in that form.
- A girl of twelve years old is worshipped in the name of *Bhairavee*. Our Devi is in that form.
- 276th name of Sri Lalita Sahasranama is also the same *Bhairavee*.

742. भीषणाकारा – *Bhīṣaṇākārā*

- One who is in the horrific form.
- This name has to be read in conjunction with 734th name above.

743. भूतिदा – *Bhūtidā*

- One who bestows wealth to her devotees.
- 71st, 480th, 483rd, 486th and 522nd names above can also be referred in this context.

744. भूतिमालिनी – *Bhūtimālinī*

- She bestows full wealth to her devotees.
- As an extension of the previous name and other names mentioned above, an adjective 'full' is prefixed in this name.

745. भामिनी – *Bhāminī*

- She gets angry and annoyed whenever needed especially during war.
- Bhamini is alluded to Devi Satyabhama the consort of Lord Krishna. She is in that form.
- She is passionate not only to her devotees, but also to all living beings, she being Jaganmata.

746. भोगनिरता – *Bhoganiratā*

- She is engaged in enjoyments.
- She is the enjoying souls, the enjoyed objects, the enjoyment, the causes of enjoyment and the feel of enjoyment.
- Only the illusion makes such a form, the status of action and enjoyment. Hence it has to be kept in mind this is only an imagination.
- She does what is sought for by the devotees. Based on the individual mindset, whether it is enjoyment or salvation.
- The devotees of *Sri Devi* have both the *Bhoga* (enjoyment) and *Moksha* (salvation) together in their hands.

747. भद्रदा – *Bhadradā*

- One who bequeaths bhadram or auspiciousness or Mangalam to her devotees.

748. भूरिविक्रमा – *Bhūrivikramā*

- She is a might lady.
- She is so mighty that no enemy can stand before her.
- She makes her devotees also mighty. Mighty need not be bodily, but also mentally strong.

749. भूतवासा – *Bhūtavāsā*

- She lives in every living being.
- She is the *jeevatman* and hence she has to be within every living thing.

750. भृगुलता – *Bhṛgulatā*

- One who is worshipped by sage Bhṛgu.
- Maharishi Bhṛgu was one of the Sapta rishis, one of the many Prajapatis (the facilitators of Creation) created by Brahma. He is the moola rishi of Bhargava Community. He was married to Khyati, one of the nine daughters of sage Kardama. One of his descendants was sage Jamadagni, who in turn was the father of Parashuraman, an avatar of Vishnu.
- Bhrigu has scripted "Bhrigu Samhita" a text on Astrology, the pioneer of its kind as a post Script of Jyotisha as one of the Six Vedangas.

751. भार्गवी – *Bhārgavī*

- She is in the form of energy (shakti) within sage Bhṛgu.
- One who is related to sage Bhṛgu.
- Sage Bhṛgu is a son of Brahma. Our Devi is a consort of Brahma. Hence Bhṛgu becomes a son of our Devi also.
- Also, in the previous name it was mentioned that sage Bhṛgu married Khyati. She was daughter of Daksha Prajapati. Our Devi also born as daughter of Daksha Prajapati. Hence sage Bhṛgu is related to Devi.

752. भूसुरार्चिता – *Bhūsurārcitā*

- One who is worshipped by Brahmins.

- In the 697th name above, it was mentioned that she is the Goddess of Brahmins. Here it is reiterated that she is worshipped by Brahmins.
- *Bhūsura* also means earth-god. Our Devi is worshipped as earth-god also.
- She is primarily worshipped by Brahmins the sons of *Bhoodevi*.

753. भागीरथी – *Bhāgīrathī*

- One who is in the form of *Bhāgīrathi* river.
- With compassion on king *Bhagīrathan*, **she** took the form of *Bhāgirathee* (river Ganges) and liberated the kings of *Sāgarā* race, arranged them to moksham.

754. भोगवती – *Bhogavatī*

- Bestower of enjoyments. She is the essence of Luxuries.
- In the 746th name above, it was mentioned that she is engaged in enjoyments. Here it is mentioned that she offers enjoyments to her devotees.
- *Bhogavatī* is a sacred river of the serpent-demons. She is in that form. In fact, she is in the form of all rivers.
- *Bhogavatī* also means night of the (*Dwitiya*) 2nd lunar day. She is in the form all *thithi nitya* Devis, including this.

755. भवनस्था – *Bhavanasthā*

- She exists in future as well as the present and past.
- She is eternal.

756. भिषग्वरा – *Bhiṣagvarā*

- She is the best physician in the world.
- She is a physician not only for the diseases pertaining to the body, but also to the disease of samsara – birth-death life cycle.
- Twins – Ashwini Devas – are Physicians of Devas. In Mahabharata Nakula and Sahadeva were sons of these twins. She is in their forms.
- 579th name of Sri Vishnu Sahasranama is *Bhiṣak* conveying the same meaning.

757. भामिनी – *Bhāminī*

- This is a repetition of 745th name above.

758. भोगिनी – *Bhoginī*

- She is in the Form of Fortunes and Happiness.
- She grants all Fortunes and Happiness to her devotees.

759. भाषा – *Bhāṣā*

- She is in the form of all Languages.
- She is the Expression, Script and Thought.
- She in the form Saraswathi, being the goddess of learning, she takes the forms of languages.

760. भवानी – *Bhavānī*

- This is a repetition of 733rd name above.

761. भूरिदक्षिणा – *Bhūridakṣiṇā*

- *Bhuri dakshina* means abundant dakshinas or gifts/ gratifications to Brahmins who conduct various functions like Yagnas, Homa kriyas, Samskaras, Vratas, Pitru Karyas, or any such Vedic and traditional tasks – She is in that form.
- Bhagavan Vishnu asserts that any Dakshina given to such Brahmins would reach Him only. She is a consort of Lord Vishnu and hence equally applicable to her also.

762. भर्गात्मिका – *Bhargātmikā*

- She is the Soul of splendour.
- She is the ultimate illumination. It has been mentioned earlier also that everything gets illuminated only from her.

763. भीमावती – *Bhīmāvatī*

- She is fuming and incensed on battle fronts ready to charge and destroy evil energies.

- She destroys evil forces; however extraordinary they might be.

764. भवबन्धविमोचिनी – *Bhavabandhavimocinī*

- She is unique in smashing the tough and harsh bonds of Samsara.
- This bondage of samsara can be relived only by her.

765. भजनीया – *Bhajanīyā*

- She is always worthy of litanies and supplications.

766. भूतधात्रीरञ्जिता – *Bhūtadhātrīrañjitā*

- She is the prime reason of existence and upkeep of all the Beings in Creation.

767. भुवनेश्वरी – *Bhuvaneśvarī*

- The Shakti due to whom the Universal evolution is made possible and the various Beings are sustained without hassles.
- One who is the sovereign ruler of the universe comprising of fourteen worlds.
- There are seven worlds beneath this earth viz., *Athalam, Vitalam, Sutalam, Talātalam, Mahātalam, Rasātalam* and *Patālam*. There are six worlds above the earth viz., *Bhuvarloka, Suvarloka, Mahālokā, Janolokā, Tapo Lokā* and *Sathya Loka*. These 13 alongwith the earth are the 14 worlds. **She** steers these 14 worlds as per **Her** wish.
- The word *Bhuvanā* has many meanings – earth, heaven, water, etc. **She** is the head of all these.
- The *Māyābeeja, Hreem* is called *Bhuvaneshvaree beeja*. **She** is the presiding deity of this. The letter *'Ha'* indicates the sky, *'R'* indicates fire and *'E'* indicates water. Since **She** only created all these and originated this world, **she** is called *Bhuvaneshwaree*.
- The word *Hreem*, has many meanings like *Hrullekā Beeja, Lajjā Beeja, Chintāmaṇi Beeja*, etc.
- There are three divisions viz., *Divya, Sidda* and *Mānvaugha* in the lineage of teachers (*Gurus*). In this, in the *Mānvaugha* division there was a teacher by name *Bhuvanānandanātha*. As per *Tripurasiddhānta*, since **She** appeared before and blessed him, **she** got the name *Bhuvaneshvaree*.

  *Bhuvanānanda Nāthasya Prasannatvāt Maheshvaree* I

*Bhuvaneshvareetivikhyātā Shambhavee Bhuvaneshvaree* II

- 294th name of Sri Lalita Sahasranama is also the same *Bhuvaneśvarī*.

768. भुजङ्गवलया – *Bhujaṅgavalayā*

- She is in the form of the Kundalini energy coiled in 3.5 rounds.
- She being in the form of a Kundalini energy has been mentioned in multiple places.
- Like a mighty coiled serpent encircles and she controls the worlds in her hands.

769. भीमा – *Bhīmā*

- She is in the ferocious form against the demons.
- 763rd name above can also be referred.

770. भेरुण्डा – *Bheruṇḍā*

- She is in the form of Bherunda.
- Sri Devi's 15 Thiti Nitya Devis being the Limbs of the Form of Pure Consciousness – The 15 Thiti Nitya Devis – *Kāmeshwaree, Bhagamālini, Nityaklinna, Bherundā, Vahnivāsini, Mahāvajreshwari, Shivadūti, Twarita, Kulasundaree, Nithya, Neelapathāka, Vijayā, Sarvamangalā, Jwālāmālini* and *Chitra*. In the center *Sri Devi* **Herself** occupies the *Bindustāna* as the 16th *Mahānitya*. In the bright half of the lunar month (*Shukla paksha*), they are worshipped starting from *Kāmeshwaree* and ending with *Chitra* and in the dark half of the lunar month (*Krishna paksha*) starting from *Chitra* and ending with *Kāmeshwaree*, in the reverse order. *Jwālāmālini* is worshipped on the fourteenth day of bright half and on the second day of the dark half.
- According to another story – Bherunda (Sarabeshwara) was the double-faced mythological bird referred to in Puranas which was a manifestation of Lord Shiva as it became impossible to restrain and tranquilize the fury of Lord Narasimha after decimating the Danava Hiranyakasipu. His consort is our Devi.

771. भागधेयिनी – *Bhāgadheyinī*

- She is the provider of excellent prosperity.

- 31, 139, 157, 483, 493 and 588th name above can also be referred.

772. माता – *Mātā*

- The supreme mother. The Singular Mother of the Universe.
- When we are in deep trouble, the first word uttered by us involuntarily is *Ma*. Human beings are afflicted by three kinds of *Tapas* (difficulties), which cannot be solved by the mother in her human form. The possession of the power to resolve these difficulties makes **Her** the "Superior Mother".
- Worshipping **Her**, who has given birth to the whole world, will prevent birth again in this world from the mother's womb. The best of love is mother's affection. Hence to contemplate and worship **Her** as the mother will give us proximity to Her.
- Merging the three letters of *Bāla Mantra* to the six consonants *ha*, *sa*, *ka*, *la*, *ra* and *ta*, we derive a three-part *Mantra*, which is indicated as *Māta*. This is contained in this name. This secret *Mantra* has to be learnt through an appropriate teacher, in a proper way.
- There is a *Shlokā* called *"Matā Kunḍaliní Kriya Madhumathee"* in the book *"Laghustuthi"* written by a great *Devi Upasakar*, *"Laghu Bhattarakar"*. The word *Mātā* mentioned here also has a special cryptic meaning. This name is an indication of that special meaning.
- Mother here also indicates that **She** has given birth to the entire universe. It indicates one of the three main functions of the Supreme Being viz. creation. *Vedas* also reflect the same sense in –
  *"Yathoo Vāimanī Bhoothānī Jāyanthee"*
- Various names in Sri Lalita Sahasranama also say that She is the mother. For instance – 1 – *Śreemātā*, 457 – *Mātā*, 823 – *Jananee*, 826 – *Prasavitree* and 985 – *Ambā*.
- In Saptashatee also we read –
  *Yā Devi Sarvabhooteśu Mātru Roopeṇa Samstitā*

773. माया – *Māyā*

- One who is in the form of illusion.
- The energy which obscures, what is plain, is *maya* or illusion. Or to make plain what is not available. Both these are the acts of *maya*.
- In addition, the acts of dream or supernatural powers are all due to *maya*. The *Devi Purana* says, "It is called *maya* because it is the instrument of marvelous actions, producing unheard of results, like dreams or jugglery".

- The same is set forth at length in the *Varāha Purana* (in 37 verses), as a dialogue between *Vishnu* and Bhoomi Devi.
- In *Shrimad Bhagavad Geeta* (VII-14) also it is mentioned that the divine illusion is made up of qualities, is hard to surmount; but those who take refuge in *Sri Krishna* alone, can cross over it.
- The *Shandilya Sutra* (86) says, "His (the Lord's) energy is *maya*".
- The power of *maya* has been explained in *Saptashatee* also.
- *Sri Muthuswami Deekshatar* also has sung addressing *Sri Devi* as '*Māye*'.
- The *Shakta Pranava*, also called as *Bhuvaneshwaree Beeja* or *Hrullekā*, is called as *Māyā Beeja*. **She** is in that form.
- In the *Mahāshoḍa Nyāsa*, illusion is being appropriated in three places – in *Prapancha Nyāsa* as *Dveeparoopā* and *Guhāroopa* and in *Devata Nyāsa* as *Sahasra Koṭigaṇeshwara Kulasevita*. **She** is in these forms.
- It is being reiterated here that the secret initiations have to done only through appropriate teachers. Only with the advice of the teacher the illusion is to be reached (according the *Shakta* method) and the illusion is to be crossed (according to non-duality philosophy).
- According to the non-duality advised by *Sri Adi Shankara*, only when the illusion is removed the knowledge of *Brahmam* can be obtained. According to *Sri Vidya* practice illusion is the energy (*shakti*) of *Brahmam* only.
- *Sree Kanchi Kamakoti Paramacharya*'s talk in this regard is (The book – Voice of God, 6th Volume) - The question, that why and how the illusion happened, does not arise according to non-duality principle. *Shakta Sastra* says that *Chit Shakti* only plays a game by reflecting the illusion in many forms. The soul, in the as is form – having the senses as tools, has to unite with the eternal *Brahmam*.

The *Brahmam* only seems as soul due to illusion. The non-duality principle says that, if the illusion is removed through knowledge then the soul will become the *Brahmam*. Basically, the soul and *Shiva* are one and the same. Again, it is same at the end of salvation also. This has been clearly accepted in *Shakta* more particularly in *Sri Vidya Tantra*. The difference between the two is the creative duality. No difference about salvation. It has to be simply ignored that it is only illusion which seem to be dual. *Shakta* says that *Sri Devi* created it. All this duality enters into that *Sri Devi* and **She** plays a game. This illusion can be overcome by worshipping and praying to **Her**. Overcome this illusion and merge with the root cause. Again, merge with that *Brahmam*, wherein this root cause itself has merged, as a single entity.

- The combined form of *Ichā*, *Gnāna* and *Kriyā shaktis* is called illusion. Further details in this regard may be seen in the explanation given in *Soota Samhita*.
- 716th name of Sri Lalita Sahasranama is also the same *Māyā*.
- 170 and 302nd names of Sri Vishnu Sahasranama – Mahamaya and Naikamaya – he is the Maya and he creates various maya-s.
- Many Puranas, Sri Lalita Sahasranamam, Srimad Bhagavat Gita, Sri Devi Bhagavatam, Sri Vishnu Bhagavatam, Saptashati and all talk in detail about illusion.

774. मधुमती – *Madhumatī*

- One who is fond of alcohol.
- The word *Madhu* means honey or alcohol. Alcohol also is one of the offerings during worship. Those who worship in religious manner offer honey, others offer alcohol itself.
- In *Saptashatee* also it has been mentioned that *Sri Devi* consumes alcohol.
- *Veda* says that the form of *Sri Devi* itself is like a honey;

  *Mahtyai Vā Etaddevatāyai Roopam Yanmatu.*
- *Chāndogya Upanishat* says that the honey of *Devas* is Sun. **She** is in that form of *Madhumatee* – *Āditryo Vai Devamadhu*.
- *Yoga shastras* mention about four types of *Yogins*. The fourth type is called *Gatikrāntyabhāvās*. These are the greatest among the four. Still they have to cross (*tāraka*) seven more stages. In that the seventh stage is called *Madhumatee*. **She** is in that form.
- The knowledge obtained at that last stage helps crossing. Hence, since that name is given to *Sri Devi*, it can be considered as *Samsara Tarika* (to cross these worldly affairs). *Yoga Sutra* (*Patanchali Yoga Sutra* 55) says about this;

  *Tārakam Sarvavishyam Sarvathā Vishyakramam Cheti Vivekajam Gnānam*
- **She** is in the form of a river called *Madhumatee*.
- 717th name of Sri Lalita Sahasranama is also the same *Madhumatī*.
- The fact that *Sri Devi* is interested in alcohol has been mentioned in many a name of Sri Lalita Sahasranama. For instance – 330–*Kādambareepriyā*, 333–*Vārunee Madavihvalā*, 432–*Madaghoorṇitaraktākshee*, 433–*Madapāṭalagaṇdabhooḥ*, 510–*Madhupreetā*, 575–*Mādhveepānālasā* and 576–*Matta*.
- Further, while commenting for the 235th name of Sri Lalita Sahasranama – *Catushshashṭiyupacārādhyā,* Sri Bhaskara Raya explains – one of the 64 offerings as vessel filled with alcohol.

775. मधुजिह्वा – *Madhujihvā*

- She is with the tongue of nectar.
- She talks so sweet. She is the goddess of speech and her speech is very sweet.
- 27th name of Sri Lalita Sahasranama – *Nijasallāpamādhurya Vinirbhartsita Kacchapee – Sri Devi*'s voice is so sweet, that it wins over the sweetness of *Sri Saraswathi's Veena*.
- 66th verse of *Soundaryalaharee* starts with *Vipanchyā Gāyanthi* – When *Sri Saraswathi* played her *Veena* in the presence of *Sri Devi*, **she** admired its sweetness and uttered the word 'awesome'. On hearing this *Sri Saraswathi* was ashamed by the sweetness of *Sri Devi*'s voice which surpassed the sound of her *Veena* and kept it inside its cover.

776. मधुप्रिया – *Madhupriyā*

- One who is totally delighted with the drink of nectar.
- 656th name above can also be referred in this regard.

777. महादेवी – *Mahādevī*

- She is the Moola Prakriti.
- One who has immense and immeasurably big body.
- *Shiva* is known as *Mahadeva*. His consort is *Mahadevi*.
- *Mahadevi* is the presiding deity at the *Salagrama Chakra Teertha* on the banks *Gandaki* river in Nepal.
- **She** has got entire energy of all *devas*. **She** is the greatest of all the *Devis*. Hence *Mahadevi*.
- 209th name of Sri Lalita Sahasranama is also the same *Mahādevī*.
- 491st name of Sri Vishnu Sahasranama is also *Mahādevaḥ*.
- 599th name of Sri Shiva Sahasranama is also *Mahādevaḥ*.

778. महाभागा – *Mahābhāgā*

- She is the Incomparable benefactor of fortune.
- In *Saptashatee* (I chapter) also we read the same message;

  *Vishayaśca Mahābhāga yāti Śaivam Prutak Prutak* II
- 370th name of Sri Vishnu Sahasranama is also *Mahābhāga*.

779. मालिनी – *Mālinī*

- One who wears different kinds of garlands ranging from flowers to jewels and even skulls as per the manifestations of Devis and Shaktis as required.
- *Malinee* is the name of the presiding deity of fifty-two letters in Samskrutam.
- In *Āmnāya Pooja* also worship is done by a *mantra* called, *Mālinee Mantra Rājam*.
- *Mālinee* is a companion of *Sri Devi*, mentioned in the *Vamana Purana*, in the section on the marriage ceremony of *Parvati*; The *Mālinee* clasped the foot of *Hara*. *Hara* said "whatever you ask I will give, release my foot". *Mālinee*, then replied to *Shiva*, "Oh *Shiva*, bestow your prosperity on my friend, then you will be released". Then *Shiva said*, "I have already given, release me, etc.".
  *Atho'vācha Mahadevo Dattam Mālinee Munchamām* II
- *Mālinee* is a certain meter. Its character is 15 letters. She is in that form.
- According to the *Vishva* dictionary, *Mālinee* means, a certain meter, a woman of the florist caste, the city of Champā, Gouree and river Ganga. She is in all these forms.
- *Mālinee*, according to *Dhaumya*, is a girl of seven years of age.
- 455th name of Sri Lalita Sahasranama is also the same *Malinī*.

780. मीनलोचना – *Mīnalocanā*

- Her looks and eyes sparkling and likening to fishes in waters.
- One whose eyes look like fish swimming in the stream of beauty of *Sri Devi*'s face.
- The motion of *Sri Devi*'s two eyes is compared to the fast movement of fish in this stream, which increases its beauty.
- Fish are not mammals but lay eggs. It is believed that fish nurse their offspring just by affectionate looks. Similarly, *Sri Devi*'s eyes, which are compared to fish swimming in the stream of beauty uplifts **Her** devotees just by a gracious look. She is therefore called *Meenakshi*.
- In the 18th name of Sri Lalita Sahasranama, it is referred to as *Meenābhalochana*.
- In the 308th name of Sri Lalita Sahasranama the same message is conveyed by the name *Rājeevalochanā*.

781. मायातीता – *Māyātītā*

- She is far beyond the realms of Maya or delusions.
- Maya or illusions are due to ignorance. She is not affected by any of the Maya or illusion.

782. मधुमती – *Madhumatī*

- She is engrossed in drinking honey or sweet liquors;
- This is a repetition of 774th name above.
- 168th name of Sri Vishnu Sahasranama is *Madhu* itself.

783. मधुमांसा – *Madhumāṃsā*

- She has the profile of the one engaged in consuming wine and meat.
- Madhu – the fire *tattva* – the fall that spreads from *Sahasrāhāra* – the *Brahmātmaikya Akanḍākāra Vruddhi*.
- Meat – the earth *tattva* – cuts with the knife of maturity, the animal form controlled by the righteousness and the wickedness. This makes the self-form integrated with the supreme being.
- In the *Navāvarṇa Pooja* there are five *articles* starting with the letter '*Ma*' – *Madhu, Māmsam, Mangai, Meen* and *Mudra* (alcohol, meat, girl, fish and signet).
- Those who are interested in the knowledge of self, have to use some representative in the place of alcohol, meat, etc., in reality.

784. मधुद्रवा – *Madhudravā*

- She is pleased with the offerings of honey/ wine.
- Earlier it was mentioned that she is pleased in drinking Madhu. Hence, she is pleased with the offerings by the devotees.

785. मानवी – *Mānavī*

- She assumes human form, when necessary. For instance, Meenakshi form is a human one.
- We know the stories of Lord Vishnu taking many incarnations in human forms.
- One who is high/ broad minded.

- *Māna* may mean the elevation of mind, regard, the expression indicating the forgiveness of sin, proof, or measurement. **She** has all these and hence *Māṇavī*.

786. मधुसम्भूता – *Madhusambhūtā*

- She takes the human form in the Chaitra month or at the beginning of the year formally.
- In continuation of the previous name, she takes the human form on the day of Vishu.

787. मिथिलापुरवासिनी – *Mithilāpuravāsinī*

- She was Sita – daughter of Janaka, princess of Mithila.
- In Ramayana she took the form of Sita, consort of Sri Rama.
- As mentioned in the 785th name above, Sita is an incarnation as a human being.

788. मधुकैटभसंहर्त्री – *Madhukaiṭabhasaṃhartrī*

- She decimated Madhu and Kaidabha Demons.
- As per chapter 1 of Durga Saptashatee, Madhu and Kaidabha were demons originated from the ears of Lord Vishnu. Actually, it was Lord Vishnu who fought with and destroyed these two demons. But Sri Devi helped him behind the scene in this battle and it is mentioned that she destroyed the demons.

789. मेदिनी – *Medinī*

- She is in the form Earth Devi (Bhooma Devi).
- 660th name above can also be referred.
- 533rd name of Sri Vishnu Sahasranama is *Medinīpati* – the Lord of the Earth.

790. मेघमालिनी – *Meghamālinī*

- She is surrounded by clouds.
- Clouds around her looks like she is wearing a garland of clouds.

791. मन्दोदरी – *Mandodarī*

- Gayatri Devi assumes the form of Mandodari the soft bellied wife of Ravana in Ramayana and daughter of Mayasura.
- Mandodari is reckoned as one of the five illustrious maidens of the yore viz., Ahalya, Draupadi, Kunti, Tara and Mandodari. This list may slightly vary from text to text.

792. महामाया – *Mahāmāyā*

- **She** is in the form of great illusion (*Mahāmāyā Swroopiṇee*).
- Since **She** creates lust to all *devas* starting from *Brahma*. *Durga Saptashatee* says;

  *Gnāninām api Chetāmsi Devee Bhagavateehisā* ।
  *Balādākrushya Mohāya Mahāmāyā Prāyacchati* ॥

- The name of the *Shakti* seed letter *Hreem* is *Māyā* or *Shakti*. The complete energy of *Sri Devi* is hidden in this. This *Hreem* seed is a knot like for all the three *kooṭās* of *Panchadashākesharee mantra*. **She** is in the form of that *Hreem* seed letter as *Mahāmāya*.
- This seed letter *Hreem* has four splits as - *'H'* + *'R'* + *'E'* + *'M'* – it is similar to - a tree's all the parts (organs) are subtly hidden within a seed. Hence *Mahāmāya*.
- The *Kalika Purana* says – **She** who always makes him devoid of knowledge, the being who possessed knowledge (of his real nature) whilst in the womb, compelled him to take birth by means of the wings of delivery and leads him by reason of the *samskara* of previous births to desire of food etc.; thence into confusion, egotism, doubt, subsequently leading him again and again to undergo (the stages of) anger, distress and greediness and then leads him into (sensual) desire causing anxiety day in and day out, producing sometimes pleasures and sometimes pain, is called the *Mahāmāyā* (great illusion).
- According to one lexicon *maya* means compassion. Hence, *Mahāmāyā* means full of compassion.
- In the 773rd name above it was mentioned that she is *Māyā*. Here it is mentioned that she is *Mahāmāyā* – prefixing the greatness to it.
- 215th name of Sri Lalita Sahasranama is also the same *Mahāmāyā*.

793. मैथिली – *Maithilī*

- Maithili is the princess of Mithila city. Our Devi is in that form.

- The same was mentioned in the 787th name above also.

794. मसृणप्रिया – *Masṛṇapriyā*

- She is fond of sweet and soft materials to eat.
- Having the quality of Sattva Guna, she likes the Sattvic foods.

795. महालक्ष्मी – *Mahālakṣmī*

- One who is in the form of a great giant (*Mahatee*) *Lakshmi*.
- **She** is in the form *Maha Lakshmi*, the consort of *Maha Vishnu*.
- As per *Padma Purana, Maha Lakshmi* is the presiding deity at the *Karaveera* in Kolhapur.
- In *Durga Saptashatee*, it is mentioned that *Sri Devi* took the form of *Maha Lakshmi* with 18 hands to kill *Mahishasura*.
- There is a story (in *Mairala tantram*) that *Maha Lakshmi*, a form of *Sri Devi* killed the demon called *Mahālan*;

  *Mahālanāmakam Daityam Sayati Kshapayateeticha* I
  *Mahālasā Mahālakshmee Ritikhyātimāgatā* II
- In many places, it has been mentioned that *Sri Devi* has the name *Maha Lakshmi*.

  *Mahālakshmeeritikhyātā Shyāmāsarvamanoharee* II
  (*Shiva Puranam*)
  *Shriyam Lakshmeem Ambigām Aoupalāngam*
  (*Ayushya Sooktam*)
- As per the saying – *Trayodashe Mahālakshmee* – a girl of thirteen years of age is called *Mahālakshmee*. She is fit to be worshipped on the thirteenth day from full or new moon day (*Thrayodashi thithi*).
- 212th name of Sri Lalita Sahasranama is also the same *Mahālakṣmī*.

796. महाकाली – *Mahākālī*

- One who is great and in the form of *Kali*.
- One who decides the time (*kala*) is called *Kali*. One who decides the time for *Kalan* (*Yama*, the deity of death) is *Mahakali*.
- The *Mahakali* is the deity worshipped at Ujjain as the consort of *Shiva* in the form of *Mahakala*.
- **She** as *Mahakali*, is worshipped as the deity of the first story in *Saptashatee*.
- *Kali* also means one who is black in colour. *Sri Devi* has been mentioned as red in colour in many a place. When **She** takes the

rude form, **She** like black in colour. *Sri Kanchi Kamakoti Paramacharya* has explained this (the book Voice of God – 1st Volume). The gist of it is given below – It is very apt that *Sri Devi* is red in colour, since **She** is very near to the pure and white Supreme Being and also since **She** is in the form of compassion.

The death is a big sleep. We are peaceful without any sorrows during sleep. In the same way, the soul after death is very peaceful without the fruits (and the corresponding enjoyments) of any of the actions and the related entanglements. Just to give us the peace by removing us temporarily from the bondage of actions, *Shiva* does the role of destroyer. Only the learned who has removed the ego "I do the actions", can permanently come out of the cycle of actions. But, to temporarily remove even the great sinners from this cycle, *Sri Devi* creates the death with compassion. Only when this world is left, one can come out of the worldly movements, reach the salvation and obtain the peace permanently. The feel of that we are in the state of peace and be in peace is called the state of *Samadhi* – the eternal state. This is the result of the task of blessings (*anugraha*) of *Sri Devi*. The next stage is to remain in peace without even this thought – either in sleep or in death. Hence the state even next to *Anugraha* is the death.

- Even in agriculture before even thinking of sowing the new seeds, the previous plants have to be harvested, to be weeded off and the ground ploughed. Death is similar to making the ground ready for next sowing.
- 737th name above can also be referred.
- 751st name of Sri Lalita Sahasranama is also the same *Mahākālī*.

797. महाकन्या – *Mahākanyā*

- One who is in the form of great and young girl. Worship is done on girl children of ages 2 to 10.
- During festival like *Navaratri*, during *Navāvarṇa Pooja* and at the end of *Chandi Homa*, worship is done on young girls (*kanya*-s) and young boys (*brahmachari*). Our Devi is worshipped in the form of those young girls.
- Worshipping young girls (*kanya*) is described in detail in the 26th chapter, third *Skanda* of Sri *Devi Bhagavatam*.
- In *Kanya pooja*, it is customary to name the girls according to their ages.

798. महेश्वरी – *Maheśvarī*

- One who is the supreme sovereign.
- One who is the consort of Lord *Maheshvara* (*Paramashiva*).
- Gayatri Devi assumes the premier forms of Devis representing Prosperity, Destruction, Virginity and Might respectively.
- The three gods *Brahma*, *Vishnu* and *Rudra* do three main functions of creation, protection and destruction. *Maheshvara* is above these three and is transcending the three characteristics (*Gunas – Rajas*, *Tamas* and *Sattva*) in equal proposition. His *Shakti* form is *Maheshwari*.
- As per *Veda*, *Maheshvara* is devoid of the three *gunas* (*nirguna*) and his consort of *Maheshwari*.
- The word *Maheshvara* means – one who is the head of all the *Bota Ganas* or by all the great practicing celibacies. His consort is *Maheshwari*.
- *Linga Purāṇā* says –

  *Tamasā Kālardrākyo Rajasā Kanakāṇṭa Jaḥ* I
  *Satvena Sarvako Viṣhṇuḥ Nairguṇyena Maheshwaraḥ* II
- 208th and 750th names of Sri Lalita Sahasranama are also *Maheśvarī* and *Maheshwari* with minor difference in spelling.

799. माहेन्द्री – *Māhendrī*

- She is of the form of Sachi Devi the consort of Indra.
- There are 8 *Prakata Yoginis* as *Matruka Devis*, in the middle layer of *Chatusrā* (*Noopurā*) of *Sri Chakra*. They are; *Brahmi, Maheshwari, Koumari, Vaishnavi, Varahi, Māhendree, Chamunda* and *Maha Lakshmi*. Each of these 8 Yoginis has one crore allied *Devis*. Hence a total of 8 x 8 = 64 crores of *Yoginis*. Hence *Sri Devi* is called as being served by these *Yoginis* – *Mahācatushshashṭikoṭi Yoginee Gaṇasevita*.

800. मेरुतनया – *Merutanayā*

- She takes the form of the daughter of Meru mountain.
- One who is daughter Himavan, the king of mountains.
- According to the saying; *Meruḥ Sumeruḥ Hemādriḥ* – *Meru* is a golden mountain. It is said that *Sri Devi*'s dwelling place, *Chintamani* house is at the top of the centre peak.

Thus ends 100 divine names on *Sri Gayatri Devi* from 701 to 800

*****

801. मन्दारकुसुमार्चिता – *Mandārakusumārcitā*

- One who is worshipped with Mandara flowers (shoe flower – Hibiscus Rosa-sinensis).
- *Mandara* is one of the five trees in the world of *Devas* and also indicates white *Erukka* (white – wild weed).
- 776th name of Sri Lalita Sahasranama is *Mandārakusumapriyā* – one who is fond of Mandara flowers.

802. मञ्जुमञ्जीरचरणा – *Mañjumañjīracaraṇā*

- She is adorned with jingling ornaments of ankles.
- The anklets worn on *Sri Devi*'s feet have bells fixed with gems. They make a sweet and soft jingle while oscillating. They add *Sri* to **Her** lotus feet. (*Sri* is one word which cannot be translated into any other language, to bring forth its entire meaning. Broadly it means "all that is good").
- 542nd name above can also be referred in this context.

803. मोक्षदा – *Mokṣadā*

- She is the Unique Shakti who is capable of bestowing Salvation.
- In the prelude to Sri Lalita Trishatee it has been mentioned that Sri Vidya is only way to reach liberation. There is no doubt in this –
  *"Mokshaika Hetu Vidyā Śreevidyāiva Na Samshayaḥ"*
- *Sri Adi Shankara* in his *Viveka Chooḍāmaṇi* (verses 32, 33) says – She is the Moksha Karana –
  *Moksha Kāraṇa Sāmagriyam Bhaktireva Gareeyasee* ।
- She bestows all stages from heaven to *moksha* as per our wish. **She** gives various stages of liberation – stages from heaven to *moksha* – as per eligibility.
- *Vāmakeshwara Tantra* says *Vāmakeshwara Tantra* says;
  *Vāgeeshwaree Gnānashaktiḥ Vāgbhave Moksharoopiṇee* ।
- Earlier it was mentioned that she provides all the four objects of human endeavour viz., *dharma* (righteousness), *arttha* (wealth), *Kama* (desires) and *moksha* (salvation).

804. मञ्जुभाषिणी – *Mañjubhāṣiṇī*

- Devi has an outstanding soft and sonorous voice.

- It is one of the qualities of ladies to speak softly. Our Devi also speaks so softly.
- 464th name of Sri Lalita Sahasranama – *Kālakaṇṭhī* – *Kāla* means a soft low sound, *kanṭha* means throat, i.e. a soft low sound proceeds from her throat and hence *Kālakaṇṭhī*.

805. मधुरद्राविणी – *Madhuradrāviṇī*

- Devi becomes happy with sweet liquids offered by her devotees.
- Hence, she talks in low, sweet and melting tones of voice.
- This name is in continuation of the previous name.

806. मुद्रा – *Mudrā*

- She is an expert in showing various mudras with her hands.
- Mudra is gestures of hand-palm fingers expressing thoughts, ideas and actions – Abhaya Mudra symbolising Protection and fearlessness, Anjali Mudra expression of respect and reverence, Jnana-Chin-Yoga Mudra displaying Dhyana and Meditation and so on.
- 51st verse of Soundaryalaharee – *Sri Devi* gestures all the emotions one at a time excepting the tranquility emotion (which **She** always shows).
- The mudra, signet, is one of the five important parts of *Sri Vidya*. By combining the fingers and showing it in a particular form is called signet. Each signet, cryptically, indicates a message or an emotion. We all know that such different signets are shown during dancing.
- The origin of the word *mudra* (signet) can be explained in two different ways. One explanation is *mudam rāti* – i.e. giving happiness. This happiness is for both – one who shows the signet and to whom it is shown. The second is *Modanāt*, *Drāvanāt* – i.e. it is called as *mudra* since it makes the person to whom it is shown as happy and it drives away the sins of the person who shows it. The meaning of the word *Drāvanāt* has been given as that it drives away the universe from the mind of the worshipper – i.e. the mind set of dualities.
- Some signets are common to all the deities – for example joining both the palms to bow.
- There are many signets in worshipping *Sri Vidya*. It is the practice to show the deer sign when chanting the *guru paduka* (chappals of teacher) *mantras* and immediately followed by the signs of

*sumukha* (good face), *suvruddha* (good development), *mudgara* and *chaturasra* (fourth) and with the *yoni* sign to pray the teacher and *Ganapati* respectively in the left and right shoulders.

- There are signs to be shown in *Navavarna* worship during *Āvāhanam, Nyāsa, Pātrasādanam* and *Nivedanam*.
- In 979th name of Sri Lalita Sahasranama – *Gnānamudra* – it is also called as *Chinmudra*.
- In 982nd name of Sri Lalita Sahasranama *Yonimudrā* has been mentioned.
- Ten signets, in a combined form, have been mentioned in 977th name of Sri Lalita Sahasranama – *Dashamudrāsamārādhya*.

807. मलया – *Malayā*

- One who is residing in the Malaya mountain (*Malayāchalam*).
- This deity is described in the *Sābara chintāmaṇi* as the famous *Malayālaya Bhagavatee*. (*Malayā* mountain is in Kerala and hence it is told as *Malayālayā Bhagavatee* or *Malayālaya Bhagavatee*).
- Malayachala mountain has been described in Devi Bhagavatam.
- 458th name of Sri Lalita Sahasranama is *Malayāchalavāsinee* – conveying the same meaning.

808. मलयान्विता – *Malayānvitā*

- She possesses the fragrance of *'Chandana'* or the paste of Sandal-wood tree bark.
- Her body scent is so famous and attracting every devotee.

809. मेधा – *Medhā*

- One who is the personification of special knowledge.
- She is the essence of Buddhi or Mental capacity.
- One of the creations was intelligence (*Medhā*). **She** is in this form.
- *Agni Purana* says *Medhā* is remembrance –
  *Dheerdhāranāvatee Medha*.
- *Sri Devi* in the form of *Medhā* has been explained in *Saptashatee* in two places – Oh *Devi*, thou art intelligence, thou art the essence of all the scriptures – *Medhāsi Devee Viditākhila Shāstra Sārā* I
  and Devee who resides in all beings in the form of intelligence –
  *Yā Devee Sarvabhooteshu Medhāroopena Samsthitā* I

- We worship *Sri Devi* through *Medhā Sooktam part of* Rig Veda also.
- According to *Padma Purana*, the deity called *Medhā* is in Kashmir.
- 538th name of Sri Lalita Sahasranama is also *Medhā*.
- 752nd name of Sri Vishnu Sahasranama is *Sumedhā* – the Lord of Pure Intelligence.

810. मरकतश्यामा – *Marakataśyāmā*

- She is of the complexion of Marakata gem.
- Marakata gem is supposed to be in green colour. But dark green sometimes resembles black and hence it is mentioned as Shyama (black) here.

811. मागधी – *Māgadhī*

- One who is specially worshipped in Magadha country, present day Bihar state.
- There are four Navaratris celebrated in a year. Out of which Vasantha navarathri is celebrated in Maga month (Feb-Mar). Since she is worshipped during Maga month, she is called as *Māgadhī*.
- The other three navarathris are – Chaitra navarathri during the month of Chaitra, Ashada or Varaha Navarathri during the month of Ashada and Sharada Navarathri during the month of September or October (this is the most popular one).

812. मेनकात्मजा – *Menakātmajā*

- Menaka is one of the divine dancers. Our Devi self-originated as Menaka.
- Maināka is a mountain. She is in that form also.

813. महामारी – *Mahāmārī*

- She is of the form of Mahamaari Shakti.
- Māri is the name of Renuka, wife of sage Jamadagni, mother of Parasuraman. She is in that form. Mahā is prefixed to add the greatness.
- Mārī also means slaughter. Since she destroys the enemies, she is Mahāmārī.

- Mārī in some language means rain. *Mahāmārī* is heavy rains. She only controls the rain and hence she is *Mahāmārī*.

814. महावीरा – *Mahāvīrā*

- One who is valorous. One with supreme valiant form of Shakti.
- Vira means a warrior. *Mahavira* is a great warrior. It is no need specifically to mention that *Sri Devi* is a great warrior – a *Mahavira*.
- **She** herself is a warrior in battles, has valour and has killed lots of demons.
- A *veerā* is a lady living with her husband and sons.
- 899th name of Sri Lalita Sahasranama is *Veerā*.
- 401st and 643rd names of Sri *Vishnu Sahasranama* is *Veeraḥ – Sri Adi Shankara* in his commentary mentions; to go, to spread, to create, to enlighten, to throw, to eat, etc. The meaning of the verb *Vee* is a person who does all these actions.

815. महाश्यामा – *Mahāśyāmā*

- She is the of the colour of thick blue clouds ready to rain.
- *Śyāmā* means black. *Mahāśyāmā* means deep black. She is of black colour.
- *Shyamala* is a *Shakti* created by *Sri Devi* out of her sugarcane bow as an embodiment of mind energy. Her complexion is that of rain-cloud and her knowledge of music is profound.
- The Veena and the parrot in the hands of *Shyamala* became the *Shaktis* known as *Yantrini* and *Tantrinee*.
- *Shyamala*, the *Mantrini Devee*, killed the demon *Vishangan*.

816. मनुस्तुता – *Manustutā*

- Gayatri Devi is worshipped by the successive lineage of all the 14 Manus
- Fourteen Manus are Swayambhu, Swarochisha, Uttama, Tamasa, Raivata, Chakshusha, Vaivasvata (the present), Savarni, Daksa Savarni, Brahma Savarni, Dharma Savarni, Rudra Savarni, Raucya or Deva Savarni and Indra Savarni.
- *Sri Devi* was adored by 12 basic devotees – Sri Vidya upasakas viz., *Manu*, Moon, *Kubera*, *Lopamudra*, Cupid, *Agastya*, Agni, Sun, *Indra*, *Skanda*, *Shiva* and *Krodha Bhattārakā* (*Durvasa*). Each of them, by

the skills of penance, felt a type of *mantra* and worshipped. *Manu* is the top most among them. *Sri Devi* is in the form of *Sri Vidya Mantra* formed by him.

817. मातृका – *Mātṛkā*

- She is of the Ashta Matruka Swaroopini.
- Ashta (8) Matrukas are Brahmi, Vaishnavi, Maheshwari, Aindri, Kaumari, Vaarahi, Chandika and Narasimhi. During the battle with Shumbha, Nishumbha and other demons, Sri Devi created 8 other Devis from her own body. They originated from different organs of her body. Hence all those forms are hers only.
- They are also called 8 *Prakata Yoginees*, in the middle layer of *Chatusrā* (*Noopurā*) of *Sri Chakra*.
- She creates the *Mātrukā* colours. In the sixth chapter of *Mātrukā Viveka*, it has been described in detail that the *Mātrukā* colours are the same as *Sri chakra*.
- Sri Adi Shankara has written a way of mentally worshiping Sri Devi called "Mantra Matruka Pushpamala".

818. मिहिराभासा – *Mihirābhāsā*

- She is of the effulgence of Surya.
- Earlier also it has been mentioned that Sun and others do not illuminate themselves. It is she who makes them to bright.

819. मुकुन्दपदविक्रमा – *Mukundapadavikramā*

- She is the follower of the footsteps of Bhagavan Vishnu.
- Mukunda is Lord Vishnu. He is lying on Adisesha snake in the ocean of milk. She as goddess Lakshmi sits by the leg side of presses Vishnu's legs.
- *Mukuḥ* means salvation. **She** bestows that *padam*.
- 838th name of Sri Lalita Sahasranama is *Mukundā* – One who bestows moksha.
- 515th name of Sri *Vishnu Sahasranama* is *Mukundaḥ*, *Sri Adi Shankara* also, in his commentary for this name confirms the above message.

820. मूलाधारस्थिता – *Mūlādhārasthitā*

- One whose main residence is *Moolādhāram*.
- She is of the form Kundalini energy or the Life Force as the coiled energy sleeping/ shining at the Moolaadhaara at the base of the spine in a human body. This symbolises memory and the sense of Time and Space and the merger point of Ida-Pingala-Sushumna Nadis.
- The backbone of the body is called *Merudhandam*. The *nadi* called *Sushumna* runs inside this. The bottom most part of this is the butt. In the midst of this, the *Linga* stays in a place called *Mooladharam*. Next the chakra called *Swadhishtanam*, which resides in the root location of the *Linga*. Third *manipoorakam* is at lower abdomen, *Anahatam* at the chest area, *Vishuddhi* in the neck and *Ajna*, the sixth one, in between two eye brows. Above all these six is the *Sahasrara Chakra*. Conventionally these are all called as Lotus (*Padmam*). Out of these six, respectively a pair of *chakras* is called as *Kandam*. These are called *Agni* (fire), *Soorya* (Sun) and *Chandra* (Moon) *Kandas*. Above and below each of the *Kandas* there are three *grantis* (knots) viz., Brahma, Vishnu and Rudra *grantis*
- Out of these, *Mooladhara* Lotus has four petals. *Kundalinee* always sleeps, keeping its head downwards, in the *bindu* called *Kulakandam*, in a *karnika* in this *chakra*. Hence it is said that, *Sri Devi*, in the form of *Kundalinee*, has *Mooladhara* as **Her** main dwelling.
- It is called *Mooladhara*, since it is the base for *Kundalinee* and also the root of *Sushumna*.
- Kundalini is the dormant cosmic energy in the form of a coiled serpent that needs to be aroused by Yogic techniques especially by meditation blocking senses. Then the Kundalini Shakti travels upwards from Moolaadhara at the base of the spine through the most significant Nadis or Body tissues viz. Ida-Pingala-Sushumna besides of course the other relevant nadis as the Sushumna Nadi extending from Mooladhara chakra between the anus and genital right upto the Brahma Randhra on the top middle point of the Head through the other chakras and grantis.
- In other words, the Cosmic Energy in the Kundalini needs to traverse in the Yogic Path from Mooladhara through the various Nadis especially the Ida-Pingala-Sushumna through the other Chakras of Swadhishtana, Manipooraka, Anaahata, Vishuddhi,

Agjnya and Sahasraara upto Brahma Randhra and three *grantis* (knots) viz., Brahma, Vishnu and Rudra *grantis.*

821. मुग्धा – *Mugdhā*

- One who is always in a pleasing mood.
- She is always joyful and makes her devotees also contented.
- Some schools prefix *'A'* - making the name *Amugdha*. In that case it has to be construed as, not-ignorant, i.e., her devotees are not ignorant and they are full of knowledge.
- 868th name of Sri Lalita Sahasranama is also *Mugdhā*.

822. मणिपूरक निवासिनी – *Maṇipūraka Nivāsinī*

- One who resides in the lotus called *Manipoora*. It is in the belly button with 10 petals.
- This is in continuation of 821st name above.
- The lotus with ten petals near the belly button is called *manipoorakam*. This is also named as *Sthithi Chakra*, place of *Vishnu* and *Soorya Kandam*. The *Kundalinee* energy pierces the knots (*Brahma granti*) between *Mooladharam* and *Swadhishtanam* and rises to *manipoorakam*. There *Sri Devi* accepts 47 *upacharams* from *Padhyam* till offering of jewels. There *Sri Devi* is decorated with various gems (*Manis*) and hence *Manipoorakam*.
- Imagining that the *Sushumna nadi* has relationship between musical sounds and the syllables of *Sri Vidya* and chanting the *mantra*, is called *nadivishwam* (*Varivasya Rahasyam* 1-45, 46).
- 101st and 495th names of Sri Lalita Sahasranamam in this connection are – *Maṇipoorāntaruditā* and *Maṇipoorābjanilayā*.

823. मृगाक्षी – *Mṛgākṣī*

- One whose eyes are like deers'. Her eyes surpass in their sparkle far superior to those of the liquid eyes of a deer.
- The eyes of the deers will not be static at one place – it wavers all the sides. This is to escape, in times of danger. Like that of the deers, the eyes of the high society ladies also will be wavering. This adds to their beauty. Since **She** belongs to the highest class, *Sri Devi*'s eyes also wavers like this.
- One other reason is – **She** wants the sympathy and compassion of her sight to fall on all her devotees on all sides and hence her eyes

are wavering.

- 561st name of Sri Lalita Sahasranamam is also *Mṛgākṣī*.
- 103rd name of Sri Lalita *Trishatee – Harinekshanā* can be compared here.

824. महिषारूढा – *Mahiṣārūḍhā*

- Devi, like Yama Dharma Raja, travels on a buffalo.
- She has a buffalo also as one of her vehicles.
- Since she killed the demon Mahishasuran (next name), she has taken the buffalo as her carrier.

825. महिषासुरमर्दिनी – *Mahiṣāsuramardinī*

- One who annihilated the demon called Mahishasuran.
- She assumed the form of Durga in annihilating the notorious Mahishasura.
- According to Sri *Devi Puranam*, the demon *Mahishan* was killed by *Sri Devi* riding on a lion. **She** thus acquired the names of *Mahishagni* (killer of *Mahishan*) and *Simhāsaneshwaree*.
- **She** killed various demons like *Bhanḍa, Shumbha, Nishumbha* and many others including *Mahishan*.

826. योगासना – *Yogāsanā*

- Sri Devi is comfortably seated in a *Yogaasana* (*padmaasana*) with crossed legs and thighs there on.
- Yogasana has been explained in detail in the 828th name below.

827. योगगम्या – *Yogagamyā*

- She aims at the accomplishment of Yoga.
- She becomes an expert in yoga shastra and enables her devotees also to be knowledgeable in yogas.
- She only aided sage Patanjali to write *yoga shastra*.

828. योगा – *Yogā*

- She is what Yoga is all about

- Yoga sadhana is the Practice of physical exercises and alignment of the body limbs and the inner consciousness deriving not only physical fitness by way of memory power, health, longevity and various direct benefits of good sight and hearing, good digestion, correctives of deficiencies of limbs like diabetes, blood pressure, cholesterol, weight control, epilepsy etc., by harnessing the Karmendriyas and Jnaanindriyas but also by pursuing the path of Realising the Supreme.
- The most significant Yoga is that of Ashtanga Yoga is not only a Physical Exercise but a Spiritual Experience and Discipline comprising *Yama, Niyama, Asana, Pranayama, Pratyahara, Dharana, Dhyana,* and *Samadhi*.
    - *Yama* comprises Ahimsa or Non-Violence, Satya or Truthfulness, Asteya or non-stealing, Brahmacharya or celibacy, and Aparigraha or non- greediness;
    - *Niyama* comprising Shoucha or Purity, Santosha or Contentment, Tapas or austerity, Swadhyaya or Self-Teaching or Introspection and Ishwara Pranidhana or inquisitiveness of Divinity;
    - *Asana* or the sitting posture of a yogi which serves five purposes viz. normal activity of limbs, exercise of limbs, mental energy, intellectual enhancement and Spiritual Awareness. There could be many postures of Asanas while standing, forward bending, supine or prostrate, inverted, abdominal or lumbar, twisting, back bending, balancing and so on. But the Padmasana is the most popular of Ashtanga yoga;
    - *Pranayama* or control of breathing – the methods being Sahita Kumbhaka or retention techniques for physical and mental soundness, Surya bhedi Pranayama or inhalation (Pooraka) through right nostril and exhalation (Rechaka) through the right nostril for good digestion and removing impurities of body and mind, Ujjayi Pranayama or travel of breathing between nose and heart to control cough and cold besides removal of impurities, Bhraamari or concentrated and fixed pattern of breathing to improve concentration and will power, Murccha Pranayama is an extreme form of breath retention which only yogis could perform as it would be a near unconscious state and finally Kewali Pranayama is temporary stoppage of breath;
    - *Pratyahara* is extraction and suppression of senses from karmendriyas and Jnanendriyas;
    - *Dharana* or retention of that stage for long durations;

  - *Dhyana* or immersion of the Self in deep meditation and Samadhi or the climactic stage of trance;
- 18th name in Sri Vishnu Sahasranama is *Yogaḥ*.
- 79th and 782nd names in Sri Shiva Sahasranama are *Yogiḥ*.

829. यौवनकाश्रया – *Yauvanakāśrayā*

- She is always surrounded by youth people.
- She is always youthful Yogi without any growth or deterioration and hence surrounded by youth.
- In Sri Lalita Sahasranama lot many names like 136 – *Nityā*, 344 – *Kshyavruddhi Vinirmuktā*, 358 – *Tarunee*, 430 – *Nityayouvanā* and 470 – *Vayovastā Vivarjitā* – all indicate that she is youthful.
- 272nd name in Sri Lalita *Trishatee* – *Labdha Youvanashālinee* also convey the same message.

830. यौवनी – *Yauvanī*

- She is the essence of youth.
- Since she is always youthful, she is the essence of youth.

831. युद्धमध्यस्था – *Yuddhamadhyasthā*

- She is right in the center stage of battles against the forces of vices and the evils.
- Whenever Devas are in trouble, they worship her and she appears before them. To protect them she is very much fond of fighting with the demons. At all other times she is niroopi (formless) and not seen by anybody. Hence, she is seemingly always in the middle of battles.
- 684th name of Sri Vishnu Sahasranama is *Ranapriya* – the Lord who is the lover of battles.
- Be it Lord Vishnu or Sri Devi – both are always ready to fight with evils and impart good things.

832. यमुना – *Yamunā*

- She is in the form sacred river Yamuna.
- 153rd name above also conveyed the same message.

833. युगधारिणी – *Yugadhāriṇī*

- She sustains the cycle of Yugas.
- During pralaya it is only she who survives and again start the process of creation, etc., through Brahma and all.

834. यक्षिणी – *Yakṣiṇī*

- She is in the form of *Yakshini*.
- Yaksha are a race among Devas. Lord Kubera is their head. Yakshini is their femineity. Sri Devi represents the benevolent Supernatural Powers controlling the malevolent Yakshas.

835. योगयुक्ता – *Yogayuktā*

- She is with and around the Yoga Practioners.
- Only through yogas she be realised. She being the head of Yogis, she likes other yogis also.
- 828th name above can also be refereed.

836. यक्षराजप्रसूतिनी – *Yakṣarājaprasūtinī*

- As mentioned in 834th name above, Kubera is the king of Yaksha-Yakshinis. She is the Mother of Kubera.

837. यात्रा – *Yātrā*

- She is the traveler to all Punya Teerthas and Kshetras.
- All devotees are lined up to and put forth their desires to these punya teerthas. She only makes them to travel to these holy places.

838. यानविधानज्ञा – *Yānavidhānajñā*

- She is a unique exponent and expert of the science of flying and aero planes.
- During the purana times there was no aero planes of today's kind. But there were Pushpaka vimanas. Also, the Devas and others were able to fly themselves like Hanuman and all. She is an expert in that technique.

839. यदुवंशसमुद्भवा – *Yaduvaṃśasamudbhavā*

- She is born in the lineage of King Yadu.
- Bhagavan Shri Krishna was born in the lineage of Yadu. Being his consort or in his form she also.

840. यकारादिहकारान्ता – *Yakārādihakārāntā*

- She is the alphabets which the total Vidya or knowledge is drawn from.
- She is in the form of Samskruta aksharas starting from *'ya'* till *'ha'*. The intrinsic meaning is she is in the form *Panchadashaaksharee* and *Shodashaakshree* (*shuddha vidya*) mantras.
- She is in the form of all the Srividya mantras.
- 204th name of Sri Lalita Sahasranama – *Sarvamantrasvaroopiṇee* – is worth comparable here.

841. याजुषी – *Yājuṣī*

- She is in the form of Yajur Veda mantras.
- She is the manifestation of all Vedas including that of Yajurveda.

842. यज्ञरूपिणी – *Yajñarūpiṇī*

- Our Devi is the form of Yagnas.
- One who is the doer of sacrifices. She is in the form of the doer of yagnas, yagnas themselves and the goddess for the yagnas.
- One who has desired and initiated to do a sacrifice is called a *yajamanar* (master). He is said to be of the form of *Paramashiva*. His consort is called *Deeksha* and their son is called *Santhanam*. **She** is in that *Deeksha* form.

843. यामिनी – *Yāminī*

- She is the Profile of Nights and Darkness too.
- She is the fund of splendour and brightness.
- She is *Antaryamini* – present in all souls – Omnipresent.

844. योगनिरता – *Yoganiratā*

- She is the high Practitioner of Yoga.
- 828 and 835th names above can also be referred in this connection.

845. यातुधानभयङ्करी – *Yātudhānabhayaṅkarī*

- One who frightens Rakshasas (demons) to their core.
- She is friendly to her devotees and frighting to her enemies.

846. रुक्मिणी – *Rukmiṇī*

- Our Devi Gayatri is the manifestations of Rukmini the prime spouse of Lord Krishna.
- Rukmini is an incarnation of Goddess Lakshmi. Our Devi is in that form also.

847. रमणी – *Ramaṇī*

- One who rejoices – simply moves happily with the devotees.
- On account of her greatness and pride, the devotees with fear, amazement and admiration, may not come close to **Her**. By making herself simple, **she** moves closely with the devotees. Thus, *Sri Devi* makes the devotees move closely without any fear.
- In *Shrimad Bhagavat Geeta* (XI–14) also, *Krishna* described to *Arjuna*, who was seeing the cosmic form, as – *Vismayāvishto Hrushtaromāḥ*. *Arjuna* describes himself as – *Bhayena Cha Pravyathitam Mano Me* (XI–45).
- *Chāndogya Upanishat* (VIII–12-3) says, laughing, playing and rejoicing.
- 310th name of Sri Lalita Sahasranama is also *Ramaṇī*.

848. रामा – *Rāmā*

- She is a woman. She is the giver of bliss to yogis.
- In *Linga Purana*, it has been mentioned that all the masculine words are *Sankara* and all the feminine words are *Sri Devi*. The same is narrated as *Hari* and *Lakshmi* in *Vishnu Purana*.
- *Bruhat Parasara Smruti* says – Just as women get pleased or dis-pleased, so are the *devas* are pleased or displeased. If they are

pleased the family grows, if they are displeased the family is spoilt.

- *Saptashatee* (XI-6) says –

*Vidyāḥ Samastāḥ Tava Devee Bhadāḥ Striyaḥ Samastāḥ Sakalā Jagatsoo*

- Since, *Yogins* delight in meditating and adoring *Sri Devi*, **she** is called *Rāma*. (*ram* = to delight, *rāmā* = woman).
- 319th name of Sri Lalita Sahasranama is also the same *Rāmā*.

849. रेवती – *Revatī*

- Revathi is the consort of Lord Balarama. Our Devi is in that form.
- Revathi is the name of a star. Our Devi is in that form too.

850. रेणुका – *Reṇukā*

- Renuka is the spouse of sage Jamadagni and mother of Lord Parashurama. Our Devi is in that form.
- **She** is worshipped twice a day during *Sandhya* times. The *Renuka Purana* says – this *Sandhya* is to be worshipped by *Devas*, the twice-born and by great souls, in sitting down, in lying down, in moving about, in eating and she is *Renuka* herself –

*Āsane Shayane Yāne Bhojane Renukaiva Hi* II

- In Renuka Purana, it is said that, three nadis viz. Idā, Pingala and Sushumna are integrated in the body. Similarly, Sandhya is an integrated form of three Devis Mahākālee, Mahālakshmee and Ekavirā. Our Devi is in the form of that Sandhya –

*Idaikāsya Mahākālee Mahālakshmeestu Pingalā* I
*Ekaveerā Shushumneyamevam Sandhyā Trayātmikā* II

- Renuka Parameshwari is the goddess to cure small pox, chicken pox, etc.

851. रती – *Ratī*

- *Rati* – beautiful lady – wife of Manmatha (Cupid) – most beautiful lady. Our Devi is in that form.
- The word *Rati* means affection. That is – *Rati* means – mind getting enjoyment and delight on anything. A person getting *Rati* on an object is due to the mind or the object? If this is researched, it can be concluded that it is only due to the mind of the enjoying person and not the object. The reason is the affection in the self. This self-affection is *Sri Devi* herself in the form of *jeevatma*. On account of ignorance people search the affection outside without

understanding that it is self in the form of affection. The person with this knowledge gets self-satisfaction within himself. *Sri Devi* is in that form of *Rati*.

852. रौद्री – *Raudrī*

- She is the counterpart of Bhagavan Rudra.
- *Tantra shastras* mention that *Vāmā, Jyeshtā* and *Roudhree shaktis* take the male form as *Brahma, Vishnu* and *Rudra* and their corresponding *Devis, Bhāratee, Lakshmee* and *Rudrāni*.
- In general *Brahma, Vishnu, Rudra* and *Eshwara* the four; according to the *Vaishnavas* they are *Pratyumnar, Anirudhar, Sankarshanar* and *Vāsudevar*. According to *Śāktas, Vāmā, Jyeshtā, Roudhree* and *Ambikā*.
- Raudree also means one with great anger. As earlier mentioned, she is annoyed with the enemies and demons.

853. रौद्रप्रियाकारा – *Raudrapriyākārā*

- She likes Rudra Deva and is liked by him.
- As mentioned in the previous name she is the counterpart of Lord Rudra. Hence they mutually like each other.

854. राममाता – *Rāmamātā*

- She is in the form of Kausalya, mother of Lord Rama.
- She takes the form of wife of Emperor Dasharatha to give birth to Rama. Not an ordinary lady can give birth to the great lord Rama. Someone like our Devi only can take that role.

855. रतिप्रिया – *Ratipriyā*

- She is liked by Rati Devi the spouse of Manmatha and she like her too.
- Lord Shiva ignited Manmatha with the fire from his third eye. Rati Devi was in distress. It is our Devi, in the form of Parvati, recommended to Lord Shiva to give life to Manmatha. Lord Shiva also bring him back from ashes. It is purely on account of liking of Rathi.
- 851st name above can also be referred.

856. रोहिणी – *Rohiṇī*

- She is in the form of Rohini the mother of Lord Balarama.
- Lord Balarama also known as Sankarshana as his virility was transferred from the womb of Devaki Devi to that of Rohini.
- Lord *Shiva* in his eighth form, out of the 12, is known as *Mahadeva*. His consort is *Rohini*.
- She was a daughter of Daksha Prajapati. *Rohini* and other constellations were also daughters of *Daksha Prajapati*. Hence, she is in that form too.

857. राज्यदा – *Rājyadā*

- One who is a giver of kingdom.
- In Durga Saptashatee, Suratan was a king. His ministers and other enemies exiled him away from the kingdom. He came to the forest. He, alongwith a businessman called Samadhi, heard the story of Sri Devi from sage Sumetas. Sri Devi (chapter XII) gave him back the kingdom and also made as one of the 14 manus (next to the present – 816th name above may be referred).

858. रेवा – *Revā*

- She is in the form of the sacred river Reva. In some schools Reva is mentioned as another name for river Narmada.
- She is in the form of all rivers including this.

859. रमा – *Ramā*

- One who is in the form of Lakshmee.
- The Soota Samhita (IV-47-66) says, she appears like a dancer in the form of Lakshmi, Sarasvati, etc.
- The fourth vowel 'Ĕ' of Samskruta letters, is indicated by this name. This is the third letter in Panchadashee mantra. She is in that form.
- In Mahashoda Nyasam (Prapancha nyasam), She is indicated as in the form of a river. She is a much beautiful Devi.
- *Ramā* means, beauty, fortune and wife of *Rāma*. She is in all these forms.
- 313th name of Sri Lalita Sahasranama is also *Ramā*.

860. राजीवलोचना – *Rājīvalocanā*

- One whose eyes are like deer, fish and red lotus flower.
- The word *Rajeeva* means deer, fish and red lotus flower. Her eyes are compared to all these.
- The word *Rajeeva* also means one who is dependent on king. Since **She** sights, with affection and blessings, the devotees of **Her** consort *Rajarajeshwara*, also get benefitted – **she** is *Rajeevalochana*.
- Earlier names in this Sahasranama itself, the eyes of Sri Devi were compared to fish, deer and all.
- 308th name of Sri Lalita Sahasranama is also *Rājīvalocanā*.
- 103rd name of Sri Lalita Trishatee *Harinekshanā* may also be referred in this context.

861. राकेशी – *Rākeśī*

- She is the presiding goddess on a full Moon day.
- One who has Moon on her forehead. Sun, Moon and Agni are the three eyes of Sri Devi. In that she has Moon as one eye in her forehead.

862. रूपसम्पन्ना – *Rūpasampannā*

- She is the embodiment of beauty and grace.
- Her beauty has been described in many a place in this Sahasranama and other texts.

863. रत्नसिंहासनस्थिता – *Ratnasiṃhāsanasthitā*

- One who is comfortably seated on a Golden Throne studded with precious gems.
- **She** controls and rules the entire world seated on a great grand throne.
- The seat of a king is a throne – *Simhasana*. The seat of kings is designed as if the ruler is seated on a lion, because the lion is the king of animals. By virtue of **Her** position as a controller and ruler of World Empire, **She** is the lord of *Simhasan*, symbolises the wealth of the empire of the Universe and seated in this throne.
- She is the empress; it is therefore appropriate that she is seated on a *Simhasana*.

- At the end of the *Devee Navavarna Pooja*, a throne (*Simhasana*) with five steps is contemplated on the *Bindu*. Five forms of *Sri Devi* are imagined on each of these five steps in the four directions north-west, north-east, south-west and south-east and in the center. This worship is called *Pancha Panchika*. In the first step are seated the five *Lakshmis viz. Sri Vidya Lakshmi, Lakshmi-Lakshmi, Mahalakshmi–Lakshmi, Trishakti-Lakshmi* and *Sarvasamrajya-Lakshmi*. Since the throne on which *Sri Devi* is seated has these five *Lakshmi*s, **she** is referred to as *Śreemat-simhāsaneshwaree* (3rd name Sri Lalita Sahasranama).

864. रक्तमाल्याम्बरधरा – *Raktamālyāmbaradharā*

- She is adorned with blood red garlands and clothes.
- Everything is red in colour for Sri Devi, including her own. Hence the attire, jewels and the garlands are also red in colour.

865. रक्तगन्धानुलेपना – *Raktagandhānulepanā*

- She is attractively smeared with red paste of sandalwood all over her body.
- Having sandal paste on all over her body has been mentioned earlier also. Here, in continuation of the previous name, it is added that it is red sandal.

866. राजहंससमारूढा – *Rājahaṃsasamārūḍhā*

- She is being carried nicely on a Swan King.
- Swan is her vehicle. She being an emperess it should be swan king with opulent luxury. That is narrated in this name.

867. रंभा – *Raṃbhā*

- Devi is like Rambha the Celestial Damsel of Glory.
- Earlier, in the 812th name it was mentioned that she is in the form of Menaka, one of the celestial dancers. Now it is Rambha, another celestial dancer.

868. रक्तवलिप्रिया – *Raktavalipriyā*

- Sri Devi is thrilled with the flows of sacrificial blood of fallen demons on battle grounds.

- When she was fighting with demon Raktabeeja, every drop of blood from him falling on the ground becomes another Raktabeejan. Hence, in the form of Kali, she drank the blood oozing out of his body, so that it does not drop on the ground. She is thrilled in drinking that blood.

869. रमणीययुगाधारा – *Ramaṇīyayugādhārā*

- She is the hinged to yuga Cycles.
- All the yugas do occur one after another as a cycle. As a controller of time, she only controls them and she is holding them.

870. राजिताखिलभूतला – *Rājitākhilabhūtalā*

- She is the grandeur of the entire Bhoo Loka.
- She is the dignity of the whole world. As Bhuwaneshwari, she is the controller of all the 14 worlds including this earth.

871. रुरुचर्मपरिधाना – *Rurucarmaparidhānā*

- She wears the skin of the Golden Deer.
- It is normal to use skin of the deers by sages and munis. Lord Shiva also wears the skin of animals and similarly our Devi also.

872. रथिनी – *Rathinī*

- One who rides a magnificent chariot.
- Being an empress, she riding in a chariot is very normal.

873. रत्नमालिका – *Ratnamālikā*

- One who wears exquisite garlands of precious gems.
- Being an empress, she has to wear jewels made of gems.

874. रोगेशी – *Rogeśī*

- One who instantly cures the ailments of her devotees.
- She cures/ alleviates all illness/ diseases. Ailments here not only mean the physical sickness, but also the mental ailments and the

ailment of birth-death cycle. She is the only medicine/ doctor for all these.

- 551st and 876th names of Sri Lalita Sahasranama, *Sarvavyādhi Prashamanee* and *Nirāmaya* also convey the same meaning.

875. रोगशमनी – *Rogaśamanī*

- She is the highest therapist and physician.
- Earlier in the 756th name above also, it was mentioned that she is the best physician.

876. राविणी – *Rāviṇī*

- Devi is like a roaring and frightful lioness to the wicked.
- Sri Devi's loud noise has been mentioned earlier also (239, 361, 364, 443, 444, 532 and 545th names above) – frightening the enemies.

877. रोमहर्षिणी – *Romaharṣiṇī*

- She is such that, even by her very thought her admirers and devotees get enraptured.

878. रामचन्द्रपदाक्रान्ता – *Rāmacandrapadākrāntā*

- She merely follows the footsteps of Sri Rama.
- Earlier in 785 and 787th names above, it was mentioned that our Devi was in the form of Sita. Hence, she always follows Rama – no questions asked.

879. रावणच्छेदकारिणी – *Rāvaṇacchedakāriṇī*

- Our Devi was the root cause for the annihilation of Ravana.
- In the form of Sita, she was the cause for destruction of Ravana and others.

880. रत्नवस्त्रपरिच्छिन्ना – *Ratnavastraparicchinvā*

- She is splendidly dressed up in the robes decorated with precious gems.
- Her attire includes expensive dresses and costly gems.

- As an empress she has every right to use high class dress with costly gems.
- 969th name of Sri Lalita Sahasranama *Suveshāḍhyā* also convey the same message.

881. रथस्था – *Rathasthā*

- She travels seated admirably in a celestial chariot.
- 872nd name above can also be referred in this regard.

882. रुक्मभूषणा – *Rukmabhūṣaṇā*

- She is festooned with grand golden ornaments.
- As mentioned in 880th name above she wears grand gold ornaments.
- 51st name of Sri Lalita Sahasranama is *Sarvābharaṇabhooshita* –who is the decked with beautiful raiment and ornaments.
- Again 163rd name of Sri Lalita *Trishatee – Hāṭakābharanojvala* – also convey the same meaning.

883. लज्जाधिदेवता – *Lajjādhidevatā*

- She is the Goddess of Modesty and Humility.
- 301st name of Sri Lalita Sahasranama is *Hreemkāree – Hree* means modesty, shyness and bashfulness. One who has all these is *Hreemkāree*.
- In *Saptashatee*, it is mentioned that we bow to *Sri Devi*, who is in the form of bashfulness in all the souls;

*Yā Devee Sarvabhooteshu Lajjāroopena Samsthitā* I
*Namastasyai Namastasyai Namastasyai Namo Nama*: II

884. लोला – *Lolā*

- She is of wobbly and attractively featured capriciousness.
- Typical of a youthful maiden she is so gorgeous.

885. ललिता – *Lalitā*

- She is the quintessence of sweetness, softness, beauty and grace.
- *Sri Devi* is very pretty (charming).

- One who is a beautiful mother called *Lalitā*.
- Since **She** is the mother of the entire universe, **she** is *Ambika*. Since **She** is also *Lalitā*, **she** is called as *Lalitāmbika*.
- Since **She** is always playful, **she** is called as *Lalitā*.
- *Padma Purana* says – in this context the word *Lokā* indicates rays or presiding deities. Controlling all of them, *Sri Devi* occupies the place *Bindu* with an unexplainable luster. Hence the name *Lalita*. –

  *Lokānateetya Lalate Lalitā Tena Sochyate* ll
- 1000th and final name of Sri *Lalitā Sahasranama* is *Lalitāmbikā* – Since **She** is always playing (the tasks like creation, etc., are themselves like sports for **Her**), **She** is called as *Lalitā*.
- 62nd of Sri Lalita Trishatee is also the same *Lalitā*.

886. लिङ्गधारिणी – *Liṅgadhāriṇī*

- She wears an outstanding emblem of Lord Shiva in Linga form.
- It is typical of Shaiva's to wear a lingam as a pendant. She also wears the same.

887. लक्ष्मी – *Lakṣmī*

- She is the emblem of Goddess of Maha Lakshmi.
- She is in the form Ashta Lakshmis and more – in several auspicious images of abundance – Dhana, Dhanya, Vidya, Santana, Keerti, Veera, Vijaya, Gaja, Aishwarya, Soubhagya, Rajya and Vara Lakshmis.
- Maha Lakshmi is the presiding deity of Madhyama Charitam (middle story) of Saptashatee. She is in that form.

888. लोला – *Lolā*

- This is a repetition of 884th name above.

889. लुप्तविषा – *Luptaviṣā*

- She is the Great Absorber and antiseptic form of poisons.
- She being a great physician she nullifies any type of poisons.

890. लोकिनी – *Lokinī*

- She is the Virat Swaroopini of Trilokas.

891. लोकविश्रुता – *Lokaviśrutā*

- She is of universally glorious Goddess of supremacy.
- She is spread across Trilokas – omnipresent.
- She is famous across the universe.

892. लज्जा – *Lajjā*

- Devi the Symbol of Modesty.
- *Vedas* indicate *Sri Devi* as shyness, mind, satisfaction, interest and cherish – *Lajjāmatee Tushțirishtā Ca Pushța*.
- Those who belong to good family race, those who have good education, those who have good character and those who move with good people, will feel ashamed to do awful actions. That is, the shame prevents them to do such acts. *Śreedevee* is in the form of shame.
- Shyness (shame or modesty) is an important character of *pathivratha* ladies. Scare or fear is also part of it. This is the form of *Sri Devi*.
- 740th name of Sri Lalita Sahasranama is the same *Lajjā*.
- 302nd name of Sri Lalita Sahasranama is *Hreematee* – One who is shy full.
- In *Saptashatee* (IV-5), *Sri Devi* is worshipped as –

  *Shraddhā Satām Kulajanaprabhavasya Lajjā*
- 883rd name above can also be referred in this regard.
- The word *Hreem* means modesty. Also, this is an important *beejam* of *Sri Devi*. Hence the word *Lajjā* is said to indicate this *beejam* cryptically. There are 60 names out of 300, in Sri Lalita *Trishatee* reflecting upon the letter *Hreem*.
- Again, in Sri Lalita *Trishatee* itself 79th name *Lajjādyā* – *Sri Adi Shankara*'s commentary – *Lajja* is modesty. This is one of the righteousness of the inner self. Hence as a sub-character all the righteousness have to be considered. *Ādyā* means one who has such righteousness as form. On account of shyness, people do not show out completely and hide themselves. In the same way, *Sri Devi* also hides herself with *Tirobhāva* energy and shows up only to her devotees by giving boons.
- Again, in Sri Lalita *Trishatee* itself 195th name *Lajjapadasamāradhya*. *Sri Adi Shankara*'s commentary – *Lajja* is a (character) tool to loathe. All the righteousness has to be considered as sub-characters. With all the righteousness in the inner self, **she** is well worshipped by the

inner mind. Amorousness, desire, skeptical doubt, interest, disinterest, help, disturbance, skepticism, indecisiveness and vacillation are all righteousness of inner self. Out of these skepticism means modesty. **She** is well thought of in these.

- The word *Lajja* is a *chakra* of soul. In this, for the development of the bliss, which is the presiding form, **she** is worthy of worship as per the system prevailing in villages.

893. लम्बोदरी देवी – *Lambodarī Devī*

- She is with a long and gigantic belly to cover up Tri Lokas.
- She is pregnant with the entire universe and naturally she has to have a long and big belly region.
- 612 and 672nd names above can also be referred in this regard.

894. ललना – *Lalanā*

- She is the empowerment of total womanhood
- She is the Shakti Swaroopa Maya.
- **She** is in the form of *Leela* as per the statement "*Lalanāt Lalita*". She is predominantly pleasure oriented. The meaning is to prattle.

895. लोकधारिणी – *Lokadhāriṇī*

- One who holds and sustains all the Lokas.
- One who supports the entire universe.
- 759th name of Sri Lalita Sahasranama *Vishvadhāriṇee* – conveys the same meaning.

896. वरदा – *Varadā*

- One who bestows boons to her devotees as per their wish.
- She grants boons to *Brahma*, *Vishnu* and other devotees. *Narada* says in *Matsya* and *Padma Puranas* – *Sri Devi*'s uplifted hand (*varada mudra*) ever confers boons. She will give boons to all *Devas*, *daityas* and ascetics. It has to be understood that the word *varada* indicate that the hand is the instrument of giving, here the hand of *Sri Devi*, is said to confer boons. In reality, the expression means simply to fulfill the desire of the *Devas* – not having the emblem of granting boons.

- *Sri Adi Shankara* says in his commentary to *Soundaryalaharee* (4th verse) – without even the emblem of boons in hands, *Sri Devi* provides the boons more than expected to her devotees;

  *Tvadanyaḥ Pānibhyā-mabhayavarado Daivatagaṇaḥ*
  *Tvamekā Naivāsi Prakatita Varābheetyabhinayā* I
  *Bhayāt Trātum Dātum Phalamapi Ca Vānchāsamadhikam*
  *Sharanye Lokānām Tava Hi Charaṇāveva Nipunou* II

- *Sri Devi Puranam* also says – **She** fulfills the desires of the *Devas* who seek boons. From the root *'Vr'* to choose, **she** is called *Varadā*, conferrer of boons, i.e. giver of the things chosen.
- In the *Varaha Purana* also in the chapter on the *Vetrāsuravadha*, *Sri Devi* is always to be worshipped, by concentration on the ninth day of the lunar fortnight; **She** will certainly become the giver of boons to all worlds.
- *Sri Adi Shankara* in his commentary for 330th name of Sri *Vishnu Sahasranama* – *Varadaḥ* mentions –
  - He gives the boons desired by the devotees in their minds.
  - He becomes the doer of sacrificial fire and gives the boons i.e. the cow as a price. *Gourvai Varaḥ* is the *Veda* saying quoted for this.

897. वन्दिता – *Vanditā*

- She is always Saluted and worshipped by all.
- 681st and 720th names above can also be referred in this regard.

898. विद्या – *Vidyā*

- **She** is the *vidyā* conferring salvation.
- *Saptashatee* (4th chapter) says – The holy supreme *Devi* is *vidyā* – *Vidyāsi Sā Bhagavatee Paramā Hi Devee*.
- Again *Saptashatee* (I chapter) says – *Sā Vidyā Paramā Mukter Hetu Bhootā Sanātanee*.
- The *Gouḍapāda* says in his *Sri Vidya Ratna Sootra* – **She** herself is *vidyā* – *Chaitanya Svaroopā Shaktiḥ Saiva Vidyā* II
- *Vidyā*, a certain kind of art, which is in the light (*tejas*) and its nature are described in the *Saiva Tantra* – By the discrimination of the products of *māyā*, one recognises the state of wisdom, that supreme art is known as *Vidyā*, consisting of knowledge and action–

  *Sā Kalā Paramā Gneyā Vidyā Gnāna Kriyātmikā* II

899. वैष्णवी – *Vaiṣṇavī*

- One who is the power of *Vishnu*.
- When Sri Devi was preparing to wage the war with demons Shumbha and others, every Deva and Gods gave power (shakti) and created their form of goddess. They are called Ashta Matas. In this regard Vaishnavi is the Shakti of Lord Vishnu. Devi Kavacam deal with this in detail in addition to Saptashatee and other texts.

900. विमलाकृती – *Vimalākṛtī*

- She is the personification of Purity.
- One who is free from any stain.
- Impurity is on account of ignorance. *Sri Devi* has no relevance to ignorance or illusion.
- There are three kinds of ignorant souls (*Pashus*):
  i. The *Vijnanākevala*, he who sees the self in the non-self and has arrogance as the only impurity;
  ii. The *Pralayakevala*, he who has the impurity of *karma*, which is unperceivable and which gives him new births; he also has the impurity mentioned in 'i' above.
  iii. The *sakala*, he who has the impurity of the illusion (*māyā*). He has the idea of duality in all matters. He also has the impurities mentioned in 'ii' above.
- *Sri Devi* has no impurities of *sakala* and hence *Vimalākṛtī*.
- **She** does not have the impurity of arrogance. Hence, **she** does not have the impurity called *Vijnanākevala*.
- **She** is free from the impurity of *Tamo* character.
- **She** does not have the impurity of un-education. Liberation is the aim of the soul.
- 133rd name of Sri Lalita Sahasranama – *Niranjanā* – convey the same message.
- 135th name of Sri Lalita Sahasranama – *Nirmalā* – can also be referred.

Thus ends 100 divine names on *Sri Gayatri Devi* from 801 to 900

*****

901. वाराहि – *Vārāhī*

- She is in the form of Matruka Devi Bhoo Devi the Consort of Varaha Deva.
- When Sri Devi was preparing to wage the war with demons Shumbha and others, every Deva and Gods gave power (shakti) and created their form of goddess. They are called Ashta Matas. In this regard Varahi is the Shakti of Lord Varaha, an incarnation of Lord Vishnu. Devi Kavacam deal with this in detail in addition to Saptashatee and other texts.
- *Ḍanḍinee Devi*, also called as *Vārāhi*, is the commander-in-chief of *Rāja Rajeshwaree*. She has twelve other names – *Panchamee, Danḍanāthā, Sankeetā, Vārāhee, Pothriṇee, Shivā, Vārttālee, Mahāsenā, Āgnachakreshwaree* and *Arighnee*.
- 538th name of Sri Vishnu Sahasranama is *Mahavaraha*.

902. विरजा – *Virajā*

- She is in the form of Homas as also that of the Viraja river.
- One who is without any stain or sin originated by the *Rajo* character.
- When such meaning is said, the prefix *'Vi'* has to be taken in the opposite sense – i.e. without the character called *Rajo*.
- The verses of *Mahā Nārāyaṇopanishat* (20th chapter) and *Tattva-soḍanā* may be connected – *Virajā Vipāpma*...
- The word *Rajas* means splendour, water and world. While accepting these meanings the prefix *'Vi'* has to be specifically considered.
- The presiding deity in the place called *Virajā* in Utkal state (present Odisha) is called *Virāja*. **She** is in that form.
- 779th name of Sri Lalita Sahasranama is also the same *Virajā*.
- 396th name of Sri Vishnu Sahasranama is *Viraja*.

903. वर्षा – *Varṣā*

- She is in the form of Showers.
- She is the kala (time) and hence she is Samvatsara (year) roopinee.

904. वरलक्ष्मी – *Varalakṣmī*

- She is in the form of Varalakshmi.

- Varalakshmi is the fulfiller of all desires of the devotees. Our Devi is in that form.
- 887th name above can also be referred.

905. विलासिनी – *Vilāsinī*

- One who is playful – showing the same thing in different forms.
- Illusion (*Māyā*) is of two types – hiding the existing one (*Āvaranam*) and showing the same things in different forms (*Vikshepam*), i.e. showing the unrealistic form as a real one.
- She who grants Mental Contentment
- *Vilāsam* means pastime, play, erotic actions, etc. **She** possesses all these.
- As per the saying *Nityā Vilāsinee Dogtree* – **She** is in the form of a *Peeṭashakti*.
- Again, as per the saying *Vabayorabhetāt* (as there is no difference between the syllable *vi* and *bi*), this name can also be had as *Bilāsinee*. *Bilā* is the cavity at the top of the *Brahmarandhra* (in *Sahasrāra*). *Svachcha Tantra* says that this is the route for liberation and the energy called *Brahmaṇee* is blocking this route. *Sri Devi* – at **Her** pleasure – either opens the way to self-realization, or closes it to the same for the devotees.
- *Vilā* is a place in *Kāmakotam* in *Kancheepuram*. **She** dwells in this place.
- 340th name of Sri Lalita Sahasranama is also the same *Vilāsinī*.

906. विनता – *Vinatā*

- She is in the form of Vinata.
- Vinata is the Mother of Garuda, the vehicle of Lord Vishnu and Aruna the charioteer of Sun God
- She is also the mother of the entire population of the aviation species.

907. व्योममध्यस्था – *Vyomamadhyasthā*

- She dwells in the center of Akasha or the Sky.
- *Vyoma* means ether. She resides in the middle.

908. वारिजासनसंस्थिता – *Vārijāsanasaṃsthitā*

- Devi is seated on the High Seat of Lotus.
- It has been mentioned in multiple places in this Sahasranama and other texts that Sri Devi is seated on a lotus.
- It can also be treated that she resides in the lotus heart of every soul.
- 111th name of Sri Vishnu Sahasranama is *Pundareekaksha* – Pervading the Lotus of the Heart.

909. वारुणी – *Vāruṇī*

- She is in the form of Vaarunee Shakti.
- Varuna is the god of water/ rain. Vaarunee is his consort. She is in that form.

910. वेणुसम्भूता – *Veṇusambhūtā*

- She is displayed with Venu (Flute).
- Lord Krishna is always portrayed with the musical instrument flute. She being his consort and she also has flute in her hand.

911. वितिहोत्रा – *Vitihotrā*

- She is a significant expression of rules.
- Viti is set of rules prescribed for any karma/ karya. She is strictly process oriented and stringently follows the rules.

912. विरूपिणी – *Virūpiṇī*

- She is without any form.
- Brahmam has no specific form. She is the Brahmam. Hence, she does not have any form (*niroopi*).
- On account of ignorance she appears to be *saroopa* – with different forms.
- One who is peerless or without any comparable person.
- Simile can be made with equal or peer objects only. There is no one equal to *Sri Devi*. Hence, **she** has no comparison.
- *Śvētāśvatara Upanishat* (IV-19) advises as – *Na Tasya Pratimā Asti* – No one is equal to him.

- In Tamil Literature it is mentioned as; *Oppārum Mikkārum Illai* – No one equal to or above is available.

913. वायुमण्डलमध्यस्था – *Vāyumaṇḍalamadhyasthā*

- She is seated in the mid region of the zone of air.
- 414th name of Sri Vishnu Sahasranama is *Vāyu* – he is the wind.

914. विष्णुरूपा – *Viṣṇurūpā*

- She is of the profile of Vishnu
- One who is in the form of *Vishnu*.
- **She** depends on *Vishnu*. The *Devi Purana* says, "She is sung as *Viṣṇurūpā* because **She** bears the conch, disc and club, the destroyer of foes".
- In the *Brahmānḍa Purana*, in the *Lalitopākhyāna*, *Sri Devi* says – my male form bewildering the milk-maids -

  *Mamaiva Pourusham Roopam Gopikā Janamohanam* ll
- In the same place *Vishnu* says to *Veerabhadra*, "The ancient *Shakti* of the Lord is divided into four forms, that *Shakti* becomes *Bhavani* in its ordinary form, in battle she takes the form of *Durga*; in anger that of *Kalee*; and she is also my female form".
- In the *Koorma Purana* when *Himavān* praises *Sri Devi* says, "I salute thy form called *Narayana*, Oh *Devi*, who has a thousand heads, who is of infinite energy, having a thousand arms, the ancient person, reclining on the waters".
- In the *Koorma Purana* itself, when *Shiva* showed his universal form to *Mankanaka*, the latter said – "What is the terrible form of thy, facing every side; who is she shining by your side?" Thus questioned, *Shiva*, after explaining the glory of his own nature, says, "She is my supreme *Māyā* (illusion) and *Prakriti* (nature) of triple qualities. She is said by sages to be the ancient womb of the universe. He bewilders the universe by the illusion, he is the knower of the universe, *Narayana*, supreme, unmanifested, in the form of illusion – thus says the *Vedas*".
- In the *Sanatkumāra Samhitā*, describing to king *Prabhākara*, the devotion to *Vishnu* and describing to his wife *Padmini*, the devotion to *Parvati*, it is said – *Janārdana* is thus in the form of *Devee* as well as in his own form, for the husband and wife being one production, the only one is worshipped as two.
- The *Bruhat Parāsara Smruti* also says, "He who with delighted mind

worships *Durga*, *Kātyāyanee* and *Vāgdevatā* obtains the world of *Vishnu*".

- In the *Padma Purana* also "One who bathes the image of *Chaṇḍikā* with the juice of the sugarcane and places her on a golden vehicle, enjoys the presence of *Vishnu* after death".
- The *Aditya* and *Shiva Puranas* say – "she who dwells by his side is the young *Parvati* and *Hari* also is a part of him".
- The *Vamana Purana* also says, "One who on the full moon day of the month *Māgha* worships *Sri Devi* according to rule, he obtains the benefits of the *Ashvamedha* sacrifices and after death he shines in the world of *Vishnu*".
- In Tamil, *Thirumazhisai Alwar* (65th verse) says –
  "*Mātāya Mālavanai... Mādhavanai*".
- 893rd name of Sri Lalita Sahasranama is *Vishnu roopiṇee* – giving the same sense.
- No need to specifically talk about Sri Vishnu Sahasranama – there are lot many names as *Viṣṇu* – omnipresent – *sarvavyapi*.

### 915. विधिप्रिया – *Vidhipriyā*

- Brahma the Creator is the destiny (*vidhi*) maker for all the Beings. She being his consort likes them.
- For everyone, vidhi is decided based on the past karmas and it is the duty of everybody to live accordingly.
- In *Soundaryalaharee*, (99th verse) also we read –
  "*Saraswatyā Lakshmyā Vidhihari Sapatno Viharate*".
- The word *Vidhiḥ* is feminine in *Moksha Dharma* in *Kām Vidhim Samupaskrutya*. It is also been reasoned it that in the phrase "*Bhāgyam Stree Niyatirvidhi*", since the word *Vidhi* is conjoined with the word *Niyati*, it is also feminine only.
- In a way this can be connected to 911th name above.

### 916. विष्णुपत्नी – *Viṣṇupatnī*

- She is a consort of Lord Vishnu.
- She in the form of Lakshmi Devi, a consort of Vishnu.
- 914th name above, it was mentioned that she is in the form of Vishnu. Here it is indicated that she is his consort.

917. विष्णुमती – *Viṣṇumatī*

- One who is the *Vishnu Māyā Shakti*.
- *Vishnu* is all-pervading, unlimited by place, time, *Brahmam*, in the form of inner self in all souls, etc.
- **She** is the *Māyā* of Universal Absolute. The *Shakti*, which limits this Absolute is illusion.
- *Sri Vishnu Sahasranama* 2nd name – *Viṣhṇuḥ* – *Sri Adi Shankara*'s commentary can also be compared.
- *Shrimad Bhagavat Gita* (VII – 14); *Daiveehyeshā Guṇamayee Mama Māyā Duratyayā* – says, this is my divine illusion, consisting of *Guṇas* is hard to surmount.
- In *Saptashatee* also we read as;
  *Yādevee Sarvabhooteshu Viṣhṇu Mayeti Shabtitā* I

918. विशालाक्षी – *Viśālākṣī*

- She is a broad visioned Devi.
- One who has long and large eyes. The eyes leading upto the ears will be beautiful.
- In *Soundaryalaharee* there are many verses describing the beauty and greatness of eyes of *Sri Devi*. Specifically, these verses may be referred; 52 to 57 – *Gate Karnābhyarnam*, *Vibhakta Traivarṇyam*, *Pavitreekartum Naḥ*, *Nimeshon Meshābhyām*, *Tavāparne Karne* and *Drushā Dragheeyasyā*.
- In this *Sahasranama* itself there were many names describing the beauty of the eyes of *Sri Devi*.
- In Sri Lalita *Trishatee* also **She** is addressed as *Kamalākshee* (7th name). That is, her eyes are like blossomed Lotus.
- According to *Padma Purana*, *Vishālākshee* is the name of the presiding goddess worshipped at *Banaras*.
- 49th verse of *Soundaryalaharee* beginning with *Vishālā Kalyanee* may also be referred. *Vishālā* means blossomed sight. In commentaries this has been mentioned as energy that creates confusion.
- The word *Vishālā* indicates *Badrikāshrama*. Since it is in the Himalayas, it also indicates *Nepala Peeṭa*. In *Laghu Shoḍa Nyāsa* (*Peeṭa Nyāsā*), *Brahmānḍa* and other *Purāṇas* say, that the *Nepala Peeṭa* should be meditated upon as situated in the eyes. The word *Akshee* indicates both the eyes. Hence it can be considered that **She** has *Vishāla Peeṭa* as her eyes.
- 936th name of Sri Lalita Sahasranama is also the same *Vishālākshee*.

919. वसुन्धरा – *Vasundharā*

- She is in the form of Bhoo Devi – goddess of the Earth.

920. वामदेवप्रिया – *Vāmadevapriyā*

- She is the beloved of Vama Deva – Parvati Devi.
- As Mahadeva split into Parama Shiva and Para Shakti, Parama Shiva assumed "Pancha Mukhas" or Five Faces viz.,
  I. *Sadhyojaatam* the West faced propagating Parama Shiva Shakti associated with Brahma signifying Earth.
  II. Vamadeva the north facing sustaining the aspect of Parama Shiva associated with Vishnu signifying Water.
  III. Aghora the South faced assumed the destructive aspect of Parama Shiva associated with Rudra signifying Agni or Fire.
  IV. Tatpurusha facing East representing Rishis and Yogis signifying Vayu or Air.
  V. Ishana facing Ishanya or North East sustaining the aspect Parama Shiva sustaining his form of Universal Existence representing Ether and signifying the Concealed Meaning of Parama Shiva.
- Vama Deva Swaroopa's **Ekadasha Rudras** are Ajayapada, Ahirbudhnya, Virupaksha, Raivata, Hara, Bahurupa, Trayambika, Savita, Pinaki and Aparajita.
- 469th name of Sri Lalita Sahasranama is *Vāmadevee* – worth comparing here.

921. वेला – *Velā*

- She is the administrator of Kala Maana or the Cycle of Time.

922. वज्रिणी – *Vajriṇī*

- Gayatri Devi in the form of a Vajrayudha the destructive weapon first ulilised by Indra to destroy Vritrasura materialised by the back bone of Maharshi Dadheechi.
- One who is the consort of *Indra*, the possessor of the weapon *Vajra* or one who has the thunderbolt in hand.
- She is adorned with jewels like diamond and other gems.

- *Kaṭopanishat* (VI-2) says, "The great terrible *Vajra*". *Vajra* means *Brahmam*. *Sri Devi* is called *Vajriṇee* as **She** is related with *Brahmam* as its limitator – *Mahadbhayam Vajramudyatam*.
- 944th name of Sri Lalita Sahasranama is also the same *Vajriṇī*.

923. वसुदोहिनी – *Vasudohinī*

- Our Devi, as Vasudevi/ Bhoodevi bestows considerable wealth by way of Food Grains and other materials.

924. वेदाक्षरपरिताङ्गी – *Vedākṣaraparitāṅgī*

- Each and every part of the body our Devi Gayatri is consummate with Vedaaksharas or innumerable Letters of Vedas.

925. वाजपेयफलप्रदा – *Vājapeyaphalapradā*

- One who worships our Devi, is returned with the fruits of executing Vajapeya Yagjna.
- Whoever does Vajapeya Yagjna is bestowed with appropriate results by our Devi.
- Vajapeya Yagna is a type of soma Yajna like Rajasooya Yagna. But is somewhere different from other Yagnas. In this Yagna, 7 horses are tied in a chariot. The other chariots were also pressed into races and after its victory, King and queen sit down on the victorious chariot and both traveled to long defined place. The chariot is welcomed by the people there gathering with the Sura of cups. Later, it is celebrated with great enthusiasm and sprit by the King and his Subjects.

926. वासवी – *Vāsavī*

- Indrani, consort of Indra is also called as *Vāsavī*. She is in that form.
- 64 and 799th names above also mentioned that She is in the form of wife of Indira.
- *Vāsavī* is another name of goddess Kanyakumari. In fact, the full name is *Vāsavi* Kanyakumari. Our Devi is in that form.

927. वामजननी – *Vāmajananī*

- One who is the mother of Vama Maharishi.

- Vama means left and Vamāchara means the "leftist path" of Sri Vidya. She gets pleased with this type of worship also.

928. वैकुण्ठनिलया – *Vaikuṇṭhanilayā*

- One who lives in Vaikuntam.
- She being a consort of Lord Vishnu lives in Vaikuntham along with him.

929. वरा – *Varā*

- One who is giving enourmous boons to her devotees.
- She is in the glorious form as Vara Lakshmi.
- 896th name above can also be referred in this regard.

930. व्यासप्रिया – *Vyāsapriyā*

- She is fond of Veda Vyasa. According to Shrimad Bhagavatam, Veda Vyasa is an incarnation of Lord Vishnu.
- Veda Vyasa is fond of her.

931. वर्मधरा – *Varmadharā*

- One who wears a body shield and armoury.
- As she appears in battle fields, she has to wear the shield and all. Hence this name.

932. वाल्मीकिपरिसेविता – *Vālmīkiparisevitā*

- She is worshipped by Valmiki Rishi.
- Valmiki Rishi is the scripter of the ever-reputed epic of 'Ramayana'. She is worshipped by him.

933. शाकम्भरी – *Śākambharī*

- She is in the form *Śākambharī* Devi, the benefactor of agricultural produce of food grains, fruits, Vegetables, flowers, etc.
- Shakambhari Devi is an incarnation of Goddess Parvati. She is the divine mother, called "the bearer of the Greens". It is said that in

times of famine, the Goddess Parvati comes down as Shakambhari and gives vegan food to the hungry.

- Shakambhari Devi is a wonderful form of Mother Parvati Devi. She is depicted as having octagonal arms on four sides and elsewhere. Our Devi is this form.

934. शिवा – *Śivā*

- She is the supreme manifestation of auspiciousness and contentment.
- *Shiva*'s consort is *Shivā* – inseparable from *Shiva*.
- Embodiment of auspiciousness, bestower of auspiciousness – the *Icchāshakti* of the Supreme Being – Liberation personified.
- Everything ultimately rests with *Sri Devi*. Hence *Shivā*.
- Lord *Parameeśhwarā* has eight forms, viz. Earth, Water, Fire, Wind, Space, Sun, Moon and Jeeva. *Shiva* in the form wind is called *Īsāna*. **His** consort is *Shivā*.
- The *Veda* says – *Yāthee Rudra Sivāthanooḥ* may be referred in this context.
- 53rd name of Sri Lalita Sahasranama is also the same *Śivā*.
- 27th and 600th names of Sri Vishnu Sahasranama are also the same *Śivā*.

935. शान्ता – *Śāntā*

- She is the flagship of Tranquility.
- The verses *Nishkalam Nishkriyam Shāntam* can be read from *Śvētāśvatara Upanishat* (VI-19). (Without organs, actionless, soothful, ...).
- It can also be construed as – it is the letter to which the letter '*Sha*' follows. In the order of Samskrutam alphabets, the letter previous to '*Sha*' is '*Va*'. This is considered as the seed of nectar (*Amruta Beejam*). Hence, **she** is in the form of seed of nectar.
- This can also be taken as *Āshānta*. The prefix '*Ā*' is understood. *Āsha* means directions. That implies **She** is spread in all directions.
- 141st name of Sri Lalita Sahasranama is also the same *Śāntā*. Other name *Shāntimatee* (131st), *Shānti* (447th) and *Shamātmikā* (963rd) are also worth comparing.

936. शारदा – *Śāradā*

- She is the Vidya-Jnana swaroopini Sharada Devi.
- One who eligible to be adored as *Shārada*.
- *Shāradā* means *Sarasvati* (consort of Lord *Brahma*) or *Vāg Devi*s beginning from *Vasinee*.
- **She** is fit to be worshipped during autumn season. The period from mid-April to mid-June is called spring season (*Vasantha Rutu*). The period from mid-October to mid-December is called autumn season (*Sharat Rutu*). The nine days (*Navarātri*) worship of *Sri Devi* during these two seasons is called *Vasantha Navarātri* and *Sharada Navaratri*. These two are most apt for adoring *Sri Devi*. *Rudrayāmalam* suggests worshiping *Rakta Danḍika* during *Vasantha Navaratri*. The devotees know that this season is a period of *Rāma Navami* and *Rakta Dandika* is *Sita* herself. In addition, *Sri Devi*'s main *devatas* are *Mantrinee* (*Shyāmalā*) and *Ḍanḍinee* (*Mahā-vārāhee*). They are to be specially adored during mid-January to mid-February and mid-July mid-August periods respectively.
- The verse in *Saptashatee* (12th Chapter) –
  *Sharatkāle Mahāpoojā Kriyate Yā Cha Vārshakee.*
- *Shārada* means *Vishāradas* – that is learned people. In particular those who have attained the abode called *Sāleenam*. **She** is fit to be adored by these.
- The below verse in *Kālikā Purana* says that **She** was awakened by *Devas* during autumn season –
  *Shāradā Sā Samākhyātā Peeṭe Loke Chanāmataḥ* ll
- The *Shāradā* (*Peeṭa*) monastery at *Sringeri* in *Karnataka* state of India is also called as *Shārada*.

937. शरणागती – *Śaraṇāgatī*

- She is the last refuge of security and assurance for all.

938. शातोदरी – *Śātodarī*

- She is with effulgent belly.
- One who has a slender waist.
- *Shātam* means slim. **She** has that type of waist. It is mentioned in the *Sāmudrikā Shāstrā* (explaining the body shapes) that ladies who have slim waists are beautiful.

- She is the daughter of *Himavān* (king of mount *Himalayās*) with hundreds of caves.
- It is mentioned in the *Gnanārnava Tantra* (16th section) of pooja method in the verse to deify *Sri Devi –*
  *Alakshyamathyamām Nimnanābhim Cātodareem Parām.*
- Similarly, in *Sri Muthusamy Deekshitar's Āvaran* (shelter) *Keertanās* (songs in classical music) the names *Sākambari* and *Sātodari* are used at the beginning and at the end.
- 130th name of Sri Lalita Sahasranama is also the same *Śātodarī*.
- 847th name of Sri Lalita Sahasranama – *Talodaree* – may also be referred.

939. शुभाचारा – *Śubhācārā*

- One with highly descipined form of propitiousness.

940. शुम्भासुरविमर्दिनी – *Śumbhāsuranardinī*

- The annihilator of Shumbha and Nishumbha brother-demons.
- In Saptashatee (chapters 9 & 10), she as Maha Saraswathi destroyed the two brother demons alongwith their team.

941. शोभावती – *Śobhāvatī*

- She is the personification of Magnificence and Splendour.
- One who is with all radiant with beauty.

942. शिवाकारा – *Śivākārā*

- One who is the everlasting bestower of auspicousness. One who dispenses happiness.
- **She** has an auspicious form.
- *Shiva* – salvation. Because salvation is the realization of the very self, she only can bestow it.
- *Shiva* means auspicious or *Kalyana*. **She** does this.
- **She** makes her devotees happy by removing the noose of *avidyā* and leads them to *Brahmam*, which is to be attained by liberated souls.

943. शङ्करार्धशरीरिणी – *Śaṅkarārdhaśarīriṇī*

- One who has a body constituting one half of Lord *Shiva*.
- The 23rd verse of *Soundaryalaharee* also conveys the same sense;
  *Shareerardham Shambhoraparamapi Shanke Hrutamabhoot* I
- *Brahadāraṇyaka Upansihat* (I-3 & 1-4) starting from *Ātmaive-damagra Āseet* till *Sa Imamevātmānam Dvetā'bhātayat Tataḥ* – explains the universal absolute (*Parabrahmam*) becoming two as husband and wife.
- It is mentioned in the *Vāyu Purana* as – Lord *Paramashiva's* body is white in colour whereas his neck is black (on account venom). Similarly, *Sri Devi*'s body is partly in the form of *Gowree*, which is white in colour and partly in the form of *Kālee*, which is black in colour.
- *Saptashatee* (V chapter) also says that *Ambikā* form came out of *Gowree* form and *Kālee* form –
  *Tasyām Vinirgatāyām Tu Krshnā'bhootsā'pi Pārvatee* I
  *Kāliketi Samākhyātā Himāchalakrutāsrayā* II
- This can also be interpreted as – *Sri Devi* having half body, filled up the remaining half body with that of Lord *Shiva*. It is mentioned as – "*Ichchā Samgnā Cha Yā Shaktiḥ Paripoorṇā Shivodara*".
- As per *Shaiva Shastras*, in *Mātrukā Nyāsam* (appropriation), half body is filled with various *shaktis* like *Poorṇodri*, etc., and other half being filled with *Shiva Mātrukās*, etc. This name indicates the same.
- When the letter '*A*' is written in Samskrutam, half form equal to *Kāma kalā* is got. Hence it can also be interpreted as that **She** has got a body nothing different from *Kāma Kala*.
- The 52nd name in Sri Lalita *Trishatee* is *Eshvarārdānga Shareera*. This has been interpreted as – **Her** body is in the form of *Ānanda*. The letter '*Ha*' in Samskrutam indicates *Eshwar*. **She** is that half body of *Eshwar* i.e., It has been interpreted as that **She** is in the form of the letter '*E*' in Samskrutam as *Shakti Beeja*. The letter '*Ha*' can also be written as ':' (*visarga*). In some schools it is mentioned that **She** is half of it (*Anusvāram*).
- 392nd name of Sri Lalita Sahasranama – *Shreekanṭhārdhashareeriṇee* – is worth comparable here.

944. शोणा – *Śoṇā*

- She is with the features of blood red profile.

- Sri Devi being red in colour has been mentioned in lot many places like the dhyana verse of Sri Lalita Sahasranama – *Sindhūrāruṇa Vigrahām....*

945. शुभाशया – *Śubhāśayā*

- She is the unique deposit of propitiousness.
- One who bestows auspicious to **Her** devotees.
- Earlier it was mentioned that **She** can be worshipped easily. The devotees might get a doubt whether any sin or annihilation will happen by not following the fasting and other requirements. To remove any such, doubt this name stresses that **She** grants auspiciousness to **Her** devotees.

946. शुभ्रा – *Śubhrā*

- She is the emblem of cleanliness.
- *Vāmana Purana* says – *Sri Devi* promotes righteousness in her devotees, like control of senses, cleanliness, wealth and devotion to god.

947. शिरःसन्धानकारिणी – *Śiraḥsandhānakāriṇī*

- She aims right at the heads of the Danavas and other evil forces.
- One who resides in the head (Sahasrara Chakra) of her devotees.
- In the *Brahmarandhra*, wherein **She** resides assuming the form of a teacher.
- **She** is in the form of the last *mahābindu* in the sound '*M*' in the seed '*Hreem*'. This has to be learnt through an appropriate teacher.

948. शरावती – *Śarāvatī*

- She is the celebrated the saviour with the flows of speedy arrows.
- Her bow and arrow skills have been explained earlier also.
- This name also means that she is happy with wine and alcoholic drinks.

949. शरानन्दा – *Śarānandā*

- She secures immense pleasure in releasing arrows and smashing enemies.

- She gives immense pleasure to Deva and other good people.
- This name has to be ready in continuation of the previous two names.

950. शरज्ज्योत्स्ना – *Śarajjyotsnā*

- Sri Devi is lustrous like the full Moon of Sharad/ Autumn Season commencing from Aashwini to Kartika Months.
- The full Moon during the Thula month is the brightest in a year. That Moon is compared here to Sri Devi. *Annabhishekam* is performed on that day to Lord Shiva.

951. शुभानना – *Śubhānanā*

- She possesses the face and looks surfeit with auspiciousness.
- The face of a normal sumangali lady will itself be auspiciousness. How about the face of Sri Devi? Do we need to mention it separately?

952. शरभा – *Śarabhā*

- *Sharabheshwarar* is one of the incarnations of *Shiva*. She is his consort.
- *Linga Purana*, *Kālikā Purana*, etc., say that *Sri Vishnu* took the incarnation of *Narasimha* and killed the demon *Hiranyakasipu*. Even after this his anger did not subside and he was about to destroy the entire world. At that time *Shiva* took the incarnation of *Sharabheshwarar* and controlled the anger of *Narasimha*. *Narasimha* is a combined form of man and lion. In the same manner *Sharabheshwarar* is a combined form of man, lion and a bird. She is his consort and hence *Śarabhā*.
- *Sharabha* kills the enemies of those who chant this Sahasranamas.

953. शूलिनी – *Śūlinī*

- Shakti with a deadly spear ready to bounce on the evil.
- *Pratyangira Devi* and *Shoolinee* are the consorts of *Sharabheshwara* mentioned in the previous name. Our Devi is in the form of that *Shoolinee* Devi.

954. शुद्धा – *Śuddhā*

- She is the full profile of Purity. One who is ever pure.
- That is, **she** is without the dirt called ignorance.
- Actual meaning is that **She** is in the form of knowledge.

955. शबरी – *Śabarī*

- She is in the form of *Śabarī*, the parama devotee of Lord Shri Rama.
- Shabari was the daughter of a hunter who developed aversion of killing animals in forests for food and left her home in search of peace till he reached Matanga Rishi Ashram. She considered him as her spiritual Guru and continued to stay in his Ashram. as the Rishi died eventually, she was asked by the rishi to patiently wait with unwavering devotion for the arrival of Rama whom she met finally and worshipped him in person by offering him fresh fruits but only after ensuring that they were sweet enough by tasting them. Rama was too happy to enjoy the pre-tasted fruits and blessed her to attain Salvation.
- That place is the present day Sabari hills (*mala*).

956. शुकवाहना – *Śukavāhanā*

- She moves about with a bright and colourful parrot as her carrier to different places.
- She has a parrot as one of her vehicles.
- It can also be construed that sage Shukhar, who has a parrot face, propagates her glory to the entire universe.
- 164th name above also conveyed the same message.

957. श्रीमती – *Śrīmatī*

- Devi Gayatri the Signage of womanhood with brightness and happiness.
- **She** is *Srimathi* (one with wealth), further **She** is one always with *Sri* (*Lakshmi*).

958. श्रीधरानन्दा – *Śrīdharānandā*

- She is the provider of joy to Bhagavan Vishnu.
- Being his consort, she provides joy to him.

959. श्रवणानन्ददायिनी – *Śravaṇānandadāyinī*

- She confers extreme pleasure of hearing about her grandeur and sublimity as also her sacred deeds.
- She is happy on those devotees who chant her puranas/ stotras and bless them more than what asked for.

960. शर्वाणी – *Śarvāṇī*

- Bhagavan Shiva's prakriti Shakti i.e. Parvati Devi.
- One of the eight forms of Lord *Paramashiva* is earth. His consort is *Sukesee*. Their son is *Angārakā* (Mars).
- In *Vāyu Purana* –

  *Sarvasya Yā Truteeyā Tu Nāma Bhoomitanuḥ Smrutā* I
  *Patnee Tasya Sukeseeti Putraschangārako Mataḥ* II
- *Sri Adi Shankara* in his commentary of Sri *Vishnu Sahasranama* for the 26th name – *Sharvaḥ* – writes that he destroys all the living beings during the great dissolution of the universe (*Pralaya* period). Here she it can be considered as the consort of *Sharvaḥ*.
- In *Mahāshoḍā Nyāsa* (*Prabancha Nyāsa*), it has been said that **She** is in the form of zodiac sign.
- 124th name of Sri Lalita Sahasranama is also the same *Śarvāṇī*.

961. शर्वरीवन्द्या – *Śarvarīvandyā*

- She is venerated daily at the pradosha kala (between 4:30 and 6:30 p.m.).
- Worshipping Sri Shiva and Sri Devi during pradosha gives much more benefits than worshipping at other times. Hence devotees' throng to worship her during pradosha time.

962. षड्भाषा – *Sabha*

- She is acclaimed as shad bhasha Swaroopini.
- She is the form of Six Vedangas viz., Siksha and Sangeeta, Kalpa Grandha, Vyaakarana, Nirukta Varnana, Chandas Shastra, and Jyotisha. These are called Shadangas or six organs to Vedas.
- She is an expert of six languages viz., Samskrutam, Prakriti, Magadhi, Paishachi, Souraseni and Apabhramsha.

963. षड्ऋतुप्रिया – *Ṣaḍṛtupriyā*

- She is fond of and active during all the Six Seasons
- Six ruthus are (96th name above can also be referred) –
  - I. Vasanta or Spring Season viz. Chaitra and Vaishakha or mid-February to mid-April;
  - II. Greeshma or Summer or Jyeshtha-Ashadha i.e. end April to end June;
  - III. Varsha or Monsoon during Shravana and Bhadrapada approximately end July-end August;
  - IV. Sharad or Autumn viz. Ashwiyuja and Kartika i.e. end August to end October approximately;
  - V. Hemanta or Pre-Winter during Margaseersha to Pushya approximating last week October to last week of December; and
  - VI. Sishira or Winter viz. Magha and Phalguna i.e. last week of Dec to mid-February approximately.

964. षडाधारस्थितादेवी – *Ṣaḍādhārasthitādevī*

- She being based on Moolaadhara, she is hinged on Shad (six) other chakras viz. Swadhishtana, Manipuraka, Anahata, Vishuddhi, Aagjna and Sahasrara.
- These have been discussed in detail earlier in other name(s).

965. षण्मुखप्रियकारिणी – *Ṣaṇmukhapriyakāriṇī*

- Devi Gayatri has immense liking for Lord Subrahmanya, the Six Headed, destroyer of Tarakasura.
- To kill the demon Tarakasuran, at the request of Devas, she incarnated as Hemavathi, daughter of Himavan and married Lord Shiva to give birth to Subrahmanya.
- His six heads and faces are stated to represent the Six Chakras mentioned in the previous name. The Six Countenances also represent Six Attributes of Maha Deva viz. –
  - I. Jnaana or Knowledge,
  - II. Vairagya or detachment,
  - III. Bala/ Might,
  - IV. Keerti or highly esteemed Fame and Glory,
  - V. Sree or wealth and
  - VI. Aishwarya or Magnificence

the Six faces also represent Pancha Karmendriyas (or five Jnanendriyas) plus Buddhi. Incidentally, the names of His consorts are Valli and Devyani. He married Valli the Gandharva way – without the consent of parents of both the sides – since he desired her but having tested with her qualities again and again. Devyani is the daughter of Indra as the latter gifted her in gratitude since Shanmukha destroyed Soora, the demon.

- 523rd name of Sri Lalita Sahasranama is *Shaḍānanā* – she herself having six faces.
- *Āgnā chakra* is the place of the mind. To exhibit the energy of the five primary elements and that of mind, **she** has six faces. To show that it is the controlling chief of all the five *chakras* from *Vishudhi* till *Moolādhāra*, **she** has six faces.

966. षडङ्ग रूप सुमति सुरासुर नमस्कृता – *Sarangi Rūpa Sumati Surāsura Namaskṛtā*

- The six countenanced and nobility incarnate Kumara worships our Devi.
- She is venerated by Deva-Danavas too.
- One who transcends the six modes of devotion. It is told that there are six methods of worshipping *Sri Devi* viz. –
    a. *Varṇātvā* is formed with the letters beginning from *'A'* till *'Ksha'*.
    b. *Padātvā* is of words – are group of letters.
    c. *Mantratvā* is of *mantra* – a group of words.
    d. *Kalātvā* is of *kalās* – abolition, etc.
    e. *Tatvādhvā* is of *tattvas* – *tattvas* are being mentioned differently in *Sivāgamam*, etc.
    f. *Bhuvātvā* is of *Bhuvanas* (worlds).
- **She** transcends all these 6 *atvās*. Worshipping of *Shiva*, *Viṣhṇu*, *Shakti*, Sun, *Ganapati* and *Kumara* (or *Indus*, which means Jainism) can be taken as six *atvās*. It has been mentioned that those who got his mind cleaned by these worships in the previous births, gets to worship *Sri Devi* in this birth. Hence it can be said as **She** transcends all these 6 *atvās*.

967. सरस्वती – *Sarasvatī*

- She is in the form of Saraswathi Devi.

- One who is in the form of Saraswathi, the presiding deity of knowledge.
- *Dhaumyar* says, Saraswathi is a girl of two years age. (In *Kanyā pooja*, it is customary to name the girls according to their ages).
- The *Bharadwaj Smruti* says, "Saraswathi is, she who ever resides in the tongues of all beings and who causes speech, hence **She** is called Saraswathi by great sages" –

  *Yā Vasetprānijihvāsu Sadā Vāgupavartanāt* I
  *Sarasvateeti Nāmneyam Samākhyātā Maharshibhi*: II
- The *Vasishta Ramayana* also says, "She is called Saraswathi because **She** is the stream of sense-impression" –

  *Saranāt Sarvdrushteenām Kathitashā Sarasvatee*.
- The three historical deities in *Saptashatee* and their group names have been mentioned in this *Sahasranāma*. They are;

  | | | |
  |---|---|---|
  | *Mahākāli* | – | 796th name |
  | *Mahālakşmī* | – | 795th name |
  | *Sarasvatī* | – | 704 (this name) |

  In *Mahāshoḍa Nyāsam* (*Prapanchanyāsam*), *Sarasvatee* is called as *Panchaprāṇaroopa*.
- **She** is in the form of *Saraswatee* river.

968. सदाधारा – *Sadādhārā*

- She is the fulcrum point of all beings always.

969. सर्वमङ्गलकारिणी – *Sarvamaṅgalakāriṇī*

- She is the benefactor to one – all depending on the results of individual karmas.
- One who is the source of all that is auspicious. **She** is the root of all those.
- *Devi Purana* says –

  *Sarvāni Hrudayasthāni Mangalāni Shubhānica* I
  *Eepsitāni Dadātheeti Tena Sā Sarvamangala* II
  *Shobhanāni Ca Sreshtāni Yā Devee Dadate Hare* I
  *Bhaktanamartiharanee Teneyam Sarvamangala* II
- *Sarvamangala* is a *Thiti Nityā Devee*. Hence it can be inferred that this name indicates the *Pranavā* (in the *mantra* of *Sarva mangalā*) sound (*Om*).
- It is mentioned as *Thiti Roopa* in *Prapancha Nyāsa* of *Mahā Shoḍā Nyāsa*.

- The 124th name of Sri *Lalita Trishatee – Sarvamangalā – Sri Devi* is the *Chit* energy nothing different from *Brahmam*. **She** gives all good fortune to those who satisfy **Her** through meditation, praising through songs and worshipping through *poojas* (even if they are stupid).
- This can be compared with *Mangalānām Mangalam* in *Viṣhṇu Sahasranāma*, first part.
- 200th name of Sri Lalita Sahasranama is *Sarvamangalā* – worth comparing here.

970. सामगानप्रिया – *Sāmagānapriyā*

- She is particularly pleased with the rendering of Saama Veda.
- One who is fond of *Samaveda* songs. Chanting of *Samaveda* is always with tune and hence it is musical. Hence it is called as *Sāmagānam*.
- Hearing *Samaveda* will be so sweet to the ears like music. It is also said that the music originates only from *Samaveda*. *Parameshwara* is also very much interested in *Samaveda* songs. It is told (*Seemed Ramayana, Uttara Kāṇḍa* – 16-33) that *Rāvanā* sang *Samaveda* and pleased *Parameshwara*. Since *Sri Devi* is an integral part of *Parameshwara*, **she** is also very much fond of *Samaveda* songs.
- It can also be said that those who follow *Samaveda* are so dear to **Her**, as **Her** own life. This meaning is taken by splitting the name as *Sāmagā* + *Ana* + *Priyā* (*Ana* means life). Like **Her** life force, **she** is interested in those who sing *Samaveda*.

971. सूक्ष्मा – *Sūkṣmā*

- Sri Devi is so minute in her appearance that one's sensory organs including Mind fail to realise her
- One who has a very subtle, not to be easily be recognised, form.
- *Kaivalyopanishat* (16) says – it is subtler than the subtle and eternal – Sookshmāt *Sookshmataram Nityam*.
- *Taitrīya Upanishat* (II-20) says – it is subtler than an atom; *Anoraneeyān*.
- The sacrificial fire done in the fire at *Kundalini*, in the midst of *Mooladhāram*, is subtle. It is called *Rahoyāgam*. This indicates, in the *Navāvarṇa Pooja*, after establishing the vessels through *mantras*, offering special *argyās*, offering prayers to teacher, the following are offered as oblations in the fire of *Kundalini*; virtues,

sins, decisions, indecisions, justice, injustice, actions and inactions. This *homa* (sacrificial fire) is explained in *Tantra Rāja Tantra* in verses starting from *"Nityā Nityodite"* ending with *"Evam Dvādashadhā Homamaksharaiḥ Syādudheeritaiḥ"*. **She** is in the form of that *homa*.

- *Sri Devi*'s gross, subtle and subtler forms were discussed in 6th name of Sri Lalita Sahasranama – *Udyadhbānu Sahasrābhā* and again in 11th name *Panchatanmātra Sāyaka*.
- *Sri Adi Shankara* in his commentary for 457th name of Sri *Viṣhṇu Sahasranāma* – *Sookshmaḥ* mentions as; the ether and all are material causes. Since there is no material cause like sound, etc., he is subtle.
- *Muṇḍakopanishat* (I-1-6) says; *"Sarvagatam Susookshmam"*.

972. सावित्री – *Sāvitrī*

- Gayatri is renowned as Bhagavati Savitri too.
- Our Devi is in the form of Savitri who redeemed Satyavan's life from Yama.
- One who is in the form of *Savitri*, the creator of the world.
- The creator of this universe is called *Savita*, a form of *Paramashiva*. His consort is *Savitri*.
- The world is seen because of Sun – i.e. it is known to all through the light of Sun. Hence, he is also called as *Savita* or *Savitri*.
- Since **She** is worshipped through all *Vedas* and since by nature, **she** is a pure form, **she** is called as *Savitri*.
- **She Herself** originates in the form of light and smoothly and continuously flows. Hence, **she** is *Savitri*.
- According to *Padma Purana*, the presiding deity at *Pushkara Kshetra* is called *Savitri* –

  *Sāvitree Pushkare Nāmnāteertthānām Pravaresubhe.*
- 699th name of Sri Lalita Sahasranama is also the same *Sāvitrī*.

973. सामसम्भवा – *Sāmasambhavā*

- She is stated to have emerged from Sama Veda.
- 970th name above mentioned that she likes Sama Veda. Here it is mentioned that she originated from Sama Veda.
- 575th and 576th names of Sri Vishnu Sahasranama are *Samaga* – The chanter of Sama hymns and *Sama* – Himself is the Sama Veda.

974. सर्वावासा – *Sarvāvāsā*

- She exists in all beings of Srishti.
- One who is omniscient in the minds of all.
- **She** fixes all the organs or provides the orders.
- *Brahadāraṇyaka Upanishat* (III-7-3) says that this is with you and eternal – *Esha Ta Ātmā Antaryāmyamrtaḥ*.
- *Māndugya Upanishat* (6th verse) also conveys the same message – *"Eshontaryāmyesha Yoniḥ Sarvasya"*.
- Or by splitting the name into *Sarvā* + *Antaryāminee*, it can be construed that **She** is in both these forms. That is, it can be said as, **she** is in all forms again inside everybody. *Taitrīya Upanishat* (II-6-1) is an evidence for this – *"Tat Shrushtvā* II *Tadevānuprāvishat Tadanu Pravishya* II *Sachcha Tyachābhavat* II"

975. सदानन्दा – *Sadānandā*

- One who is always happy.
- Sage *Sadānandā* is the family guru of King Janaka. He is a son sage Goutama and Akalika (in Ramayana).
- 407th name above may also be referred.

976. सुस्तनी – *Sustanī*

- One who has beautiful breasts.
- Her figure is well curved and excellently shaped.
- The beauty of the breasts of Sri Devi have been described in many a place in this Sahasranama and other Shakta texts as well.

977. सागराम्बरा – *Sāgarāmbarā*

- She has the appearance of oceans
- She supports the sky as well.
- Earlier it has been mentioned in more than once that she lives in the midst of the ocean.

978. सर्वैश्वर्यप्रिया – *Sarvaiśvaryapriyā*

- She loves being the deposits of all kinds of fortunes and abundances.

- She loves to bestow all the Aishwarya to her devotees. This has also been mentioned in multiple places.

979. सिद्धिः – *Siddhīḥ*

- She is the manifestation of all Siddhis.
- She is the accomplishments like of Ashta Siddhis.
- She bestows Ashtamaa Siddhis to all.
- The Ashta Siddhis have been discussed in details in the 08th name above.

980. साधुबन्धुपराक्रमा – *Sādhubandhuparākramā*

- She displays her heroism for the sake of the virtuous and noble.
- One who does penance or devotion on her will definitely achieve the results/ fruits.

981. सप्तर्षिमण्डलगता – *Saptarṣimaṇḍalagatā*

- Sri Devi sometimes sojourns in the Sapta Rishi Mandala.
- The Sapta Rishi Mandala is above *Bhuḥ*, *Bhuvaḥ* and *Swaḥ* Lokas. Antariksha Surya, Chandra, Shukra, Budha, Mangala, Guru and Shani Mandalas where the well-wishers of the Lokas beneath reside as the Sapta Rishis. Present list of Sapta Rishis – Atri, Brugu, Kutsa, Vashishta, Kashyapa, Vamadeva and Angirasa. The list of Sapta Rishis is subject to revision by every manvantaram.

982. सोममण्डलवासिनी – *Somamaṇḍalavāsinī*

- Sri Devi resides in Soma Mandala as per her choice and convenience too.
- As mentioned in the previous name it can be considered that she resides in the Moon Mandala also.

983. सर्वज्ञा – *Sarvajñā*

- One who is omniscient.
- *Mundaka Upanishat* (I-1-9) says – one who perceives all and knows all – *"Yaḥ Sarvagnaḥ Sarva Vid"*.
- In *Devee Puranam* it is said as; *Sarvagna Sarva Vetrutvāt* – As **she**

knows everything, **she** is called omniscient.

- 196th name of Sri Lalita Sahasranama is also the same *Sarvajñā*.

984. सान्द्रकरुणा – *Sāndrakaruṇā*

- She is the replete with unreserved compassion.
- One who shows intense compassion.
- 197th name of Sri Lalita Sahasranama is also the same *Sāndrakaruṇā*.

985. समानाधिकवर्जिता – *Samānādhikavarjitā*

- She is fully non-discriminatory
- One who neither has equal nor a superior.
- *Svetaswatara Upanishat* (VI-8) – No one is seen equal or superior to him – *Na Tat Samas Capyadhikas Ca Drushyate*.
- 198th name of Sri Lalita Sahasranama is also the same *Samānādhikavarjitā*.

986. सर्वोत्तुङ्गा – *Sarvottuṅgā*

- She is the common occupant of all the species.

987. सङ्गहीना – *Saṅgahīnā*

- She has no special interest in any except among her keen followers.
- She has no prejudice among her devotees.

988. सद्गुणा – *Sadguṇā*

- She is the signage of all noble features and qualities.
- In reality she is the Brahmam – Nirguna (without any qualities). But in Saguna form, she is treated with various qualities.

989. सकलेष्टदा – *Sakaleṣṭadā*

- She is ready to fulfill all the desires of every devotee.
- She fulfilling the desires and wises of the devotees have been mentioned in multiple places.

990. सरघा – *Saraghā*

- She is omnipresent including within the honey bees and flies.
- 285th name of Sri Lalita Sahasranamam – *Ābrahmakeeṭajananee* – she is the mother of every living beings right from Brahma till a worm. Hence honey bees and flies are also included in this list.

991. सूर्यतनया – *Sūryatanayā*

- She is of a daughter of the Sun God.
- Yamuna Devi the daughter of Surya Deva. She is in that form and hence this name.

992. सुकेशी – *Sukeśī*

- She is possessive of gorgeous hair style.

993. सोमसंहती – *Somasaṃhatī*

- She has of the unique brightness of several Moons.
- The brightness of a Moon is cool. But the brightness of one Moon may not be enough to compare with that of Sri Devi. Hence it has been mentioned that several Moons – cool and much bright.

994. हिरण्यवर्णा – *Hiraṇyavarṇā*

- Sri Devi's physical complexion is golden.
- Her golden complexion has been mentioned earlier also.
- The very dhyana verse of Sri Lalita Sahasranama starts with '*Hiraṇyavarṇām*'.

995. हरिणी – *Hariṇī*

- She is distinct with the yellowish colour of a golden deer.
- 635th name of Sri Lalita Sahasranama is *Gowree* – Yellowish white colour is called as *Gowraḥ* i.e. of gold colour.
- Again the dhyana verse of Sri Lalita Sahasranama reads *Hiraṇyavarṇā* <u>*Hariṇīm.*</u>

996. ह्रीङ्कारी – *Hrīṅkārī*

- She is of the *Beeja Swaroopa* called *'Hreem'* – *'H'* is stated to represent *Mahadeva* and *'R'* for *Parashakti*. Hence it is unison of *Shiva* and *Shakti*.
- *'Hree'* means modesty, shyness and bashfulness. One who does this is *Hreenkāree*.
- In *Swatantra Tantra* it is mentioned as; since *Sri Devi* takes care of creation, protection and destruction tasks, **she** is called as *Hreenkāree*. The letters in the corresponding verse here is deliberately in a dispersed manner.
- *Hreem* itself is one of the names of *Sree Devee* – 99th name in Sri *Lalita Trishatee* also. *Sri Adi Shankara*, in his commentary mentions – all energies are attributes of *Sri Devi*. By disconnecting them we get **Her** liberated form. **She** is seen as a complete liberated goddess.
- *Hreem* is the *Maya beeja – a*lso called as *Bhuvaneshvaree beeja*.
- This *beeja*, in the *Panchadashee mantra*, is suffixed to every division. The letters *'Ka'* and *'Ha'* in the *Panchadashee mantra* correspond to *Shiva*. The letters *'A'*, *'E'*, *'La'* and *'Sa'*, correspond to *Shakti*. In Sri Lalita *Trishatee* itself, it is mentioned as *"Hreem Upayātmakam"*.
- *'Oṃ'* in general is called as *Praṇavam*. *'Hreem'* is called as *Shakta Praṇavam*.
- Sri *Lalita Trishatee* has 300 names corresponding 20 names for each of the letters in Panchadashee mantra. It has 60 names corresponding to *Hreem*.
- In *Purusha Sookta* we read – *Hreeshcha Te Lakshmeeshcha Patnyou.*
- 301st name of Sri Lalita Sahasranama is also the same *Hrīṅkārī*.

997. हंसवाहिनी – *Haṃsavāhinī*

- She has an illustrious Swan as her carrier.
- Swan birds are famous for their beauty in walking. It is the practice of poets to compare the gait of great ladies to that of swan birds. Great gentlemen's gait is compared to that of elephants or lions.
- *Sri Adi Shankara*, in his *Soundaryalaharee*, (91st verse beginning with *"Padanyāsa Kreedā"*) describes that the swans are inspired by *Sri Devi*'s gait beauty and go behind **Her**.
- A type of *sanyasis* called *Paramahamsā* is indifferent to **Her** (i.e. those great *sanyasis* are always meditating upon **Her**). Hence **She** is called as *Hamsinee*.

- During pranayama, exhale and inhale of breath together has to be done with a mantra. That mantra is called *Hamsa Mantra* or *Ajapā Mantra*. This is a *mantra* about *Sri Devi* and hence **She** is *Hamsinee*.

998. क्षौमवस्त्रपरिताङ्गी – *Kṣaumavastraparitāngī*

- Sri Devi is magnificent in the apparel of bright silks.
- As an emperes her dress is always magnificent. Also, she is a goddess and hence more qualified to have amusing dress.

999. क्षीराब्धितनया – *Kṣīrābdhitanayā*

- When the milky ocean was churned for nectar, Goddess Lakshmi appeared from it. Lord Vishnu married her.
- Our Devi is in the form Lakshmi and hence named as the daughter of milky ocean.

1000. क्षमा – *Kṣamā*

- Devi Gayatri is the embodiment of Forgiveness and Tolerance.
- The quality of compassion is to forgive the sins and protect. She is to the core in this regard.
- **She** is the highest in all these – the elevation of mind, regard, the expression indicating the forgiveness of sin, proof, or measurement.
- She is our mother and we are her children. She does not mind the mistakes done by children, forgives them and still bless us.

Thus ends 100 divine names on *Sri Gayatri Devi* from 901 to 1000

*****

1001. गायत्री – *Gāyatrī*

- This name is repetition of 200th name above.

1002. सावित्री – *Sāvitrī*

- She is also the same manifestation of Savitri.
- This name is repetition of 972nd name above.

1003. पार्वती – *Pārvatī*

- Our Devi is another form of Parvati.
- This name is repetition of 548th name above.

1004. सरस्वती – *Sarasvatī*

- Sri Devi is in the form of Saraswathi also.
- This name is repetition of 967th name above.

1005. वेदगर्भा – *Vedagarbhā*

- She is the one who created the *Vedas*.
- Sri Devi is celebrated all over the Universe as the Veda Garbha.
- She is the very originator of one Veda which was further divided and edited subsequently into four branches as Rig, Yajus, Sama and Atharvarva.
- It has been mentioned in many a place in *Vedas* that they originated from *Brahmam* – Yasya *Nisvasitam Vedāḥ, Asya Mahato Bhootasya Nisvashitametadrugvedo Yajurveda, Ruchaḥ Sāmāni Jagjire*, etc.
- 338th name of Sri Lalita Sahasranama is *Vedajananee* – giving the same meaning.
- The Sri *Devi Purana* says – because, there arose from the *Kundalini*, which is triangular in form. Hence, **she** is the mother of all the *Vedas* and hence *Vedajananee*.
- 386th name of Sri Lalita Sahasranama is *Shadangadevatā Yuktā* – may also be referred in this context.

1006. वरारोहा – *Varārohā*

- She is the outstanding bestower of Boons to her devotees.

- She not only bestows what is asked for, but also something more. As a mother she knows what is to be offered to her children and what we are eligible for.

1007. श्रीगायत्री – *Śrīgāyatrī*

- She is the Maha Gayatri Devi.
- This name is repetition of 200th and 1001st names above.
- This is her Sahasranama Stora. It never gets bored, no matter how many times her name is mentioned like Gayatri japam.

1008. परांविका – *Parāṃvikā*

- She is the supreme Maha Mother Shakti.
- One who is the object of Supreme devotion.
- It has to be taken as **She** is worshipped as the supreme deity and the ultimate Godhead to be meditated upon.

|| *Iti Śrīdevībhāgavate Mahāpurāṇe Dvādaśaskandhe*

*Gāyatrī Aśtotra Sahasranāmā Samāptaḥ* ||

*****

## *Śrī Gāyatri Sahasranāma Uttara Bhāgaḥ*

उत्तर भागः – फल श्रुतिः । *Uttara Bhāgaḥ – Phala Śrutiḥ* ।

*Uttara Bhāgaḥ* – Last Part and *Phala Śrutiḥ* – fruits/ results of chanting the Gayatri Sahasranama Stotram.

इति साहस्त्रकं नाम्नां गायत्र्याश्चैव नारद ।
पुण्यदं सर्वपापघ्नं महासम्पत्तिदायकम् ॥ १

*Iti Sāhasrakaṃ Nāmnāṃ Gāyatryāścaiva Nārada* ।

*Puṇyadaṃ Sarvapāpaghnaṃ Mahāsampattidāyakam* ॥ 1

Oh Narada! Thus, I have described to you one thousand and eight names of Gayatri; the hearing of which yields merits and destroys all sins and gives all prosperity and wealth.

एवं नामानि गायत्र्यास्तोषोत्पत्तिकराणि हि ।
अष्टम्यां च विशेषेण पठितव्यं द्विजैः सह ॥ २

*Evaṃ Nāmāni Gāyatryāstoṣotpattikarāṇi Hi* ।

*Aṣṭamyāṃ Ca Viśeṣeṇa Paṭhitavyaṃ Dvijaiḥ Saha* ॥ 2

जपं कृत्वा होम पूजाध्यानं कृत्वा विशेषतः ।
यस्मै कस्मै न दातव्यं गायत्र्यास्तु विशेषतः ॥ ३

*Japaṃ Kṛtvā Homa Pūjādhyānaṃ Kṛtvā Viśeṣataḥ* ।

*Yasmai Kasmai Na Dātavyaṃ Gāyatryāstu Viśeṣataḥ* ॥ 3

Specially on an Ashtami tithi (eighth lunar day) if after one's meditation (Dhyanam) worship, Homa, and Japam, one recites this in company with the Brahmanas, one gets all sorts of satisfactions.

सुभक्ताय सुशिष्याय वक्तव्यं भूसु राय वै ।
भ्रष्टेभ्यः साधकेभ्यश्च बान्धवेभ्यो न दर्शयेत् ॥ ४

*Subhaktāya Suśiṣyāya Vaktavyaṃ Bhūsu Rāya Vai* ।

*Bhraṣṭebhyaḥ Sādhakebhyaśca Bāndhavebhyo Na Darśayet* ॥ 4

These one thousand and eight names of the Gayatri ought not to be given to anybody indiscriminately. Speak this out to him only who is very devoted, who is a Brahmana and who is an obedient disciple. Even if any devotee, fallen from the observances of Achara (right way of living), be a great friend, still do not disclose this to him.

यद्गृहे लिखितं शास्त्रं भयं तस्य न कस्यचित् ।
चञ्चलापिस्थिरा भूत्वा कमला तत्र तिष्ठति ॥ ५

*Yadgṛhe Likhitaṃ Śāstraṃ Bhayaṃ Tasya Na Kasyacit |*

*Cañcalāpisthirā Bhūtvā Kamalā Tatra Tiṣṭhati* || 5

इदं रहस्यं परमं गुह्याद्गुह्यतरं महत् ।
पुण्यप्रदं मनुष्याणां दरिद्राणांनिधिप्रदम् ॥ ६

*Idaṃ Rahasyaṃ Paramaṃ Guhyādguhyataraṃ Mahat |*

*Puṇyapradaṃ Manuṣyāṇāṃ Daridrāṇāṃnidhipradam* || 6

In whatever house, these names are kept written, no cause of fear can creep in there and Lakshmi, the Goddess of wealth, though unsteady, remains steady in that house.

मोक्षप्रदं मुमुक्षूणां कामिनां सर्वकामदम् ।
रोगाद्वै मुच्यते रोगी बद्धो मुच्येत बन्धनात् ॥ ७

*Mokṣapradaṃ Mumukṣūṇāṃ Kāmināṃ Sarvakāmadam |*

*Rogādvai Mucyate Rogī Baddho Mucyeta Bandhanāt* || 7

These great sacred names yield merits to persons, gives wealth to the poor, yields moksha to those who are desirous of it, and grants all desires. If anybody reads this, he gets cured of his diseases and becomes freed from bondages and imprisonment.

ब्रह्महत्या सुरापानं सुवर्णस्तेयिनो नराः ।
गुरुतल्पगतो वापि पातकातन्मुच्यते सकृत् ॥ ८

*Brahmahatyā Surāpānaṃ Suvarṇasteyino Narāḥ |*

*Gurutalpagato Vāpi Pātakātanmucyate Sakṛt* || 8

असत्प्रतिग्रहाच्चैवाऽभक्ष्यभक्षाद्विशेषतः ।
पाखण्डानृत्यमुख्यभ्यः पाठनादेव मुच्यते ॥ ९

*Asatpratigrahāccaivā'bhakṣyabhakṣādviśeṣataḥ |*

*Pākhaṇḍānṛtyamukhyabhyaḥ Pāṭhanādeva Mucyate* || 9

इदं रहस्यममलं मयोक्तं पद्मजोद्भव ।
ब्रह्मसायुज्यदं नॄनां सत्यं सन्त्य न संशय ॥ १०

*Idaṃ Rahasyamamalaṃ Mayoktaṃ Padmajodbhava* |
*Brahmasāyujyadaṃ Nṝnāṃ Satyaṃ Santya Na Saṃśaya* || 10

All the Great Sins, for example, murdering Brahmanas, drinking wine, stealing gold, going to the wife of one's Guru, taking gifts from bad persons, and eating the uneatable, all are destroyed, yea, verily destroyed!

Oh Narada! Thus, I have recited to you this Great Secret. All persons get, indeed, united with Brahma (Brahma–sayujya) by this. True. True. True. There is not the least trace of doubt here.

Note: In almost all the stotras the *phala shruti* part will be an addendum – added separately later on. But in the case the *phala shruti* is part and parcel of the stotra itself.

The greatest benefits of reciting each stotra are mentioned in the phala shruti portion – most people will doubt whether it is correct. Is it exaggerated in a way? Certainly not – these are certain benefits if the stotras are recited with store focus/ attention (*ananya chinta*) and devotion.

Author's concluding remarks

This book was started with an intention to provide meaning for each of 1000 names for easy and proper understanding and reading. But after starting writing, with enthusiasm, the author was passioned and of course with the blessings of Sri Devi, it ended up as commentary (*Bhashyam*) of each of the names.

From the above commentaries, it can be concluded that there is no difference between Goddess Gayatri, Lalita, Lord Vishnu, Shiva and all. All are equal – all are the different forms of Brahmam. Let us comprehend the meanings, inner tattvas, etc., and get most benefit.

As already mentioned, let us read this Sahasranama and after completing the daily Gayatri Japa and all. This will reap the best results.

Lord Narayana as if says to Narada, says to all of us – This Sahasranama of Bhagavati Gayatri is very significant, provider of Maha Punya and abundant prosperity, reliever of all the sins committed. This is the best way of making Gayatri happy especially if it is sincerely read and heard in the company of Brahmanas on Ashtami Tithis. If this deed is accompanied by Japa, Homa, Puja and Dhyana the effort secures manifold benefits. However, there should be a word of precaution that Gayatri Sahasranama should not be instructed in a formal manner to a non deserving person but required to be taught to ideal and sincere devotees, let alone even close relatives who are not committed. Indeed, there needs to be no publicity about it as it might be counter-productive. Those who practice the rendition and interpretation of the Sahasranama suffer no fear and apprehension. The results can be summarised as;

- A waving Lakshmi would settle down in their homes for good.
- Human beings would turn out to be highly virtuous and those from abject poverty would gradually become prosperous.
- Yogis and Seekers would traverse on the path of Salvation with firm footsteps.
- Persons steeped in illnesses would recover rapidly.
- Those in imprisonment would instantly release.
- Even those who might have committed the proverbial Pancha Maha Patakas or Five inexcusable sins (Brahma Hatya, Sura Pana or Intoxication, Suvarna Chourya or thieving especially of gold, Guru Patni Gamana or adultery especially with the wife of Guru and keeping company or abetting of any of these vices) could be rescinded by the reading, hearing and absorbing the meaning of Sri Gayatri Sahasranama.
- Acceptance of disqualified offerings as renumerations, consumption of forbidden eats and drinks, indulgence in untruth and ingratitude, waywardly and errant behavior verging on impropriety and anti-socialism could be quashed too by the recourse of Sri Devi Gayatri Sahasranama!
- The above does not mean that one can do any type of sin or wrong and chant this Sahasranama and get rid of it. It has to be construed that these are for wrong doings unknowing done.

May we sincerely meditate and worship Gayatri Devi with –

- Five Faces of the complexions of Pearls, Corals, Golden Yellow, Blue Nila and Milky White;

- Three Eyed representing Tri Lokas, Trigunas and Three Actions of Srishti, Sthithi, and Samhara;
- Ornamented with a gem-studded headgear with a Symbol of Half Moon;
- Possessive of Eight Arms adorned with Varadaabhaya Mudra or a Protective Hand Sign, Ankusha or Goad, Gada or Mace, Shankha or Conch Shell, Chakra or the Mighty Disc, Kapala Gunam or a Skull and two Lotus Flowers each signifying Purity and Vidya or Knowledge and Wisdom.

*****

## *Śrī Gāyatri Sahasranāma Storam* – Samskrutam

श्री गायत्री सहस्रनाम स्तोत्रम्

पूर्व भागः।

नारद उवाच।

भगवन् सर्व धर्मज्ञ सर्व शास्त्र विशारद।
श्रुति स्मृति पुराणानाम् रहस्यम् त्वन्मुखाच्छ्रुतम्॥ १

सर्वपापहरम् देव येन विद्या प्रवर्तते।
केन वा ब्रह्म्विज्ञानं किं नु वा मोक्षसाधनम्॥ २

ब्राह्मणानां गतिः केन केन वा मृत्युनाशनम्।
ऐहिकामुष्मिक फलं केन वा पद्मलोचन॥ ३

वक्तुमर्हस्यशेषेण सर्वं निखिलमादितः।

श्रीनारायण उवाच।

साधु साधु महाप्राज्ञ सम्यक् पृष्टं त्वयानघ॥ ४

शृणु वक्ष्यामि यत्नेन गायत्र्यष्ट सहस्रकम्।
नाम्नां शुभानां दिव्यानां सर्वपाप विनाशनम्॥ ५

सृष्ट्यादौ यद्भगवता पूर्वं प्रोक्तं ब्रवीमि ते।
अष्टोत्तर सहस्रस्य ऋषिर्ब्रह्मा प्रकीर्तितः॥ ६

छन्दोऽनुष्टुप् तथा देवी गायत्री देवता स्मृता।
हलो बीजानि तस्यैव स्वराः शक्तय ईरिताः॥ ७

अङ्गन्यास करन्यासावुच्येते मातृकाक्षरैः।
अथ ध्यानं प्रवक्ष्यामि साधकानां हिताय वै॥ ८

ध्यानम्

रक्त श्वेत हिरण्य नील धवलैर्युक्तां त्रिनेत्रोज्ज्वलां
रक्तां रक्तनवस्रजं मणिगणैर्युक्तां कुमारीमिमाम्।
गायत्रीं कमलासनां करतल व्यानद्ध कुण्डाम्बुजां
पद्माक्षीं च वरस्रजं च दधातीं हंसाधि रूढां भजे॥ ९

अथ स्तोत्रः ।

ॐ अचिन्त्य लक्षणाव्यक्ताप्यर्थ मातृ महेश्वरी ।
अमृतार्णवमध्यस्थाप्यजिता चापराजिता ॥ १०

अणिमादि गुणा धाराप्यर्क मण्डल संस्थिता ।
अजराजापराधर्मा अक्षसूत्रधराधरा ॥ ११

अकारादि क्षकारान्ताप्यरिषड्वर्ग भेदिनी ।
अञ्जनाद्रि प्रतीकाशाप्यञ्जनाद्रि निवासिनी ॥ १२

अदितिश्चा जपा विद्याप्यरविन्द निभेक्षणा ।
अन्तर्बहिः स्थिता विद्याध्वंसिनी चान्तरात्मिका ॥ १३

अजा चाजमुखा वासाप्यरविन्द निभानना ।
अर्धमात्रार्थदानज्ञाप्यरि मण्डल मर्दिनी ॥ १४

असुरघ्नी ह्यमावास्याप्य लक्ष्मीघ्न्यन्त्यजार्चिता ।
आदि लक्ष्मीश्चादि शक्तिराकृतिश्चायतानना ॥ १५

आदित्य पदवी चाराप्यादित्य परि सेविता ।
आचार्या वर्तनाचाराप्यादि मूर्ति निवासिनी ॥ १६

आग्नेयी चामरी चाद्या चाराध्या चासनस्थिता ।
आधार निलयाधारा चाकाशान्त निवासिनी ॥ १७

आद्याक्षर समायुक्ता चान्तराकाश रूपिणी ।
आदित्य मण्डल गता चान्तरध्वान्त नाशिनी ॥ १८

इन्दिरा चेष्टदा चेष्टा चेन्दी वर निभेक्षणा ।
इरावती चेन्द्रपदा चेन्द्राणी चेन्दु रूपिणी ॥ १९

इक्षु कोदण्ड संयुक्ता चेषु संधान कारिणी ।
इन्द्र नील समाकारा चेडापिङ्गल रूपिणी ॥ २०

इन्द्राक्षीचेश्वरी देवी चेहात्रय विवर्जिता ।
उमा चोषा ह्युडुनिभा उर्वारुक फलानना ॥ २१

उडुप्रभा चोडुमती ह्युडुपा ह्युडु मध्यगा ।
ऊर्ध्वा चाप्यूर्ध्व केशी चाप्यूर्ध्वाधो गति भेदिनी ॥ २२

ऊर्ध्व बाहुप्रिया चोर्मिमालावाग्ग्रन्थ दायिनी ।
ऋतं चर्षिरृतुमती ऋषिदेवनमस्कृता ॥ २३

ऋग्वेदा ऋणहर्त्री च ऋषि मण्डल चारिणी ।
ऋद्धिदा ऋजुमार्गस्था ऋजुधर्मा ऋतुप्रदा ॥ २४

ऋग्वेद निलया ऋज्वी लुप्त धर्म प्रवर्तिनी ।
लूतारि वर सम्भूता लूतादि विष हारिणी ॥ २५

एकाक्षरा चैकमात्रा चैका चैकैकनिष्ठिता ।
ऐन्द्री ह्यैरावतारूढा चैहिकामुष्मिकप्रदा ॥ २६

ओंकारा ह्योषधी चोता चोतप्रोतनिवासिनी ।
और्वा ह्यौषधसम्पन्ना औपासनफलप्रदा ॥ २७

अण्ड मध्यस्थिता देवी चाःकार मनुरूपिणी ।
कात्यायनी कालरात्रिः कामाक्षी कामसुन्दरी ॥ २८

कमला कामिनी कान्ता कामदा कालकण्ठिनी ।
करि कुम्भस्तनभरा करवीर सुवासिनी ॥ २९

कल्याणी कुण्डलवती कुरुक्षेत्र निवासिनी ।
कुरुविन्द दलाकारा कुण्डली कुमुदालया ॥ ३०

कालजिह्वा करालास्या कालिका कालरूपिणी ।
कमनीयगुणा कान्तिः कलाधारा कुमुद्वती ॥ ३१

कौशिकी कमलाकारा कामचार प्रभञ्जिनी ।
कौमारी करुणापाङ्गी ककुबन्ता करिप्रिया ॥ ३२

केसरी केशवनुता कदम्ब कुसुम प्रिया ।
कालिन्दी कालिका काञ्ची कलशोद्भव संस्तुता ॥ ३३

काम माता क्रतुमती कामरूपा कृपावती ।
कुमारी कुण्डनिलया किराती कीरवाहना ॥ ३४

कैकेयी कोकिलालापा केतकी कुसुमप्रिया।
कमण्डलुधरा काली कर्म निर्मूल कारिणी ॥ ३५

कलहंसगतिः कक्षा कृत कौतुक मङ्गला।
कस्तूरीतिलका कम्प्रा करीन्द्र गमना कुहूः ॥ ३६

कर्पूरलेपना कृष्णा कपिला कुहराश्रया।
कूटस्था कुधरा कम्रा कुक्षिस्थाखिलविष्टपा ॥ ३७

खड्गखेटकरा खर्वा खेचरी खगवाहना।
खट्वाङ्ग धारिणी ख्याता खगराजोपरिस्थिता ॥ ३८
खलघ्नी खण्डितजरा खण्डाख्यान प्रदायिनी।
खण्डेन्दुतिलका गङ्गा गणेश गुह पूजिता ॥ ३९

गायत्री गोमती गीता गान्धारी गानलोलुपा।
गौतमी गामिनी गाधा गन्धर्वाप्सर सेविता ॥ ४०

गोविन्द चरणा क्रान्ता गुणत्रय विभाविता।
गन्धर्वी गह्वरी गोत्रा गिरीशा गहना गमी ॥ ४१

गुहावासा गुणवती गुरु पाप प्रणाशिनी।
गुर्वी गुणवती गुह्या गोप्तव्या गुणदायिनी ॥ ४२

गिरिजा गुह्य मातङ्गी गरुडध्वज वल्लभा।
गर्वा पहारिणी गोदा गोकुलस्था गदाधरा ॥ ४३

गोकर्ण निलया सक्ता गुह्यमण्डल वर्तिनी।
घर्मदा घनदा घण्टा घोर दानव मर्दिनी ॥ ४४

घृणि मन्त्रमयी घोषा घनसम्पात दायिनी।
घण्टारव प्रिया घ्राणा घृणिसंतुष्टकारिणी ॥ ४५

घनारि मण्डला घूर्णा घृताची घनवेगिनी।
ज्ञान धातुमयी चर्चा चर्चिता चारुहासिनी ॥ ४६

चटुला चण्डिका चित्रा चित्रमाल्य विभूषिता।
चतुर्भुजा चारुदन्ता चातुरी चरितप्रदा ॥ ४७

चूलिका चित्र वस्त्रान्ता चन्द्रमःकर्ण कुण्डला।
चन्द्रहासा चारुदात्री चकोरी चन्द्र हासिनी ॥ ४८

चन्द्रिका चन्द्र धात्री च चौरी चौरा च चण्डिका।
चञ्चद्वाग्वादिनी चन्द्रचूडा चोर विनाशिनी ॥ ४९

चारु चन्दन लिप्ताङ्गी चञ्चच्चामर वीजिता।
चारु मध्या चारु गतिश्चन्दिला चन्द्र रूपिणी ॥ ५०

चारु होम प्रिया चार्वा चरिता चक्र बाहुका।
चन्द्र मण्डल मध्यस्था चन्द्र मण्डल दर्पणा ॥ ५१

चक्रवाक स्तनी चेष्टा चित्रा चारु विलासिनी।
चित्स्वरूपा चन्द्र वती चन्द्रमाश्चन्दन प्रिया ॥ ५२

चोदयित्री चिरप्रज्ञा चातका चारुहेतुकी।
छत्रयाता छत्रधरा छाया छन्दःपरिच्छदा ॥ ५३
छायादेवी छिद्रनखा छन्नेन्द्रियविसर्पिणी।
छन्दोऽनुष्टुप्प्रतिष्ठान्ता छिद्रोपद्रव भेदिनी ॥ ५४

छेदा छत्रेश्वरी छिन्ना छुरिका छेदन प्रिया।
जननी जन्मरहिता जातवेदा जगन्मयी ॥ ५५

जाह्नवी जटिला जेत्री जरा मरण वर्जिता।
जम्बूद्वीप वती ज्वाला जयन्ती जलशालिनी ॥ ५६

जितेन्द्रिया जितक्रोधा जितामित्रा जगत्प्रिया।
जातरूपमयी जिह्वा जानकी जगती जरा ॥ ५७

जनित्री जह्नुतनया जगत्त्रय हितैषिणी।
ज्वालामुखी जपवती ज्वरघ्नी जितविष्टपा ॥ ५८

जिताक्रान्तमयी ज्वाला जाग्रती ज्वरदेवता।
ज्वलन्ती जलदा ज्येष्ठा ज्याघोषास्फोटदिङ्मुखी ॥ ५९

जम्भिनी जृम्भणा जृम्भा ज्वलन्माणिक्य कुण्डला।
झिंझिका झणनिर्घोषा झंझामारुतवेगिनी ॥ ६०

झल्लरीवाद्यकुशला अरूपा अभुजा स्मृता ।
टङ्कबाण समायुक्ता टङ्किनी टङ्क भेदिनी ॥ ६१

टङ्कीगण कृताघोषा टङ्कनीय महोरसा ।
टङ्कार कारिणी देवी ठठशब्द निनादिनी ॥ ६२

डामरी डाकिनी डिम्भा डुण्डमारैक निर्जिता ।
डामरी तन्त्र मार्गस्था डमड्डमरु नादिनी ॥ ६३

डिण्डीरवसहा डिम्भल सत्क्रीडा परायणा ।
ढुण्ढि विघ्नेशजननी ढक्काहस्ता ढिलिव्रजा ॥ ६४

नित्यज्ञाना निरुपमा निर्गुणा नर्मदा नदी ।
त्रिगुणा त्रिपदा तन्त्री तुलसी तरुणा तरुः ॥ ६५

त्रिविक्रम पदाक्रान्ता तुरीय पदगामिनी ।
तरुणादित्य संकाशा तामसी तुहिना तुरा ॥ ६६

त्रिकालज्ञान सम्पन्ना त्रिवली च त्रिलोचना ।
त्रिशक्तिस्त्रिपुरा तुङ्गा तुरङ्ग वदना तथा ॥ ६७

तिमिङ्गिलगिला तीव्रा त्रिस्रोता तामसादिनी ।
तन्त्र मन्त्र विशेषज्ञा तनुमध्या त्रिविष्टपा ॥ ६८
त्रिसन्ध्या त्रिस्तनी तोषासंस्था तालप्रतापिनी ।
ताटङ्किनी तुषाराभा तुहिनाचलवासिनी ॥ ६९

तन्तुजाल समायुक्ता तारहारा वलिप्रिया ।
तिल होम प्रिया तीर्था तमाल कुसुमाकृतिः ॥ ७०

तारका त्रियुता तन्वी त्रिशङ्कुपरिवारिता ।
तलोदरी तिलाभूषा ताटङ्कप्रियवादिनी ॥ ७१

त्रिजटा तित्तिरी तृष्णा त्रिविधा तरुणा कृतिः ।
तप्त काञ्चन संकाशा तप्त काञ्चन भूषणा ॥ ७२

त्रैयम्बका त्रिवर्गा च त्रिकालज्ञानदायिनी ।
तर्पणा तृप्तिदा तृप्ता तामसी तुम्बुरुस्तुता ॥ ७३

तार्क्ष्यस्था त्रिगुणाकारा त्रिभङ्गी तनुवल्लरिः ।
थात्कारी थारवा थान्ता दोहिनी दीनवत्सला ॥ ७४

दानवान्तकरी दुर्गा दुर्गासुरनिबर्हिणी ।
देवरीतिर्दिवारात्रिर्द्रौपदी दुन्दुभिस्वना ॥ ७५

देवयानी दुरावासा दारिद्र्योद्भेदिनी दिवा ।
दामोदरप्रिया दीप्ता दिग्वासा दिग्विमोहिनी ॥ ७६

दण्डकारण्यनिलया दण्डिनी देवपूजिता ।
देववन्द्या दिविषदा द्वेषिणी दानवाकृतिः ॥ ७७

दीनानाथस्तुता दीक्षा दैवतादिस्वरूपिणी ।
धात्री धनुर्धरा धेनुर्धारिणी धर्मचारिणी ॥ ७८

धरन्धरा धराधारा धनदा धान्यदोहिनी ।
धर्मशीला धनाध्यक्षा धनुर्वेद विशारदा ॥ ७९

धृतिर्धन्या धृतपदा धर्मराजप्रिया ध्रुवा ।
धूमावती धूमकेशी धर्मशास्त्र प्रकाशिनी ॥ ८०

नन्दा नन्दप्रिया निद्रा नृनुता नन्दनात्मिका ।
नर्मदा नलिनी नीला नीलकण्ठसमाश्रया ॥ ८१

नारायणप्रिया नित्या निर्मला निर्गुणा निधिः ।
निराधारा निरुपमा नित्यशुद्धा निरञ्जना ॥ ८२

नादबिन्दु कलातीता नादबिन्दु कलात्मिका ।
नृसिंहिनी नगधरा नृपनाग विभूषिता ॥ ८३
नरक क्लेश शमनी नारायण पदोद्भवा ।
निरवद्या निराकारा नारद प्रिय कारिणी ॥ ८४

नानाज्योतिः समाख्याता निधिदा निर्मलात्मिका ।
नवसूत्रधरा नीतिर्निरुपद्रवकारिणी ॥ ८५

नन्दजा नवरत्नाढ्या नैमिषारण्य वासिनी ।
नवनीतप्रिया नारी नीलजीमूतनिस्वना ॥ ८६

निमेषिणी नदीरूपा नीलग्रीवा निशीश्वरी ।
नामावलिर्निशुम्भघ्नी नागलोक निवासिनी ॥ ८७

नवजाम्बूनद प्रख्या नागलोकाधि देवता ।
नूपुराक्रान्त चरणा नरचित्त प्रमोदिनी ॥ ८८

निमग्ना रक्त नयना निर्घात समनिस्वना ।
नन्दनोद्यान निलया निर्व्यूहोपरिचारिणी ॥ ८९

पार्वती परमोदारा परब्रह्मात्मिका परा ।
पञ्चकोश विनिर्मुक्ता पञ्चपातक नाशिनी ॥ ९०

परचित्तविधानज्ञा पञ्चिका पञ्चरूपिणी ।
पूर्णिमा परमा प्रीतिः परतेजः प्रकाशिनी ॥ ९१

पुराणी पौरुषी पुण्या पुण्डरीक निभेक्षणा ।
पाताल तल निर्मग्ना प्रीता प्रीति विवर्धिनी ॥ ९२

पावनी पादसहिता पेशला पवनाशिनी ।
प्रजापतिः परिश्रान्ता पर्वत स्तन मण्डला ॥ ९३

पद्मप्रिया पद्मसंस्था पद्माक्षी पद्मसम्भवा ।
पद्मपत्रा पद्मपदा पद्मिनी प्रियभाषिणी ॥ ९४

पशुपाश विनिर्मुक्ता पुरन्ध्री पुरवासिनी ।
पुष्कला पुरुषा पर्वा पारिजात सुमप्रिया ॥ ९५

पतिव्रता पवित्राङ्गी पुष्प हास परायणा ।
प्रज्ञावतीसुता पौत्री पुत्रपूज्या पयस्विनी ॥ ९६

पट्टिपाशधरा पङ्क्तिः पितृलोकप्रदायिनी ।
पुराणी पुण्यशीला च प्रणतार्ति विनाशिनी ॥ ९७

प्रद्युम्न जननी पुष्टा पितामह परिग्रहा ।
पुण्डरीकपुरावासा पुण्डरीकसमानना ॥ ९८

पृथुजङ्घा पृथुभुजा पृथुपादा पृथूदरी ।
प्रवालशोभा पिङ्गाक्षी पीतवासाः प्रचापला ॥ ९९

प्रसवा पुष्टिदा पुण्या प्रतिष्ठा प्रणवागतिः ।
पञ्चवर्णा पञ्चवाणी पञ्चिका पञ्चरस्थिता ॥ १००

परमाया परज्योतिः परप्रीतिः परागतिः ।
पराकाष्ठा परेशानी पाविनी पावकद्युतिः ॥ १०१

पुण्यभद्रा परिच्छेद्या पुष्पहासा पृथूदरी ।
पीताङ्गी पीतवसना पीतशय्या पिशाचिनी ॥ १०२

पीतक्रिया पिशाचघ्नी पाटलाक्षी पटुक्रिया ।
पञ्चभक्षप्रियाचारा पूतनाप्राणघातिनी ॥ १०३

पुन्नागवनमध्यस्था पुण्यतीर्थनिषेविता ।
पञ्चाङ्गी च पराशक्तिः परमाह्लादकारिणी ॥ १०४

पुष्पकाण्डस्थिता पूषा पोषिताखिल विष्टपा ।
पानप्रिया पञ्चशिखा पन्नगोपरिशायिनी ॥ १०५

पञ्चमात्रात्मिका पृथ्वी पथिका पृथुदोहिनी ।
पुराण न्याय मीमांसा पाटली पुष्प गन्धिनी ॥ १०६

पुण्यप्रजा पारदात्री परमार्गैकगोचरा ।
प्रवालशोभा पूर्णाशा प्रणवा पल्लवोदरी ॥ १०७

फलिनी फलदा फल्गुः फूत्कारी फलकाकृतिः ।
फणीन्द्र भोगशयना फणिमण्डल मण्डिता ॥ १०८

बालबाला बहुमता बालातपनिभांशुका ।
बलभद्रप्रिया वन्द्या वडवा बुद्धिसंस्तुता ॥ १०९

बन्दीदेवी बिलवती बडिशघ्नी बलिप्रिया ।
बान्धवी बोधिता बुद्धिर्बन्धूक कुसुमप्रिया ॥ ११०

बालभानुप्रभाकारा ब्राह्मी ब्राह्मणदेवता ।
बृहस्पतिस्तुता वृन्दा वृन्दावनविहारिणी ॥ १११

बालाकिनी बिलाहारा बिलवासा बहूदका ।
बहुनेत्रा बहुपदा बहुकर्णावतंसिका ॥ ११२

बहुबाहुयुता बीजरूपिणी बहुरूपिणी ।
बिन्दुनाद कलातीता बिन्दुनाद स्वरूपिणी ॥ ११३

बद्धगोधाङ्गुलित्राणा बदर्याश्रमवासिनी ।
बृन्दारका बृहत्स्कन्धा बृहती बाणपातिनी ॥ ११४

बृन्दाध्यक्षा बहुनुता वनिता बहुविक्रमा ।
बद्धपद्मासनासीना बिल्वपत्रतलस्थिता ॥ ११५

बोधिद्रुमनिजावासा बडिस्था बिन्दुदर्पणा ।
बाला बाणासनवती बडवानलवेगिनी ॥ ११६

ब्रह्माण्डबहिरन्तःस्था ब्रह्मकङ्कणसूत्रिणी ।
भवानी भीषणवती भाविनी भयहारिणी ॥ ११७

भद्रकाली भुजङ्गाक्षी भारती भारताशया ।
भैरवी भीषणाकारा भूतिदा भूतिमालिनी ॥ ११८

भामिनी भोगनिरता भद्रदा भूरिविक्रमा ।
भूतवासा भृगुलता भार्गवी भूसुरार्चिता ॥ ११९

भागीरथी भोगवती भवनस्था भिषग्वरा ।
भामिनी भोगिनी भाषा भवानी भूरिदक्षिणा ॥ १२०

भर्गात्मिका भीमवती भवबन्धविमोचिनी ।
भजनीया भूतधात्रीरञ्जिता भुवनेश्वरी ॥ १२१

भुजङ्गवलया भीमा भेरुण्डा भागधेयिनी ।
माता माया मधुमती मधुजिह्वा मधुप्रिया ॥ १२२

महादेवी महाभागा मालिनी मीनलोचना ।
मायातीता मधुमती मधुमांसा मधुद्रवा ॥ १२३

मानवी मधुसम्भूता मिथिलापुरवासिनी ।
मधुकैटभसंहर्त्री मेदिनी मेघमालिनी ॥ १२४

मन्दोदरी महामाया मैथिली मसृणप्रिया ।
महालक्ष्मीर्महाकाली महाकन्या महेश्वरी ॥ १२५

माहेन्द्री मेरुतनया मन्दारकुसुमार्चिता ।
मञ्जुमञ्जीरचरणा मोक्षदा मञ्जुभाषिणी ॥ १२६

मधुरद्राविणी मुद्रा मलया मलयान्विता ।
मेधा मरकतश्यामा मागधी मेनकात्मजा ॥ १२७

महामारी महावीरा महाश्यामा मनुस्तुता ।
मातृका मिहिराभासा मुकुन्दपदविक्रमा ॥ १२८
मूलाधारस्थिता मुग्धा मणिपूरकवासिनी ।
मृगाक्षी महिषारूढा महिषासुरमर्दिनी ॥ १२९

योगासना योगगम्या योगा यौवनकाश्रया ।
यौवनी युद्धमध्यस्था यमुना युगधारिणी ॥ १३०

यक्षिणी योगयुक्ता च यक्षराज प्रसूतिनी ।
यात्रा यानविधानज्ञा यदुवंश समुद्भवा ॥ १३१

यकारादिहकारान्ता याजुषी यज्ञरूपिणी ।
यामिनी योगनिरता यातुधानभयङ्करी ॥ १३२

रुक्मिणी रमणी रामा रेवती रेणुका रतिः ।
रौद्री रौद्रप्रियाकारा राममाता रतिप्रिया ॥ १३३

रोहिणी राज्यदा रेवा रमा राजीवलोचना ।
राकेशी रूपसम्पन्ना रत्नसिंहासनस्थिता ॥ १३४

रक्तमाल्याम्बरधरा रक्तगन्धानुलेपना ।
राजहंससमारूढा रम्भा रक्तबलिप्रिया ॥ १३५

रमणीययुगाधारा राजिताखिलभूतला ।
रुरुचर्मपरीधाना रथिनी रत्नमालिका ॥ १३६

रोगेशी रोगशमनी राविणी रोमहर्षिणी ।
रामचन्द्रपदाक्रान्ता रावणच्छेदकारिणी ॥ १३७

रत्नवस्त्रपरिच्छन्ना रथस्था रुक्मभूषणा ।
लज्जाधिदेवता लोला ललिता लिङ्गधारिणी ॥ १३८

लक्ष्मीर्लोला लुप्तविषा लोकिनी लोकविश्रुता।
लज्जा लम्बोदरी देवी ललना लोकधारिणी॥ १३९

वरदा वन्दिता विद्या वैष्णवी विमलाकृतिः।
वाराही विरजा वर्षा वरलक्ष्मीर्विलासिनी॥ १४०

विनता व्योम मध्यस्था वारिजा सनसंस्थिता।
वारुणी वेणुसम्भूता वीतिहोत्रा विरूपिणी॥ १४१

वायुमण्डलमध्यस्था विष्णुरूपा विधिप्रिया।
विष्णुपत्नी विष्णुमती विशालाक्षी वसुन्धरा॥ १४२

वामदेवप्रिया वेला वज्रिणी वसुदोहिनी।
वेदाक्षरपरीताङ्गी वाजपेयफलप्रदा॥ १४३
वासवी वामजननी वैकुण्ठनिलया वरा।
व्यासप्रिया वर्मधरा वाल्मीकिपरिसेविता॥ १४४

शाकम्भरी शिवा शान्ता शारदा शरणागतिः।
शातोदरी शुभाचारा शुम्भासुरविमर्दिनी॥ १४५

शोभावती शिवाकारा शंकरार्ध शरीरिणी।
शोणा शुभाशया शुभ्रा शिरःसन्धानकारिणी॥ १४६

शरावती शरानन्दा शरज्ज्योत्स्ना शुभानना।
शरभा शूलिनी शुद्धा शबरी शुकवाहना॥ १४७

श्रीमती श्रीधरानन्दा श्रवणानन्ददायिनी।
शर्वाणी शर्वरीवन्द्या षड्भाषा षड्तुप्रिया॥ १४८

षडाधारस्थिता देवी षण्मुखप्रियकारिणी।
षडङ्गरूपसुमतिसुरासुरनमस्कृता॥ १४९

सरस्वती सदाधारा सर्वमङ्गलकारिणी।
सामगानप्रिया सूक्ष्मा सावित्री सामसम्भवा॥ १५०

सर्वावासा सदानन्दा सुस्तनी सागराम्बरा।
सर्वैश्वर्यप्रिया सिद्धिः साधुबन्धुपराक्रमा॥ १५१

सप्तर्षिमण्डलगता सोममण्डलवासिनी ।
सर्वज्ञा सान्द्रकरुणा समानाधिकवर्जिता ॥ १५२

सर्वोत्तुङ्गा सङ्गहीना सद्गुणा सकलेष्टदा ।
सरधा सूर्यतनया सुकेशी सोमसंहतिः ॥ १५३

हिरण्यवर्णा हरिणी ह्रींकारी हंसवाहिनी ।
क्षौमवस्त्रपरीताङ्गी क्षीराब्धितनया क्षमा ॥ १५४

गायत्री चैव सावित्री पार्वती च सरस्वती ।
वेदगर्भा वरारोहा श्रीगायत्री पराम्बिका ॥ १५५

फल श्रुतिः

इति साहस्रकं नाम्नां गायत्र्याश्चैव नारद ।
पुण्यदं सर्वपापघ्नं महासम्पत्तिदायकम् ॥ १५६

एवं नामानि गायत्र्यास्तोषोत्पत्तिकराणि हि ।
अष्टम्यां च विशेषेण पठितव्यं द्विजैः सह ॥ १५७

जपं कृत्वा होम पूजाध्यानं कृत्वा विशेषतः ।
यस्मै कस्मै न दातव्यं गायत्र्यास्तु विशेषतः ॥ १५८

सुभक्ताय सुशिष्याय वक्तव्यं भूसु राय वै ।
भ्रष्टेभ्यः साधकेभ्यश्च बान्धवेभ्यो न दर्शयेत् ॥ १५९

यद्गृहे लिखितं शास्त्रं भयं तस्य न कस्यचित् ।
चञ्चलापिस्थिरा भूत्वा कमला तत्र तिष्ठति ॥ १६०

इदं रहस्यं परमं गुह्याद्गुह्यतरं महत् ।
पुण्यप्रदं मनुष्याणां दरिद्राणांनिधिप्रदम् ॥ १६१

मोक्षप्रदं मुमुक्षूणां कामिनां सर्वकामदम् ।
रोगाद्वै मुच्यते रोगी बद्धो मुच्येत बन्धनात् ॥ १६२

ब्रह्महत्या सुरापानं सुवर्णस्तेयिनो नराः ।
गुरुतल्पगतो वापि पातकातन्मुच्यते सकृत् ॥ १६३

असत्प्रतिग्रहाच्चैवाऽभक्ष्यभक्षाद्विशेषतः ।
पाखण्डानृत्यमुख्यभ्यः पाठनादेव मुच्यते ॥ १६४

इदं रहस्यममलं मयोक्तं पद्मजोद्भव ।
ब्रह्मसायुज्यदं नृणां सत्यं सन्त्य न संशय ॥ १६५

इति श्रीदेवीभागवते महापुराणे द्वादशस्कन्धे गायत्रीसहस्रनाम
स्तोत्रकथनं नाम षष्ठोऽध्यायः ॥

*****

## *Śrī Gāyatri Sahasranāma Storam* – English

*Pūrva Bhāgaḥ* I

*Nārada Uvāca* I

*Bhagavan Sarva Dharmajña Sarva Śāstraviśārada* I
*Śruti Smṛtipurāṇānāṃ Rahasyaṃ Tvanmukhācchrutam* II 1

*Sarvapāpaharaṃ Deva Yena Vidyā Pravareate* I
*Kena Vā Brahmavijñānaṃ Kiṃ Nu Vā Mokṣasādhanam* II 2

*Brāhmaṇānāṃ Gatiḥ Kena Kena Vā Mṛtyu Nāśanam* I
*Aihikāmuṣmika Phalaṃ Kena Vā Padmalocana* II 3

*Vaktumarhasyaśeṣeṇa Sarve Nikhilamāditaḥ* I

*Śrīnārāyaṇa Uvāca* I

*Sādhu Sādhu Mahāprājña Samyak Pṛṣṭaṃ Tvayā'nagha* II 4

*Śṛṇu Vakṣyāmi Yatnena Gāyatryaṣṭasahasrakam* I
*Nāmnāṃ Śubhānāṃ Divyānāṃ Sarvapāpavināśanam* II 5

*Sṛṣṭyādau Yadbhagavatā Pūrve Proktaṃ Bravīmi Te* I
*Aṣṭottarasahasrasya Ṛṣirbrahmā Prakīrtitaḥ* II 6

*Chando'nuṣṭup Tathā Devī Gāyatrīṃ Devatā Smṛtā* I
*Halo Bījāni Tasyaiva Svarāḥ Śaktaya Īritāḥ* II 7

*Aṅganyāsa Karanyāsāvucyete Mātṛkākṣaraiḥ* I
*Atha Dhyānaṃ Pravakṣyāmi Sādhakānāṃ Hitāya Vai* II 8

*Dhyānam*

*Rakta Śveta Hiraṇya Nīla Dhavalairyuktā Trinītrojjvalāṃ*
*Raktāṃ Raktanavasrajaṃ Maṇigaṇairyuktāṃ Kumārīmimām* I
*Gāyatrīṃ Kamalāsanāṃ Karatalavyānaddhakuṇḍāmbujāṃ*
*Padmākṣī Ca Varasrajaṃ Ca Dadhatīṃ Haṃsādhirūḍhāṃ Bhaje* II 9

*Atha Stotraḥ* ।

*Oṃ Acintya Lakṣaṇāvyaktāpyartha Mātṛ Maheśvarī* ।
*Amṛtārṇavamadhyasthāpyajitā Cāparājitā* ॥ 10

*Aṇimādi Guṇā Dhārāpyarka Maṇḍala Saṃsthitā* ।
*Ajarājāparādharmā Akṣasūtradharādharā* ॥ 11

*Akārādik Ṣakārāntāpyariṣaḍvarga Bhedinī* ।
*Añjanādri Pratīkāśāpyañjanādri Nivāsinī* ॥ 12

*Aditiścā Japā Vidyāpyaravinda Nibhekṣaṇā* ।
*Antarbahiḥ Sthitā Vidyādhvaṃsinī Cāntarātmikā* ॥ 13

*Ajā Cājamukhā Vāsāpyaravinda Nibhānanā* ।
*Ardhamātrārthadānajñāpyari Maṇḍala Mardinī* ॥ 14

*Asuraghnī Hyamāvāsyāpya Lakṣmīghnyantyajārcitā* ।
*Ādi Lakṣmīścādi Śaktirākṛtiścāyatānanā* ॥ 15

*Āditya Padavī Cārāpyāditya Pari Sevitā* ।
*Ācāryā Vareanācārāpyādi Mūrti Nivāsinī* ॥ 16

*Āgneyī Cāmarī Cādyā Cārādhyā Cāsanasthitā* ।
*Ādhāra Nilayādhārā Cākāśānta Nivāsinī* ॥ 17

*Ādyākṣara Samāyuktā Cāntarākāśa Rūpiṇī* ।
*Āditya Maṇḍala Gatā Cāntaradhvānta Nāśinī* ॥ 18

*Indirā Ceṣṭadā Ceṣṭā Cendī Vara Nibhekṣaṇā* ।
*Irāvatī Cendrapadā Cendrāṇī Cendu Rūpiṇī* ॥ 19

*Ikṣu Kodaṇḍa Saṃyuktā Ceṣu Sandhāna Kāriṇī* ।
*Indra Nīla Samākārā Ceḍāpiṅgala Rūpiṇī* ॥ 20

*Indrākṣīceśvarī Devī Cehātraya Vivarjitā* ।
*Umā Coṣā Hyuḍunibhā Urvāruka Phalānanā* ॥ 21

*Uḍuprabhā Coḍumatī Hyuḍupā Hyuḍu Madhyagā* ।
*Ūrdhvā Cāpyūrdhva Keśī Cāpyūrdhvādho Gati Bhedinī* ॥ 22

*Ūrdhva Bāhupriyā Cormimālāvāggrantha Dāyinī* ।
*Ṛtaṃ Carṣirṛtumatī Ṛṣidevanamaskṛtā* ॥ 23

*Ṛgvedā Ṛṇaharerī Ca Ṛṣi Maṇḍala Cāriṇī* ।
*Ṛddhidā Ṛjumārgasthā Ṛjudharmā Ṛtupradā* ॥ 24

*Ṛgveda Nilayā Ṛjvī Lupta Dharma Pravartinī* ।
*Lūtāri Vara Sambhūtā Lūtādi Viṣa Hāriṇī* ॥ 25

*Ekākṣarā Caikamātrā Caikā Caikaikaniṣṭhitā* ।
*Aindrī Hyairāvatārūḍhā Caihikāmuṣmikapradā* ॥ 26

*Oṃkārā Hyoṣadhī Cotā Cotaprotanivāsinī* ।
*Aurvā Hyauṣadhasampannā Aupāsanaphalapradā* ॥ 27

*Aṇḍamadhyasthitā Devī Cāḥkāra Manurūpiṇī* ।
*Kātyāyanī Kālarātriḥ Kāmākṣī Kāmasundarī* ॥ 28

*Kamalā Kāminī Kāntā Kāmadā Kālakaṇṭhinī* ।
*Kari Kumbhastanabharā Karavīra Suvāsinī* ॥ 29

*Kalyāṇī Kuṇḍalavatī Kurukṣetra Nivāsinī* ।
*Kuruvinda Dalākārā Kuṇḍalī Kumudālayā* ॥ 30

*Kālajihvā Karālāsyā Kālikā Kālarūpiṇī* ।
*Kamanīyaguṇā Kāntiḥ Kalādhārā Kumudvatī* ॥ 31

*Kauśikī Kamalākārā Kāmacāra Prabhañjinī |*

*Kaumārī Karuṇāpāṅgī Kakubantā Karipriyā* || 32

*Kesarī Keśavanutā Kadamba Kusuma Priyā |*

*Kālindī Kālikā Kāñcī Kalaśodbhava Saṃstutā* || 33

*Kāma Mātā Kratumatī Kāmarūpā Kṛpāvatī |*

*Kumārī Kuṇḍanilayā Kirātī Kīravāhanā* || 34

*Kaikeyī Kokilālāpā Ketakī Kusumapriyā |*

*Kamaṇḍaludharā Kālī Karma Nirmūlakāriṇī* || 35

*Kalahaṃsagatiḥ Kakṣā Kṛta Kautuka Maṅgalā |*

*Kastūrītilakā Kamprā Karīndra Gamanā Kuhūḥ* || 36

*Karpūralepanā Kṛṣṇā Kapilā Kuharāśrayā |*

*Kūṭasthā Kudharā Kamrā Kukṣisthākhilaviṣṭapā* || 37

*Khaḍgakheṭakarā Kharvā Khecarī Khagavāhanā |*

*Khaṭvāṅga Dhāriṇī Khyātā Khagarājoparisthitā* || 38

*Khalaghnī Khaṇḍitajarā Khaṇḍākhyānapradāyinī |*

*Khaṇḍendutilakā Gaṅgā Gaṇeśa Guha Pūjitā* || 39

*Gāyatrī Gomatī Gītā Gāndhārī Gānalolupā |*

*Gautamī Gāminī Gādhā Gandharvāpsara Sevitā* || 40

*Govinda Caraṇā Krāntā Guṇatraya Vibhāvitā |*

*Gandharvī Gahvarī Gotrā Girīśā Gahanā Gamī* || 41

*Guhāvāsā Guṇavatī Guru Pāpa Praṇāśinī |*

*Gurvī Guṇavatī Guhyā Goptavyā Guṇadāyinī* || 42

*Girijā Guhya Mātaṅgī Garuḍadhvaja Vallabhā* I
*Garvā Pahāriṇī Godā Gokulasthā Gadādharā* II 43

*Gokarṇa Nilayā Saktā Guhyamaṇḍala Vartinī* I
*Gharmadā Ghanadā Ghaṇṭā Ghora Dānava Mardinī* II 44

*Ghṛṇi Mantramayī Ghoṣā Ghanasampāta Dāyinī* I
*Ghaṇṭārava Priyā Ghrāṇā Ghṛṇisaṃtuṣṭakāriṇī* II 45

*Ghanāri Maṇḍalā Ghūrṇā Ghṛtācī Ghanaveginī* I
*Jñāna Dhātumayī Carcā Carcitā Cāruhāsinī* II 46

*Caṭulā Caṇḍikā Citrā Citramālya Vibhūṣitā* I
*Caturbhujā Cārudantā Cāturī Caritapradā* II 47

*Cūlikā Citra Vastrāntā Candramaḥ Karṇa Kuṇḍalā* I
*Candrahāsā Cārudātrī Cakorī Candra Hāsinī* II 48

*Candrikā Candra Dhātrī Ca Caurī Caurā Ca Caṇḍikā* I
*Cañcadvāgvādinī Candracūḍā Cora Vināśinī* II 49

*Cāru Candana Liptāṅgī Cañcaccāmara Vījitā* I
*Cāru Madhyā Cāru Gatiścandilā Candra Rūpiṇī* II 50

*Cāru Homa Priyā Cārvā Caritā Cakra Bāhukā* I
*Candra Maṇḍala Madhyasthā Candra Maṇḍala Darpaṇā* II 51

*Cakravāka Stanī Ceṣṭā Citrā Cāru Vilāsinī* I
*Citsvarūpā Candra Vatī Candramāścandana Priyā* II 52

*Codayitrī Ciraprajñā Cātakā Cāruhetukī* I
*Chatrayātā Chatradharā Chāyā Chandaḥparicchadā* II 53

*Chāyādevī Chidranakhā Channendriyavisarpiṇī* I
*Chando'nuṣṭuppratiṣṭhāntā Chidropadrava Bhedinī* II 54

*Chedā Chatreśvarī Chinnā Churikā Chedanapriyā* I
*Jananī Janmarahitā Jātavedā Jaganmayī* II 55

*Jāhnavī Jaṭilā Jetrī Jarā Maraṇa Varjitā* I
*Jambūdvīpa Vatī Jvālā Jayantī Jalaśālinī* II 56

*Jitendriyā Jitakrodhā Jitāmitrā Jagatpriyā* I
*Jātarūpamayī Jihvā Jānakī Jagatī Jarā* II 57

*Janitrī Jahnutanayā Jagattraya Hitaiṣiṇī* I
*Jwālāmukhī Japavatī Jvaraghnī Jitaviṣṭapā* II 58

*Jitākrāntamayī Jvālā Jāgratī Jvaradevatā* I
*Jvalantī Jaladā Jyeṣṭhā Jyāghoṣāsphoṭadiṅmukhī* II 59

*Jambhinī Jṛmbhaṇā Jṛmbhā Jvalanmāṇikya Kuṇḍalā* I
*Jhiṃjhikā Jhaṇanirghoṣā Jhaṃjhāmārutaveginī* II 60

*Jhallarīvādyakuśalā Ñarūpā Ñabhujā Smṛtā* I
*Ṭaṅkabāṇa Samāyuktā Ṭaṅkinī Ṭaṅka Bhedinī* II 61

*Ṭaṅkīgaṇa Kṛtāghoṣā Ṭaṅkanīya Mahorasā* I
*Ṭaṅkārakāriṇī Devī Ṭhaṭhaśabda Ninādinī* II 62

*Ḍāmarī Ḍākinī Ḍimbhā Ḍuṇḍamāraika Nirjitā* I
*Ḍāmarī Tantra Mārgasthā Ḍamaḍḍamaru Nādinī* II 63

*Ḍiṇḍīravasahā Ḍimbhala Satkrīḍā Parāyaṇā* I
*Ḍhuṇḍhi Vighneśajananī Ḍhakkāhastā Ḍhilivrajā* II 64

*Nityajñānā Nirupamā Nirguṇā Narmadā Nadī* I
*Triguṇā Tripadā Tantrī Tulasī Taruṇā Taruḥ* II 65

*Trivikrama Padākrāntā Turīya Padagāminī* I
*Taruṇāditya Saṃkāśā Tāmasī Tuhinā Turā* II 66

*Trikālajñāna Sampannā Trivalī Ca Trilocanā* I
*Triśaktistripurā Tuṅgā Turaṅga Vadanā Tathā* II 67

*Timiṅgilagilā Tīvrā Trisrotā Tāmasādinī* I
*Tantra Mantra Viśeṣajñā Tanumadhyā Triviṣṭapā* II 68

*Trisandhyā Tristanī Toṣāsaṃsthā Tālapratāpinī* I
*Tāṭaṅkinī Tuṣārābhā Tuhinācalavāsinī* II 69

*Tantujāla Samāyuktā Tārahārā Valipriyā* I
*Tila Homa Priyā Tīrthā Tamāla Kusumākṛtiḥ* II 70

*Tārakā Triyutā Tanvī Triśaṅkuparivāritā* I
*Talodarī Tilābhūṣā Tāṭaṅkapriyavādinī* II 71

*Trijaṭā Tittirī Tṛṣṇā Trividhā Taruṇā Kṛtiḥ* I
*Tapta Kāñcana Saṃkāśā Tapta Kāñcana Bhūṣaṇā* II 72

*Traiyambakā Trivargā Ca Trikālajñānadāyinī* I
*Tarpaṇā Tṛptidā Tṛptā Tāmasī Tumburustutā* II 73

*Tārkṣyasthā Triguṇākārā Tribhaṅgī Tanuvallariḥ* I
*Thātkārī Thāravā Thāntā Dohinī Dīnavatsalā* II 74

*Dānavāntakarī Durgā Durgāsuranibarhiṇī* I
*Devarītirdivārātrirdraupadī Dundubhisvanā* II 75

*Devayānī Durāvāsā Dāridryodbhedinī Divā* |
*Dāmodarapriyā Dīptā Digvāsā Digvimohinī* || 76

*Daṇḍakāraṇyanilayā Daṇḍinī Devapūjitā* |
*Devavandyā Diviṣadā Dveṣiṇī Dānavākṛtiḥ* || 77

*Dīnānāthastutā Dīkṣā Daivatādisvarūpiṇī* |
*Dhātrī Dhanurdharā Dhenurdhāriṇī Dharmacāriṇī* || 78

*Dharandharā Dharādhārā Dhanadā Dhānyadohinī* |
*Dharmaśīlā Dhanādhyakṣā Dhanurveda Viśāradā* || 79

*Dhṛtirdhanyā Dhṛtapadā Dharmarājapriyā Dhruvā* |
*Dhūmāvatī Dhūmakeśī Dharmaśāstra Prakāśinī* || 80

*Nandā Nandapriyā Nidrā Nṛnutā Nandanātmikā* |
*Narmadā Nalinī Nīlā Nīlakaṇṭhasamāśrayā* || 81

*Nārāyaṇapriyā Nityā Nirmalā Nirguṇā Nidhiḥ* |
*Nirādhārā Nirupamā Nityaśuddhā Nirañjanā* || 82

*Nādabindu Kalātītā Nādabindu Kalātmikā* |
*Nṛsiṃhinī Nagadharā Nṛpanāga Vibhūṣitā* || 83

*Naraka Kleśa Śamanī Nārāyaṇa Padodbhavā* |
*Niravadyā Nirākārā Nārada Priyakāriṇī* || 84

*Nānājyotiḥ Samākhyātā Nidhidā Nirmalātmikā* |
*Navasūtradharā Nītirnirupadravakāriṇī* || 85

*Nandajā Navaratnāḍhyā Naimiṣāraṇya Vāsinī* |
*Navanītapriyā Nārī Nīlajīmūtanisvanā* || 86

*Nimeṣiṇī Nadīrūpā Nīlagrīvā Niśīśvarī* |
*Nāmāvalirniśumbhaghnī Nāgalokanivāsinī* || 87

*Navajāmbūnada Prakhyā Nāgalokādhi Devatā* |
*Nūpurākrānta Caraṇā Naracitta Pramodinī* || 88

*Nimagnā Rakta Nayanā Nirghāta Samanisvanā* |
*Nandanodyāna Nilayā Nirvyūhoparicāriṇī* || 89

*Pārvatī Paramodārā Parabrahmātmikā Parā* |
*Pañcakośavi Nirmuktā Pañcapātaka Nāśinī* || 90

*Paracittavidhānajñā Pañcikā Pañcarūpiṇī* |
*Pūrṇimā Paramā Prītiḥ Paratejaḥ Prakāśinī* || 91

*Purāṇī Pauruṣī Puṇyā Puṇḍarīka Nibhekṣaṇā* |
*Pātāla Tala Nirmagnā Prītā Prīti Vivardhinī* || 92

*Pāvanī Pādasahitā Peśalā Pavanāśinī* |
*Prajāpatiḥ Pariśrāntā Parvata Stana Maṇḍalā* || 93

*Padmapriyā Padmasaṃsthā Padmākṣī Padmasambhavā* |
*Padmapatrā Padmapadā Padminī Priyabhāṣiṇī* || 94

*Paśupāśavinirmuktā Purandhrī Puravāsinī* |
*Puṣkalā Puruṣā Parvā Pārijāta Sumapriyā* || 95

*Pativratā Pavitrāṅgī Puṣpa Hāsa Parāyaṇā* |
*Prajñāvatīsutā Pautrī Putrapūjyā Payasvinī* || 96

*Paṭṭipāśadharā Paṅktiḥ Pitṛlokapradāyinī* |
*Purāṇī Puṇyaśīlā Ca Praṇatārti Vināśinī* || 97

*Pradyumna Jananī Puṣṭā Pitāmaha Parigrahā* I
*Puṇḍarīkapurāvāsā Puṇḍarīkasamānanā* II 98

*Pṛthujaṅghā Pṛthubhujā Pṛthupādā Pṛthūdarī* I
*Pravālaśobhā Piṅgākṣī Pītavāsāḥ Pracāpalā* II 99

*Prasavā Puṣṭidā Puṇyā Pratiṣṭhā Praṇavāgatiḥ* I
*Pañcavarṇā Pañcavāṇī Pañcikā Pañcarasthitā* II 100

*Paramāyā Parajyotiḥ Paraprītiḥ Parāgatiḥ* I
*Parākāṣṭhā Pareśānī Pāvinī Pāvakadyutiḥ* II 101

*Puṇyabhadrā Paricchedyā Puṣpahāsā Pṛthūdarī* I
*Pītāṅgī Pītavasanā Pītaśayyā Piśācinī* II 102

*Pītakriyā Piśācaghnī Pāṭalākṣī Paṭukriyā* I
*Pañcabhakṣapriyācārā Pūtanāprāṇaghātinī* II 103

*Punnāgavanamadhyasthā Puṇyatīrthaniṣevitā* I
*Pañcāṅgī Ca Parāśaktiḥ Paramāhlādakāriṇī* II 104

*Puṣpakāṇḍasthitā Pūṣā Poṣitākhila Viṣṭapā* I
*Pānapriyā Pañcaśikhā Pannagopariśāyinī* II 105

*Pañcamātrātmikā Pṛthvī Pathikā Pṛthudohinī* I
*Purāṇa Nyāya Mīmāṃsā Pāṭalī Puṣpa Gandhinī* II 106

*Puṇyaprajā Pāradātrī Paramārgaikagocarā* I
*Pravālaśobhā Pūrṇāśā Praṇavā Pallavodarī* II 107

*Phalinī Phaladā Phalguḥ Phūtkārī Phalakākṛtiḥ* I
*Phaṇīndra Bhogaśayanā Phaṇimaṇḍala Maṇḍitā* II 108

*Bālabālā Bahumatā Bālātapanibhāṃśukā* I

*Balabhadrapriyā Vandyā Vaḍavā Buddhisaṃstutā* II 109

*Bandīdevī Bilavatī Baḍiśaghnī Balipriyā* I

*Bāndhavī Bodhitā Buddhirbandhūka Kusumapriyā* II 110

*Bālabhānuprabhākārā Brāhmī Brāhmaṇadevatā* I

*Bṛhaspatistutā Vṛndā Vṛndāvanavihāriṇī* II 111

*Bālākinī Bilāhārā Bilavāsā Bahūdakā* I

*Bahunetrā Bahupadā Bahukarṇāvataṃsikā* II 112

*Bahubāhuyutā Bījarūpiṇī Bahurūpiṇī* I

*Bindunāda Kalātītā Bindunāda Svarūpiṇī* II 113

*Baddhagodhāṅgulitrāṇā Badaryāśramavāsinī* I

*Bṛndārakā Bṛhatskandhā Bṛhatī Bāṇapātinī* II 114

*Bṛndādhyakṣā Bahunutā Vanitā Bahuvikramā* I

*Baddhapadmāsanāsīnā Bilvapatratalasthitā* II 115

*Bodhidrumanijāvāsā Baḍisthā Bindudarpaṇā* I

*Bālā Bāṇāsanavatī Baḍavānalaveginī* II 116

*Brahmāṇḍabahirantaḥsthā Brahmakaṅkaṇasūtriṇī* I

*Bhavānī Bhīṣaṇavatī Bhāvinī Bhayahāriṇī* II 117

*Bhadrakālī Bhujaṅgākṣī Bhāratī Bhāratāśayā* I

*Bhairavī Bhīṣaṇākārā Bhūtidā Bhūtimālinī* II 118

*Bhāminī Bhoganiratā Bhadradā Bhūrivikramā* I

*Bhūtavāsā Bhṛgulatā Bhārgavī Bhūsurārcitā* II 119

*Bhāgīrathī Bhogavatī Bhavanasthā Bhiṣagvarā* |

*Bhāminī Bhoginī Bhāṣā Bhavānī Bhūridakṣiṇā* || 120

*Bhargātmikā Bhīmavatī Bhavabandhavimocinī* |

*Bhajanīyā Bhūtadhātrīrañjitā Bhuvaneśvarī* || 121

*Bhujaṅgavalayā Bhīmā Bheruṇḍā Bhāgadheyinī* |

*Mātā Māyā Madhumatī Madhujihvā Madhupriyā* || 122

*Mahādevī Mahābhāgā Mālinī Mīnalocanā* |

*Māyātītā Madhumatī Madhumāṃsā Madhudravā* || 123

*Mānavī Madhusambhūtā Mithilāpuravāsinī* |

*Madhukaiṭabhasaṃhartrī Medinī Meghamālinī* || 124

*Mandodarī Mahāmāyā Maithilī Masṛṇapriyā* |

*Mahālakṣmīrmahākālī Mahākanyā Maheśvarī* || 125

*Māhendrī Merutanayā Mandārakusumārcitā* |

*Mañjumañjīracaraṇā Mokṣadā Mañjubhāṣiṇī* || 126

*Madhuradrāviṇī Mudrā Malayā Malayānvitā* |

*Medhā Marakataśyāmā Māgadhī Menakātmajā* || 127

*Mahāmārī Mahāvīrā Mahāśyāmā Manustutā* |

*Mātṛkā Mihirābhāsā Mukundapadavikramā* || 128

*Mūlādhārasthitā Mugdhā Maṇipūrakavāsinī* |

*Mṛgākṣī Mahiṣārūḍhā Mahiṣāsuramardinī* || 129

*Yogāsanā Yogagamyā Yogā Yauvanakāśrayā* |

*Yauvanī Yuddhamadhyasthā Yamunā Yugadhāriṇī* || 130

*Yakṣiṇī Yogayuktā Ca Yakṣarājaprasūtinī* ।
*Yātrā Yānavidhānajñā Yaduvaṃśa Samudbhavā* ॥ 131

*Yakārādihakārāntā Yājuṣī Yajñarūpiṇī* ।
*Yāminī Yoganiratā Yātudhānabhayaṅkarī* ॥ 132

*Rukmiṇī Ramaṇī Rāmā Revatī Reṇukā Ratiḥ* ।
*Raudrī Raudrapriyākārā Rāmamātā Ratipriyā* ॥ 133

*Rohiṇī Rājyadā Revā Ramā Rājīvalocanā* ।
*Rākeśī Rūpasampannā Ratnasiṃhāsanasthitā* ॥ 134

*Raktamālyāmbaradharā Raktagandhānulepanā* ।
*Rājahaṃsasamārūḍhā Rambhā Raktabalipriyā* ॥ 135

*Ramaṇīyayugādhārā Rājitākhilabhūtalā* ।
*Rurucarmaparīdhānā Rathinī Ratnamālikā* ॥ 136

*Rogeśī Rogaśamanī Rāviṇī Romaharṣiṇī* ।
*Rāmacandrapadākrāntā Rāvaṇacchedakāriṇī* ॥ 137

*Ratnavastraparicchannā Rathasthā Rukmabhūṣaṇā* ।
*Lajjādhidevatā Lolā Lalitā Liṅgadhāriṇī* ॥ 138

*Lakṣmīrlolā Luptaviṣā Lokinī Lokaviśrutā* ।
*Lajjā Lambodarī Devī Lalanā Lokadhāriṇī* ॥ 139

*Varadā Vanditā Vidyā Vaiṣṇavī Vimalākṛtiḥ* ।
*Vārāhī Virajā Varṣā Varalakṣmīrvilāsinī* ॥ 140

*Vinatā Vyoma Madhyasthā Vārijā Sanasaṃsthitā* ।
*Vāruṇī Veṇusambhūtā Vītihotrā Virūpiṇī* ॥ 141

*Vāyumaṇḍalamadhyasthā Viṣṇurūpā Vidhipriyā* |
*Viṣṇupatnī Viṣṇumatī Viśālākṣī Vasundharā* || 142

*Vāmadevapriyā Velā Vajriṇī Vasudohinī* |
*Vedākṣaraparītāṅgī Vājapeyaphalapradā* || 143

*Vāsavī Vāmajananī Vaikuṇṭhanilayā Varā* |
*Vyāsapriyā Varmadharā Vālmīkiparisevitā* || 144

*Śākambharī Śivā Śāntā Śaradā Śaraṇāgatiḥ* |
*Śātodarī Śubhācārā Śumbhāsuravimardinī* || 145

*Śobhāvatī Śivākārā Śaṃkarārdha Śarīriṇī* |
*Śoṇā Śubhāśayā Śubhrā Śiraḥsandhānakāriṇī* || 146

*Śarāvatī Śarānandā Śarajjyotsnā Śubhānanā* |
*Śarabhā Śūlinī Śuddhā Śabarī Śukavāhanā* || 147

*Śrīmatī Śrīdharānandā Śravaṇānandadāyinī* |
*Śarvāṇī Śarvarīvandyā Ṣaḍbhāṣā Ṣaḍṛtupriyā* || 148

*Ṣaḍādhārasthitā Devī Ṣaṇmukhapriyakāriṇī* |
*Ṣaḍaṅgarūpasumatisurāsuranamaskṛtā* || 149

*Sarasvatī Sadādhārā Sarvamaṅgalakāriṇī* |
*Sāmagānapriyā Sūkṣmā Sāvitrī Sāmasambhavā* || 150

*Sarvāvāsā Sadānandā Sustanī Sāgarāmbarā* |
*Sarvaiśvaryapriyā Siddhiḥ Sādhubandhuparākramā* || 151

*Saptarṣimaṇḍalagatā Somamaṇḍalavāsinī* |
*Sarvajñā Sāndrakaruṇā Samānādhikavarjitā* || 152

*Sarvottuṅgā Saṅgahīnā Sadguṇā Sakaleṣṭadā* ।
*Saradhā Sūryatanayā Sukeśī Somasaṃhatiḥ* ॥ 153

*Hiraṇyavarṇā Hariṇī Hrīṃkārī Haṃsavāhinī* ।
*Kṣaumavastraparītāṅgī Kṣīrābdhitanayā Kṣamā* ॥ 154

*Gāyatrī Caiva Sāvitrī Pārvatī Ca Sarasvatī* ।
*Vedagarbhā Varārohā Śrīgāyatrī Parāmbikā* ॥ 155

*Uttara Bhāgaḥ – Phala Śrutiḥ* ।

*Iti Sāhasrakaṃ Nāmnāṃ Gāyatryāścaiva Nārada* ।
*Puṇyadaṃ Sarvapāpaghnaṃ Mahāsampattidāyakam* ॥ 156

*Evaṃ Nāmāni Gāyatryāstoṣotpattikarāṇi Hi* ।
*Aṣṭamyāṃ Ca Viśeṣeṇa Paṭhitavyaṃ Dvijaiḥ Saha* ॥ 157

*Japaṃ Kṛtvā Homa Pūjādhyānaṃ Kṛtvā Viśeṣataḥ* ।
*Yasmai Kasmai Na Dātavyaṃ Gāyatryāstu Viśeṣataḥ* ॥ 158

*Subhaktāya Suśiṣyāya Vaktavyaṃ Bhūsu Rāya Vai* ।
*Bhraṣṭebhyaḥ Sādhakebhyaśca Bāndhavebhyo Na Darśayet* ॥ 159

*Yadgṛhe Likhitaṃ Śāstraṃ Bhayaṃ Tasya Na Kasyacit* ।
*Cañcalāpisthirā Bhūtvā Kamalā Tatra Tiṣṭhati* ॥ 160

*Idaṃ Rahasyaṃ Paramaṃ Guhyādguhyataraṃ Mahat* ।
*Puṇyapradaṃ Manuṣyāṇāṃ Daridrāṇāṃnidhipradam* ॥ 161

*Mokṣapradaṃ Mumukṣūṇāṃ Kāmināṃ Sarvakāmadam* ।
*Rogādvai Mucyate Rogī Baddho Mucyeta Bandhanāt* ॥ 162

*Brahmahatyā Surāpānaṃ Suvarṇasteyino Narāḥ* ।
*Gurutalpagato Vāpi Pātakātanmucyate Sakṛt* ॥ 163

*Asatpratigrahāccaivā'bhakṣyabhakṣādviśeṣataḥ* ।
*Pākhaṇḍānṛtyamukhyabhyaḥ Pāṭhanādeva Mucyate* ॥ 164

*Idaṃ Rahasyamamalaṃ Mayoktaṃ Padmajodbhava* ।
*Brahmasāyujyadaṃ Nṛnāṃ Satyaṃ Santya Na Saṃśaya* ॥ 165

॥ *Iti Śrīdevībhāgavate Mahāpurāṇe Dvādaśaskandhe*
*Gāyatrīsahasranāma Stotrakathanaṃ Nāma Ṣaṣṭho'dhyāyaḥ* ॥

*****

## *Śrī Gāyatri Sahasranāmavaḷi* – Samskrutam

श्री गायत्री सहस्र नामावलिः ।

ध्यानम् ।

रक्तश्वेतहिरण्यनीलधवलैर्युक्ता त्रिनीत्रोज्ज्वलां रक्तां
रक्तनवस्रजं मणिगणैर्युक्तां कुमारीमिमाम् ।
गायत्रीं कमलासनां करतलव्यानद्धकुण्डाम्बुजां
पद्माक्षी च वरस्रजं च दधतीं हंसाधिरूढां भजे ॥

अथ नामावलिः ।

1. ॐ अचिन्त्यलक्षणायै नमः ।
2. ॐ अव्यक्तायै नमः ।
3. ॐ अर्थमातृमहेश्वर्यै नमः ।
4. ॐ अमृतायै नमः ।
5. ॐ अर्णवमध्यस्थायै नमः ।
6. ॐ अजितायै नमः ।
7. ॐ अपराजितायै नमः ।
8. ॐ अणिमादिगुणाधारायै नमः ।
9. ॐ अर्कमण्डलसंस्थितायै नमः।
10. ॐ अजरायै नमः ।
11. ॐ अजायै नमः ।
12. ॐ अपरायै नमः ।
13. ॐ अधर्मायै नमः ।
14. ॐ अक्षसूत्र धरायै नमः ।
15. ॐ अधरायै नमः ।
16. ॐ अकारादि क्षकारान्तायै नमः।
17. ॐ अरिषड्वर्ग भेदिन्यै नमः ।
18. ॐ अञ्जनाद्रि प्रतिकाशायै नमः ।
19. ॐ अञ्जनाद्रि निवासिन्यै नमः।
20. ॐ अदित्यै नमः ।

21. ॐ अजपायै नमः ।
22. ॐ अविद्यायै नमः ।
23. ॐ अरविन्द निभेक्षणायै नमः ।
24. ॐ अन्तर्बहिः:स्थितायै नमः ।
25. ॐ अविद्याध्वंसिन्यै नमः ।
26. ॐ अन्तरात्मिकायै नमः ।
27. ॐ अजायै नमः ।
28. ॐ अजमुखावासायै नमः ।
29. ॐ अरविन्दनिभाननायै नमः ।
30. ॐ अर्धमात्रायै नमः ।

31. ॐ अर्थदानज्ञायै नमः ।
32. ॐ अरिमण्डलमर्दिन्यै नमः ।
33. ॐ असुरघ्न्यै नमः ।
34. ॐ अमावास्यायै नमः ।
35. ॐ अलक्ष्मीघ्न्त्यजार्चितायै नमः ।
36. ॐ आदिलक्ष्म्यै नमः ।
37. ॐ आदिशक्त्यै नमः ।
38. ॐ आकृत्यै नमः ।
39. ॐ आयताननायै नमः ।
40. ॐ आदित्य पद विचारायै नमः ।

41. ॐ आदित्य परि सेवितायै नमः ।
42. ॐ आचार्यायै नमः ।
43. ॐ आवर्तनायै नमः ।
44. ॐ आचारायै नमः ।
45. ॐ आदि मूर्ति निवासिन्यै नमः।
46. ॐ आग्नेय्यै नमः ।
47. ॐ आमर्यै नमः ।
48. ॐ आद्यायै नमः ।
49. ॐ आराध्यायै नमः ।

50. ॐ आसन स्थितायै नमः ।

51. ॐ आधार निलयायै नमः ।
52. ॐ आधारायै नमः ।
53. ॐ आकाशान्त निवासिन्यै नमः।
54. ॐ आद्याक्षर समयुक्तायै नमः ।
55. ॐ आन्त राकाश रूपिण्यै नमः।
56. ॐ आदित्य मण्डल गतायै नमः।
57. ॐ आन्तरध्वान्तनाशिन्यै नमः ।
58. ॐ इन्दिरायै नमः ।
59. ॐ इष्टदायै नमः ।
60. ॐ इष्टायै नमः ।

61. ॐ इन्दीवरनिभेक्षणायै नमः ।
62. ॐ इरावत्यै नमः ।
63. ॐ इन्द्रपदायै नमः ।
64. ॐ इन्द्राण्यै नमः ।
65. ॐ इन्दुरूपिण्यै नमः ।
66. ॐ इक्षु कोदण्ड संयुक्तायै नमः ।
67. ॐ इषु सन्धान कारिण्यै नमः ।
68. ॐ इन्द्रनील समाकारायै नमः ।
69. ॐ इडा पिङ्गल रूपिण्यै नमः ।
70. ॐ इन्द्राक्ष्यै नमः ।

71. ॐ ईश्वरी देव्यै नमः ।
72. ॐ ईहात्रय विवर्जितायै नमः ।
73. ॐ उमायै नमः ।
74. ॐ उषायै नमः ।
75. ॐ उडुनिभायै नमः ।
76. ॐ उर्वारुक फलाननायै नमः ।
77. ॐ उडुप्रभायै नमः ।
78. ॐ उडुमत्यै नमः ।

79. ॐ उडुपायै नमः ।
80. ॐ उडुमध्यगायै नमः ।
81. ॐ ऊर्ध्व्यायै नमः ।
82. ॐ ऊर्ध्वकेश्यै नमः ।
83. ॐ ऊर्ध्वाधो गति भेदिन्यै नमः।
84. ॐ ऊर्ध्व बाहु प्रियायै नमः ।
85. ॐ ऊर्मि माला वाग्ग्रन्थदा यिन्यै नमः ।
86. ॐ ऋतायै नमः ।
87. ॐ ऋष्यै नमः ।
88. ॐ ऋतुमत्यै नमः ।
89. ॐ ऋषि देव नमस्कृतायै नमः ।
90. ॐ ऋग्वेदायै नमः ।
91. ॐ ऋणहर्त्र्यै नमः ।
92. ॐ ऋषि मण्डल चारिण्यै नमः ।
93. ॐ ऋद्धिदायै नमः ।
94. ॐ ऋजुमार्गस्थायै नमः ।
95. ॐ ऋजुधर्मायै नमः ।
96. ॐ ऋतुप्रदायै नमः ।
97. ॐ ऋग्वेद निलयायै नमः ।
98. ॐ ऋज्व्यै नमः ।
99. ॐ लुप्त धर्म प्रवर्तिन्यै नमः ।
100. ॐ लूतारि वर सम्भूतायै नमः ।
101. ॐ लूतादि विष हारिण्यै नमः ।
102. ॐ एकाक्षरायै नमः ।
103. ॐ एकमात्रायै नमः ।
104. ॐ एकायै नमः ।
105. ॐ एक निष्ठायै नमः ।
106. ॐ ऐन्द्र्यै नमः ।
107. ॐ ऐरावता रूढायै नमः ।

108. ॐ ऐहिका मुष्मिक प्रदायै नमः ।
109. ॐ ओङ्कारायै नमः ।
110. ॐ ओषध्यै नमः ।

111. ॐ ओतायै नमः ।
112. ॐ ओतप्रोत निवासिन्यै नमः ।
113. ॐ और्वायै नमः ।
114. ॐ औषध सम्पन्नायै नमः।
115. ॐ औपासन फल प्रदायै नमः ।
116. ॐ अण्डमध्यस्थिता देव्यै नमः ।
117. ॐ अःकारमनु रूपिण्यै नमः ।
118. ॐ कात्यायन्यै नमः ।
119. ॐ कालरात्र्यै नमः ।
120. ॐ कामाक्ष्यै नमः ।

121. ॐ काम सुन्दर्यै नमः ।
122. ॐ कमलायै नमः ।
123. ॐ कामिन्यै नमः ।
124. ॐ कान्तायै नमः ।
125. ॐ कामदायै नमः ।
126. ॐ कालकण्ठिन्यै नमः ।
127. ॐ करिकुम्भ स्तन भरायै नमः ।
128. ॐ करवीर सुवासिन्यै नमः।
129. ॐ कल्याण्यै नमः ।
130. ॐ कुण्डलवत्यै नमः ।

131. ॐ कुरुक्षेत्र निवासिन्यै नमः ।
132. ॐ कुरुविन्द दलाकारायै नमः ।
133. ॐ कुण्डल्यै नमः ।
134. ॐ कुमुदालयायै नमः ।
135. ॐ कालजिह्वायै नमः ।
136. ॐ करालास्यायै नमः ।
137. ॐ कालिकायै नमः ।

138. ॐ कालरूपिण्यै नमः ।
139. ॐ कमनीय गुणायै नमः ।
140. ॐ कान्त्यै नमः ।

141. ॐ कलाधारायै नमः ।
142. ॐ कुमुद्वत्यै नमः ।
143. ॐ कौशिक्यै नमः ।
144. ॐ कमलाकारायै नमः ।
145. ॐ कामचारप्रभञ्जिन्यै नमः ।
146. ॐ कौमार्यै नमः ।
147. ॐ करुणापाङ्ग्यै नमः ।
148. ॐ ककुबन्तायै नमः ।
149. ॐ करिप्रियायै नमः ।
150. ॐ केसर्यै नमः ।

151. ॐ केशवनुतायै नमः ।
152. ॐ कदम्ब कुसुमप्रियायै नमः ।
153. ॐ कालिन्द्यै नमः ।
154. ॐ कालिकायै नमः ।
155. ॐ काञ्च्यै नमः ।
156. ॐ कलशोद्भव संस्तुतायै नमः ।
157. ॐ काममातायै नमः ।
158. ॐ क्रतुमत्यै नमः ।
159. ॐ कामरूपायै नमः ।
160. ॐ कृपावत्यै नमः ।

161. ॐ कुमार्यै नमः ।
162. ॐ कुण्डनिलयायै नमः ।
163. ॐ किरात्यै नमः ।
164. ॐ कीरवाहनायै नमः ।
165. ॐ कैकेय्यै नमः ।
166. ॐ कोकिलालापायै नमः ।
167. ॐ केतकीयै नमः ।

168. ॐ कुसुमप्रियायै नमः ।
169. ॐ कमण्डलुधरायै नमः ।
170. ॐ काल्यै नमः ।
171. ॐ कर्मनिर्मूल कारिण्यै नमः ।
172. ॐ कलहंसगत्यै नमः ।
173. ॐ कक्षायै नमः ।
174. ॐ कृतकौतुक मङ्गलायै नमः ।
175. ॐ कस्तुरी तिलकायै नमः।
176. ॐ कम्रायै नमः ।
177. ॐ करिन्द्रगमनायै नमः ।
178. ॐ कुह्वै नमः ।
179. ॐ कर्पूर लेपनायै नमः ।
180. ॐ कृष्णायै नमः ।
181. ॐ कपिलायै नमः ।
182. ॐ कुहराश्रयायै नमः ।
183. ॐ कूटस्थायै नमः ।
184. ॐ कुधरायै नमः ।
185. ॐ कम्रायै नमः ।
186. ॐ कुक्षिस्थाखिलविष्टपायै नमः ।
187. ॐ खड्गखेटकरायै नमः ।
188. ॐ खर्वायै नमः ।
189. ॐ खेचर्यै नमः ।
190. ॐ खगवाहनायै नमः ।
191. ॐ खट्वाङ्गधारिण्यै नमः।
192. ॐ ख्यातायै नमः ।
193. ॐ खगराजोपरिस्थितायै नमः ।
194. ॐ खलघ्न्यै नमः ।
195. ॐ खण्डितजरायै नमः ।
196. ॐ खण्डाख्यान प्रदायिन्यै नमः ।

197. ॐ खण्डेन्दुतिलकायै नमः।
198. ॐ गङ्गायै नमः ।
199. ॐ गणेश गुह पूजितायै नमः ।
200. ॐ गायत्र्यै नमः ।

201. ॐ गोमत्यै नमः ।
202. ॐ गीतायै नमः ।
203. ॐ गान्धार्यै नमः ।
204. ॐ गानलोलुपायै नमः ।
205. ॐ गौतम्यै नमः ।
206. ॐ गामिन्यै नमः ।
207. ॐ गाधायै नमः ।
208. ॐ गन्धर्वाप्सर सेवितायै नमः ।
209. ॐ गोविन्द चरणा क्रान्तायै नमः ।
210. ॐ गुणत्रय विभावितायै नमः ।

211. ॐ गन्धर्व्यै नमः ।
212. ॐ गह्वर्यै नमः ।
213. ॐ गोत्रायै नमः ।
214. ॐ गिरीशायै नमः ।
215. ॐ गहनायै नमः ।
216. ॐ गम्यै नमः ।
217. ॐ गुहावासायै नमः ।
218. ॐ गुणवत्यै नमः ।
219. ॐ गुरुपाप प्रणासिन्यै नमः।
220. ॐ गुर्व्यै नमः ।

221. ॐ गुणवत्यै नमः ।
222. ॐ गुह्यायै नमः ।
223. ॐ गोप्तव्यायै नमः ।
224. ॐ गुणदायिन्यै नमः ।
225. ॐ गिरिजायै नमः ।
226. ॐ गुह्यमातङ्ग्यै नमः ।

227. ॐ गरुडध्वज वल्लभायै नमः ।
228. ॐ गर्वापहारिण्यै नमः ।
229. ॐ गोदायै नमः ।
230. ॐ गोकुलस्थायै नमः ।

231. ॐ गदाधरायै नमः ।
232. ॐ गोकर्ण निलया सक्तायै नमः ।
233. ॐ गुह्य मण्डल वर्तिन्यै नमः ।
234. ॐ घर्मदायै नमः ।
235. ॐ घनदायै नमः ।
236. ॐ घण्टायै नमः ।
237. ॐ घोरदानव मर्दिन्यै नमः ।
238. ॐ घृणिमन्त्रमय्यै नमः ।
239. ॐ घोषायै नमः ।
240. ॐ घनसम्पातदायिन्यै नमः।

241. ॐ घण्टारवप्रियायै नमः ।
242. ॐ घ्राणायै नमः ।
243. ॐ घृणिसन्तुष्टकारिण्यै नमः ।
244. ॐ घनारिमण्डलायै नमः ।
245. ॐ घूर्णायै नमः ।
246. ॐ घृताच्यै नमः ।
247. ॐ घणवेगिन्यै नमः ।
248. ॐ ज्ञानधातुमय्यै नमः ।
249. ॐ चर्चायै नमः ।
250. ॐ चर्चितायै नमः ।

251. ॐ चारुहासिन्यै नमः ।
252. ॐ चटुलायै नमः ।
253. ॐ चण्डिकायै नमः ।
254. ॐ चित्रायै नमः ।
255. ॐ चित्रमाल्य विभूषितायै नमः ।
256. ॐ चतुर्भुजायै नमः ।

257. ॐ चारुदन्तायै नमः ।
258. ॐ चातुर्यै नमः ।
259. ॐ चरितप्रदायै नमः ।
260. ॐ चूलिकायै नमः ।

261. ॐ चित्रवस्त्रान्तायै नमः ।
262. ॐ चन्द्रमःकर्णकुण्डलायै नमः ।
263. ॐ चन्द्रहासायै नमः ।
264. ॐ चारुदात्र्यै नमः ।
265. ॐ चकोर्यै नमः ।
266. ॐ चन्द्रहासिन्यै नमः ।
267. ॐ चन्द्रिकायै नमः ।
268. ॐ चन्द्रधात्र्यै नमः ।
269. ॐ चौर्यै नमः ।
270. ॐ चौरायै नमः ।

271. ॐ चण्डिकायै नमः ।
272. ॐ चञ्चद्वागवादिन्यै नमः।
273. ॐ चन्द्र चूडायै नमः ।
274. ॐ चोर विनाशिन्यै नमः ।
275. ॐ चारु चन्दन लिप्ताङ्ग्यै नमः ।
276. ॐ चञ्चच्चामरवीजितायै नमः ।
277. ॐ चारुमध्यायै नमः ।
278. ॐ चारुगत्यै नमः ।
279. ॐ चन्दिलायै नमः ।
280. ॐ चन्द्ररूपिण्यै नमः ।

281. ॐ चारुहोमप्रियायै नमः ।
282. ॐ चार्वाचरितायै नमः ।
283. ॐ चक्रबाहुकायै नमः ।
284. ॐ चन्द्रमण्डलमध्यस्थायै नमः ।
285. ॐ चन्द्रमण्डलदर्पणायै नमः ।
286. ॐ चक्रवाकस्तन्यै नमः ।

287. ॐ चेष्टायै नमः ।
288. ॐ चित्रायै नमः ।
289. ॐ चारुविलासिन्यै नमः ।
290. ॐ चित्स्वरूपायै नमः ।
291. ॐ चन्द्रवत्यै नमः ।
292. ॐ चन्द्रमायै नमः ।
293. ॐ चन्दनप्रियायै नमः ।
294. ॐ चोदयित्र्यै नमः ।
295. ॐ चिरप्रज्ञायै नमः ।
296. ॐ चातकायै नमः ।
297. ॐ चारुहेतुक्यै नमः ।
298. ॐ छत्रयातायै नमः ।
299. ॐ छत्रधरायै नमः ।
300. ॐ छायायै नमः ।
301. ॐ छन्दः परिच्छदायै नमः।
302. ॐ छायादेव्यै नमः ।
303. ॐ छिद्रनखायै नमः ।
304. ॐ छन्नेन्द्रियविसर्पिण्यै नमः ।
305. ॐ छन्दोऽनुष्टुप्प्रतिष्ठान्तायै नमः ।
306. ॐ छिद्रोपद्रवभेदिन्यै नमः।
307. ॐ छेदायै नमः ।
308. ॐ छत्रेश्वर्यै नमः ।
309. ॐ छिन्नायै नमः ।
310. ॐ छुरिकायै नमः ।
311. ॐ छेदनप्रियायै नमः ।
312. ॐ जनन्यै नमः ।
313. ॐ जन्मरहितायै नमः ।
314. ॐ जातवेदायै नमः ।
315. ॐ जगन्मय्यै नमः ।
316. ॐ जाह्नव्यै नमः ।

317. ॐ जटिलायै नमः ।
318. ॐ जेत्र्यै नमः ।
319. ॐ जरा मरण वर्जितायै नमः ।
320. ॐ जम्बुद्वीपवत्यै नमः ।

321. ॐ ज्वालायै नमः ।
322. ॐ जयन्त्यै नमः ।
323. ॐ जलशालिन्यै नमः ।
324. ॐ जितेन्द्रियायै नमः ।
325. ॐ जितक्रोधायै नमः ।
326. ॐ जितामित्रायै नमः ।
327. ॐ जगत्प्रियायै नमः ।
328. ॐ जातरूपमय्यै नमः ।
329. ॐ जिह्वायै नमः ।
330. ॐ जानक्यै नमः ।

331. ॐ जगत्यै नमः ।
332. ॐ जरायै नमः ।
333. ॐ जनित्र्यै नमः ।
334. ॐ जह्नुतनयायै नमः ।
335. ॐ जगत्त्रय हितैषिण्यै नमः।
336. ॐ ज्वालामुख्यै नमः ।
337. ॐ जपवत्यै नमः ।
338. ॐ ज्वरघ्न्यै नमः ।
339. ॐ जितविष्टपायै नमः ।
340. ॐ जिताक्रान्तमय्यै नमः ।

341. ॐ ज्वालायै नमः ।
342. ॐ जाग्रत्यै नमः ।
343. ॐ ज्वरदेवतायै नमः ।
344. ॐ ज्वलन्त्यै नमः ।
345. ॐ जलदायै नमः ।
346. ॐ ज्येष्ठायै नमः ।

347. ॐ ज्याघोषस्फोटदिङ्मुख्यै नमः ।
348. ॐ जम्भिन्यै नमः ।
349. ॐ जृम्भणायै नमः ।
350. ॐ जृम्भायै नमः ।

351. ॐ ज्वलन्माणिक्य कुण्डलायै नमः ।
352. ॐ झिञ्झिकायै नमः ।
353. ॐ झणनिर्घोषायै नमः ।
354. ॐ झंझामारुतवेगिन्यै नमः।
355. ॐ झल्लरीवाद्यकुशलायै नमः ।
356. ॐ ञरूपायै नमः ।
357. ॐ ञभुजायै नमः ।
358. ॐ टङ्कबाणसमायुक्तायै नमः ।
359. ॐ टङ्किन्यै नमः ।
360. ॐ टङ्कभेदिन्यै नमः ।

361. ॐ टङ्कीगणकृताघोषायै नमः ।
362. ॐ टङ्कनीयमहोरसायै नमः ।
363. ॐ टङ्कारकारिणीदेव्यै नमः ।
364. ॐ ठठशब्दनिनादिन्यै नमः।
365. ॐ डामर्यै नमः ।
366. ॐ डाकिन्यै नमः ।
367. ॐ डिम्भायै नमः ।
368. ॐ डुण्डमारैकनिर्जितायै नमः ।
369. ॐ डामरीतन्त्रमार्गस्थायै नमः ।
370. ॐ डमड्डमरुनादिन्यै नमः।

371. ॐ डिण्डीरवसहायै नमः ।
372. ॐ डिम्भ लसत्क्रीडा परायणायै नमः।
373. ॐ ढुण्ढिविघ्नेशजनन्यै नमः ।
374. ॐ ढक्काहस्तायै नमः ।
375. ॐ ढिलिव्रजायै नमः ।
376. ॐ नित्यज्ञानायै नमः ।

377. ॐ निरुपमायै नमः ।
378. ॐ निर्गुणायै नमः ।
379. ॐ नर्मदायै नमः ।
380. ॐ नद्यायै नमः ।

381. ॐ त्रिगुणायै नमः ।
382. ॐ त्रिपदायै नमः ।
383. ॐ तन्त्र्यै नमः ।
384. ॐ तुलसीतरुणातरुव्यै नमः ।
385. ॐ त्रिविक्रमपदाक्रान्तायै नमः ।
386. ॐ तुरीयपदगामिन्यै नमः ।
387. ॐ तरुणादित्य शङ्काश्यै नमः ।
388. ॐ तामस्यै नमः ।
389. ॐ तुहिनायै नमः ।
390. ॐ तुरायै नमः ।

391. ॐ त्रिकालज्ञानसम्पन्नायै नमः ।
392. ॐ त्रिवेण्यै नमः ।
393. ॐ त्रिलोचनायै नमः ।
394. ॐ त्रिशक्त्यै नमः ।
395. ॐ त्रिपुरायै नमः ।
396. ॐ तुङ्गायै नमः ।
397. ॐ तुरङ्ग वदनायै नमः ।
398. ॐ तिमिङ्गिलगिलायै नमः ।
399. ॐ तीव्रायै नमः ।
400. ॐ त्रिश्रोतायै नमः ।

401. ॐ तामसादिन्यै नमः ।
402. ॐ तन्त्रमन्त्रविशेषज्ञायै नमः ।
403. ॐ तनुमध्यायै नमः ।
404. ॐ त्रिविष्टपायै नमः ।
405. ॐ त्रिसन्ध्यायै नमः ।
406. ॐ त्रिस्तन्यै नमः ।

407. ॐ तोषासंस्थायै नमः ।
408. ॐ तालप्रतापिन्यै नमः ।
409. ॐ ताटङ्किन्यै नमः ।
410. ॐ तुषाराभायै नमः ।

411. ॐ तुहिनाचलवासिन्यै नमः ।
412. ॐ तन्तुजालसमायुक्तायै नमः ।
413. ॐ तारहारावलिप्रियायै नमः ।
414. ॐ तिलहोमप्रियायै नमः ।
415. ॐ तीर्थायै नमः ।
416. ॐ तमालकुसुमाकृत्यै नमः।
417. ॐ तारकायै नमः ।
418. ॐ त्रियुतायै नमः ।
419. ॐ तन्व्यै नमः ।
420. ॐ त्रिशङ्कुपरिवारितायै नमः ।

421. ॐ तलोदर्यै नमः ।
422. ॐ तिलाभूषायै नमः ।
423. ॐ ताटङ्कप्रियवादिन्यै नमः ।
424. ॐ त्रिजटायै नमः ।
425. ॐ तित्तिर्यै नमः ।
426. ॐ तृष्णायै नमः ।
427. ॐ त्रिविधायै नमः ।
428. ॐ तरुणाकृत्यै नमः ।
429. ॐ तप्तकाञ्चनसङ्काशायै नमः ।
430. ॐ तप्तकाञ्चनभूषणायै नमः ।

431. ॐ त्रयम्बकायै नमः ।
432. ॐ त्रिवर्गायै नमः ।
433. ॐ त्रिकालज्ञानदायिन्यै नमः ।
434. ॐ तर्पणायै नमः ।
435. ॐ तृप्तिदायै नमः ।
436. ॐ तृप्तायै नमः ।

437. ॐ तामस्यै नमः ।
438. ॐ तुम्बरुस्तुतायै नमः ।
439. ॐ तार्क्ष्यस्थायै नमः ।
440. ॐ त्रिगुणाकारायै नमः ।

441. ॐ त्रिभङ्ग्यै नमः ।
442. ॐ तनुवल्लर्यै नमः ।
443. ॐ थात्कार्यै नमः ।
444. ॐ थारवायै नमः ।
445. ॐ थान्तायै नमः ।
446. ॐ दोहिन्यै नमः ।
447. ॐ दीनवत्सलायै नमः ।
448. ॐ दानवान्तकर्यै नमः ।
449. ॐ दुर्गायै नमः ।
450. ॐ दुर्गासुरनिबर्हिण्यै नमः ।

451. ॐ देवरीत्यै नमः ।
452. ॐ दिवारात्र्यै नमः ।
453. ॐ द्रौपद्यै नमः ।
454. ॐ दुन्दुभिस्वनायै नमः ।
455. ॐ देवयान्यै नमः ।
456. ॐ दुरावासायै नमः ।
457. ॐ दारिद्र्योभेदिन्यै नमः ।
458. ॐ दिवायै नमः ।
459. ॐ दामोदरप्रियायै नमः ।
460. ॐ दीप्तायै नमः ।

461. ॐ दिग्वासायै नमः ।
462. ॐ दिग्विमोहिन्यै नमः ।
463. ॐ दण्डकारण्यनिलयायै नमः ।
464. ॐ दण्डिन्यै नमः ।
465. ॐ देवपूजितायै नमः ।
466. ॐ देववन्द्यायै नमः ।

467. ॐ दिविषदायै नमः ।
468. ॐ द्वेषिण्यै नमः ।
469. ॐ दानावाकृत्यै नमः ।
470. ॐ दीननाथस्तुतायै नमः ।
471. ॐ दीक्षायै नमः ।
472. ॐ दैवतादिस्वरूपिण्यै नमः ।
473. ॐ धात्र्यै नमः ।
474. ॐ धनुर्धरायै नमः ।
475. ॐ धेनुण्यै नमः ।
476. ॐ धारिण्यै नमः ।
477. ॐ धर्मचारिण्यै नमः ।
478. ॐ धरन्धरायै नमः ।
479. ॐ धराधारायै नमः ।
480. ॐ धनदायै नमः ।
481. ॐ धान्यदोहिन्यै नमः ।
482. ॐ धर्मशीलायै नमः ।
483. ॐ धनाध्यक्षायै नमः ।
484. ॐ धनुर्वेदविशारदायै नमः।
485. ॐ धृत्यै नमः ।
486. ॐ धन्यायै नमः ।
487. ॐ धृतपदायै नमः ।
488. ॐ धर्मराजप्रियायै नमः ।
489. ॐ ध्रुवायै नमः ।
490. ॐ धूमावत्यै नमः ।
491. ॐ धूमकेश्यै नमः ।
492. ॐ धर्मशास्त्रप्रकाशिन्यै नमः ।
493. ॐ नन्दायै नमः ।
494. ॐ नन्दप्रियायै नमः ।
495. ॐ निद्रायै नमः ।
496. ॐ नृनुतायै नमः ।

497. ॐ नन्दनात्मिकायै नमः ।

498. ॐ नर्मदायै नमः ।

499. ॐ नलिन्यै नमः ।

500. ॐ नीलायै नमः ।

501. ॐ नील कण्ठ समाश्रयायै नमः ।

502. ॐ नारायणप्रियायै नमः ।

503. ॐ नित्यायै नमः ।

504. ॐ निर्मलायै नमः ।

505. ॐ निर्गुणायै नमः ।

506. ॐ निध्यै नमः ।

507. ॐ निराधारायै नमः ।

508. ॐ निरुपमायै नमः ।

509. ॐ नित्यशुद्धायै नमः ।

510. ॐ निरञ्जनायै नमः ।

511. ॐ नादबिन्दुकलातीतायै नमः ।

512. ॐ नादबिन्दुकलात्मिकायै नमः ।

513. ॐ नृसिंह्यै नमः ।

514. ॐ नगधरायै नमः ।

515. ॐ नृपनागविभूषितायै नमः।

516. ॐ नरकक्लेशशमन्यै नमः।

517. ॐ नारायणपदोद्भवायै नमः।

518. ॐ निरवद्यायै नमः ।

519. ॐ निराकारायै नमः ।

520. ॐ नारदप्रियकारिण्यै नमः।

521. ॐ नानाज्योतिः समाख्यातायै नमः ।

522. ॐ निधिदायै नमः ।

523. ॐ निर्मलात्मिकायै नमः ।

524. ॐ नवसूत्रधरायै नमः ।

525. ॐ नीत्यै नमः ।

526. ॐ निरुपद्रवकारिण्यै नमः ।

527. ॐ नन्दजायै नमः ।
528. ॐ नवरत्नाढ्यायै नमः ।
529. ॐ नैमिषारण्यवासिन्यै नमः ।
530. ॐ नवनीतप्रियायै नमः ।
531. ॐ नार्यै नमः ।
532. ॐ नीलजीमूतनिस्वनायै नमः ।
533. ॐ निमेषिण्यै नमः ।
534. ॐ नदीरूपायै नमः ।
535. ॐ नीलग्रीवायै नमः ।
536. ॐ निशिश्वर्यै नमः ।
537. ॐ नामावल्यै नमः ।
538. ॐ निशुम्भघ्न्यै नमः ।
539. ॐ नागलोकनिवासिन्यै नमः ।
540. ॐ नवजाम्बूनदप्रख्यायै नमः ।
541. ॐ नागलोकाधिदेवतायै नमः ।
542. ॐ नूपूराक्रान्तचरणायै नमः।
543. ॐ नरचित्तप्रमोदिन्यै नमः ।
544. ॐ निमग्नारक्तनयनायै नमः।
545. ॐ निर्घातसमनिःस्वनायै नमः ।
546. ॐ नन्दनोद्यानानिलयायै नमः ।
547. ॐ निर्व्यूहोपरिचारिण्यै नमः ।
548. ॐ पार्वत्यै नमः ।
549. ॐ परमोदारायै नमः ।
550. ॐ परब्रह्मात्मिकायै नमः ।
551. ॐ परायै नमः ।
552. ॐ पञ्चकोशविनिर्मुक्तायै नमः ।
553. ॐ पञ्चपातकनाशिन्यै नमः ।
554. ॐ परचित्तविधानज्ञायै नमः ।
555. ॐ पञ्चिकायै नमः ।
556. ॐ पञ्चरूपिण्यै नमः ।

557. ॐ पूर्णिमायै नमः ।
558. ॐ परमायै नमः ।
559. ॐ प्रीत्यै नमः ।
560. ॐ परतेज्यै नमः ।

561. ॐ प्रकाशिन्यै नमः ।
562. ॐ पुराण्यै नमः ।
563. ॐ पौरुष्यै नमः ।
564. ॐ पुण्यायै नमः ।
565. ॐ पुण्डरीकनिभेक्षणायै नमः ।
566. ॐ पातालतलनिर्मग्नायै नमः ।
567. ॐ प्रीतायै नमः ।
568. ॐ प्रीतिविवर्धिन्यै नमः ।
569. ॐ पावन्यै नमः ।
570. ॐ पादसहितायै नमः ।

571. ॐ पेशलायै नमः ।
572. ॐ पवनाशिन्यै नमः ।
573. ॐ प्रजापत्यै नमः ।
574. ॐ परिश्रान्तायै नमः ।
575. ॐ पर्वतस्तन मण्डलायै नमः ।
576. ॐ पद्मप्रियायै नमः ।
577. ॐ पद्मसंस्थायै नमः ।
578. ॐ पद्माक्ष्यै नमः ।
579. ॐ पद्मसम्भवायै नमः ।
580. ॐ पद्मपत्रायै नमः ।

581. ॐ पद्मपदायै नमः ।
582. ॐ पद्मिन्यै नमः ।
583. ॐ प्रियभाषिण्यै नमः ।
584. ॐ पशुपाशविनिर्मुक्तायै नमः ।
585. ॐ पुरन्ध्र्यै नमः ।
586. ॐ पुरवासिन्यै नमः ।

587. ॐ पुष्कलायै नमः ।
588. ॐ पुरुषायै नमः ।
589. ॐ पर्वायै नमः ।
590. ॐ पारिजातसुमप्रियायै नमः ।
591. ॐ पतिव्रतायै नमः ।
592. ॐ पवित्राङ्ग्यै नमः ।
593. ॐ पुष्पहासपरायणायै नमः।
594. ॐ प्रज्ञावतीसुतायै नमः ।
595. ॐ पौत्र्यै नमः ।
596. ॐ पुत्रपूज्यायै नमः ।
597. ॐ पयस्विन्यै नमः ।
598. ॐ पट्टिपाशधरायै नमः ।
599. ॐ पङ्क्त्यै नमः ।
600. ॐ पितृलोकप्रदायिन्यै नमः।
601. ॐ पुराण्यै नमः ।
602. ॐ पुण्यशीलायै नमः ।
603. ॐ प्रणतार्ति विनाशिन्यै नमः ।
604. ॐ प्रद्युम्न जनन्यै नमः ।
605. ॐ पुष्टायै नमः ।
606. ॐ पितामह परिग्रहायै नमः।
607. ॐ पुण्डरीक पुरावासायै नमः ।
608. ॐ पुण्डरीक समाननायै नमः ।
609. ॐ पृथुजङ्घायै नमः ।
610. ॐ पृथुभुजायै नमः ।
611. ॐ पृथुपादायै नमः ।
612. ॐ पृथूदर्यै नमः ।
613. ॐ प्रवाल शोभायै नमः ।
614. ॐ पिङ्गाक्ष्यै नमः ।
615. ॐ पीतवासाः नमः ।
616. ॐ प्रचापलायै नमः ।

617. ॐ प्रसवायै नमः ।
618. ॐ पुष्टिदायै नमः ।
619. ॐ पुण्यायै नमः ।
620. ॐ प्रतिष्ठायै नमः ।

621. ॐ प्रणवागत्यै नमः ।
622. ॐ पञ्चवर्णायै नमः ।
623. ॐ पञ्चवाण्यै नमः ।
624. ॐ पञ्चिकायै नमः ।
625. ॐ पञ्जरस्थितायै नमः ।
626. ॐ परमायै नमः ।
627. ॐ परज्योतिः नमः ।
628. ॐ परप्रीत्यै नमः ।
629. ॐ परागत्यै नमः ।
630. ॐ पराकाष्ठायै नमः ।

631. ॐ परेशान्यै नमः ।
632. ॐ पावन्यै नमः ।
633. ॐ पावकद्युत्यै नमः ।
634. ॐ पुण्यभद्रायै नमः ।
635. ॐ परिच्छेद्यायै नमः ।
636. ॐ पुष्पहासायै नमः ।
637. ॐ पृथूदर्यै नमः ।
638. ॐ पीताङ्ग्यै नमः ।
639. ॐ पीतवसनायै नमः ।
640. ॐ पीतशय्यायै नमः ।

641. ॐ पिशाचिन्यै नमः ।
642. ॐ पीतक्रियायै नमः ।
643. ॐ पिशाचघ्न्यै नमः ।
644. ॐ पाटलाक्ष्यै नमः ।
645. ॐ पटुक्रियायै नमः ।
646. ॐ पञ्चभक्षप्रियाचारायै नमः ।

647. ॐ पूतना प्राण घातिन्यै नमः।
648. ॐ पुन्नाग वन मध्यस्थायै नमः ।
649. ॐ पुण्य तीर्थ निषेवितायै नमः ।
650. ॐ पञ्चाङ्ग्यै नमः ।

651. ॐ पराशक्त्यै नमः ।
652. ॐ परमाह्लादकारिण्यै नमः।
653. ॐ पुष्प काण्ड स्थितायै नमः ।
654. ॐ पूषायै नमः ।
655. ॐ पोषिताखिल विष्टपायै नमः ।
656. ॐ पानप्रियायै नमः ।
657. ॐ पञ्चशिखायै नमः ।
658. ॐ पन्न गोपरिशायिन्यै नमः ।
659. ॐ पञ्च मात्रात्मिकायै नमः ।
660. ॐ पृथ्व्यै नमः ।

661. ॐ पथिकायै नमः ।
662. ॐ पृथुदोहिन्यै नमः ।
663. ॐ पुराण न्याय मीमांसायै नमः ।
664. ॐ पाटल्यै नमः ।
665. ॐ पुष्प गन्धिन्यै नमः ।
666. ॐ पुण्य प्रजायै नमः ।
667. ॐ पार दात्र्यै नमः ।
668. ॐ परमार्गैकगोचरायै नमः।
669. ॐ प्रवाल शोभायै नमः ।
670. ॐ पूर्णाशायै नमः ।

671. ॐ प्रणवायै नमः ।
672. ॐ पल्लवोदर्यै नमः ।
673. ॐ फलिन्यै नमः ।
674. ॐ फलदायै नमः ।
675. ॐ फल्ग्वै नमः ।
676. ॐ फुत्कार्यै नमः ।

677. ॐ फलकाकृत्यै नमः ।
678. ॐ फणिन्द्र भोग शयनायै नमः ।
679. ॐ फणि मण्डल मण्डितायै नमः ।
680. ॐ बालबालायै नमः ।

681. ॐ बहुमतायै नमः ।
682. ॐ बाला तपनीभांशुकायै नमः ।
683. ॐ बल भद्र प्रियायै नमः ।
684. ॐ बन्द्यायै नमः ।
685. ॐ बडवायै नमः ।
686. ॐ बुद्धिसंस्तुतायै नमः ।
687. ॐ बन्दीदेव्यै नमः ।
688. ॐ बिलवत्यै नमः ।
689. ॐ बडिशघ्निये नमः ।
690. ॐ बलिप्रियायै नमः ।

691. ॐ बान्धव्यै नमः ।
692. ॐ बोधितायै नमः ।
693. ॐ बुद्धियै नमः ।
694. ॐ बन्धूक कुसुम प्रियायै नमः ।
695. ॐ बालभानु प्रभाकरायै नमः ।
696. ॐ ब्राह्म्यै नमः ।
697. ॐ ब्राह्मण देवतायै नमः ।
698. ॐ बृहस्पति स्तुतायै नमः ।
699. ॐ बृन्दायै नमः ।
700. ॐ बृन्दावन विहारिण्यै नमः ।

701. ॐ बालाकिन्यै नमः ।
702. ॐ बिलाहारायै नमः ।
703. ॐ बिलवसायै नमः ।
704. ॐ बहूदकायै नमः ।
705. ॐ बहुनेत्रायै नमः ।
706. ॐ बहुपदायै नमः ।

707. ॐ बहुकर्णावतंसिकायै नमः ।
708. ॐ बहुबाहुयुतायै नमः ।
709. ॐ बीज रूपिण्यै नमः ।
710. ॐ बहु रूपिण्यै नमः ।

711. ॐ बिन्दुनाद कलातीतायै नमः ।
712. ॐ बिन्दुनाद स्वरूपिण्यै नमः ।
713. ॐ बद्धगोधाङ्गुलित्राणायै नमः ।
714. ॐ बदर्याश्रमवासिन्यै नमः।
715. ॐ बृन्दारकायै नमः ।
716. ॐ बृहत्स्कन्धायै नमः ।
717. ॐ बृहत्यै नमः ।
718. ॐ बाणपातिन्यै नमः ।
719. ॐ बृन्दाध्यक्षायै नमः ।
720. ॐ बहुनुतायै नमः ।

721. ॐ वनितायै नमः ।
722. ॐ बहुविक्रमायै नमः ।
723. ॐ बद्धपद्मा सनासीनायै नमः ।
724. ॐ बिल्व पत्रतल स्थितायै नमः ।
725. ॐ बोधिद्रुम निजावासायै नमः ।
726. ॐ बडिस्थायै नमः ।
727. ॐ बिन्दु दर्पणायै नमः ।
728. ॐ बालायै नमः ।
729. ॐ बाणासनवत्यै नमः ।
730. ॐ बडवानलवेगिन्यै नमः ।

731. ॐ ब्रह्माण्ड बहिरन्तस्थायै नमः ।
732. ॐ ब्रह्म कङ्कणसूत्रिण्यै नमः ।
733. ॐ भवान्यै नमः ।
734. ॐ भीषणवत्यै नमः ।
735. ॐ भाविन्यै नमः ।
736. ॐ भयहारिण्यै नमः ।

737. ॐ भद्रकाल्यै नमः ।
738. ॐ भुजङ्गाक्ष्यै नमः ।
739. ॐ भारत्यै नमः ।
740. ॐ भारताशयायै नमः ।

741. ॐ भैरव्यै नमः ।
742. ॐ भीषणाकारायै नमः ।
743. ॐ भूतिदायै नमः ।
744. ॐ भूतिमालिन्यै नमः ।
745. ॐ भामिन्यै नमः ।
746. ॐ भोगनिरतायै नमः ।
747. ॐ भद्रदायै नमः ।
748. ॐ भूरिविक्रमायै नमः ।
749. ॐ भूतवासायै नमः ।
750. ॐ भृगुलतायै नमः ।

751. ॐ भार्गव्यै नमः ।
752. ॐ भूसुरार्चितायै नमः ।
753. ॐ भागीरथ्यै नमः ।
754. ॐ भोगवत्यै नमः ।
755. ॐ भवनस्थायै नमः ।
756. ॐ भिषग्वरायै नमः ।
757. ॐ भामिन्यै नमः ।
758. ॐ भोगिन्यै नमः ।
759. ॐ भाषायै नमः ।
760. ॐ भवान्यै नमः ।

761. ॐ भूरिदक्षिणायै नमः ।
762. ॐ भर्गात्मिकायै नमः ।
763. ॐ भीमावत्यै नमः ।
764. ॐ भव बन्ध विमोचिन्यै नमः ।
765. ॐ भजनीयायै नमः ।
766. ॐ भूत धात्री रञ्जितायै नमः ।

767. ॐ भुवनेश्वर्यै नमः ।
768. ॐ भुजङ्गवलयायै नमः ।
769. ॐ भीमायै नमः ।
770. ॐ भेरुण्डायै नमः ।

771. ॐ भागधेयिन्यै नमः ।
772. ॐ मातायै नमः ।
773. ॐ मायायै नमः ।
774. ॐ मधुमत्यै नमः ।
775. ॐ मधुजिह्वायै नमः ।
776. ॐ मधुप्रियायै नमः ।
777. ॐ महादेव्यै नमः ।
778. ॐ महाभागायै नमः ।
779. ॐ मालिन्यै नमः ।
780. ॐ मीनलोचनायै नमः ।

781. ॐ मायातीतायै नमः ।
782. ॐ मधुमत्यै नमः ।
783. ॐ मधुमांसायै नमः ।
784. ॐ मधुद्रवायै नमः ।
785. ॐ मानव्यै नमः ।
786. ॐ मधुसम्भूतायै नमः ।
787. ॐ मिथिला पुर वासिन्यै नमः ।
788. ॐ मधुकैटभसंहर्त्र्यै नमः ।
789. ॐ मेदिन्यै नमः ।
790. ॐ मेघमालिन्यै नमः ।

791. ॐ मन्दोदर्यै नमः ।
792. ॐ महामायायै नमः ।
793. ॐ मैथिल्यै नमः ।
794. ॐ मसृणप्रियायै नमः ।
795. ॐ महालक्ष्म्यै नमः ।
796. ॐ महाकाल्यै नमः ।

797. ॐ महाकन्यायै नमः ।
798. ॐ महेश्वर्यै नमः ।
799. ॐ माहेन्द्र्यै नमः ।
800. ॐ मेरुतनयायै नमः ।

801. ॐ मन्दार कुसुमार्चितायै नमः ।
802. ॐ मञ्जुमञ्जीर चरणायै नमः ।
803. ॐ मोक्षदायै नमः ।
804. ॐ मञ्जु भाषिण्यै नमः ।
805. ॐ मधुरद्राविण्यै नमः ।
806. ॐ मुद्रायै नमः ।
807. ॐ मलयायै नमः ।
808. ॐ मलयान्वितायै नमः ।
809. ॐ मेधायै नमः ।
810. ॐ मरकत श्यामायै नमः ।

811. ॐ मागध्यै नमः ।
812. ॐ मेनकात्मजायै नमः ।
813. ॐ महामायै नमः ।
814. ॐ महावीरायै नमः ।
815. ॐ महाश्यामायै नमः ।
816. ॐ मनुस्तुतायै नमः ।
817. ॐ मातृकायै नमः ।
818. ॐ मिहिराभासायै नमः ।
819. ॐ मुकुन्द पद विक्रमायै नमः ।
820. ॐ मूलाधारस्थितायै नमः ।

821. ॐ मुग्धायै नमः ।
822. ॐ मणिपूरक निवासिन्यै नमः ।
823. ॐ मृगाक्ष्यै नमः ।
824. ॐ महिषारूढायै नमः ।
825. ॐ महिषासुरमर्दिन्यै नमः ।
826. ॐ योगासनायै नमः ।

827. ॐ योगगम्यायै नमः ।
828. ॐ योगायै नमः ।
829. ॐ यौवनकाश्रयायै नमः ।
830. ॐ यौवन्यै नमः ।

831. ॐ युद्ध मध्यस्थायै नमः ।
832. ॐ यमुनायै नमः ।
833. ॐ युगधारिण्यै नमः ।
834. ॐ यक्षिण्यै नमः ।
835. ॐ योग युक्तायै नमः ।
836. ॐ यक्षराजप्रसूतिन्यै नमः ।
837. ॐ यात्रायै नमः ।
838. ॐ यानविधानज्ञायै नमः ।
839. ॐ यदुवंशसमुद्भवायै नमः।
840. ॐ यकारादि हकारान्तायै नमः ।

841. ॐ याजुष्यै नमः ।
842. ॐ यज्ञरूपिण्यै नमः ।
843. ॐ यामिन्यै नमः ।
844. ॐ योगनिरतायै नमः ।
845. ॐ यातुधान भयङ्कर्यै नमः ।
846. ॐ रुक्मिण्यै नमः ।
847. ॐ रमण्यै नमः ।
848. ॐ रामायै नमः ।
849. ॐ रेवत्यै नमः ।
850. ॐ रेणुकायै नमः ।

851. ॐ रत्यै नमः ।
852. ॐ रौद्र्यै नमः ।
853. ॐ रौद्रप्रियाकारायै नमः ।
854. ॐ राममातायै नमः ।
855. ॐ रतिप्रियायै नमः ।
856. ॐ रोहिण्यै नमः ।

857. ॐ राज्यदायै नमः ।

858. ॐ रेवायै नमः ।

859. ॐ रमायै नमः ।

860. ॐ राजीवलोचनायै नमः ।

861. ॐ राकेश्यै नमः ।

862. ॐ रूपसम्पन्नायै नमः ।

863. ॐ रत्नसिंहासनस्थितायै नमः ।

864. ॐ रक्तमाल्याम्बरधरायै नमः ।

865. ॐ रक्त गन्धानु लेपनायै नमः ।

866. ॐ राज हंस समारूढायै नमः ।

867. ॐ रंभायै नमः ।

868. ॐ रक्तवलिप्रियायै नमः ।

869. ॐ रमणीय युगा धारायै नमः ।

870. ॐ राजिताखिल भूतलायै नमः ।

871. ॐ रुरुचर्मपरिधानायै नमः।

872. ॐ रथिन्यै नमः ।

873. ॐ रत्नमालिकायै नमः ।

874. ॐ रोगेश्यै नमः ।

875. ॐ रोगशमन्यै नमः ।

876. ॐ राविण्यै नमः ।

877. ॐ रोमहर्षिण्यै नमः ।

878. ॐ रामचन्द्रपदाक्रान्तायै नमः ।

879. ॐ रावणच्छेदकारिण्यै नमः ।

880. ॐ रत्नवस्त्रपरिच्छिन्नायै नमः ।

881. ॐ रथस्थायै नमः ।

882. ॐ रुक्मभूषणायै नमः ।

883. ॐ लज्जाधिदेवतायै नमः ।

884. ॐ लोलायै नमः ।

885. ॐ ललितायै नमः ।

886. ॐ लिङ्गधारिण्यै नमः ।

887. ॐ लक्ष्म्यै नमः ।

888. ॐ लोलायै नमः ।

889. ॐ लुप्तविषायै नमः ।

890. ॐ लोकिन्यै नमः ।

891. ॐ लोकविश्रुतायै नमः ।

892. ॐ लज्जायै नमः ।

893. ॐ लम्बोदरीदेव्यै नमः ।

894. ॐ ललनायै नमः ।

895. ॐ लोकधारिण्यै नमः ।

896. ॐ वरदायै नमः ।

897. ॐ वन्दितायै नमः ।

898. ॐ विद्यायै नमः ।

899. ॐ वैष्णव्यै नमः ।

900. ॐ विमलाकृत्यै नमः ।

901. ॐ वाराह्यै नमः ।

902. ॐ विरजायै नमः ।

903. ॐ वर्षायै नमः ।

904. ॐ वरलक्ष्म्यै नमः ।

905. ॐ विलासिन्यै नमः ।

906. ॐ विनतायै नमः ।

907. ॐ व्योममध्यस्थायै नमः ।

908. ॐ वारिजासन संस्थितायै नमः ।

909. ॐ वारुण्यै नमः ।

910. ॐ वेणुसम्भूतायै नमः ।

911. ॐ वितिहोत्रायै नमः ।

912. ॐ विरूपिण्यै नमः ।

913. ॐ वायु मण्डल मध्यस्थायै नमः ।

914. ॐ विष्णुरूपायै नमः ।

915. ॐ विधिप्रियायै नमः ।

916. ॐ विष्णुपत्न्यै नमः ।

917. ॐ विष्णुमत्यै नमः ।
918. ॐ विशालाक्ष्यै नमः ।
919. ॐ वसुन्धरायै नमः ।
920. ॐ वामदेवप्रियायै नमः ।

921. ॐ वेलायै नमः ।
922. ॐ वज्रिण्यै नमः ।
923. ॐ वसुदोहिन्यै नमः ।
924. ॐ वेदाक्षर परिताङ्ग्यै नमः ।
925. ॐ वाजपेय फलप्रदायै नमः ।
926. ॐ वासव्यै नमः ।
927. ॐ वामजनन्यै नमः ।
928. ॐ वैकुण्ठनिलयायै नमः ।
929. ॐ वरायै नमः ।
930. ॐ व्यासप्रियायै नमः ।

931. ॐ वर्मधरायै नमः ।
932. ॐ वाल्मीकिपरिसेवितायै नमः ।
933. ॐ शाकम्भर्यै नमः ।
934. ॐ शिवायै नमः ।
935. ॐ शान्तायै नमः ।
936. ॐ शारदायै नमः ।
937. ॐ शरणागत्यै नमः ।
938. ॐ शातोदर्यै नमः ।
939. ॐ शुभाचारायै नमः ।
940. ॐ शुम्भासुर विमर्दिन्यै नमः ।

941. ॐ शोभावत्यै नमः ।
942. ॐ शिवाकारायै नमः ।
943. ॐ शङ्करार्ध शरीरिण्यै नमः ।
944. ॐ शोणायै नमः ।
945. ॐ शुभाशयायै नमः ।
946. ॐ शुभ्रायै नमः ।

947. ॐ शिरःसन्धानकारिण्यै नमः ।

948. ॐ शरावत्यै नमः ।

949. ॐ शरानन्दायै नमः ।

950. ॐ शरज्ज्योत्स्नायै नमः ।

951. ॐ शुभाननायै नमः ।

952. ॐ शरभायै नमः ।

953. ॐ शूलिन्यै नमः ।

954. ॐ शुद्धायै नमः ।

955. ॐ शबर्यै नमः ।

956. ॐ शुकवाहनायै नमः ।

957. ॐ श्रीमत्यै नमः ।

958. ॐ श्रीधरानन्दायै नमः ।

959. ॐ श्रवणानन्द दायिन्यै नमः ।

960. ॐ शर्वाण्यै नमः ।

961. ॐ शर्वरीवन्द्यायै नमः ।

962. ॐ षड्भाषायै नमः ।

963. ॐ षड्ऋतुप्रियायै नमः ।

964. ॐ षडाधारस्थितादेव्यै नमः ।

965. ॐ षण्मुखप्रियकारिण्यै नमः ।

966. ॐ षडङ्गरूपसुमति सुरासुर नमस्कृतायै नमः ।

967. ॐ सरस्वत्यै नमः ।

968. ॐ सदाधारायै नमः ।

969. ॐ सर्वमङ्गल कारिण्यै नमः ।

970. ॐ सामगान प्रियायै नमः ।

971. ॐ सूक्ष्मायै नमः ।

972. ॐ सावित्र्यै नमः ।

973. ॐ सामसम्भवायै नमः ।

974. ॐ सर्वावासायै नमः ।

975. ॐ सदानन्दायै नमः ।

976. ॐ सुस्तन्यै नमः ।

977. ॐ सागराम्बरायै नमः ।
978. ॐ सर्वैश्वर्यप्रियायै नमः ।
979. ॐ सिद्ध्यै नमः ।
980. ॐ साधुबन्धुपराक्रमायै नमः ।
981. ॐ सप्तर्षिमण्डलगतायै नमः ।
982. ॐ सोममण्डलवासिन्यै नमः ।
983. ॐ सर्वज्ञायै नमः ।
984. ॐ सान्द्रकरुणायै नमः ।
985. ॐ समानाधिकवर्जितायै नमः ।
986. ॐ सर्वोत्तुङ्गायै नमः ।
987. ॐ सङ्गहीनायै नमः ।
988. ॐ सद्गुणायै नमः ।
989. ॐ सकलेष्टदायै नमः ।
990. ॐ सरघायै नमः ।
991. ॐ सूर्यतनयायै नमः ।
992. ॐ सुकेश्यै नमः ।
993. ॐ सोमसंहत्यै नमः ।
994. ॐ हिरण्यवर्णायै नमः ।
995. ॐ हरिण्यै नमः ।
996. ॐ ह्रीङ्कार्यै नमः ।
997. ॐ हंसवाहिन्यै नमः ।
998. ॐ क्षौमवस्त्रपरिताङ्ग्यै नमः ।
999. ॐ क्षीराब्धितनयायै नमः ।
1000. ॐ क्षमायै नमः ।
1001. ॐ गायत्र्यै नमः ।
1002. ॐ सावित्र्यै नमः ।
1003. ॐ पार्वत्यै नमः ।
1004. ॐ सरस्वत्यै नमः ।
1005. ॐ वेदगर्भायै नमः ।
1006. ॐ वरारोहायै नमः ।

1007. ॐ श्रीगायत्र्यै नमः ।

1008. ॐ परांविकायै नमः ।

इति श्रीदेवीभागवते महापुराणे द्वादशस्कन्धे श्रीगायत्रीसहस्रनामआवलीः समाप्ता ॥

*****

## *Śrī Gāyatri Sahasranāmavaļi* – English

*Śrī Gāyatrī Sahasranāmāvaliḥ*

*Dhyānam*

*Raktaśvetahiraṇyanīladhavalairyuktā Trinītrojjvalāṃ*
*Raktāṃ Raktanavasrajaṃ Maṇigaṇairyuktāṃ Kumārīmimām* I
*Gāyatrīṃ Kamalāsanāṃ Karatalavyānaddhakuṇḍāmbujāṃ*
*Padmākṣī Ca Varasrajaṃ Ca Dadhatīṃ Haṃsādhirūḍhāṃ Bhaje* II

*Atha Nāmāḥ* I

1. *Oṃ Acintyalakṣaṇāyai Namaḥ* I
2. *Oṃ Avyaktāyai Namaḥ* I
3. *Oṃ Arthamātṛmaheśvaryai Namaḥ* I
4. *Oṃ Amṛtāyai Namaḥ* I
5. *Oṃ Arṇavamadhyasthāyai Namaḥ* I
6. *Oṃ Ajitāyai Namaḥ* I
7. *Oṃ Aparājitāyai Namaḥ* I
8. *Oṃ Aṇimādiguṇādhārāyai Namaḥ* I
9. *Oṃ Arkamaṇḍalasaṃsthitāyai Namaḥ* I
10. *Oṃ Ajarāyai Namaḥ* I

11. *Oṃ Ajāyai Namaḥ* I
12. *Oṃ Aparāyai Namaḥ* I
13. *Oṃ Adharmāyai Namaḥ* I
14. *Oṃ Akṣasūtradharāyai Namaḥ* I
15. *Oṃ Adharāyai Namaḥ* I
16. *Oṃ Akārādikṣakārāntāyai Namaḥ* I
17. *Oṃ Ariṣadvargabhedinyai Namaḥ* I
18. *Oṃ Añjanādripratikāśāyai Namaḥ* I
19. *Oṃ Añjanādrinivāsinyai Namaḥ* I
20. *Oṃ Adityai Namaḥ* I

21. *Oṃ Ajapāyai Namaḥ* |
22. *Oṃ Avidyāyai Namaḥ* |
23. *Oṃ Aravindanibhekṣaṇāyai Namaḥ* |
24. *Oṃ Antarbahisthitāyai Namaḥ* |
25. *Oṃ Avidyādhvaṃsinyai Namaḥ* |
26. *Oṃ Antarātmikāyai Namaḥ* |
27. *Oṃ Ajāyai Namaḥ* |
28. *Oṃ Ajamukhavāsāyai Namaḥ* |
29. *Oṃ Aravindanibhānanāyai Namaḥ* |
30. *Oṃ Ardhamātrāyai Namaḥ* |

31. *Oṃ Arthadānajñāyai Namaḥ* |
32. *Oṃ Arimaṇḍalamardinyai Namaḥ* |
33. *Oṃ Asurāghnyai Namaḥ* |
34. *Oṃ Amāvāsyāyai Namaḥ* |
35. *Oṃ Alākṣmīghnyajārcitāyai Namaḥ* |
36. *Oṃ Ādilakṣmyai Namaḥ* |
37. *Oṃ Ādiśaktyai Namaḥ* |
38. *Oṃ Ākṛtyai Namaḥ* |
39. *Oṃ Āyatānanāyai Namaḥ* |
40. *Oṃ Ādityapadavicārāyai Namaḥ* |

41. *Oṃ Ādityaparisevitāyai Namaḥ* |
42. *Oṃ Ācāryāyai Namaḥ* |
43. *Oṃ Āvartanāyai Namaḥ* |
44. *Oṃ Ācārāyai Namaḥ* |
45. *Oṃ Ādimūrtinivāsinyai Namaḥ* |
46. *Oṃ Āgneyyai Namaḥ* |
47. *Oṃ Āmaryai Namaḥ* |
48. *Oṃ Ādyāyai Namaḥ* |
49. *Oṃ Ārādhyāyai Namaḥ* |

50. *Oṃ Āsanasthitāyai Namaḥ* ।

51. *Oṃ Ādhāranilayāyai Namaḥ* ।
52. *Oṃ Ādhārāyai Namaḥ* ।
53. *Oṃ Ākāśāntanivāsinyai Namaḥ* ।
54. *Oṃ ĀdyākṣaraSamayuktāyai Namaḥ* ।
55. *Oṃ Āntarākāśarūpiṇyai Namaḥ* ।
56. *Oṃ Ādityamaṇḍalagatāyai Namaḥ* ।
57. *Oṃ Āntaradhvāntanāśinyai Namaḥ* ।
58. *Oṃ Indirāyai Namaḥ* ।
59. *Oṃ Iṣṭadāyai Namaḥ* ।
60. *Oṃ Iṣṭāyai Namaḥ* ।

61. *Oṃ Indivaranibhekṣaṇāyai Namaḥ* ।
62. *Oṃ Irāvatyai Namaḥ* ।
63. *Oṃ Indrapadāyai Namaḥ* ।
64. *Oṃ Indrāṇyai Namaḥ* ।
65. *Oṃ Indurūpiṇyai Namaḥ* ।
66. *Oṃ Ikṣukodaṇḍasaṃyuktāyai Namaḥ* ।
67. *Oṃ Iṣusandhānakāriṇyai Namaḥ* ।
68. *Oṃ Indranīlasamākārāyai Namaḥ* ।
69. *Oṃ Iḍāpiṅgalarūpiṇyai Namaḥ* ।
70. *Oṃ Indrākṣyai Namaḥ* ।

71. *Oṃ Īśvarī Devyai Namaḥ* ।
72. *Oṃ Īhātrayavivarjitāyai Namaḥ* ।
73. *Oṃ Umāyai Namaḥ* ।
74. *Oṃ Uṣāyai Namaḥ* ।
75. *Oṃ Uḍunibhāyai Namaḥ* ।
76. *Oṃ Urvārukaphalānanāyai Namaḥ* ।
77. *Oṃ Uḍuprabhāyai Namaḥ* ।

78. *Oṃ Uḍumatyai Namaḥ* ।
79. *Oṃ Uḍupāyai Namaḥ* ।
80. *Oṃ Uḍumadhyagāyai Namaḥ* ।

81. *Oṃ Ūrdhvāyai Namaḥ* ।
82. *Oṃ Ūrdhvakeśyai Namaḥ* ।
83. *Oṃ Ūrdhvādhogatibhedinyai Namaḥ* ।
84. *Oṃ Ūrdhva Bāhupriyāyai Namaḥ* ।
85. *Oṃ Ūrmimālāvāggranthadāyinyai Namaḥ* ।
86. *Oṃ Ṛtāyai Namaḥ* ।
87. *Oṃ Ṛṣyai Namaḥ* ।
88. *Oṃ Ṛtumatyai Namaḥ* ।
89. *Oṃ Ṛṣidevanāmasakṛtāyai Namaḥ* ।
90. *Oṃ Ṛgvedāyai Namaḥ* ।

91. *Oṃ Ṛṇahareryai Namaḥ* ।
92. *Oṃ Ṛṣimaṇḍalacāriṇyai Namaḥ* ।
93. *Oṃ Ṛddhidāyai Namaḥ* ।
94. *Oṃ Ṛjumārgasthāyai Namaḥ* ।
95. *Oṃ Ṛjudharmāyai Namaḥ* ।
96. *Oṃ Ṛtupradāyai Namaḥ* ।
97. *Oṃ Ṛgvedanilayāyai Namaḥ* ।
98. *Oṃ Ṛjvyai Namaḥ* ।
99. *Oṃ Luptadharmapravartinyai Namaḥ* ।
100. *Oṃ Lūtārivarasambhūtāyai Namaḥ* ।

101. *Oṃ Lūtādiviṣahāriṇyai Namaḥ* ।
102. *Oṃ Ekākṣarāyai Namaḥ* ।
103. *Oṃ Ekamātrāyai Namaḥ* ।
104. *Oṃ Ekāyai Namaḥ* ।
105. *Oṃ Ekaniṣṭhāyai Namaḥ* ।

106. *Oṃ Aindryai Namaḥ* |
107. *Oṃ Airāvatārūḍhāyai Namaḥ* |
108. *Oṃ Aihikāmuṣmikapradāyai Namaḥ* |
109. *Oṃ Oṅkārāyai Namaḥ* |
110. *Oṃ Oṣadhyai Namaḥ* |

111. *Oṃ Otāyai Namaḥ* |
112. *Oṃ Otaprotanivāsinyai Namaḥ* |
113. *Oṃ Aurvāyai Namaḥ* |
114. *Oṃ Auṣadhasampannāyai Namaḥ* |
115. *Oṃ Aupāsanaphalapradāyai Namaḥ* |
116. *Oṃ Aṇḍamadhyasthitā Devyai Namaḥ* |
117. *Oṃ Aḥkāramanurūpiṇyai[Visargarūpiṇyai] Namaḥ* |
118. *Oṃ Kātyāyanyai Namaḥ* |
119. *Oṃ Kālarātryai Namaḥ* |
120. *Oṃ Kāmākṣyai Namaḥ* |

121. *Oṃ Kāmasundaryai Namaḥ* |
122. *Oṃ Kamalāyai Namaḥ* |
123. *Oṃ Kāminyai Namaḥ* |
124. *Oṃ Kāntāyai Namaḥ* |
125. *Oṃ Kāmadāyai Namaḥ* |
126. *Oṃ Kālakaṇṭhinyai Namaḥ* |
127. *Oṃ Karikumbhastanabharāyai Namaḥ* |
128. *Oṃ Karavīrasuvāsinyai Namaḥ* |
129. *Oṃ Kalyāṇyai Namaḥ* |
130. *Oṃ Kuṇḍalavatyai Namaḥ* |

131. *Oṃ Kurukṣetranivāsinyai Namaḥ* |
132. *Oṃ Kuruvindadalākārāyai Namaḥ* |
133. *Oṃ Kuṇḍalyai Namaḥ* |

134. *Oṃ Kumudālayāyai Namaḥ* |
135. *Oṃ Kālajihvāyai Namaḥ* |
136. *Oṃ Karālāsyāyai Namaḥ* |
137. *Oṃ Kālikāyai Namaḥ* |
138. *Oṃ Kālarūpiṇyai Namaḥ* |
139. *Oṃ Kamanīyaguṇāyai Namaḥ* |
140. *Oṃ Kāntyai Namaḥ* |

141. *Oṃ Kalādhārāyai Namaḥ* |
142. *Oṃ Kumudvatyai Namaḥ* |
143. *Oṃ Kauśikyai Namaḥ* |
144. *Oṃ Kamalākārāyai Namaḥ* |
145. *Oṃ Kāmacāraprabhañjinyai Namaḥ* |
146. *Oṃ Kaumāryai Namaḥ* |
147. *Oṃ Karuṇāpāṅgyai Namaḥ* |
148. *Oṃ Kakubantāyai Namaḥ* |
149. *Oṃ Karipriyāyai Namaḥ* |
150. *Oṃ Keśaryai Namaḥ* |

151. *Oṃ Keśavanutāyai Namaḥ* |
152. *Oṃ Kadamba Kusumapriyāyai Namaḥ* |
153. *Oṃ Kālindyai Namaḥ* |
154. *Oṃ Kālikāyai Namaḥ* |
155. *Oṃ Kāñcyai Namaḥ* |
156. *Oṃ Kalaśodbhavasaṃstutāyai Namaḥ* |
157. *Oṃ Kāmamātāyai Namaḥ* |
158. *Oṃ Kratumatyai Namaḥ* |
159. *Oṃ Kāmarūpāyai Namaḥ* |
160. *Oṃ Kṛpāvatyai Namaḥ* |

161. *Oṃ Kumāryai Namaḥ* |

162. *Oṃ Kuṇḍanilayāyai Namaḥ* |
163. *Oṃ Kirātyai Namaḥ* |
164. *Oṃ Kīravāhanāyai Namaḥ* |
165. *Oṃ Kaikeyyai Namaḥ* |
166. *Oṃ Kokilālāpāyai Namaḥ* |
167. *Oṃ Ketakīyai Namaḥ* |
168. *Oṃ Kusumapriyāyai Namaḥ* |
169. *Oṃ Kamaṇḍaludharāyai Namaḥ* |
170. *Oṃ Kālyai Namaḥ* |

171. *Oṃ Karmanirmūlakāriṇyai Namaḥ* |
172. *Oṃ Kalahaṃsagatyai Namaḥ* |
173. *Oṃ Kakṣāyai Namaḥ* |
174. *Oṃ Kṛtakautukamaṅgalāyai Namaḥ* |
175. *Oṃ Kasturītilakāyai Namaḥ* |
176. *Oṃ Kamrāyai Namaḥ* |
177. *Oṃ Karindragamanāyai Namaḥ* |
178. *Oṃ Kuhvai Namaḥ* |
179. *Oṃ Karpūralepanāyai Namaḥ* |
180. *Oṃ Kṛṣṇāyai Namaḥ* |

181. *Oṃ Kapilāyai Namaḥ* |
182. *Oṃ Kuharāśrayāyai Namaḥ* |
183. *Oṃ Kūṭasthāyai Namaḥ* |
184. *Oṃ Kudharāyai Namaḥ* |
185. *Oṃ Kamrāyai Namaḥ* |
186. *Oṃ Kukṣisthākhilaviṣṭapāyai Namaḥ* |
187. *Oṃ Khaḍgakheṭadharāyai Namaḥ* |
188. *Oṃ Kharvāyai Namaḥ* |
189. *Oṃ Khecaryai Namaḥ* |
190. *Oṃ Khagavāhanāyai Namaḥ* |

191. *Oṃ Khaṭvāṅgadhāriṇyai Namaḥ* |

192. *Oṃ Khyātāyai Namaḥ* |

193. *Oṃ Khagarājoparisthitāyai Namaḥ* |

194. *Oṃ Khalaghnyai Namaḥ* |

195. *Oṃ Khaṇḍitajarāyai Namaḥ* |

196. *Oṃ Khaṇḍākhyānapradāyinyai Namaḥ* |

197. *Oṃ Khaṇḍendutilakāyai Namaḥ* |

198. *Oṃ Gaṅgāyai Namaḥ* |

199. *Oṃ Gaṇeśaguhapūjitāyai Namaḥ* |

200. *Oṃ Gāyatryai Namaḥ* |

201. *Oṃ Gomatyai Namaḥ* |

202. *Oṃ Gītāyai Namaḥ* |

203. *Oṃ Gāndhāryai Namaḥ* |

204. *Oṃ Gānalolupāyai Namaḥ* |

205. *Oṃ Gautamyai Namaḥ* |

206. *Oṃ Gāminyai Namaḥ* |

207. *Oṃ Gādhāyai Namaḥ* |

208. *Oṃ Gandharvāpsarasevitāyai Namaḥ* |

209. *Oṃ Govindacaraṇākrāntāyai Namaḥ* |

210. *Oṃ Guṇatrayavibhāvitāyai Namaḥ* |

211. *Oṃ Gandharvyai Namaḥ* |

212. *Oṃ Gahvaryai Namaḥ* |

213. *Oṃ Gotrāyai Namaḥ* |

214. *Oṃ Girīśāyai Namaḥ* |

215. *Oṃ Gahanāyai Namaḥ* |

216. *Oṃ Gamyai Namaḥ* |

217. *Oṃ Guhāvāsāyai Namaḥ* |

218. *Oṃ Guṇavatyai Namaḥ* |

219. *Oṃ Gurupāpapraṇāsinyai Namaḥ* |

220. *Oṃ Gurvyai Namaḥ* ।

221. *Oṃ Guṇavatyai Namaḥ* ।
222. *Oṃ Guhyāyai Namaḥ* ।
223. *Oṃ Goptavyāyai Namaḥ* ।
224. *Oṃ Guṇadāyinyai Namaḥ* ।
225. *Oṃ Girijāyai Namaḥ* ।
226. *Oṃ Guhyamātaṅgyai Namaḥ* ।
227. *Oṃ Garuḍadhvajavallabhāyai Namaḥ* ।
228. *Oṃ Garvāpahāriṇyai Namaḥ* ।
229. *Oṃ Godāyai Namaḥ* ।
230. *Oṃ Gokulasthāyai Namaḥ* ।

231. *Oṃ Gadādharāyai Namaḥ* ।
232. *Oṃ Gokarṇanilayāsaktāyai Namaḥ* ।
233. *Oṃ Guhyamaṇḍalavartinyai Namaḥ* ।
234. *Oṃ Gharmadāyai Namaḥ* ।
235. *Oṃ Ghanadāyai Namaḥ* ।
236. *Oṃ Ghaṇṭāyai Namaḥ* ।
237. *Oṃ Ghoradānavamardinyai Namaḥ* ।
238. *Oṃ Ghṛṇimantramayyai Namaḥ* ।
239. *Oṃ Ghoṣāyai Namaḥ* ।
240. *Oṃ Ghanasampātadāyinyai Namaḥ* ।

241. *Oṃ Ghaṇṭāravapriyāyai Namaḥ* ।
242. *Oṃ Ghrāṇāyai Namaḥ* ।
243. *Oṃ Ghṛṇisantuṣṭikāriṇyai Namaḥ* ।
244. *Oṃ Ghanārimaṇḍalāyai Namaḥ* ।
245. *Oṃ Ghūrṇāyai Namaḥ* ।
246. *Oṃ Ghṛtācyai Namaḥ* ।
247. *Oṃ Ghaṇaveginyai Namaḥ* ।

248. *Oṃ Jñānadhātumayyai Namaḥ* I
249. *Oṃ Carcāyai Namaḥ* I
250. *Oṃ Carcitāyai Namaḥ* I

251. *Oṃ Cāruhāsinyai Namaḥ* I
252. *Oṃ Caṭulāyai Namaḥ* I
253. *Oṃ Caṇḍikāyai Namaḥ* I
254. *Oṃ Citrāyai Namaḥ* I
255. *Oṃ Citramālyavibhūṣitāyai Namaḥ* I
256. *Oṃ Caturbhujāyai Namaḥ* I
257. *Oṃ Cārudantāyai Namaḥ* I
258. *Oṃ Cāturyai Namaḥ* I
259. *Oṃ Caritapradāyai Namaḥ* I
260. *Oṃ Cūlikāyai Namaḥ* I

261. *Oṃ Citravastrāntāyai Namaḥ* I
262. *Oṃ Candramaḥkarṇakuṇḍalāyai Namaḥ* I
263. *Oṃ Candrahāsāyai Namaḥ* I
264. *Oṃ Cārudātryai Namaḥ* I
265. *Oṃ Cakoryai Namaḥ* I
266. *Oṃ Candrahāsinyai Namaḥ* I
267. *Oṃ Candrikāyai Namaḥ* I
268. *Oṃ Candradhātryai Namaḥ* I
269. *Oṃ Cauryai Namaḥ* I
270. *Oṃ Caurāyai Namaḥ* I

271. *Oṃ Caṇḍikāyai Namaḥ* I
272. *Oṃ Cañcadvāgavādinyai Namaḥ* I
273. *Oṃ Candracūḍāyai Namaḥ* I
274. *Oṃ Coravināśinyai Namaḥ* I
275. *Oṃ Cārucandanaliptāṅgyai Namaḥ* I

276. *Oṃ Cañcaccāmaravījitāyai Namaḥ* I
277. *Oṃ Cārumadhyāyai Namaḥ* I
278. *Oṃ Cārugatyai Namaḥ* I
279. *Oṃ Candilāyai Namaḥ* I
280. *Oṃ Candrarūpiṇyai Namaḥ* I

281. *Oṃ Cāruhomapriyāyai Namaḥ* I
282. *Oṃ Cārvācaritāyai Namaḥ* I
283. *Oṃ Cakrabāhukāyai Namaḥ* I
284. *Oṃ Candramaṇḍalamadhyasthāyai Namaḥ* I
285. *Oṃ Candramaṇḍaladarpaṇāyai Namaḥ* I
286. *Oṃ Cakravākastanyai Namaḥ* I
287. *Oṃ Ceṣṭāyai Namaḥ* I
288. *Oṃ Citrāyai Namaḥ* I
289. *Oṃ Cāruvilāsinyai Namaḥ* I
290. *Oṃ Citsvarūpāyai Namaḥ* I

291. *Oṃ Candravatyai Namaḥ* I
292. *Oṃ Candramāyai Namaḥ* I
293. *Oṃ Candanapriyāyai Namaḥ* I
294. *Oṃ Codayitryai Namaḥ* I
295. *Oṃ Ciraprajñāyai Namaḥ* I
296. *Oṃ Cātakāyai Namaḥ* I
297. *Oṃ Cāruhetukyai Namaḥ* I
298. *Oṃ Chatrayātāyai Namaḥ* I
299. *Oṃ Chatradharāyai Namaḥ* I
300. *Oṃ Chāyāyai Namaḥ* I

301. *Oṃ Chandaḥparicchadāyai Namaḥ* I
302. *Oṃ Chāyādevyai Namaḥ* I
303. *Oṃ Chidranakhāyai Namaḥ* I

304. *Oṃ Channendriyavisarpiṇyai Namaḥ* |
305. *Oṃ Chando'nuṣṭuppratiṣṭhāntāyai Namaḥ* |
306. *Oṃ Chidropadravabhedinyai Namaḥ* |
307. *Oṃ Chedāyai Namaḥ* |
308. *Oṃ Chatreśvaryai Namaḥ* |
309. *Oṃ Chinnāyai Namaḥ* |
310. *Oṃ Churikāyai Namaḥ* |

311. *Oṃ Chedanapriyāyai Namaḥ* |
312. *Oṃ Jananyai Namaḥ* |
313. *Oṃ Janmarahitāyai Namaḥ* |
314. *Oṃ Jātavedāyai Namaḥ* |
315. *Oṃ Jaganmayyai Namaḥ* |
316. *Oṃ Jāhnavyai Namaḥ* |
317. *Oṃ Jaṭilāyai Namaḥ* |
318. *Oṃ Jetryai Namaḥ* |
319. *Oṃ Jarāmaraṇavarjitāyai Namaḥ* |
320. *Oṃ Jambudvīpavatyai Namaḥ* |

321. *Oṃ Jvālāyai Namaḥ* |
322. *Oṃ Jayantyai Namaḥ* |
323. *Oṃ Jalaśālinyai Namaḥ* |
324. *Oṃ Jitendriyāyai Namaḥ* |
325. *Oṃ Jitakrodhāyai Namaḥ* |
326. *Oṃ Jitāmitrāyai Namaḥ* |
327. *Oṃ Jagatpriyāyai Namaḥ* |
328. *Oṃ Jātarūpamayyai Namaḥ* |
329. *Oṃ Jihvāyai Namaḥ* |
330. *Oṃ Jānakyai Namaḥ* |

331. *Oṃ Jagatyai Namaḥ* |

332. *Oṃ Jarāyai Namaḥ* |

333. *Oṃ Janitryai Namaḥ* |

334. *Oṃ Jahnutanayāyai Namaḥ* |

335. *Oṃ Jagattrayahitaiṣiṇyai Namaḥ* |

336. *Oṃ Jwālāmukhyai Namaḥ* |

337. *Oṃ Japavatyai Namaḥ* |

338. *Oṃ Jvaraghnyai Namaḥ* |

339. *Oṃ Jitaviṣṭapāyai Namaḥ* |

340. *Oṃ Jitākrāntamayyai Namaḥ* |

341. *Oṃ Jvālāyai Namaḥ* |

342. *Oṃ Jāgratyai Namaḥ* |

343. *Oṃ Jvaradevatāyai Namaḥ* |

344. *Oṃ Jvalantyai Namaḥ* |

345. *Oṃ Jaladāyai Namaḥ* |

346. *Oṃ Jyeṣṭhāyai Namaḥ* |

347. *Oṃ Jyāghoṣasphoṭadiṅmukhyai Namaḥ* |

348. *Oṃ Jambhinyai Namaḥ* |

349. *Oṃ Jṛmbhanāyai Namaḥ* |

350. *Oṃ Jṛmbhāyai Namaḥ* |

351. *Oṃ Jvalanmaṇikyakuṇḍalāyai Namaḥ* |

352. *Oṃ Jhiñjhikāyai Namaḥ* |

353. *Oṃ Jhaṇanirghoṣāyai Namaḥ* |

354. *Oṃ Jhañjhāmārutaveginyai Namaḥ* |

355. *Oṃ Jhallarīvādyakuśalāyai Namaḥ* |

356. *Oṃ Ñarūpāyai Namaḥ* |

357. *Oṃ Ñabhujāyai Namaḥ* |

358. *Oṃ Ṭaṅkabāṇasamāyuktāyai Namaḥ* |

359. *Oṃ Ṭaṅkinyai Namaḥ* |

360. *Oṃ Ṭaṅkabhedinyai Namaḥ* |

361. *Oṃ Ṭaṅkīgaṇakṛtāghoṣāyai Namaḥ* |

362. *Oṃ Ṭaṅkanīyamahorasāyai Namaḥ* |

363. *Oṃ Ṭaṅkārakāriṇī Devyai Namaḥ* |

364. *Oṃ ṬhaṬhaŚabdaninādinyai Namaḥ* |

365. *Oṃ Ḍāmaryai Namaḥ* |

366. *Oṃ Ḍākinyai Namaḥ* |

367. *Oṃ Ḍimbhāyai Namaḥ* |

368. *Oṃ Ḍuṇḍamāraikanirjitāyai Namaḥ* |

369. *Oṃ Ḍāmarītantramārgasthāyai Namaḥ* |

370. *Oṃ Ḍamaḍḍamarunādinyai Namaḥ* |

371. *Oṃ Ḍiṇḍīravasahāyai Namaḥ* |

372. *Oṃ Ḍimbhalasākrīḍāparāyaṇāyai Namaḥ* |

373. *Oṃ Ḍhuṇḍhivighneśajananyai Namaḥ* |

374. *Oṃ Ḍhakkāhastāyai Namaḥ* |

375. *Oṃ Ḍhilivrajāyai Namaḥ* |

376. *Oṃ Nityajñānāyai Namaḥ* |

377. *Oṃ Nirupamāyai Namaḥ* |

378. *Oṃ Nirguṇāyai Namaḥ* |

379. *Oṃ Narmadāyai Namaḥ* |

380. *Oṃ Nadyāyai Namaḥ* |

381. *Oṃ Triguṇāyai Namaḥ* |

382. *Oṃ Tripadāyai Namaḥ* |

383. *Oṃ Tantryai Namaḥ* |

384. *Oṃ Tulasītaruṇātaruvyai Namaḥ* |

385. *Oṃ Trivikrama Padākrāntāyai Namaḥ* |

386. *Oṃ Turīyapadagāminyai Namaḥ* |

387. *Oṃ Taruṇādityasaṅkaśāyai Namaḥ* |

388. *Oṃ Tāmasyai Namaḥ* |

389. *Oṃ Tuhināyai Namaḥ* |

390. *Oṃ Turāyai Namaḥ* I

391. *Oṃ Trikālajñānasampannāyai Namaḥ* I
392. *Oṃ Triveṇyai Namaḥ* I
393. *Oṃ Trilocanāyai Namaḥ* I
394. *Oṃ Triśaktyai Namaḥ* I
395. *Oṃ Tripurāyai Namaḥ* I
396. *Oṃ Tuṅgāyai Namaḥ* I
397. *Oṃ Turaṅgavadanāyai Namaḥ* I
398. *Oṃ Timiṅgilagilāyai Namaḥ* I
399. *Oṃ Tīvrāyai Namaḥ* I
400. *Oṃ Triśrotāyai Namaḥ* I

401. *Oṃ Tāmasādinyai Namaḥ* I
402. *Oṃ Tantramantraviśeṣajñāyai Namaḥ* I
403. *Oṃ Tanumadhyāyai Namaḥ* I
404. *Oṃ Triviṣṭapāyai Namaḥ* I
405. *Oṃ Trisandhyāyai Namaḥ* I
406. *Oṃ Tristanyai Namaḥ* I
407. *Oṃ Toṣāsaṃsthāyai Namaḥ* I
408. *Oṃ Tālapratāpinyai Namaḥ* I
409. *Oṃ Tāṭaṅkinyai Namaḥ* I
410. *Oṃ Tuṣārābhāyai Namaḥ* I

411. *Oṃ Tuhinācalavāsinyai Namaḥ* I
412. *Oṃ Tantujālasamāyuktāyai Namaḥ* I
413. *Oṃ Tārahārāvalipriyāyai Namaḥ* I
414. *Oṃ Tilahomapriyāyai Namaḥ* I
415. *Oṃ Tīrthāyai Namaḥ* I
416. *Oṃ Tamālakusumākṛtyai Namaḥ* I
417. *Oṃ Tārakāyai Namaḥ* I

418. *Oṃ Triyutāyai Namaḥ* I

419. *Oṃ Tanvyai Namaḥ* I

420. *Oṃ Triśaṅkuparivāritāyai Namaḥ* I

421. *Oṃ Talodaryai Namaḥ* I

422. *Oṃ Tilābhūṣāyai Namaḥ* I

423. *Oṃ Tāṭaṅkapriyavādinyai Namaḥ* I

424. *Oṃ Trijaṭāyai Namaḥ* I

425. *Oṃ Tittiryai Namaḥ* I

426. *Oṃ Tṛṣṇāyai Namaḥ* I

427. *Oṃ Trividhāyai Namaḥ* I

428. *Oṃ Taruṇākṛtyai Namaḥ* I

429. *Oṃ Taptakāñcanasankāśāyai Namaḥ* I

430. *Oṃ Taptakāñcanabhūṣaṇāyai Namaḥ* I

431. *Oṃ Trayambakāyai Namaḥ* I

432. *Oṃ Trivargāyai Namaḥ* I

433. *Oṃ Trikālajñānadāyinyai Namaḥ* I

434. *Oṃ Tarpaṇāyai Namaḥ* I

435. *Oṃ Tṛptidāyai Namaḥ* I

436. *Oṃ Tṛptāyai Namaḥ* I

437. *Oṃ Tāmasyai Namaḥ* I

438. *Oṃ Tumbarustutāyai Namaḥ* I

439. *Oṃ Tārkṣyasthāyai Namaḥ* I

440. *Oṃ Triguṇākārāyai Namaḥ* I

441. *Oṃ Tribhaṅgyai Namaḥ* I

442. *Oṃ Tanuvallaryai Namaḥ* I

443. *Oṃ Thātkāryai Namaḥ* I

444. *Oṃ Thāravāyai Namaḥ* I

445. *Oṃ Thāntāyai Namaḥ* I

446. *Oṃ Dohinyai Namaḥ* |
447. *Oṃ Dīnavatsalāyai Namaḥ* |
448. *Oṃ Dānavāntakaryai Namaḥ* |
449. *Oṃ Durgāyai Namaḥ* |
450. *Oṃ Durgāsuranibarhiṇyai Namaḥ* |

451. *Oṃ Devarītyai Namaḥ* |
452. *Oṃ Divārātryai Namaḥ* |
453. *Oṃ Draupadyai Namaḥ* |
454. *Oṃ Dundubhisvanāyai Namaḥ* |
455. *Oṃ Devayānyai Namaḥ* |
456. *Oṃ Durāvāsāyai Namaḥ* |
457. *Oṃ Dāridryobhedinyai Namaḥ* |
458. *Oṃ Divāyai Namaḥ* |
459. *Oṃ Dāmodarapriyāyai Namaḥ* |
460. *Oṃ Dīptāyai Namaḥ* |

461. *Oṃ Digvāsāyai Namaḥ* |
462. *Oṃ Digvimohinyai Namaḥ* |
463. *Oṃ Daṇḍakāraṇyanilayāyai Namaḥ* |
464. *Oṃ Daṇḍinyai Namaḥ* |
465. *Oṃ Devapūjitāyai Namaḥ* |
466. *Oṃ Devavandyāyai Namaḥ* |
467. *Oṃ Diviṣadāyai Namaḥ* |
468. *Oṃ Dveṣiṇyai Namaḥ* |
469. *Oṃ Dānāvākṛtyai Namaḥ* |
470. *Oṃ Dīnanāthastutāyai Namaḥ* |

471. *Oṃ Dīkṣāyai Namaḥ* |
472. *Oṃ Daivatādisvarūpiṇyai Namaḥ* |
473. *Oṃ Dhātryai Namaḥ* |

474. *Oṃ Dhanurdharāyai Namaḥ* I
475. *Oṃ Dhenuṇyai Namaḥ* I
476. *Oṃ Dhāriṇyai Namaḥ* I
477. *Oṃ Dharmacāriṇyai Namaḥ* I
478. *Oṃ Dharandharāyai Namaḥ* I
479. *Oṃ Dharādhārāyai Namaḥ* I
480. *Oṃ Dhanadāyai Namaḥ* I

481. *Oṃ Dhānyadohinyai Namaḥ* I
482. *Oṃ Dharmaśīlāyai Namaḥ* I
483. *Oṃ Dhanādhyakṣāyai Namaḥ* I
484. *Oṃ Dhanurvedaviśāradāyai Namaḥ* I
485. *Oṃ Dhṛtyai Namaḥ* I
486. *Oṃ Dhanyāyai Namaḥ* I
487. *Oṃ Dhṛtapadāyai Namaḥ* I
488. *Oṃ Dharmarājapriyāyai Namaḥ* I
489. *Oṃ Dhruvāyai Namaḥ* I
490. *Oṃ Dhūmāvatyai Namaḥ* I

491. *Oṃ Dhūmakeśyai Namaḥ* I
492. *Oṃ Dharmaśāstraprakāśinyai Namaḥ* I
493. *Oṃ Nandāyai Namaḥ* I
494. *Oṃ Nandapriyāyai Namaḥ* I
495. *Oṃ Nidrāyai Namaḥ* I
496. *Oṃ Nṛnutāyai Namaḥ* I
497. *Oṃ Nandanātmikāyai Namaḥ* I
498. *Oṃ Narmadāyai Namaḥ* I
499. *Oṃ Nalinyai Namaḥ* I
500. *Oṃ Nīlāyai Namaḥ* I

501. *Oṃ Nīlakaṇṭhasamāśrayāyai Namaḥ* I

502. *Oṃ Nārāyaṇapriyāyai Namaḥ* |

503. *Oṃ Nityāyai Namaḥ* |

504. *Oṃ Nirmalāyai Namaḥ* |

505. *Oṃ Nirguṇāyai Namaḥ* |

506. *Oṃ Nidhyai Namaḥ* |

507. *Oṃ Nirādhārāyai Namaḥ* |

508. *Oṃ Nirupamāyai Namaḥ* |

509. *Oṃ Nityaśuddhāyai Namaḥ* |

510. *Oṃ Nirañjanāyai Namaḥ* |

511. *Oṃ Nādabindukalātītāyai Namaḥ* |

512. *Oṃ Nādabindukalātmikāyai Namaḥ* |

513. *Oṃ Nṛsiṃhinyai Namaḥ* |

514. *Oṃ Nagadharāyai Namaḥ* |

515. *Oṃ Nṛpanāgavibhūṣitāyai Namaḥ* |

516. *Oṃ Narakakleśa Śamanyai Namaḥ* |

517. *Oṃ Nārāyaṇapadodbhavāyai Namaḥ* |

518. *Oṃ Niravadyāyai Namaḥ* |

519. *Oṃ Nirākārāyai Namaḥ* |

520. *Oṃ Nāradapriyakāriṇyai Namaḥ* |

521. *Oṃ Nānājyotiḥ Namaḥ* |

522. *Oṃ Nidhidāyai Namaḥ* |

523. *Oṃ Nirmalātmikāyai Namaḥ* |

524. *Oṃ Navasūtradharāyai Namaḥ* |

525. *Oṃ Nītyai Namaḥ* |

526. *Oṃ Nirupadravakāriṇyai Namaḥ* |

527. *Oṃ Nandajāyai Namaḥ* |

528. *Oṃ Navaratnāḍhyāyai Namaḥ* |

529. *Oṃ Naimiṣāraṇyavāsinyai Namaḥ* |

530. *Oṃ Navanītapriyāyai Namaḥ* |

531. *Oṃ Nāryai Namaḥ* I
532. *Oṃ Nīlajīmūtanisvanāyai Namaḥ* I
533. *Oṃ Nimeṣiṇyai Namaḥ* I
534. *Oṃ Nadīrūpāyai Namaḥ* I
535. *Oṃ Nīlagrīvāyai Namaḥ* I
536. *Oṃ Niśiśvaryai Namaḥ* I
537. *Oṃ Nāmāvalyai Namaḥ* I
538. *Oṃ Niśumbhagnyai Namaḥ* I
539. *Oṃ Nāgalokanivāsinyai Namaḥ* I
540. *Oṃ Navajāmbūnadaprakhyāyai Namaḥ* I

541. *Oṃ Nāgalokādhidevatāyai Namaḥ* I
542. *Oṃ Nūpūrākrāntacaraṇāyai Namaḥ* I
543. *Oṃ Naracittapramodinyai Namaḥ* I
544. *Oṃ Nimagnāraktanayanāyai Namaḥ* I
545. *Oṃ Nirghātasamaniḥsvanāyai Namaḥ* I
546. *Oṃ Nandanodyanilayāyai Namaḥ* I
547. *Oṃ Nirvyūhoparicāriṇyai Namaḥ* I
548. *Oṃ Pārvatyai Namaḥ* I
549. *Oṃ Paramodārāyai Namaḥ* I
550. *Oṃ Parabrahmātmikāyai Namaḥ* I

551. *Oṃ Parāyai Namaḥ* I
552. *Oṃ Pañcakośavinirmuktāyai Namaḥ* I
553. *Oṃ Pañcapātakanāśinyai Namaḥ* I
554. *Oṃ Paracittavidhānajñāyai Namaḥ* I
555. *Oṃ Pañcikāyai Namaḥ* I
556. *Oṃ Pañcarūpiṇyai Namaḥ* I
557. *Oṃ Pūrṇimāyai Namaḥ* I
558. *Oṃ Paramāyai Namaḥ* I
559. *Oṃ Prītyai Namaḥ* I

560. *Oṃ Paratejyai Namaḥ* I

561. *Oṃ Prakāśinyai Namaḥ* I

562. *Oṃ Purāṇyai Namaḥ* I

563. *Oṃ Pauruṣyai Namaḥ* I

564. *Oṃ Puṇyāyai Namaḥ* I

565. *Oṃ Puṇḍarīkanibhakṣanāyai Namaḥ* I

566. *Oṃ Pātālatalanirmagnāyai Namaḥ* I

567. *Oṃ Prītāyai Namaḥ* I

568. *Oṃ Prītivivardhinyai Namaḥ* I

569. *Oṃ Pāvanyai Namaḥ* I

570. *Oṃ Pādasahitāyai Namaḥ* I

571. *Oṃ Peśalāyai Namaḥ* I

572. *Oṃ Pavanāśinyai Namaḥ* I

573. *Oṃ Prajāpatyai Namaḥ* I

574. *Oṃ Pariśrāntāyai Namaḥ* I

575. *Oṃ Parvatastanamaṇḍalāyai Namaḥ* I

576. *Oṃ Padmapriyāyai Namaḥ* I

577. *Oṃ Padmasaṃsthāyai Namaḥ* I

578. *Oṃ Padmākṣyai Namaḥ* I

579. *Oṃ Padmasambhavāyai Namaḥ* I

580. *Oṃ Padmapatrāyai Namaḥ* I

581. *Oṃ Padmapadāyai Namaḥ* I

582. *Oṃ Padminyai Namaḥ* I

583. *Oṃ Priyabhāṣiṇyai Namaḥ* I

584. *Oṃ Paśupāśavinirmuktāyai Namaḥ* I

585. *Oṃ Purandhryai Namaḥ* I

586. *Oṃ Puravāsinyai Namaḥ* I

587. *Oṃ Puṣkalāyai Namaḥ* I

588. *Oṃ Puruṣāyai Namaḥ* I

589. *Oṃ Parvāyai Namaḥ* |

590. *Oṃ Pārijāta Sumapriyāyai Namaḥ* |

591. *Oṃ Pativratāyai Namaḥ* |

592. *Oṃ Pavitrāṅgyai Namaḥ* |

593. *Oṃ Puṣpahāsaparāyaṇāyai Namaḥ* |

594. *Oṃ Prajñāvatīsutāyai Namaḥ* |

595. *Oṃ Pautryai Namaḥ* |

596. *Oṃ Putrapūjyāyai Namaḥ* |

597. *Oṃ Payasvinyai Namaḥ* |

598. *Oṃ Paṭṭipāśadharāyai Namaḥ* |

599. *Oṃ Paṅktyai Namaḥ* |

600. *Oṃ Pitṛlokapradāyinyai Namaḥ* |

601. *Oṃ Purāṇyai Namaḥ* |

602. *Oṃ Puṇyaśilāyai Namaḥ* |

603. *Oṃ Praṇatārtivināśinyai Namaḥ* |

604. *Oṃ Pradyumnajananyai Namaḥ* |

605. *Oṃ Puṣṭāyai Namaḥ* |

606. *Oṃ Pitāmahaparigrahāyai Namaḥ* |

607. *Oṃ Puṇḍarīkapurāvāsāyai Namaḥ* |

608. *Oṃ Puṇḍarīkasamānanāyai Namaḥ* |

609. *Oṃ Pṛthujaṅghāyai Namaḥ* |

610. *Oṃ Pṛthubhujāyai Namaḥ* |

611. *Oṃ Pṛthupādāyai Namaḥ* |

612. *Oṃ Pṛthūdaryai Namaḥ* |

613. *Oṃ Pravālaśobhāyai Namaḥ* |

614. *Oṃ Piṅgākṣyai Namaḥ* |

615. *Oṃ Pītavāsāḥ Namaḥ* |

616. *Oṃ Pracāpalāyai Namaḥ* |

617. *Oṃ Prasavāyai Namaḥ* I

618. *Oṃ Puṣṭidāyai Namaḥ* I

619. *Oṃ Puṇyāyai Namaḥ* I

620. *Oṃ Pratiṣṭhāyai Namaḥ* I

621. *Oṃ Praṇavāgatyai Namaḥ* I

622. *Oṃ Pañcavarṇāyai Namaḥ* I

623. *Oṃ Pañcavāṇyai Namaḥ* I

624. *Oṃ Pañcikāyai Namaḥ* I

625. *Oṃ Pañjarasthitāyai Namaḥ* I

626. *Oṃ Paramāyāyai Namaḥ* I

627. *Oṃ Parajyotiḥ Namaḥ* I

628. *Oṃ Paraprītyai Namaḥ* I

629. *Oṃ Parāgatyai Namaḥ* I

630. *Oṃ Parākāṣṭhāyai Namaḥ* I

631. *Oṃ Pareśanyai Namaḥ* I

632. *Oṃ Pāvanyai Namaḥ* I

633. *Oṃ Pāvakadyutyai Namaḥ* I

634. *Oṃ Puṇyabhadrāyai Namaḥ* I

635. *Oṃ Paricchedyāyai Namaḥ* I

636. *Oṃ Puṣpahāsāyai Namaḥ* I

637. *Oṃ Pṛthūdarāyai Namaḥ* I

638. *Oṃ Pītāṅgyai Namaḥ* I

639. *Oṃ Pītavasanāyai Namaḥ* I

640. *Oṃ Pītaśayāyai Namaḥ* I

641. *Oṃ Piśācinyai Namaḥ* I

642. *Oṃ Pītakriyāyai Namaḥ* I

643. *Oṃ Piśācaghnyai Namaḥ* I

644. *Oṃ Pāṭalākṣyai Namaḥ* I

645. *Oṃ Paṭukriyāyai Namaḥ* |
646. *Oṃ Pañcabhakṣapriyācārāyai Namaḥ* |
647. *Oṃ Pūtanāprāṇaghātinyai Namaḥ* |
648. *Oṃ Punnāgavanamadhyasthāyai Namaḥ* |
649. *Oṃ Puṇyatīrthaniṣevitāyai Namaḥ* |
650. *Oṃ Pañcāṅgyai Namaḥ* |

651. *Oṃ Parāśaktyai Namaḥ* |
652. *Oṃ Paramāhlādakāriṇyai Namaḥ* |
653. *Oṃ Puṣpakāṇḍasthitāyai Namaḥ* |
654. *Oṃ Pūṣāyai Namaḥ* |
655. *Oṃ Poṣitākhilaviṣṭapāyai Namaḥ* |
656. *Oṃ Pānapriyāyai Namaḥ* |
657. *Oṃ Pañcaśikhāyai Namaḥ* |
658. *Oṃ Pannagopariśāyinyai Namaḥ* |
659. *Oṃ Pañcamātrātmikāyai Namaḥ* |
660. *Oṃ Pṛthvyai Namaḥ* |

661. *Oṃ Pathikāyai Namaḥ* |
662. *Oṃ Pṛthudohinyai Namaḥ* |
663. *Oṃ Purāṇanyāyamīmāṃsāyai Namaḥ* |
664. *Oṃ Pāṭalyai Namaḥ* |
665. *Oṃ Puṣpagandhinyai Namaḥ* |
666. *Oṃ Puṇyaprajāyai Namaḥ* |
667. *Oṃ Pāradātryai Namaḥ* |
668. *Oṃ Paramārgaikagocarāyai Namaḥ* |
669. *Oṃ Pravālaśobhāyai Namaḥ* |
670. *Oṃ Pūrṇāśāyai Namaḥ* |

671. *Oṃ Praṇavāyai Namaḥ* |
672. *Oṃ Pallavodaryai Namaḥ* |

673. *Oṃ Phalinyai Namaḥ* |
674. *Oṃ Phaladāyai Namaḥ* |
675. *Oṃ Phalgvai Namaḥ* |
676. *Oṃ Phutkāryai Namaḥ* |
677. *Oṃ Phalakākṛtyai Namaḥ* |
678. *Oṃ Phaṇindrabhogaśayanāyai Namaḥ* |
679. *Oṃ Phaṇimaṇḍalamaṇḍitāyai Namaḥ* |
680. *Oṃ Bālabālāyai Namaḥ* |

681. *Oṃ Bahumatāyai Namaḥ* |
682. *Oṃ Bālātapanībhāṃśukāyai Namaḥ* |
683. *Oṃ Balabhadrapriyāyai Namaḥ* |
684. *Oṃ Bandyāyai Namaḥ* |
685. *Oṃ Baḍavāyai Namaḥ* |
686. *Oṃ Buddhisaṃstutāyai Namaḥ* |
687. *Oṃ Bandīdevyai Namaḥ* |
688. *Oṃ Bilavatyai Namaḥ* |
689. *Oṃ Baḍiśaghnyai Namaḥ* |
690. *Oṃ Balipriyāyai Namaḥ* |

691. *Oṃ Bāndhavyai Namaḥ* |
692. *Oṃ Bodhitāyai Namaḥ* |
693. *Oṃ Buddhiyai Namaḥ* |
694. *Oṃ Bandhūkakusumapriyāyai Namaḥ* |
695. *Oṃ Bālabhānuprabhākarāyai Namaḥ* |
696. *Oṃ Brāhmyai Namaḥ* |
697. *Oṃ Brāhmaṇadevatāyai Namaḥ* |
698. *Oṃ Bṛhaspatistutāyai Namaḥ* |
699. *Oṃ Bṛndāyai Namaḥ* |
700. *Oṃ Bṛndāvanavihāriṇyai Namaḥ* |

701. *Oṃ Bālākinyai Namaḥ* I
702. *Oṃ Bilāhārāyai Namaḥ* I
703. *Oṃ Bilavasāyai Namaḥ* I
704. *Oṃ Bahūdakāyai Namaḥ* I
705. *Oṃ Bahunetrāyai Namaḥ* I
706. *Oṃ Bahupadāyai Namaḥ* I
707. *Oṃ Bahukarṇāvataṃsikāyai Namaḥ* I
708. *Oṃ Bahubāhuyutāyai Namaḥ* I
709. *Oṃ Bījarūpiṇyai Namaḥ* I
710. *Oṃ Bahurūpiṇyai Namaḥ* I

711. *Oṃ Bindunādakalātītāyai Namaḥ* I
712. *Oṃ Bindunādasvarūpiṇyai Namaḥ* I
713. *Oṃ Baddhagodhāṅgulitrāṇāyai Namaḥ* I
714. *Oṃ Badaryāśramavāsinyai Namaḥ* I
715. *Oṃ Bṛndārakāyai Namaḥ* I
716. *Oṃ Bṛhatskandhāyai Namaḥ* I
717. *Oṃ Bṛhatyai Namaḥ* I
718. *Oṃ Bāṇapātinyai Namaḥ* I
719. *Oṃ Bṛndādhyakṣāyai Namaḥ* I
720. *Oṃ Bahunutāyai Namaḥ* I

721. *Oṃ Vanitāyai Namaḥ* I
722. *Oṃ Bahuvikramāyai Namaḥ* I
723. *Oṃ Baddhapadmāsanāsīnāyai Namaḥ* I
724. *Oṃ Bilvapatratalasthitāyai Namaḥ* I
725. *Oṃ Bodhidrumanijāvāsāyai Namaḥ* I
726. *Oṃ Baḍiṣṭhāyai Namaḥ* I
727. *Oṃ Bindudarpaṇāyai Namaḥ* I
728. *Oṃ Bālāyai Namaḥ* I
729. *Oṃ Bāṇāsanavatyai Namaḥ* I

730. *Oṃ Baḍavānalaveginyai Namaḥ* I

731. *Oṃ Brahmāṇḍabahirantasthāyai Namaḥ* I

732. *Oṃ Brahmakaṅkaṇasūtriṇyai Namaḥ* I

733. *Oṃ Bhavānyai Namaḥ* I

734. *Oṃ Bhīṣṇavatyai Namaḥ* I

735. *Oṃ Bhāvinyai Namaḥ* I

736. *Oṃ Bhayahāriṇyai Namaḥ* I

737. *Oṃ Bhadrakālyai Namaḥ* I

738. *Oṃ Bhujaṅgākṣyai Namaḥ* I

739. *Oṃ Bhāratyai Namaḥ* I

740. *Oṃ Bhāratāśayāyai Namaḥ* I

741. *Oṃ Bhairavyai Namaḥ* I

742. *Oṃ Bhīṣaṇākārāyai Namaḥ* I

743. *Oṃ Bhūtidāyai Namaḥ* I

744. *Oṃ Bhūtimālinyai Namaḥ* I

745. *Oṃ Bhāminyai Namaḥ* I

746. *Oṃ Bhoganiratāyai Namaḥ* I

747. *Oṃ Bhadradāyai Namaḥ* I

748. *Oṃ Bhūrivikramāyai Namaḥ* I

749. *Oṃ Bhūtavāsāyai Namaḥ* I

750. *Oṃ Bhṛgulatāyai Namaḥ* I

751. *Oṃ Bhārgavyai Namaḥ* I

752. *Oṃ Bhūsurārcitāyai Namaḥ* I

753. *Oṃ Bhāgīrathyai Namaḥ* I

754. *Oṃ Bhogavatyai Namaḥ* I

755. *Oṃ Bhavanasthāyai Namaḥ* I

756. *Oṃ Bhiṣagvarāyai Namaḥ* I

757. *Oṃ Bhāminyai Namaḥ* I

758. *Oṃ Bhoginyai Namaḥ* |
759. *Oṃ Bhāṣāyai Namaḥ* |
760. *Oṃ Bhavānyai Namaḥ* |

761. *Oṃ Bhūridakṣiṇāyai Namaḥ* |
762. *Oṃ Bhargātmikāyai Namaḥ* |
763. *Oṃ Bhīmāvatyai Namaḥ* |
764. *Oṃ Bhavabandhavimocinyai Namaḥ* |
765. *Oṃ Bhajanīyāyai Namaḥ* |
766. *Oṃ Bhūtadhātrīrañjitāyai Namaḥ* |
767. *Oṃ Bhuvaneśvaryai Namaḥ* |
768. *Oṃ Bhujaṅgavalayāyai Namaḥ* |
769. *Oṃ Bhīmāyai Namaḥ* |
770. *Oṃ Bheruṇḍāyai Namaḥ* |

771. *Oṃ Bhāgadheyinyai Namaḥ* |
772. *Oṃ Mātāyai Namaḥ* |
773. *Oṃ Māyāyai Namaḥ* |
774. *Oṃ Madhumatyai Namaḥ* |
775. *Oṃ Madhujihvāyai Namaḥ* |
776. *Oṃ Madhupriyāyai Namaḥ* |
777. *Oṃ Mahādevyai Namaḥ* |
778. *Oṃ Mahābhāgāyai Namaḥ* |
779. *Oṃ Mālinyai Namaḥ* |
780. *Oṃ Mīnalocanāyai Namaḥ* |

781. *Oṃ Māyātītāyai Namaḥ* |
782. *Oṃ Madhumatyai Namaḥ* |
783. *Oṃ Madhumāṃsāyai Namaḥ* |
784. *Oṃ Madhudravāyai Namaḥ* |
785. *Oṃ Mānavyai Namaḥ* |

786. *Oṃ Madhusambhūtāyai Namaḥ* I
787. *Oṃ Mithilāpuravāsinyai Namaḥ* I
788. *Oṃ Madhukaiṭabhasaṃhartryai Namaḥ* I
789. *Oṃ Medinyai Namaḥ* I
790. *Oṃ Meghamālinyai Namaḥ* I

791. *Oṃ Mandodaryai Namaḥ* I
792. *Oṃ Mahāmāyāyai Namaḥ* I
793. *Oṃ Maithilyai Namaḥ* I
794. *Oṃ Masṛṇapriyāyai Namaḥ* I
795. *Oṃ Mahālakṣmyai Namaḥ* I
796. *Oṃ Mahākālyai Namaḥ* I
797. *Oṃ Mahākanyāyai Namaḥ* I
798. *Oṃ Maheśvaryai Namaḥ* I
799. *Oṃ Māhendryai Namaḥ* I
800. *Oṃ Merutanayāyai Namaḥ* I

801. *Oṃ Mandārakusumārcitāyai Namaḥ* I
802. *Oṃ Mañjumañjīracaraṇāyai Namaḥ* I
803. *Oṃ Mokṣadāyai Namaḥ* I
804. *Oṃ Mañjubhāṣiṇyai Namaḥ* I
805. *Oṃ Madhuradrāviṇyai Namaḥ* I
806. *Oṃ Mudrāyai Namaḥ* I
807. *Oṃ Malayāyai Namaḥ* I
808. *Oṃ Malayānvitāyai Namaḥ* I
809. *Oṃ Medhāyai Namaḥ* I
810. *Oṃ Marakataśyāmāyai Namaḥ* I

811. *Oṃ Magadhyai Namaḥ* I
812. *Oṃ Menakātmajāyai Namaḥ* I
813. *Oṃ Mahāmāryai Namaḥ* I

814. *Oṃ Mahāvīrāyai Namaḥ* I
815. *Oṃ Mahāśyāmāyai Namaḥ* I
816. *Oṃ Manustutāyai Namaḥ* I
817. *Oṃ Mātṛkāyai Namaḥ* I
818. *Oṃ Mihirābhāsāyai Namaḥ* I
819. *Oṃ Mukundapadavikramāyai Namaḥ* I
820. *Oṃ Mūlādhārasthitāyai Namaḥ* I

821. *Oṃ Mugdhāyai Namaḥ* I
822. *Oṃ Maṇipūraka Nivāsinyai Namaḥ* I
823. *Oṃ Mṛgākṣyai Namaḥ* I
824. *Oṃ Mahiṣārūḍhāyai Namaḥ* I
825. *Oṃ Mahiṣāsuramardinyai Namaḥ* I
826. *Oṃ Yogāsanāyai Namaḥ* I
827. *Oṃ Yogagamyāyai Namaḥ* I
828. *Oṃ Yogāyai Namaḥ* I
829. *Oṃ Yauvanakāśrayāyai Namaḥ* I
830. *Oṃ Yauvanyai Namaḥ* I

831. *Oṃ Yuddhamadhyasthāyai Namaḥ* I
832. *Oṃ Yamunāyai Namaḥ* I
833. *Oṃ Yugadhāriṇyai Namaḥ* I
834. *Oṃ Yakṣiṇyai Namaḥ* I
835. *Oṃ Yogayuktāyai Namaḥ* I
836. *Oṃ Yakṣarājaprasūtinyai Namaḥ* I
837. *Oṃ Yātrāyai Namaḥ* I
838. *Oṃ Yānavidhānajñāyai Namaḥ* I
839. *Oṃ Yaduvaṃśasamudbhavāyai Namaḥ* I
840. *Oṃ Yakārādihakārāntāyai Namaḥ* I

841. *Oṃ Yājuṣyai Namaḥ* I

842. *Oṃ Yajñarūpiṇyai Namaḥ* ǀ

843. *Oṃ Yāminyai Namaḥ* ǀ

844. *Oṃ Yoganiratāyai Namaḥ* ǀ

845. *Oṃ Yātudhānabhayaṅkaryai Namaḥ* ǀ

846. *Oṃ Rukmiṇyai Namaḥ* ǀ

847. *Oṃ Ramaṇyai Namaḥ* ǀ

848. *Oṃ Rāmāyai Namaḥ* ǀ

849. *Oṃ Revatyai Namaḥ* ǀ

850. *Oṃ Reṇukāyai Namaḥ* ǀ

851. *Oṃ Ratyai Namaḥ* ǀ

852. *Oṃ Raudryai Namaḥ* ǀ

853. *Oṃ Raudrapriyākārāyai Namaḥ* ǀ

854. *Oṃ Rāmamātāyai Namaḥ* ǀ

855. *Oṃ Ratipriyāyai Namaḥ* ǀ

856. *Oṃ Rohiṇyai Namaḥ* ǀ

857. *Oṃ Rājyadāyai Namaḥ* ǀ

858. *Oṃ Revāyai Namaḥ* ǀ

859. *Oṃ Ramāyai Namaḥ* ǀ

860. *Oṃ Rājīvalocanāyai Namaḥ* ǀ

861. *Oṃ Rākeśyai Namaḥ* ǀ

862. *Oṃ Rūpasampannāyai Namaḥ* ǀ

863. *Oṃ Ratnasiṃhāsanasthitāyai Namaḥ* ǀ

864. *Oṃ Raktamālyāmbaradharāyai Namaḥ* ǀ

865. *Oṃ Raktagandhānulepanāyai Namaḥ* ǀ

866. *Oṃ Rājahaṃsasamārūḍhāyai Namaḥ* ǀ

867. *Oṃ Raṃbhāyai Namaḥ* ǀ

868. *Oṃ Raktavalipriyāyai Namaḥ* ǀ

869. *Oṃ Ramaṇīyayugādhārāyai Namaḥ* ǀ

870. *Oṃ Rājitākhilabhūtalāyai Namaḥ* ǀ

871. *Oṃ Rurucarmaparidhānāyai Namaḥ* I
872. *Oṃ Rathinyai Namaḥ* I
873. *Oṃ Ratnamālikāyai Namaḥ* I
874. *Oṃ Rogeśyai Namaḥ* I
875. *Oṃ Rogaśamanyai Namaḥ* I
876. *Oṃ Rāviṇyai Namaḥ* I
877. *Oṃ Romaharṣiṇyai Namaḥ* I
878. *Oṃ Rāmacandrapadākrāntāyai Namaḥ* I
879. *Oṃ Rāvaṇacchedakāriṇyai Namaḥ* I
880. *Oṃ Ratnavastraparicchinvāyai Namaḥ* I

881. *Oṃ Rathasthāyai Namaḥ* I
882. *Oṃ Rukmabhūṣaṇāyai Namaḥ* I
883. *Oṃ Lajjādhidevatāyai Namaḥ* I
884. *Oṃ Lolāyai Namaḥ* I
885. *Oṃ Lalitāyai Namaḥ* I
886. *Oṃ Liṅgadhāriṇyai Namaḥ* I
887. *Oṃ Lakṣmyai Namaḥ* I
888. *Oṃ Lolāyai Namaḥ* I
889. *Oṃ Luptaviṣāyai Namaḥ* I
890. *Oṃ Lokinyai Namaḥ* I

891. *Oṃ Lokaviśrutāyai Namaḥ* I
892. *Oṃ Lajjāyai Namaḥ* I
893. *Oṃ Lambodarī Devyai Namaḥ* I
894. *Oṃ Lalanāyai Namaḥ* I
895. *Oṃ Lokadhāriṇyai Namaḥ* I
896. *Oṃ Varadāyai Namaḥ* I
897. *Oṃ Vanditāyai Namaḥ* I
898. *Oṃ Vidyāyai Namaḥ* I
899. *Oṃ Vaiṣṇavyai Namaḥ* I

900. *Oṃ Vimalākṛtyai Namaḥ* I

901. *Oṃ Vārāhyai Namaḥ* I

902. *Oṃ Virajāyai Namaḥ* I

903. *Oṃ Varṣāyai Namaḥ* I

904. *Oṃ Varalakṣmyai Namaḥ* I

905. *Oṃ Vilāsinyai Namaḥ* I

906. *Oṃ Vinatāyai Namaḥ* I

907. *Oṃ Vyomamadhyasthāyai Namaḥ* I

908. *Oṃ Vārijāsanasaṃsthitāyai Namaḥ* I

909. *Oṃ Vāruṇyai Namaḥ* I

910. *Oṃ Veṇusambhūtāyai Namaḥ* I

911. *Oṃ Vitihotrāyai Namaḥ* I

912. *Oṃ Virūpiṇyai Namaḥ* I

913. *Oṃ Vāyumaṇḍalamadhyasthāyai Namaḥ* I

914. *Oṃ Viṣṇurūpāyai Namaḥ* I

915. *Oṃ Vidhipriyāyai Namaḥ* I

916. *Oṃ Viṣṇupatnyai Namaḥ* I

917. *Oṃ Viṣṇumatyai Namaḥ* I

918. *Oṃ Viśālākṣyai Namaḥ* I

919. *Oṃ Vasundharāyai Namaḥ* I

920. *Oṃ Vāmadevapriyāyai Namaḥ* I

921. *Oṃ Velāyai Namaḥ* I

922. *Oṃ Vajriṇyai Namaḥ* I

923. *Oṃ Vasudohinyai Namaḥ* I

924. *Oṃ Vedākṣaraparitāṅgyai Namaḥ* I

925. *Oṃ Vājapeyaphalapradāyai Namaḥ* I

926. *Oṃ Vāsavyai Namaḥ* I

927. *Oṃ Vāmajananyai Namaḥ* I

928. *Oṃ Vaikuṇṭhanilayāyai Namaḥ* I

929. *Oṃ Varāyai Namaḥ* |
930. *Oṃ Vyāsapriyāyai Namaḥ* |

931. *Oṃ Varmadharāyai Namaḥ* |
932. *Oṃ Vālmīkiparisevitāyai Namaḥ* |
933. *Oṃ Śākambharyai Namaḥ* |
934. *Oṃ Śivāyai Namaḥ* |
935. *Oṃ Śāntāyai Namaḥ* |
936. *Oṃ Śāradāyai Namaḥ* |
937. *Oṃ Śaraṇāgatyai Namaḥ* |
938. *Oṃ Śātodaryai Namaḥ* |
939. *Oṃ Śubhācārāyai Namaḥ* |
940. *Oṃ Śumbhāsuranardinyai Namaḥ* |

941. *Oṃ Śobhāvatyai Namaḥ* |
942. *Oṃ Śivākārāyai Namaḥ* |
943. *Oṃ Śaṅkarārdhaśarīriṇyai Namaḥ* |
944. *Oṃ Śoṇāyai Namaḥ* |
945. *Oṃ Śubhāśayāyai Namaḥ* |
946. *Oṃ Śubhrāyai Namaḥ* |
947. *Oṃ Śiraḥsandhānakāriṇyai Namaḥ* |
948. *Oṃ Śarāvatyai Namaḥ* |
949. *Oṃ Śarānandāyai Namaḥ* |
950. *Oṃ Śarajjyotsnāyai Namaḥ* |

951. *Oṃ Śubhānanāyai Namaḥ* |
952. *Oṃ Śarabhāyai Namaḥ* |
953. *Oṃ Śūlinyai Namaḥ* |
954. *Oṃ Śuddhāyai Namaḥ* |
955. *Oṃ Śabaryai Namaḥ* |
956. *Oṃ Śukavāhanāyai Namaḥ* |

957. *Oṃ Śrīmatyai Namaḥ* |
958. *Oṃ Śrīdharānandāyai Namaḥ* |
959. *Oṃ Śravaṇānandadāyinyai Namaḥ* |
960. *Oṃ Śarvāṇyai Namaḥ* |

961. *Oṃ Śarvarīvandyāyai Namaḥ* |
962. *Oṃ Ṣaḍbhāśāyai Namaḥ* |
963. *Oṃ Ṣaḍṛtupriyāyai Namaḥ* |
964. *Oṃ Ṣaḍādhārasthitādevyai Namaḥ* |
965. *Oṃ Ṣaṇmukhapriyakāriṇyai Namaḥ* |
966. *Oṃ Ṣaḍaṅgarūpasumati Surāsuranamaskṛtāyai Namaḥ* |
967. *Oṃ Sarasvatyai Namaḥ* |
968. *Oṃ Sadādhārāyai Namaḥ* |
969. *Oṃ Sarvamaṅgalakāriṇyai Namaḥ* |
970. *Oṃ Sāmagānapriyāyai Namaḥ* |

971. *Oṃ Sūkṣmāyai Namaḥ* |
972. *Oṃ Sāvitryai Namaḥ* |
973. *Oṃ Sāmasambhavāyai Namaḥ* |
974. *Oṃ Sarvāvāsāyai Namaḥ* |
975. *Oṃ Sadānandāyai Namaḥ* |
976. *Oṃ Sustanyai Namaḥ* |
977. *Oṃ Sāgarāmbarāyai Namaḥ* |
978. *Oṃ Sarvaiśvaryapriyāyai Namaḥ* |
979. *Oṃ Siddhyai Namaḥ* |
980. *Oṃ Sādhubandhuparākramāyai Namaḥ* |

981. *Oṃ Saptarṣimaṇḍalagatāyai Namaḥ* |
982. *Oṃ Somamaṇḍalavāsinyai Namaḥ* |
983. *Oṃ Sarvajñāyai Namaḥ* |
984. *Oṃ Sāndrakaruṇāyai Namaḥ* |

985. *Oṃ Samānādhikavarjitāyai Namaḥ* I

986. *Oṃ Sarvottuṅgāyai Namaḥ* I

987. *Oṃ Saṅgahīnāyai Namaḥ* I

988. *Oṃ Sadguṇāyai Namaḥ* I

989. *Oṃ Sakaleṣṭadāyai Namaḥ* I

990. *Oṃ Saraghāyai Namaḥ* I

991. *Oṃ Sūryatanayāyai Namaḥ* I

992. *Oṃ Sukeśyai Namaḥ* I

993. *Oṃ Somasaṃhatyai Namaḥ* I

994. *Oṃ Hiraṇyavarṇāyai Namaḥ* I

995. *Oṃ Hariṇyai Namaḥ* I

996. *Oṃ Hrīṅkāryai Namaḥ* I

997. *Oṃ Haṃsavāhinyai Namaḥ* I

998. *Oṃ Kṣaumavastraparitāṅgyai Namaḥ* I

999. *Oṃ Kṣīrābdhitanayāyai Namaḥ* I

1000. *Oṃ Kṣamāyai Namaḥ* I

1001. *Oṃ Gāyatryai Namaḥ* I

1002. *Oṃ Sāvitryai Namaḥ* I

1003. *Oṃ Pārvatyai Namaḥ* I

1004. *Oṃ Sarasvatyai Namaḥ* I

1005. *Oṃ Vedagarbhāyai Namaḥ* I

1006. *Oṃ Varārohāyai Namaḥ* I

1007. *Oṃ Śrīgāyatryai Namaḥ* I

1008. *Oṃ Parāṃvikāyai Namaḥ* I

*Iti Śrīdevībhāgavate Mahāpurāṇe*
*Dvādaśaskandhe*
*Śrī Gāyatrī Sahasranāmāvalīḥ*
*Samāptā* II

*****

# Other Books of the Author

http://ramamurthy.jaagruti.co.in/

| # | Title | Remarks | Pages |
|---|---|---|---|
| | | **Indology Related** | |
| 1. | *Shrī Lalitā Sahasranāmam* | English translation of Shrī *Bhāskararāya's Bhāśyam* | 750 |
| 2. | Power of *Shrī Vidyā* | The secrets demystified – with lucid English rendering and commentaries | 80 |
| 3. | *Samatā* | An exposition of Similarities in *Lalitā Sahasranāma* with *Soundaryalaharī*, *Saptaśatī*, *Viṣṇu Sahasranāma* and *Shrīmad Bhagavad Gīta* | 172 |
| 4. | *Advaita* in *Shākta* | Advaita Philosophy discussed in Shakta related Books | 80 |
| 5. | *Shrī Lalitā Triśatī* | 300 divine names of the celestial Mother – **English** translation of *Shrī Ādi Śaṅkara's Bhāśyam* | 193 |
| 6. | Secrets of *Mahāśakti* | Chandi demystified | 78 |
| 7. | *Daśa Mahā Vidyā* | Ten cosmic forms of the Divine mother | 60 |
| 8. | ஸ்ரீவித்யா பேதங்கள் | ஸ்ரீவித்யா உபாசனையின் படிகள் - கோவை ஶதச் சண்டீ மலர் | 51 |
| 9. | ஸ்ரீ தேவீ ஸ்துதிகள் | பல முக்கிய அம்பாள் ஸ்தோத்ரங்கள் | 133 |
| 10. | Śrī Devī Stutis – श्री देवी स्तुति: | Various important stotras of Sri Devi | 223 |
| 11. | ஷண்மத மந்த்ரங்–கள் – षण्मत मन्त्रा: | பொள்ளாச்சி ஸ்ரீ ஸஹஸ்ரசண்டீ மஹாயாக நினைவு மலர் | 145 |
| 12. | *Śanmata Mantras* – षण्मत मन्त्रा: | Important Mantras relating to Gods of six religions | 87 |
| 13. | தேவதா மந்த்ரங்கள் | அக்கரைப்பட்டி ஸஹஸ்ரசண்டீ மஹாயாக நினைவு மலர் | 32 |
| 14. | ஆதி ஶங்கரரும் ஷண்மதமும் | ஷண்மதங்களைப் பற்றிய ஒரு அறிமுகம் | 32 |
| 15. | ஸ்ரீ ஷண்மத தேவதா அர்ச்சனை | ஸ்ரீ மஹா கும்பாபிஷேக மலர் | 64 |
| 16. | *Vaidhīka* Wedding | Typical Wedding process in English | 56 |
| 17. | வைதீகத் திருமணம் | Typical Wedding process in Tamil | 57 |
| 18. | ஸ்ரீ லலிதா திரிஶதி | 300 divine names of the celestial Mother – Tamil translation of *Shrī Ādi Śaṅkara's Bhāśyam* | 234 |
| 19. | ஸ்ரீகுரு பாத பூஜா விதானம் | சித்தகிரி ஸஹஸ்ரசண்டீ மலர் | 44 |

| # | Title | Remarks | Pages |
|---|---|---|---|
| 20. | ஸ்ரீவித்யா ஷடாம்னாய மந்த்ரங்கள் | சித்தகிரி ஸஹஸ்ரசண்டீ மலர் | 60 |
| 21. | *Ekatā* | Oneness among Shiva, Vishnu and Shakti | 277 |
| 22. | *Vedas* – An Analytical Perspective | A description of Veda, Vedanta, Vedanga, Jyotisha, Shastra, etc. | 240 |
| 23. | *Shrīvidya* Variances | Variances in Srividya Upasana | 50 |
| 24. | வேதங்கள் – ஒரு பகுப்பாய்வு | A description of Veda, Vedanta, Vedanga, Jyotisha, Shastra, etc. | 280 |
| 25. | பரமாச்சார்யாள் நோக்கில் ஸ்ரீலலிதாம்பிகா | The explanation given by Paramacharya on some of the names in Sri Lalita Sahasranama | 175 |
| 26. | *Ṣaṇṇavati Tarpaṇa* | Repaying Debts to Ancestors | 42 |
| 27. | ஷண்ணவதி தர்பணம் | முன்னோர் கடன் தீர்த்தல் | 48 |
| 28. | *Śrī Mahā Pratyangirā Devī* | Holy Divine mother in ferocious form | 41 |
| 29. | ஸ்ரீ மஹா ப்ரத்யங்கிரா தேவீ | தெய்வீக அன்னையின் பயங்கர வடிவம் | 51 |
| 30. | *Śrī Chakra Navāvarṇam* | Marvels of *Śrī Chakra* | 115 |
| 31. | ஸ்ரீ சக்ர நவாவர்ணம் | ஸ்ரீ சக்ரத்தின் அதிசயங்கள் | 130 |
| 32. | அம்பிகையின் (திரு) அவதாரங்கள் | ஸ்ரீ தேவியின் பல்வேறு அவதாரங்கள் | 142 |
| 33. | Incarnations of Holy Mother | Different Incarnations of *Śrī Devī* | 140 |
| 34. | ஸ்ரீ பிரணவானந்தர் – ஒரு சரிதம் | ஒரு அரிய ஸ்வாமிகளின் திவ்ய சரிதம் | 91 |
| 35. | ஸன்யாஸம் – ஓர் அலசல் | ஹிந்து மத ஸன்யாஸ பேதங்கள் – ஒரு பகுப்பாய்வு | 140 |
| 36. | Asceticism – an Analysis | A Study of Hindu *Sanyasam* | 140 |
| 37. | ஶாந்தமும் ப்ரணவமும் | (ஸ்ரீ ஶாந்தானந்தரும் ஸ்ரீ ப்ரணவானந்தரும்) குரு சிஷ்யருக்கு உபதேசங்கள் | 120 |
| 38. | ஸ்ரீ ஸஹஸ்ராக்ஷரீ வித்யா | 2020 சாதுர்மாஸ்ய மலர் | 84 |

| # | Title | Remarks | Pages |
|---|---|---|---|
| 39. | ஶாக்த உபநிஷதங்கள் | ஸ்ரீ தேவியைப் பற்றிய உபநிஷதங்கள் | 400 |
| 40. | *Shakta Upanishats* | *Upanishats* about *Sri Devi* | 385 |
| 41. | ஸ்ரீ தேவீ கீதை | Sri Devi Geeta | 193 |
| 42. | *Śrī Devī Gīta* | Sri Devi Geeta | 180 |
| 43. | *Śrī Gāyatrī Sahasranamam* | 1000 Divine Names of *Śrī Gāyatrī Mātā* | 392 |
| 44. | ஸ்ரீ காயத்ரீ ஸஹஸ்ரநாமம் | ஸ்ரீ காயத்ரி மாதாவின் 1000 திவ்ய நாமங்கள் | 450 |
| | | **Applied Samskrutam Based** | |
| 45. | *Paribhāshā Stora*—s | An exploration of *Lalitā Sahasranāmam* | 96 |
| 46. | *Shrī Cakra*, An Esoteric Approach | Mathematical Construction to draw *Shrī Cakra* | 64 |
| 47. | Number System in Samskrutam | An overview of Mathematics based on Samskrutam | 123 |
| 48. | *Vedic* Mathematics | 30 formulae elucidated | 146 |
| 49. | Vedic IT | Information Technology and Samskrutam | 162 |
| | | **IT Based** | |
| 50. | Orthogonal Array | A Statistical Tool for Software Testing | 180 |
| | | **Banking Based** | |
| 51. | Retail Banking | A guide book for Novice | 213 |
| 52. | Corporate Banking | A guide book for Novice | 232 |
| 53. | Dictionary of Financial Terms | A Guide Book for all – Demystifying Myriad Global Financial Terms | 215 |
| 54. | GRC in BFS Industry | (**G**overnance, **R**isk Management and **Com**pliance by Banking & Finance Industry) | 200 |

Let him be blessed to share his knowledge and experience with others through more books. Let us wish him all the best.

*****

# Bibliography

The following books were referred to write this book. Lot many thanks to the authors and the publishers. They were very useful.



| # | Title of the book | Author/ Publishers |
|---|---|---|
| 1. | श्रीमद्देवीभागवतमहापुराणम् | Gita Press, Gorakhpur |
| 2. | ஸ்ரீமத் தேவி பாகவதம் | ஸ்ரீ ராம நாம வங்கியின் பகவன் நாமா பப்ளிகேஷன்ஸ் |
| 3. | ஸ்ரீ தேவீ பாகவதம் | ஸ்ரீ டி. எஸ். கிருஷ்ண ஐயர் |
| 4. | Other books of the same author. | |

*Om Tat Sat* ॐ तत् सत्

*****

www.ingramcontent.com/pod-product-compliance
Lightning Source LLC
Chambersburg PA
CBHW011802160726
48282CB00035B/1229

* 9 7 8 9 3 8 2 2 3 7 7 4 7 *